Lecture Notes in Computer Science 4376

Commenced Publication in 1973
Founding and Former Series Editors:
Gerhard Goos, Juris Hartmanis, and Jan van Leeuwen

Eitan Frachtenberg   Uwe Schwiegelshohn (Eds.)

Job Scheduling Strategies for Parallel Processing

12th International Workshop, JSSPP 2006
Saint-Malo, France, June 26, 2006
Revised Selected Papers

 Springer

Volume Editors

Eitan Frachtenberg
Los Alamos National Laboratory
Computer and Computational Sciences Division, Los Alamos, NM 87545, USA
E-mail: eitanf@lanl.gov

Uwe Schwiegelshohn
University of Dortmund
Robotics Research Institute (IRF-IT), 44221 Dortmund, Germany
E-mail: uwe.schwiegelshohn@udo.edu

Library of Congress Control Number: 2007920905

CR Subject Classification (1998): D.4, D.1.3, F.2.2, C.1.2, B.2.1, B.6, F.1.2

LNCS Sublibrary: SL 1 – Theoretical Computer Science and General Issues

ISSN   0302-9743
ISBN-10   3-540-71034-5 Springer Berlin Heidelberg New York
ISBN-13   978-3-540-71034-9 Springer Berlin Heidelberg New York

Springer is a part of Springer Science+Business Media

springer.com

© Springer-Verlag Berlin Heidelberg 2007
Printed in Germany

Typesetting: Camera-ready by author, data conversion by Scientific Publishing Services, Chennai, India
Printed on acid-free paper   SPIN: 11980940   06/3142   5 4 3 2 1 0

Preface

This volume contains the papers presented at the 12th workshop on Job Scheduling Strategies for Parallel Processing. The workshop was held in Saint-Malo, France, on June 16, 2006, in conjunction with SIGMETRICS 2006.

This year, the presented papers covered a large variety of topics. The first three papers address workflow problems. "Provably efficient two-level adaptive scheduling" by Yuxiong He et al. provides a theoretical analysis of a scheduling approach for independent jobs consisting of threads, that are represented by a DAG. Job and thread scheduling are separately addressed with different algorithms. The task graph is not known a priori in the paper "Scheduling dynamically spawned processes in MPI-2" by Márcia Cera et al., but processes are spawned dynamically. This paper is based on the features of MPI-2 and evaluates its scheduler with the help of an experiment. The DAG of a Grid job is known at submission time in the problem discussed in the paper "Advance reservation policies for workflows" by Henan Zhao and Rizos Sakellariou. Here, the tasks of this job are automatically scheduled on heterogeneous machines using advance reservation such that the overall execution time frame of the user is obeyed. The proposed approach is again experimentally evaluated.

The next three papers describe classical job scheduling problems that arise when parallel jobs are submitted to parallel systems with little or no node heterogeneity. The paper "On advantages of scheduling using Genetic Fuzzy systems" by Carsten Franke et al. presents scheduling algorithms that support arbitrary scheduling criteria. The algorithms are trained with recorded workloads using Fuzzy concepts. Their performances are evaluated by simulations with those workloads. In their paper "Moldable parallel job scheduling using job efficiency: An iterative approach," Gerald Sabin et al. show that scalability information of a job can help to improve the efficiency of this job. As in the previous paper, they use real workload traces for evaluation. The missing scalability information is provided with the help of a well-established speedup model. This model is also used in the paper "Adaptive job scheduling via predictive job resource allocation" by Lawrence Barsanti and Angela Sodan. Similar to the previous paper, the scalability of jobs improves the schedule performance. In addition, the resource allocation considers future job submissions based on a suitable prediction.

Many scientific applications are data intensive. For those applications, it is important to consider the network latency to transfer data from the storage facility to the parallel processing system. It is possible to improve schedule performance by scheduling those jobs on compute resources that are local to the storage resources. This is the subject of the paper "A data locality-aware online scheduling approach for I/O-intensive jobs with file sharing" by Gaurav Kanna et al. The next two papers address job migration issues. "Volunteer computing on clusters" by Deepti Vyas and Jaspal Subhlok demonstrates that nodes of a compute cluster are often underutilized while executing parallel applications. Exploiting this observation by a cycle stealing approach will lead only to a small slowdown of the parallel host application while system throughput increases significantly. Idleness of processors is also the subject of the paper "Load balancing: Toward the Infinite Network and Beyond" by Javier Bustos-Jiménez. There, active objects are sent to underutilized processors that are determined with the help of a peer-to-peer approach. The performance of the approach is evaluated by an experiment with a real application and also by simulations. Jonathan Weinberg and Allan Snavely observed in their paper "Symbiotic space-sharing on SDSC's DataStar system" that the hierarchical architecture of modern parallel processing systems leads to a significant amount of resource sharing among independent jobs and thus to performance degradation. They propose to generate better schedules by considering combinations of jobs with minimum interference between them. Again the performance is evaluated with the help of experiments with real applications.

The last two papers address job modeling issues in Grid computing. "Modeling job arrivals in a data-intensive Grid" by Hui Li et al. analyzes job arrival processes in workloads from high-energy physics and uses a special Markov process to model them. Virtual organizations determine the granularity of the model. The paper "On Grid performance evaluation using synthetic workloads" by Alexandru Iosup et al. discusses various aspects of performance analysis. The authors review different performance metrics and show important properties of existing workloads. Then, they present workload modeling requirements that are specific for Grid computing.

All submitted papers went through a complete review process, with the full version being read and evaluated by an average of five reviewers. We would like to thank the Program Committee members for their willingness to participate in this effort and their excellent, detailed reviews: Su-Hui Chiang, Walfredo Cirne, Allen Downey, Dror Feitelson, Allan Gottlieb, Andrew Grimshaw, Moe Jette, Richard Lagerstrom, Virginia Lo, Jose Moreira, Bill Nitzberg, Mark Squillante, John Towns, Jon Weissman, and Ramin Yahyapour.

The continued interest in this area is reflected by the longevity of this workshop, which has now reached its 12th consecutive year. The proceedings of previous workshops are available from Springer as LNCS volumes 949, 1162, 1291, 1459, 1659, 1911, 2221, 2537, 2862, 3277, and 3834 (and since 1998 they have also been available online).

Finally, we would like to give our warmest thanks to Dror Feitelson and Larry Rudolph, the founding co-organizers of the workshop. Their efforts to promote this field are evidenced by the continuing success of this workshop.

November 2006   Eitan Frachtenberg
                                                                Uwe Schwiegelshohn

Table of Contents

Provably Efficient
Two-Level Adaptive Scheduling*

Yuxiong He[1], Wen-Jing Hsu[1], and Charles E. Leiserson[2]

[1] Nanyang Technological University, Nanyang Avenue 639798, Singapore
yxhe@mit.edu, hsu@ntu.edu.sg
[2] Massachusetts Institute of Technology, Cambridge, MA 02139, USA
cel@mit.edu

Abstract. Multiprocessor scheduling in a shared multiprogramming environment can be structured in two levels, where a kernel-level job scheduler allots processors to jobs and a user-level thread scheduler maps the ready threads of a job onto the allotted processors. This paper presents two-level scheduling schemes for scheduling "adaptive" multithreaded jobs whose parallelism can change during execution. The AGDEQ algorithm uses dynamic-equipartioning (DEQ) as a job-scheduling policy and an adaptive greedy algorithm (A-GREEDY) as the thread scheduler. The ASDEQ algorithm uses DEQ for job scheduling and an adaptive work-stealing algorithm (A-STEAL) as the thread scheduler. AGDEQ is suitable for scheduling in centralized scheduling environments, and ASDEQ is suitable for more decentralized settings. Both two-level schedulers achieve $O(1)$-competitiveness with respect to makespan for any set of multithreaded jobs with arbitrary release time. They are also $O(1)$-competitive for any batched jobs with respect to mean response time. Moreover, because the length of the scheduling quantum can be adjusted to amortize the cost of context-switching during processor reallocation, our schedulers provide control over the scheduling overhead and ensure effective utilization of processors.

1   Introduction

Multiprocessors are often used for multiprogrammed workloads where many parallel applications share the same machine. As Feitelson points out in his excellent survey [27], schedulers for these machines can be implemented using two levels: a kernel-level *job scheduler* which allots processors to jobs, and a user-level *thread scheduler* which maps the threads belonging to a given job onto the allotted processors. The job schedulers may implement either *space-sharing*, where jobs occupy disjoint processor resources, or *time-sharing*, where different jobs may share the same processor resources at different times. Moreover, both the thread scheduler and the job scheduler may be either *adaptive* (called "dynamic" in [19]), allowing the number of processors allotted to a job to vary

---

* This research was supported in part by the Singapore-MIT Alliance and NSF Grants ACI-0324974 and CNS-0540248.

E. Frachtenberg and U. Schwiegelshohn (Eds.): JSSPP 2006, LNCS 4376, pp. 1–32, 2007.

while the job is running, or **nonadaptive** (called "static" in [19]), where a job runs on a fixed number of processors over its lifetime. A **clairvoyant** scheduling algorithm may use knowledge of the jobs' execution time, whereas a **nonclairvoyant** algorithm assumes nothing about the execution time of the jobs. This paper presents two provably efficient two-level adaptive schedulers, each of which schedules jobs nonpreemptively and without clairvoyance.

With **adaptive** scheduling [4] (called "dynamic" scheduling in many other papers [27,60,41,58,37]), the job scheduler can change the number of processors allotted to a job while the job executes. Thus, new jobs can enter the system, because the job scheduler can simply recruit processors from the already executing jobs and allot them to the new jobs. Without an adequate feedback mechanism, however, both adaptive and nonadaptive schedulers may waste processor cycles, because a job with low parallelism may be allotted more processors than it can productively use.

If individual jobs provide **parallelism feedback** to the job scheduler, waste can be avoided. When a job does not require many processors, it can release the excess processors to the job scheduler to be reallotted to jobs in need. When a job needs more processors, it can make a request to the job scheduler. Based on this parallelism feedback, the job scheduler can adaptively change the allotment of processors according to the availability of processors and the system administrative policy.

A two-level scheduler communicates the parallelism feedback by each job requesting processors from a job scheduler at regular intervals, called **quanta**. The quantum length is typically chosen to be long enough to amortize the scheduling overheads, including the cost of reallotting processors among the jobs. The job scheduler uses the parallelism feedback to assign the available processors to the jobs according to its administrative policy. During the quantum, the job's allotment does not typically change. Once a job is allotted processors, the job's thread scheduler maps the job's threads onto the allotted processors, reallocating them if necessary as threads are spawned and terminated.

Various researchers [21,20,29,41,59] have proposed the use of **instantaneous parallelism** — the number of processors the job can effectively use at the current moment — as the parallelism feedback to the job scheduler. Unfortunately, using instantaneous parallelism as feedback can either cause gross misallocation of processor resources [49] or introduce significant scheduling overhead. For example, the parallelism of a job may change substantially during a scheduling quantum, alternating between parallel and serial phases. Depending on which phase is currently active, the sampling of instantaneous parallelism may lead the task scheduler to request either too many or too few processors. Consequently, the job may either waste processor cycles or take too long to complete. On the other hand, if the quantum length is set to be small enough to capture frequent changes in instantaneous parallelism, the proportion of time spent reallotting processors among the jobs increases, resulting in a high scheduling overhead.

A-GREEDY [1] and A-STEAL [2,3] are two adaptive thread schedulers that provide the parallelism feedback to the job scheduler. Rather than using instantaneous parallelism, these thread schedulers employ a single summary statistic and the job's behavior in the previous quantum to make processor requests of the job scheduler. Even though this parallelism feedback is generated based on the job's history and may not be correlated to the job's future parallelism, A-GREEDY and A-STEAL still guarantee to make effective use of the available processors.

Intuitively, if each job provides good parallelism feedback and makes productive use of available processors, a good job scheduler should ensure that *all* the jobs perform well. In this paper, we affirm this intuition for A-GREEDY and A-STEAL in the case when the job scheduler implements dynamic equipartitioning (DEQ) [55,41]. DEQ gives each job a fair allotment of processors based on the job's request, while allowing processors that cannot be used by a job to be reallocated. DEQ was introduced by McCann, Vaswani, and Zahorjan [41] based on earlier work on equipartitioning by Tucker and Gupta [55], and it has been studied extensively [21,20,29,42,41,24,36,46,45,59,40,25].

This paper shows that efficient two-level adaptive schedulers can ensure that all jobs can perform well. AGDEQ, which couples DEQ with A-GREEDY, is suitable for centralized thread scheduling, such as might be used to schedule data-parallel jobs, wherein each job's thread scheduler can dispatch all the ready threads to the allotted processors in a centralized manner. ASDEQ, which couples DEQ with A-STEAL, is suitable when each job distributes threads over the allotted processors using decentralized work-stealing [16,31,47,13].

The main contributions of this paper are as follows. In a centralized environment, AGDEQ guarantees $O(1)$-competitiveness against an optimal clairvoyant scheduler with respect to makespan. For any set of batched jobs, where all jobs have the same release time, AGDEQ also achieves $O(1)$-competitiveness with respect to mean response time. In a decentralized settings where the scheduler has no knowledge of all the available threads at the current moment, ASDEQ guarantees $O(1)$-competitiveness with respect to makespan for any set of jobs with arbitrary job release time. It is also $O(1)$-competitive with respect to the mean response time for batched jobs. Unlike many previous results, which either assume clairvoyance [38,18,43,33,34,56,48,50,57] or use instantaneous parallelism [21,14,22], our schedulers remove these restrictive assumptions. We generate parallelism feedback after each quantum based on the job's behavior in the past quantum. Even though job's future parallelism may not be correlated with its history of parallelism, our schedulers can still guarantee constant competitiveness for both the makespan and the mean response time. Moreover, because the quantum length can be adjusted to amortize the cost of context-switching during processor reallocation, our schedulers provide control over the scheduling overhead and ensure effective utilization of processors.

The remainder of this paper is organized as follows. Section 2 describes the job model, scheduling model, and objective functions. Section 3 describes the AGDEQ algorithm. Section 4 and 5 analyze the competitiveness of AGDEQ with respect to makespan and mean response time, respectively. Section 6 presents the ASDEQ algorithm and analyzes its performance. Section 7 gives a lower bound on the competitiveness for mean response time. Section 9 concludes the paper by raising issues for future research.

2   Models and Objective Functions

This section provides the background formalisms for two-level scheduling, which will be used to study AGDEQ and ASDEQ. We formalize the job model, define the scheduling model, and present the optimization criteria of makespan and mean response time.

Job Model

A **two-level scheduling problem** consists of a collection of independent jobs $\mathcal{J} = \{J_1, J_2, \ldots, J_{|\mathcal{J}|}\}$ to be scheduled on a collection of P identical processors. This paper restricts its attention to the situation where $|\mathcal{J}| \leq P$, that is, the number of jobs does not exceed the number of processors. (The situation where the parallel computer may sometimes be heavily loaded with jobs remains an interesting open problem.) Like prior work on scheduling of multithreaded jobs [12,13,11,10,8,26,32,44], we model the execution of a multithreaded job J_i as a dynamically unfolding directed acyclic graph (dag) such that $J_i = (V(J_i), E(J_i))$ where $V(J_i)$ and $E(J_i)$ represent the sets of J_i's vertices and edges, respectively. Similarly, let $V(\mathcal{J}) = \bigcup_{J_i \in \mathcal{J}} V(J_i)$. Each vertex $v \in V(\mathcal{J})$ represents a unit-time instruction. The **work** $T_1(i)$ of the job J_i corresponds to the total number of vertices in the dag, that is, $T_1(i) = |V(J_i)|$. Each edge $(u, v) \in E(J_i)$ represents a dependency between the two vertices. The precedence relationship $u \prec v$ holds if and only if there exists a path from vertex u to vertex v in $E(J_i)$. The **critical-path length** $T_\infty(i)$ corresponds to the length of the longest chain of precedence dependencies. The **release time** $r(i)$ of the job J_i is the time immediately after which J_i becomes first available for processing. For a **batched** job set $\mathcal{J}$, all jobs in $\mathcal{J}$ have the same release time. (Without loss of generality, we assume that $r(i) = 0$ for all $J_i \in \mathcal{J}$.)

Scheduling Model

Our scheduling model assumes that time is broken into a sequence of equal-sized **scheduling quanta** $1, 2, \ldots$, each of length L, where each quantum q includes the interval $[Lq, Lq+1, \ldots, L(q+1)-1]$ of time steps. The quantum length L is a system configuration parameter chosen to be long enough to amortize scheduling overheads. These overheads might include the time to reallocate processors among the various jobs and the time for the thread scheduler to communicate with the job scheduler, which typically involves a system call.

The job scheduler and thread schedulers interact as follows. The job scheduler may reallocate processors between quanta. Between quantum $q - 1$ and quantum q, the thread scheduler (for example, A-GREEDY or A-STEAL) of a given job J_i determines the job's **desire** $d(i, q)$, which is the number of processors J_i wants for quantum q. The thread scheduler provides the desire $d(i, q)$ to the job scheduler as its parallelism feedback. Based on the desire of all running jobs, the job scheduler follows its processor-allocation policy (for example, dynamic equi-partitioning) to determine the **allotment** $a(i, q)$ of the job with the constraint that $a(i, q) \leq d(i, q)$. Once a job is allotted its processors, the allotment does not change during the quantum. Consequently, the thread scheduler must do a good job in estimating how many processors it will need in the next quantum, as well as scheduling the ready threads on the allotted processors. Moreover, the thread scheduler must operate in an online and nonclairvoyant manner, oblivious to the future characteristics of the dynamically unfolding dag.

A **schedule** $\chi = (\tau, \pi)$ of a job set $\mathcal{J}$ on P processors is defined as two mappings $\tau : V(\mathcal{J}) \rightarrow \{1, 2, \ldots, \infty\}$ and $\pi : V(\mathcal{J}) \rightarrow \{1, 2, \ldots, P\}$, which map the vertices in the job set $\mathcal{J}$ to the set of time steps and to the set of processors in the machine, respectively. A valid mapping must preserve the precedence relationship of each job: for any two vertices $u, v \in V(\mathcal{J})$, if $u \prec v$, then $\tau(u) < \tau(v)$, that is, the vertex u must be executed before the vertex v. A valid mapping must also ensure that a processor is only assigned to one job at any time: for any two distinct vertices $u, v \in V(\mathcal{J})$, we have $\tau(u) \neq \tau(v)$ or $\pi(u) \neq \pi(v)$.

Objective Functions

We can now define the objective functions that a two-level scheduler should minimize.

Definition 1. Let χ be a schedule of a job set $\mathcal{J}$ on P processors. The **completion time** a job $J_i \in \mathcal{J}$ is

$$T_\chi(i) = \max_{v \in V_i} \tau(v) ,$$

and the **makespan** of $\mathcal{J}$ is

$$T_\chi(\mathcal{J}) = \max_{J_i \in \mathcal{J}} T_\chi(i) .$$

The **response time** of a job $J_i \in \mathcal{J}$ is

$$R_\chi(i) = T_\chi(i) - r(i) ,$$

the **total response time** of $\mathcal{J}$ is

$$R_\chi(\mathcal{J}) = \sum_{J_i \in \mathcal{J}} R_\chi(i) ,$$

and the **mean response time** of $\mathcal{J}$ is

$$\overline{R}_\chi(\mathcal{J}) = R_\chi(\mathcal{J}) / |\mathcal{J}| .$$

That is, the completion time of J_i is simply the time at which the schedule completes the execution of J_i. The makespan of $\mathcal{J}$ is the time taken to complete all jobs in the job set. The response time of a job J_i is the duration between its release time $r(i)$ and the completion time $T_\chi(i)$. The total response time of a job set is the sum of the response times of the individual jobs, and the mean response time is the arithmetic average of the jobs' response times. For batched jobs where $r(i) = 0$ for all $J_i \in \mathcal{J}$, the total response time simplifies to $R_\chi(\mathcal{J}) = \sum_{J_i \in \mathcal{J}} T_\chi(i)$.

Competitiveness
The competitive analysis of an online scheduling algorithm compares the algorithm against an optimal clairvoyant algorithm. Let $T^*(\mathcal{J})$ denote the makespan of the jobset $\mathcal{J}$ scheduled by an optimal clairvoyant scheduler, and $\chi(A)$ denote the schedule produced by an algorithm A for the job set $\mathcal{J}$. A deterministic algorithm A is said to be **c-competitive** if there exist constants $c > 0$ and $b \geq 0$ such that $T_{\chi(A)}(\mathcal{J}) \leq c \cdot T^*(\mathcal{J}) + b$ holds for the schedule $\chi(A)$ of each job set. A randomized algorithm A is said to be **c-competitive** if there exists constants $c > 0$ and $b \geq 0$ such that $E\left[T_{\chi(A)}(\mathcal{J})\right] \leq c \cdot T^*(\mathcal{J}) + b$ holds for the schedule $\chi(A)$ of each job set. Thus, for each job set $\mathcal{J}$, a c-competitive algorithm is guaranteed to have makespan (or expected makespan) within a factor c of that incurred in the optimal clairvoyant algorithm (up to the additive constant b). We shall show that AGDEQ and ASDEQ are c-competitive with respect to makespan, where $c > 0$ is a small constant. For the mean response time, we shall show that our algorithm is $O(1)$-competitive for batched jobs.

3   The AGDEQ Algorithm

AGDEQ is a two-level adaptive scheduler, which uses A-GREEDY [1] as its thread scheduler and DEQ [41] as its job scheduler. Given a set $\mathcal{J}$ of jobs and P processors, DEQ works at the kernel level, partitioning the P processors among the jobs. Within each job, A-GREEDY schedules threads at user level onto the allotted processors. The interactions between DEQ and A-GREEDY follow the scheduling model described in Section 2. At the beginning of each quantum q, the A-GREEDY thread scheduler for each job $J_i \in \mathcal{J}$ provides its desire $d(i, q)$ as parallelism feedback to the DEQ job scheduler. DEQ collects the desire information from all jobs and decides the allotment $a(i, q)$ for each job J_i. In this section, we briefly overview the basic properties of A-GREEDY and DEQ.

The Adaptive Greedy Thread Scheduler
A-GREEDY [1] is an adaptive greedy thread scheduler with parallelism feedback. In a two-level adaptive scheduling system, A-GREEDY performs the following functions.

- Between quanta, it estimates its job's desire and requests processors from the job scheduler using its **desire-estimation algorithm**.

- During the quantum, it schedules the ready threads of the job onto the allotted processors using its **thread-scheduling algorithm**.

We now describe each of these algorithms.

A-GREEDY's desire-estimation algorithm is parameterized in terms of a **utilization parameter** $\delta > 0$ and a **responsiveness parameter** $\rho > 1$, both of which can be tuned to affect variations in guaranteed bounds for waste and completion time.

Before each quantum, A-GREEDY for a job $J_i \in \mathcal{J}$ provides parallelism feedback to the job scheduler based on the J_i's history of utilization for the previous quantum. A-GREEDY classifies quanta as "satisfied" versus "deprived" and "efficient" versus "inefficient." A quantum q is **satisfied** if $a(i,q) = d(i,q)$, in which case J_i's allotment is equal to its desire. Otherwise, the quantum is **deprived**. The quantum q is **efficient** if A-GREEDY utilizes no less than a δ fraction of the total allotted processor cycles during the quantum, where δ is the utilization parameter. Otherwise, the quantum is **inefficient**. Of the four possibilities of classification, however, A-GREEDY only uses three: inefficient, efficient-and-satisfied, and efficient-and-deprived.

Using this three-way classification and the job's desire for the previous quantum, A-GREEDY computes the desire for the next quantum using a simple multiplicative-increase, multiplicative-decrease strategy. If quantum $q-1$ was inefficient, A-GREEDY decreases the desire, setting $d(i,q) = d(i,q-1)/\rho$, where ρ is the responsiveness parameter. If quantum $q-1$ was efficient and satisfied, A-GREEDY increases the desire, setting $d(i,q) = \rho d(i,q-1)$. If quantum $q-1$ was efficient but deprived, A-GREEDY keeps desire unchanged, setting $d(i,q) = d(i,q-1)$.

A-GREEDY's thread-scheduling algorithm is based on greedy scheduling [28, 15,12]. After A-GREEDY for a job $J_i \in \mathcal{J}$ receives its allotment $a(i,q)$ of processors from the job scheduler, it simply attempts to keep the allotted processors as busy as possible. During each time step, if there are more than $a(i,q)$ ready threads, A-GREEDY schedules any $a(i,q)$ of them. Otherwise, it schedules all of them.

The Dynamic-Equipartitioning Job Scheduler

DEQ is a dynamic-equipartitioning job scheduler [55,41] which attempts to give each job a fair share of processors. If a job cannot use its fair share, however, DEQ distributes the extra processors across the other jobs. More precisely, upon receiving the desires $\{d(i,q)\}$ from the thread schedulers of all jobs $J_i \in \mathcal{J}$, DEQ executes the following **processor-allocation algorithm**:

1. Set $n = |\mathcal{J}|$. If $n = 0$, return.
2. If the desire for every job $J_i \in \mathcal{J}$ satisfies $d(i,q) \geq P/n$, assign each job $a(i,q) = P/n$ processors.
3. Otherwise, let $\mathcal{J}' = \{J_i \in \mathcal{J} : d(i,q) < P/n\}$. Allot $a(i,q) = d(i,q)$ processors to each $J_i \in \mathcal{J}'$. Update $\mathcal{J} = \mathcal{J} - \mathcal{J}'$. Go to Step 1.

Accordingly, for a given quantum all jobs receive the same number of processors to within 1, unless their desire is less. To simplify the analysis in this paper, we shall assume that all deprived jobs receive exactly the same number of processors, which we term the **mean deprived allotment** for the quantum. Relaxing this assumption may double the execution-time bound of a job, but our algorithms remain $O(1)$-competitive. A tighter but messier analysis retains the constants of the simpler analysis presented here.

4   Makespan of AGDEQ

This section shows that AGDEQ is c-competitive with respect to makespan for a constant $c \geq 1$. The exact value of c is related to the choice of the utilization parameter and responsiveness parameter in A-GREEDY. In this section, we first review lower bounds for makespan. Then, we analyze the competitiveness of AGDEQ in the simple case where all jobs are released at time step 0 and the scheduling quantum length is $L = 1$. Finally, we analyze the competitiveness of AGDEQ for the general case.

Lower Bounds
Given a job set $\mathcal{J}$ and P processors, lower bounds on the makespan of any job scheduler can be obtained based on release time, work, and critical-path length. Recall that for a job $J_i \in \mathcal{J}$, the quantities $r(i)$, $T_1(i)$, and $T_\infty(i)$ represent the release time, work, and critical-path length of J_i, respectively. Let $\mathrm{T}^*(\mathcal{J})$ denote the makespan produced by an optimal scheduler on a job set $\mathcal{J}$ scheduled on P processors. Let $T_1(\mathcal{J}) = \sum_{J_i \in \mathcal{J}} T_1(i)$ denote the total work of the job set. The following two inequalities give two lower bounds on the makespan [14]:

$$\mathrm{T}^*(\mathcal{J}) \geq \max_{J_i \in \mathcal{J}} \{r(i) + T_\infty(i)\} \ , \tag{1}$$

$$\mathrm{T}^*(\mathcal{J}) \geq T_1(\mathcal{J})/P \ . \tag{2}$$

Analysis of a Simple Case
To ease the understanding of the analysis, we first consider the simple case where all jobs are released at time step 0 and the quantum length $L = 1$. We show that in this case, AGDEQ is $O(1)$-competitive with respect to makespan. Afterward, we shall extend the analysis to the general case.

The next two lemmas, proved in [1], bound the satisfied steps and the waste of any single job scheduled by A-GREEDY when the quantum length is $L = 1$. We restate them as a starting point for our analysis.

Lemma 1. *[1] Suppose that* A-GREEDY *schedules a job* J_i *with critical-path length* $T_\infty(i)$ *on a machine with* P *processors. Let* $\rho = 2$ *denote* A-GREEDY*'s responsiveness parameter,* $\delta = 1$ *its utilization parameter, and* $L = 1$ *the quantum length. Then,* A-GREEDY *produces at most* $2T_\infty(i) + \lg P + 1$ *satisfied steps.* $\square$

Lemma 2. *[1] Suppose that* A-GREEDY *schedules a job* J_i *with work* $T_1(i)$ *on a machine. If* $\rho = 2$ *is* A-GREEDY*'s responsiveness parameter,* $\delta = 1$ *is its utilization parameter, and* $L = 1$ *is the quantum length, then* A-GREEDY *wastes no more than* $2T_1(i)$ *processor cycles in the course of the computation.* $\square$

The next lemma shows that for the simple case, AGDEQ is $O(1)$-competitive with respect to makespan. Let $\chi = (\tau, \pi)$ be the schedule of a job set $\mathcal{J}$ produced by AGDEQ. For simplicity we shall use the notation $\mathrm{T}(\mathcal{J}) = \mathrm{T}_\chi(\mathcal{J})$ for the remaining of the section.

Lemma 3. *Suppose that a job set $\mathcal{J}$ is scheduled by AGDEQ on a machine with P processors, and suppose that all jobs arrive at time 0. Let $\rho = 2$ denote A-GREEDY's responsiveness parameter, $\delta = 1$ its utilization parameter, and L the quantum length. Then, the makespan of $\mathcal{J}$ is bounded by*

$$\mathrm{T}(\mathcal{J}) \leq 5\mathrm{T}^*(\mathcal{J}) + \lg P + 1 \;,$$

where $\mathrm{T}^*(\mathcal{J})$ is the makespan produced by an optimal clairvoyant scheduler.

Proof. Suppose that the job J_k is the last job completed in the execution of the job set $\mathcal{J}$ scheduled by AGDEQ. Since the scheduling quantum length is $L = 1$, we can treat each scheduling quantum as a time step. Let $S(k)$ and $D(k)$ denote the set of satisfied steps and the set of deprived steps respectively for job J_k. Since J_k is the last job completed in the job set, we have $\mathrm{T}(\mathcal{J}) = |S(k)| + |D(k)|$. We bound $|S(k)|$ and $|D(k)|$ separately.

By Lemma 1, we know that the number of satisfied steps for job J_k is $|S(k)| \leq 2T_\infty(i) + \lg P + 1$.

We now bound the number of deprived steps for J_k. If a step t is deprived for job J_k, the job gets fewer processors than it requested. On such a step $t \in D(k)$, DEQ must have allotted all the processors, and so we have $\sum_{J_i \in \mathcal{J}} a(i, t) = P$, where $a(i, t)$ denotes the allotment of the job J_i on step t. Let $a(\mathcal{J}, D(k)) = \sum_{t \in D(k)} \sum_{J_i \in \mathcal{J}} a(i, t)$ denote the total processor allotment of all jobs in $\mathcal{J}$ over J_k's deprived steps $D(k)$. We have $a(\mathcal{J}, D(k)) = \sum_{t \in D(k)} \sum_{J_i \in \mathcal{J}} a(i, t) = \sum_{t \in D(k)} P = P|D(k)|$. Since any allotted processor is either working on the ready threads of the job or wasted because of insufficient parallelism, the total allotment for any job J_i is bounded by the sum of its total work $T_1(i)$ and its total waste $w(i)$. By Lemma 2, the waste for the job J_i is $w(i) \leq 2T_1(i)$, which is at most twice its work. Thus, the total allotment for job J_i is at most $3T_1(i)$, and the total allotment for all jobs is at most $\sum_{J_i \in \mathcal{J}} 3T_1(i) = 3T_1(\mathcal{J})$. Therefore, we have $a(\mathcal{J}, D(k)) \leq 3T_1(\mathcal{J})$. Given that $a(\mathcal{J}, D(k)) \leq 3T_1(\mathcal{J})$ and $a(\mathcal{J}, D(k)) = P|D(k)|$, we have $|D(k)| \leq 3T_1(\mathcal{J})/P$.

Thus, we have $\mathrm{T}(\mathcal{J}) = |S(k)| + |D(k)| \leq 3T_1(\mathcal{J})/P + 2T_\infty(k) + \lg P + 1$. Combining this bound with Inequalities (1) and (2), we obtain $\mathrm{T}(\mathcal{J}) \leq 5\mathrm{T}^*(\mathcal{J}) + \lg P + 1$.

Since P is the number of processors on the machine, which is an independent variable with respect to any job set $\mathcal{J}$, Lemma 3 indicates that AGDEQ is 5-competitive with respect to makespan.

Analysis of the General Case

With the intuition from the simple case in hand, we now generalize the makespan analysis of AGDEQ to job sets with arbitrary job release times and scheduled with any quantum length L. First, we state two lemmas from [1] that describe the satisfied steps and the waste of a single job scheduled by A-GREEDY. Then, we show that AGDEQ is $O(1)$-competitive with respect to makespan in the general case.

Lemma 4. *[1] Suppose that* A-GREEDY *schedules a job* J_i *with critical-path length* $T_\infty(i)$ *on a machine with* P *processors. Let* ρ *denote* A-GREEDY*'s responsiveness parameter,* δ *its utilization parameter, and* L *the quantum length,. Then,* A-GREEDY *produces at most* $2T_\infty(i)/(1-\delta)+L\log_\rho P+L$ *satisfied steps.* □

Lemma 5. *[1] Suppose that* A-GREEDY *schedules a job* J_i *with work* $T_1(i)$ *on a machine. Let* ρ *denote* A-GREEDY*'s responsiveness parameter,* δ *its utilization parameter, and* L *the quantum length. Then,* A-GREEDY *wastes at most* $(1+\rho-\delta)T_1(i)/\delta$ *processor cycles in the course of the computation.* □

The following theorem analyzes the makespan of any job set $\mathcal{J}$ with arbitrary release times, when $\mathcal{J}$ is scheduled by AGDEQ with quantum length L. The makespan bound is based on the release time $r(i)$, critical-path length $T_\infty(i)$, and work $T_1(i)$ of individual job J_i, and the total work $T_1(\mathcal{J})$ of the job set $\mathcal{J}$.

Theorem 1. *Suppose* AGDEQ *schedules a job set* $\mathcal{J}$ *on a machine with* P *processors. Let* ρ *denote* A-GREEDY*'s responsiveness parameter,* δ *its utilization parameter, and* L *the quantum length. Then,* AGDEQ *completes the job set in*

$$\mathrm{T}(\mathcal{J}) \le \frac{\rho+1}{\delta}\frac{T_1(\mathcal{J})}{P} + \frac{2}{1-\delta}\max_{J_i\in\mathcal{J}}\{T_\infty(i)+r(i)\} + L\log_\rho P + 2L$$

time steps.

Proof. The proof is similar to that in the simple case for Lemma 3. Let job J_k be the last job to complete among the jobs in $\mathcal{J}$. Let $S(k)$ and $D(k)$ denote the set of satisfied steps and the set of deprived steps for J_k, respectively. The earliest that the job J_k can start its execution is at the beginning of the quantum immediately after J_k's release, which is the quantum q satisfying $Lq < r(k) \le L(q+1)$. Thus, we have $\mathrm{T}(\mathcal{J}) < r(k) + L + |S(k)| + |D(k)|$. From Lemma 4, we know that the number of satisfied steps is $|S(k)| \le 2T_\infty(k)/(1-\delta) + L\log_\rho P + L$. It remains to bound the quantity $|D(k)|$.

By definition, DEQ must have allotted all processors to jobs on any step $t \in D(k)$ where J_k is deprived. Thus, the total allotment of $\mathcal{J}$ over J_k's deprived steps $D(k)$ is $a(\mathcal{J}, D(k)) = \sum_{t\in D(k)}\sum_{J_i\in\mathcal{J}}a(i,t) = P|D(k)|$. Since any allotted processor is either working or wasted, the total allotment for any job J_i is bounded by the sum of its total work $T_1(i)$ and total waste $w(i)$. By Lemma 5, the waste for the job J_i is at most $(\rho-\delta+1)/\delta$ times its work, and hence, the total allotment for job J_i is at most $T_1(i)+w(i) \le (\rho+1)T_1(i)/\delta$, and the total allotment for all jobs is at most $\sum_{J_i\in\mathcal{J}}(\rho+1)T_1(i)/\delta = ((\rho+1)/\delta)T_1(\mathcal{J})$. Consequently, we have $a(\mathcal{J}, D(k)) \le ((\rho+1)/\delta)T_1(\mathcal{J})$. Since $a(\mathcal{J}, D(k)) = P|D(k)|$, it follows that

$$|D(k)| < \frac{\rho+1}{\delta}\frac{T_1(\mathcal{J})}{P}.$$

Combining these bounds, we obtain

$$
\begin{aligned}
\mathrm{T}(\mathcal{J}) &< r(k) + L + |D(k)| + |S(k)| \\
&\leq r(k) + L + \frac{\rho+1}{\delta}\frac{T_1(\mathcal{J})}{P} + \frac{2}{1-\delta}T_\infty(k) + L\log_\rho P + L \\
&\leq \frac{\rho+1}{\delta}\frac{T_1(\mathcal{J})}{P} + \frac{2}{1-\delta}(r(k) + T_\infty(k)) + L\log_\rho P + 2L \\
&\leq \frac{\rho+1}{\delta}\frac{T_1(\mathcal{J})}{P} + \frac{2}{1-\delta}\max_{J_i\in\mathcal{J}}\{T_\infty(i) + r(i)\} + L\log_\rho P + 2L \; .
\end{aligned}
$$

Since both $T_1(\mathcal{J})/P$ and $\max_{J_i\in\mathcal{J}}\{T_\infty(i) + r(i)\}$ are lower bounds of $\mathrm{T}^*(\mathcal{J})$, we obtain the following corollary.

Corollary 1. *Suppose that* AGDEQ *schedules a job set* $\mathcal{J}$ *on a machine with* P *processors. Let* ρ *denote* A-GREEDY*'s responsiveness parameter,* δ *its utilization parameter, and* L *the quantum length. Then,* AGDEQ *completes the job set in*

$$
\mathrm{T}(\mathcal{J}) \leq \left(\frac{\rho+1}{\delta} + \frac{2}{1-\delta}\right)\mathrm{T}^*(\mathcal{J}) + L\log_\rho P + 2L
$$

time steps, where $\mathrm{T}^*(\mathcal{J})$ *is the makespan of* $\mathcal{J}$ *produced by an optimal clairvoyant scheduler.* $\qquad\square$

When $\delta = 0.5$ and ρ is approaching 1, the competitiveness ratio $(\rho+1)/\delta + 2/(1-\delta)$ approaches its minimum value 8. Thus, AGDEQ is $(8+\epsilon)$-competitive with respect to makespan for any constant $\epsilon > 0$.

5   Mean Response Time of AGDEQ for Batched Jobs

This section shows that AGDEQ is $O(1)$-competitive for batched jobs with respect to the mean response time, an important measure for multiuser environments where we desire as many users as possible to get fast response from the system. To analyze the mean response time of job sets scheduled by AGDEQ, we first describe lower bounds and some preliminary concepts. Then, we prove that AGDEQ is $O(1)$-competitive with respect to mean response time for batched jobs.

Lower Bounds and Preliminaries
Before stating the lower bounds on mean response time for a batched job set, we first define some terms.

Definition 2. *Given a finite list* $\mathcal{A} = \langle\alpha_i\rangle$ *of* $n = |\mathcal{A}|$ *integers, define* $f :$ $\{1, 2, \ldots, n\} \rightarrow \{1, 2, \ldots, n\}$ *to be a permutation satisfying* $\alpha_{f(1)} \leq \alpha_{f(2)} \leq \cdots \leq \alpha_{f(n)}$. *The **squashed sum** of* $\mathcal{A}$ *is defined as*

$$
\text{sq-sum}(\mathcal{A}) = \sum_{i=1}^{n}(n - i + 1)\alpha_{f(i)} \; .
$$

*The **squashed work area** of a job set $\mathcal{J}$ on a set of P processors is*

$$\text{swa}\,(\mathcal{J}) = \frac{1}{P}\,\text{sq-sum}(\langle T_1(i)\rangle)\ ,$$

*where $T_1(i)$ is the work of job $J_i \in \mathcal{J}$. The **aggregate critical-path length** of $\mathcal{J}$ is*

$$T_\infty(\mathcal{J}) = \sum_{J_i \in \mathcal{J}} T_\infty(i)\ ,$$

where $T_\infty(i)$ is the critical-path length of job $J_i \in \mathcal{J}$.

The research in [56, 57, 22] establishes two lower bounds for the mean response time:

$$\overline{R^*}(\mathcal{J}) \geq T_\infty(\mathcal{J})/|\mathcal{J}|\ , \tag{3}$$
$$\overline{R^*}(\mathcal{J}) \geq \text{swa}\,(\mathcal{J})/|\mathcal{J}|\ , \tag{4}$$

where $\overline{R^*}(\mathcal{J})$ denotes the mean response time of $\mathcal{J}$ scheduled by an optimal clairvoyant scheduler. Both the aggregate critical-path length $T_\infty(\mathcal{J})$ and the squashed work area $\text{swa}\,(\mathcal{J})$ are lower bounds for the total response time $R^*(\mathcal{J})$ under an optimal clairvoyant scheduler.

We extend the classification of "satisfied" versus "deprived" from quanta to time steps. A job J_i is **satisfied** at step $t \in [Lq, Lq+1, \ldots, L(q+1)-1]$ if J_i is satisfied at the quantum q. Otherwise, the time step t is **deprived**. At time step t, let $\mathcal{JS}(t)$ denote the set of jobs that are satisfied, and let $\mathcal{JD}(t)$ denote the set of jobs that are deprived. According to DEQ, all deprived jobs receive the mean deprived allotment.

To assist in the analysis of the mean response time, we now define some auxiliary concepts.

Definition 3. *Suppose that a job set $\mathcal{J}$ is scheduled by AGDEQ on P processors. For any job $J_i \in \mathcal{J}$, let $S(i)$ and $D(i)$ denote the sets of satisfied and deprived time steps, respectively. The **total satisfied time** of $\mathcal{J}$ is*

$$\text{sat}\,(\mathcal{J}) = \sum_{J_i \in \mathcal{J}} |S(i)|\ .$$

*The **accumulated allotment** of J_i is*

$$a(i) = \sum_{t=1}^{\infty} a\,(i,t)\ .$$

*The **accumulated deprived allotment** of J_i is*

$$a\,(i, D(i)) = \sum_{t \in D(i)} a\,(i,t)\ .$$

*The **squashed deprived allotment area** of $\mathcal{J}$ is*

$$\text{sdaa}\,(\mathcal{J}) = \frac{1}{P}\,\text{sq-sum}(\langle a\,(i, D(i))\rangle)\ .$$

Thus, sat $(\mathcal{J})$ is the total number of satisfied steps of all jobs in $\mathcal{J}$, $a(i)$ is the job J_i's total allotment on all time steps, $a\left(i, D(i)\right)$ is its total allotment during all its deprived steps, and sdaa $(\mathcal{J})$ is $1/P$ of the squashed sum of the accumulated deprived allotments for all jobs in $\mathcal{J}$.

Analysis

We now turn to show that AGDEQ is $O(1)$-competitive with respect to mean response time for batched jobs. Let $\chi = (\tau, \pi)$ be the schedule of a job set $\mathcal{J}$ produced by AGDEQ. For simplicity we shall use the notations $R(\mathcal{J}) = R_\chi(\mathcal{J})$ and $\overline{R}(\mathcal{J}) = \overline{R}_\chi(\mathcal{J})$. Let ρ and δ be A-GREEDY's responsiveness and utilization parameters, respectively. We shall establish the bound

$$\overline{R}(\mathcal{J}) \leq \left(2 - \frac{2}{|\mathcal{J}|+1}\right) \left(\left(\frac{\rho+1}{\delta} + \frac{2}{1-\delta}\right) \overline{R}^*(\mathcal{J}) + L\log_\rho P + L\right) ,$$

where $\overline{R}^*(\mathcal{J})$ is the mean response time produced by an optimal clairvoyant scheduler.

Our analysis comprises four major steps. First, we prove three technical lemmas concerning squashed sums. Second, we prove that

$$R(\mathcal{J}) \leq \left(2 - \frac{2}{|\mathcal{J}|+1}\right) (\text{sdaa}\,(\mathcal{J}) + \text{sat}\,(\mathcal{J})) , \tag{5}$$

thereby relating the total response time $R(\mathcal{J})$ to the squashed deprived allotment area sdaa $(\mathcal{J})$ and the total satisfied time sat $(\mathcal{J})$. Third, we relate the squashed deprived allotment area sdaa $(\mathcal{J})$ and the squashed work area swa $(\mathcal{J})$. Finally, we relate the total satisfied time sat $(\mathcal{J})$ to the aggregate critical-path length $T_\infty(\mathcal{J})$. Since both swa $(\mathcal{J})$ and $T_\infty(\mathcal{J})$ are lower bounds on the total response time, we can derive an upper bound of the mean response time against the optimal.

We begin with three technical lemmas that describe properties of the squashed sum.

Lemma 6. *Let $\langle \alpha_i \rangle$ and $\langle \beta_i \rangle$ be two lists of nonnegative integers with m elements each, and suppose that $\alpha_i \leq \beta_i$ for $i = 1, 2, \ldots, m$. Then, we have* sq-sum($\langle \alpha_i \rangle$) $\leq$ sq-sum($\langle \beta_i \rangle$).

Proof. Let $f : \{1, 2, \ldots, m\} \rightarrow \{1, 2, \ldots, m\}$ be the permutation satisfying $\alpha_{f(1)} \leq \alpha_{f(2)} \leq \cdots \leq \alpha_{f(m)}$, and let $g : \{1, 2, \ldots, m\} \rightarrow \{1, 2, \ldots, m\}$ be the permutation satisfying $\beta_{g(1)} \leq \beta_{g(2)} \leq \cdots \leq \beta_{g(m)}$.

We first show that $\alpha_{f(i)} \leq \beta_{g(i)}$ for $i = 1, 2, \ldots, m$. Suppose for the purpose of contradiction that there exists a $j \in \{1, 2, \ldots, m\}$ such that $\alpha_{f(j)} > \beta_{g(j)}$. Then, there must be at least j integers smaller than $\alpha_{f(j)}$ in $\langle \beta_i \rangle$, namely $\beta_{g(1)}, \beta_{g(2)}, \ldots, \beta_{g(j)}$. Since $\alpha_i \leq \beta_i$ for $i = 1, 2, \ldots, m$, we have $\alpha_{g(i)} \leq \beta_{g(i)}$ for $i = 1, 2, \ldots, j$. Thus, there are at least j elements smaller than $\alpha_{f(j)}$ in $\langle \alpha_i \rangle$, namely $\alpha_{g(1)}, \alpha_{g(2)}, \ldots, \alpha_{g(j)}$. But, since $\alpha_{f(j)}$ is the jth smallest number in $\langle \alpha_i \rangle$, we obtain the contradiction that there are at most $j - 1$ integers smaller than $\alpha_{f(j)}$ in $\langle \alpha_i \rangle$, thereby establishing that that $\alpha_{f(i)} \leq \beta_{g(i)}$ for $i = 1, 2, \ldots, m$.

Consequently, by Definition 2, we have

$$\text{sq-sum}(\langle \alpha_i \rangle) = \sum_{i=1}^{m} (m - i + 1)\alpha_{f(i)}$$

$$\leq \sum_{i=1}^{m} (m - i + 1)\beta_{g(i)}$$

$$= \text{sq-sum}(\langle \beta_i \rangle) .$$

Lemma 7. *Let l, h, and m be nonnegative integers such that $l \leq m$. Suppose that a list $\langle \alpha_i \rangle$ of m nonnegative integers has total value $\sum_{i=1}^{m} \alpha_i = lh$ and that each α_i satisfies $\alpha_i \leq h$. Assume that the elements in $\langle \alpha_i \rangle$ are sorted such that $\alpha_1 \leq \alpha_2 \leq \cdots \leq \alpha_m$. Then, the list's squashed sum satisfies $\text{sq-sum}(\langle \alpha_i \rangle) \geq hl(l + 1)/2$, and its minimum occurs when $\alpha_1 = \alpha_2 = \cdots = \alpha_{m-l} = 0$ and $\alpha_{m-l+1} = \alpha_{m-l+2} = \cdots = \alpha_m = h$.*

Proof. Suppose for the purpose of contradiction that a given list $\langle \alpha_i \rangle$ of integers minimizes the function $\text{sq-sum}(\langle \alpha_i \rangle)$ but does not satisfy $\alpha_1 = \alpha_2 = \cdots = \alpha_{m-l} = 0$ and $\alpha_{m-l+1} = \alpha_{m-l+2} = \cdots = \alpha_m = h$. Then, there must exist at least one integer $\alpha_i > 0$ with index $i < m-l+1$, i.e. $S = \{i \mid \alpha_i > 0, i < m - l + 1\} \neq \emptyset$. Similarly, there must exist at least one integer $\alpha_j > 0$ with index $j \geq m-l+1$, i.e. $S' = \{j \mid \alpha_j < h, j \geq m - l + 1\} \neq \emptyset$. Let $x = \min\{S\}$ and $y = \max\{S'\}$. Because $x = \min\{S\}$ is the smallest index such that $\alpha_x > 0$, we have $\alpha_1 = \alpha_2 = \cdots = \alpha_{x-1} = 0$. Since $\alpha_x > 0$ and it is an integer, we get $\alpha_1 = \alpha_2 = \cdots = \alpha_{x-1} \leq \alpha_x - 1$. Similarly, given $y = \max\{S'\}$, we can show $\alpha_y + 1 \leq \alpha_{y+1} = \cdots = \alpha_m$. Then we have

$$\alpha_1 \leq \cdots \leq \alpha_{x-1} \leq \alpha_x - 1 \leq \alpha_{x+1} \leq \cdots \leq \alpha_y + 1 \leq \alpha_{y+1} \leq \cdots \leq \alpha_m \quad (6)$$

Define another list $\langle \alpha_i' \rangle$ of integers such that $\alpha_x' = \alpha_x - 1$, $\alpha_y' = \alpha_y + 1$, and $\alpha_i' = \alpha_i$ if $i \neq x$ and $i \neq y$. Given Inequality (6), we have $\alpha_1' \leq \alpha_2' \leq \cdots \leq \alpha_m'$. We know that $\sum_{i=1}^{m} \alpha_i' = lh$ and $\alpha_i' \leq h$ for each index $i = 1, 2, \ldots, m$. The squashed sum difference of these two lists is given by

$$\text{sq-sum}(\langle \alpha_i' \rangle) - \text{sq-sum}(\langle \alpha_i \rangle)$$
$$= (m - x + 1)\alpha_x' + (m - y + 1)\alpha_y' - ((m - x + 1)\alpha_x + (m - y + 1)\alpha_y)$$
$$= (m - x + 1)(\alpha_x' - \alpha_x) + (m - y + 1)(\alpha_y' - \alpha_y)$$
$$= -(m - x + 1) + (m - y + 1)$$
$$= x - y .$$

Since $x < m - l + 1$ and $y \geq m - l + 1$, we have $x < y$, and thus we obtain the contradiction $\text{sq-sum}(\langle \alpha_i' \rangle) < \text{sq-sum}(\langle \alpha_i \rangle)$. Since the minimum of the squashed sum occurs when $\alpha_1 = \alpha_2 = \cdots = \alpha_{m-l} = 0$ and $\alpha_{m-l+1} = \alpha_{m-l+2} = \cdots = \alpha_m = h$, the minimum value of the squashed sum is $\sum_{i=1}^{m} (m - i + 1)\alpha_i = \sum_{i=m-l+1}^{m} (m - i + 1)h = hl(l + 1)/2$.

Lemma 8. *Let $\langle \alpha_i \rangle$ be a list of m nonnegative integers, and let $h \geq 0$ be another integer. Generate another list of integers $\langle \beta_i \rangle$ by choosing any l integers from $\langle \alpha_i \rangle$ and increasing each of their values by h. Then, we have*

$$\text{sq-sum}(\langle \beta_i \rangle) \geq \text{sq-sum}(\langle \alpha_i \rangle) + hl(l+1)/2 .$$

Proof. Assume that the elements in both $\langle \alpha_i \rangle$ and $\langle \beta_i \rangle$ are sorted such that $\alpha_1 \leq \alpha_2 \leq \cdots \leq \alpha_m$ and $\beta_1 \leq \beta_2 \leq \cdots \leq \beta_m$. Observe that when viewed in sorted order, if an element of $\langle \beta_i \rangle$ was produced by increasing an element of $\langle \alpha_i \rangle$ by h, their indexes may now no longer correspond.

First, we show by contradiction that $\beta_i \geq \alpha_i$. If there exists an index j such that $\beta_j < \alpha_j$, there must exist at least j integers strictly less than α_j in the list $\langle \beta_i \rangle$, namely $\beta_1, \beta_2, \ldots, \beta_j$. Each β_x among these j integers corresponds to a distinct $\alpha_y \in \langle \alpha_i \rangle$, where $\beta_x = \alpha_y$ or $\beta_x = \alpha_y + h$. Thus, there are at least j integers strictly less than α_j in the list $\langle \alpha_i \rangle$. But, there can be only at most $j - 1$ integers less than α_j in the list $\langle \alpha_i \rangle$, namely $\alpha_1, \alpha_2, \ldots, \alpha_{j-1}$. Contradiction.

Second, we show by contradiction that $\beta_i \leq \alpha_i + h$. If there exists an index j such that $\beta_j > \alpha_j + h$, there must exist at least $m - j + 1$ integers strictly greater than $\alpha_j + h$ in the list $\langle \beta_i \rangle$, namely $\beta_j, \beta_{j+1}, \ldots, \beta_m$. Each β_x of these $m - j + 1$ integers corresponds to a distinct $\alpha_y \in \langle \alpha_i \rangle$, where $\beta_x = \alpha_y$ or $\beta_x = \alpha_y + h$. Thus, there are at least $m - j + 1$ integers strictly greater than α_j in the list $\langle \alpha_i \rangle$. But, there can be at most $m - j$ integers greater than α_j in $\langle \alpha_i \rangle$, namely $\alpha_{j+1}, \alpha_{j+2}, \ldots, \alpha_m$. Contradiction.

Now, define another list $\langle \gamma_i \rangle$ of integers by $\gamma_i = \beta_i - \alpha_i$ for $i = 1, 2, \ldots, m$. From Definition 2 we have

$$\text{sq-sum}(\langle \beta_i \rangle) - \text{sq-sum}(\langle \alpha_i \rangle) = \sum_{i=1}^{m} (m - i + 1)(\beta_i - \alpha_i)$$
$$= \sum_{i=1}^{m} (m - i + 1)\gamma_i$$
$$= \text{sq-sum}(\langle \gamma_i \rangle) .$$

Since we obtain $\langle \beta_i \rangle$ from $\langle \alpha_i \rangle$ by choosing l numbers and increasing each of them by h, we have

$$\sum_{i=1}^{m} \gamma_i = \sum_{i=1}^{m} \beta_i - \sum_{i=1}^{m} \alpha_i$$
$$= lh .$$

Because we have $0 \leq \beta_i - \alpha_i \leq h$, it follows that $0 \leq \gamma_i \leq h$. From Lemma 7, we know that the squashed sum of the list $\langle \gamma_i \rangle$ is $\text{sq-sum}(\langle \gamma_i \rangle) \geq hl(l+1)/2$, and its minimum occurs when $\gamma_1 = \gamma_2 = \cdots = \gamma_{m-l} = 0$ and for $\gamma_{m-l+1} = \gamma_{m-l+2} = \cdots = \gamma_m = h$. Thus, we have $\text{sq-sum}(\langle \beta_i \rangle) - \text{sq-sum}(\langle \alpha_i \rangle) \geq hl(l+1)/2$, and the minimum occurs when

$$\beta_i = \begin{cases} \alpha_i & \text{if } i = 1, 2, \ldots, m - l, \\ \alpha_i + h & \text{if } i = m - l + 1, m - l + 2, \ldots, m. \end{cases}$$

The second step of our analysis bounds the total response time $R(\mathcal{J})$ of AGDEQ in terms of the squashed deprived allotment area sdaa $(\mathcal{J})$ and total satisfied time sat $(\mathcal{J})$.

Lemma 9. *Suppose that a job set $\mathcal{J}$ is scheduled by AGDEQ. The total response time of $\mathcal{J}$ can be bounded as*

$$R(\mathcal{J}) \leq \left(2 - \frac{2}{|\mathcal{J}| + 1}\right) (\text{sdaa}\,(\mathcal{J}) + \text{sat}\,(\mathcal{J})) \,, \tag{7}$$

where sdaa $(\mathcal{J})$ is the squashed deprived allotment area of $\mathcal{J}$ and sat $(\mathcal{J})$ is the total satisfied time of $\mathcal{J}$.

Proof. Suppose that AGDEQ produces a schedule $\chi = (\tau, \pi)$ for $\mathcal{J}$. Let $T = T_\chi(\mathcal{J})$ be the completion time of the job set $\mathcal{J}$.

First, let us define some notation. For any time step t, represent set of time steps from t to the completion of $\mathcal{J}$ by $\overrightarrow{t} = \{t, t+1, \ldots, T\}$. We shall be interested in "suffixes" of jobs, namely, the portions of jobs that remain after some number of steps have been executed. To that end, define the *t-suffix* of a job $J_i \in \mathcal{J}$ to be the job $J_i\left(\overrightarrow{t}\right)$ induced by those vertices in $V(J_i)$ that execute on or after time t, that is,

$$J_i\left(\overrightarrow{t}\right) = \left(V\left(J_i\left(\overrightarrow{t}\right)\right), E\left(J_i\left(\overrightarrow{t}\right)\right)\right) \,,$$

where $v \in V\left(J_i\left(\overrightarrow{t}\right)\right)$ if $v \in V(J_i)$ and $\tau(v) \geq t$, and $(u, v) \in E\left(J_i\left(\overrightarrow{t}\right)\right)$ if $(u, v) \in E(J_i)$ and $u, v \in V\left(J_i\left(\overrightarrow{t}\right)\right)$. The t-suffix of the job set $\mathcal{J}$ is

$$\mathcal{J}\left(\overrightarrow{t}\right) = \left\{J_i\left(\overrightarrow{t}\right) : J_i \in \mathcal{J} \text{ and } V\left(J_i\left(\overrightarrow{t}\right)\right) \neq \emptyset\right\} \,.$$

Thus, we have $\mathcal{J} = \mathcal{J}\left(\overrightarrow{1}\right)$, and the number of incomplete jobs at time step t is the number $\left|\mathcal{J}\left(\overrightarrow{t}\right)\right|$ of nonempty jobs in $\mathcal{J}\left(\overrightarrow{t}\right)$. Since we only consider batched jobs, the number of incomplete jobs is decreasing monotonically, and hence, we have

$$\left|\mathcal{J}\left(\overrightarrow{t+1}\right)\right| \leq \left|\mathcal{J}\left(\overrightarrow{t}\right)\right| \,. \tag{8}$$

The total response times of $\mathcal{J}\left(\overrightarrow{t}\right)$ and $\mathcal{J}\left(\overrightarrow{t+1}\right)$ can also be related using this notation. Since each incomplete job of $\mathcal{J}\left(\overrightarrow{t}\right)$ adds one time step into its total response time during step t, we have

$$R\left(\mathcal{J}\left(\overrightarrow{t}\right)\right) = R\left(\mathcal{J}\left(\overrightarrow{t+1}\right)\right) + \left|\mathcal{J}\left(\overrightarrow{t}\right)\right| \,. \tag{9}$$

We shall prove the lemma by induction on the remaining execution time of the job set $\mathcal{J}\left(\overrightarrow{t}\right)$.

Basis: $t = T+1$. Since we have $\mathcal{J}\left(\overrightarrow{T+1}\right) = \emptyset$, it follows that $R\left(\mathcal{J}\left(\overrightarrow{T+1}\right)\right) = 0$, sdaa $\left(\mathcal{J}\left(\overrightarrow{T+1}\right)\right) = 0$, and sat $\left(\mathcal{J}\left(\overrightarrow{T+1}\right)\right) = 0$. Thus, the claim holds trivially.

Induction: $1 \leq t \leq T$. Suppose that the lemma holds for $\mathcal{J}\left(\overrightarrow{t+1}\right)$. We shall prove that it holds for $\mathcal{J}\left(\overrightarrow{t}\right)$.

We first define some notation. At any time step t, the incomplete jobs can be partitioned as $\mathcal{J}\left(\overrightarrow{t}\right) = \mathcal{JS}(t) \cup \mathcal{JD}(t)$, representing the set of satisfied and deprived jobs at time t, respectively. For any job $J_i \in \mathcal{J}$ and time t, define

$$S\left(i,t\right) = \begin{cases} \{t\} & \text{if } J_i \in \mathcal{JS}(t) \text{ ,} \\ \emptyset & \text{if } J_i \notin \mathcal{JS}(t) \text{ ;} \end{cases}$$

and similarly, define

$$D\left(i,t\right) = \begin{cases} \{t\} & \text{if } J_i \in \mathcal{JD}(t) \text{ ,} \\ \emptyset & \text{if } J_i \notin \mathcal{JD}(t) \text{ .} \end{cases}$$

We can extend these definitions to suffix ranges:

$$S\left(i,\overrightarrow{t}\right) = \bigcup_{t'=t}^{T} S\left(i,t'\right) \text{ ,}$$

$$D\left(i,\overrightarrow{t}\right) = \bigcup_{t'=t}^{T} D\left(i,t'\right) \text{ .}$$

We now relate the total satisfied times of $\mathcal{J}\left(\overrightarrow{t}\right)$ and $\mathcal{J}\left(\overrightarrow{t+1}\right)$. By definition of total satisfied time and using the fact that $\sum_{J_i \in \mathcal{J}} |S\left(i,t\right)| = |\mathcal{JS}(t)|$, we have

$$\begin{aligned} \text{sat}\left(\mathcal{J}\left(\overrightarrow{t}\right)\right) &= \sum_{J_i \in \mathcal{J}} \left|S\left(i,\overrightarrow{t}\right)\right| \\ &= \sum_{J_i \in \mathcal{J}} \left|S\left(i,t\right)\right| + \sum_{J_i \in \mathcal{J}} \left|S\left(i,\overrightarrow{t+1}\right)\right| \\ &= \left|\mathcal{JS}(t)\right| + \text{sat}\left(\mathcal{J}\left(\overrightarrow{t+1}\right)\right) \text{ .} \end{aligned} \tag{10}$$

We next relate the accumulated deprived allotments $a\left(i, D\left(i,\overrightarrow{t}\right)\right)$ and $a\left(i, D\left(i,\overrightarrow{t+1}\right)\right)$. Job J_i's accumulated deprived allotment on $\overrightarrow{t}$ is given by

$$a\left(i, D\left(i,\overrightarrow{t}\right)\right) = \sum_{t' \in D\left(i,\overrightarrow{t}\right)} a\left(i,t'\right) \text{ .}$$

We consider two cases depending on whether $J_i \in \mathcal{JS}(t)$ or $J_i \in \mathcal{JD}(t)$. If $J_i \in \mathcal{JS}(t)$, we have $D\left(i,t\right) = \emptyset$ and $D\left(i,\overrightarrow{t}\right) = D\left(i,\overrightarrow{t+1}\right)$, and thus, J_i's accumulated deprived allotment is

$$\begin{aligned} a\left(i, D\left(i,\overrightarrow{t}\right)\right) &= \sum_{t' \in D\left(i,\overrightarrow{t}\right)} a\left(i,t'\right) \\ &= \sum_{t' \in D\left(i,\overrightarrow{t+1}\right)} a\left(i,t'\right) \\ &= a\left(i, D\left(i,\overrightarrow{t+1}\right)\right) \text{ .} \end{aligned} \tag{11}$$

If $J_i \in \mathcal{JD}(t)$, we have $D\left(i, t\right) = \{t\}$ and $D\left(i, \overrightarrow{t}\right) = D\left(i, \overrightarrow{t+1}\right) \cup \{t\}$. Moreover, J_i has allotment $a\left(i, t\right) = p\left(t\right)$, where $p\left(t\right)$ denotes the mean deprived allotment at time step t. Thus, J_i's accumulated deprived allotment is

$$
\begin{aligned}
a\left(i, D\left(i, \overrightarrow{t}\right)\right) &= \sum_{t' \in D(i, \overrightarrow{t})} a\left(i, t'\right) \\
&= \sum_{t' \in D(i, \overrightarrow{t+1})} a\left(i, t'\right) + a\left(i, t\right) \\
&= a\left(i, D\left(i, \overrightarrow{t+1}\right)\right) + a\left(i, t\right) \\
&= a\left(i, D\left(i, \overrightarrow{t+1}\right)\right) + p\left(t\right) .
\end{aligned}
\tag{12}
$$

Thus, going backwards from step $t+1$ to step t, the accumulated deprived allotment either stays the same or increases by $p\left(t\right)$, depending on whether step t is satisfied or deprived, respectively.

We now use Lemma 8 to relate the squashed deprived allotment areas of $\mathcal{J}\left(\overrightarrow{t}\right)$ and $\mathcal{J}\left(\overrightarrow{t+1}\right)$. Let $n = \left|\mathcal{J}\left(\overrightarrow{t}\right)\right|$ denote the number of incomplete jobs before step t. For $i = 1, 2, \ldots, n$, let $\alpha_i = a\left(i, D\left(i, \overrightarrow{t+1}\right)\right)$, and let $\beta_i = a\left(i, D\left(i, \overrightarrow{t}\right)\right)$. If $J_i \in \mathcal{JS}(t)$, Equation (11) implies that $\beta_i = \alpha_i$. If $J_i \in \mathcal{JD}(t)$, Equation (12) implies that $\beta_i = \alpha_i + p\left(t\right)$. Thus, the list $\langle \beta_i \rangle$ can be generated by choosing $l = \left|\mathcal{JD}(t)\right|$ integers from $\langle \alpha_i \rangle$ and increasing each of them by $h = p\left(t\right)$. Applying Lemma 8 and the definition of squashed deprived allotment area, we obtain

$$
\begin{aligned}
& \text{sdaa}\left(\mathcal{J}\left(\overrightarrow{t}\right)\right) \\
&= \frac{1}{P} \text{sq-sum}\left(\left\langle a\left(i, D\left(i, \overrightarrow{t}\right)\right)\right\rangle\right) \\
&\geq \frac{1}{P}\left(\text{sq-sum}\left(\left\langle a\left(i, D\left(i, \overrightarrow{t+1}\right)\right)\right\rangle\right) + p\left(t\right)\left|\mathcal{JD}(t)\right|\left(\left|\mathcal{JD}(t)\right| + 1\right)/2\right) \\
&= \text{sdaa}\left(\mathcal{J}\left(\overrightarrow{t+1}\right)\right) + p\left(t\right)\left|\mathcal{JD}(t)\right|\left(\left|\mathcal{JD}(t)\right| + 1\right)/2P .
\end{aligned}
\tag{13}
$$

We now can complete the proof of the lemma by using Inequality (8), Equations (9) and (10), and Inequality (13) to bound the total response time of $\mathcal{J}\left(\overrightarrow{t}\right)$:

$$
\begin{aligned}
& R\left(\mathcal{J}\left(\overrightarrow{t}\right)\right) \\
&= R\left(\mathcal{J}\left(\overrightarrow{t+1}\right)\right) + \left|\mathcal{J}\left(\overrightarrow{t}\right)\right| \\
&\leq \left(2 - \frac{2}{\left|\mathcal{J}\left(\overrightarrow{t+1}\right)\right| + 1}\right)\left(\text{sdaa}\left(\mathcal{J}\left(\overrightarrow{t+1}\right)\right) + \text{sat}\left(\mathcal{J}\left(\overrightarrow{t+1}\right)\right)\right) + \left|\mathcal{J}\left(\overrightarrow{t}\right)\right| \\
&\leq \left(2 - \frac{2}{\left|\mathcal{J}\left(\overrightarrow{t}\right)\right| + 1}\right)\left(\text{sdaa}\left(\mathcal{J}\left(\overrightarrow{t+1}\right)\right) + \text{sat}\left(\mathcal{J}\left(\overrightarrow{t+1}\right)\right)\right) + \left|\mathcal{J}\left(\overrightarrow{t}\right)\right| \\
&\leq \left(2 - \frac{2}{n+1}\right)\left(\text{sdaa}\left(\mathcal{J}\left(\overrightarrow{t}\right)\right) - \frac{p\left(t\right)\left|\mathcal{JD}(t)\right|\left(\left|\mathcal{JD}(t)\right| + 1\right)}{2P}\right)
\end{aligned}
$$

$$+ \left(2 - \frac{2}{n+1} \right) \left(\text{sat} \left(\mathcal{J} \left(\overrightarrow{t} \right) \right) - |\mathcal{JS}(t)| \right) + n$$

$$\leq \left(2 - \frac{2}{n+1} \right) \left(\text{sdaa} \left(\mathcal{J} \left(\overrightarrow{t} \right) \right) + \text{sat} \left(\mathcal{J} \left(\overrightarrow{t} \right) \right) \right)$$

$$- \left(2 - \frac{2}{n+1} \right) \left(\frac{p\,(t)\,|\mathcal{JD}(t)|\,(|\mathcal{JD}(t)|+1)}{2P} + |\mathcal{JS}(t)| \right) + n$$

We must show that

$$\left(2 - \frac{2}{n+1} \right) \left(\frac{p\,(t)\,|\mathcal{JD}(t)|\,(|\mathcal{JD}(t)|+1)}{2P} + |\mathcal{JS}(t)| \right) - n \geq 0$$

Using the facts that $p\,(t) \geq P/n$, $|\mathcal{JD}(t)| = n - |\mathcal{JS}(t)|$, $|\mathcal{JS}(t)|$ is an integer, and $0 \leq |\mathcal{JS}(t)| \leq n$, we obtain

$$\left(2 - \frac{2}{n+1} \right) \left(\frac{p\,(t)\,|\mathcal{JD}(t)|\,(|\mathcal{JD}(t)|+1)}{2P} + |\mathcal{JS}(t)| \right) - n$$

$$\geq \frac{n}{n+1} \left(\frac{p\,(t)}{P} |\mathcal{JD}(t)|\,(|\mathcal{JD}(t)|+1) + 2\,|\mathcal{JS}(t)| - (n+1) \right)$$

$$\geq \frac{n}{n+1} \left(\frac{|\mathcal{JD}(t)|\,(|\mathcal{JD}(t)|+1)}{n} + 2\,|\mathcal{JS}(t)| - n - 1 \right)$$

$$= \frac{1}{n+1} \left(|\mathcal{JD}(t)|\,(|\mathcal{JD}(t)|+1) + 2n\,|\mathcal{JS}(t)| - n^2 - n \right)$$

$$= \frac{1}{n+1} \left((n - |\mathcal{JS}(t)|)\,(n - |\mathcal{JS}(t)| + 1) + 2n\,|\mathcal{JS}(t)| - n^2 - n \right)$$

$$= \frac{1}{n+1} |\mathcal{JS}(t)|\,(|\mathcal{JS}(t)| - 1)$$

$$\geq 0 \,.$$

The third step of our analysis bounds the squashed deprived allotment area in terms of the squashed work area.

Lemma 10. *Suppose that a job set $\mathcal{J}$ is scheduled by* AGDEQ, *where ρ and δ are* A-GREEDY*'s responsiveness and utilization parameters, respectively. The squashed deprived allotment area of $\mathcal{J}$ can be bounded as*

$$\text{sdaa}\,(\mathcal{J}) \leq \frac{\rho+1}{\delta} \text{swa}\,(\mathcal{J}) \,,$$

where $\text{swa}\,(\mathcal{J})$ *is the squashed work area of the job set $\mathcal{J}$.*

Proof. We first show that $a\,(i, D(i)) \leq cT_1(i)$ for every job $J_i \in \mathcal{J}$, where $a(i)$ and $a\,(i, D(i))$ are J_i's accumulated allotment and accumulated deprived allotment, respectively, and $c = (\rho + 1)/\delta$. By Definition 3, we have $a\,(i, D(i)) = \sum_{t \in D(i)} a\,(i,t) \leq \sum_{t=0}^{\infty} a\,(i,t) = a(i)$, since $D(i) \subseteq \{1, 2, \ldots, \infty\}$ and $a\,(i,t) \geq 0$. The processor allotments to any job are either used to make progress on the total work $T_1(i)$ or wasted. According to Lemma 5, any job J_i wastes at most $w(i) = ((\rho + 1 - \delta)/\delta)T_1(i)$ processor cycles. For each job J_i, we have

$$
\begin{aligned}
a\,(i, D(i)) &\le a(i) \\
&= T_1(i) + w(i) \\
&\le ((\rho + 1 - \delta)/\delta)T_1(i) + T_1(i) \\
&= cT_1(i) \; .
\end{aligned}
$$

To complete the proof, we use Definition 2 and apply Lemma 6:

$$
\begin{aligned}
\mathrm{sdaa}\,(\mathcal{J}) &= (1/P)\,\mathrm{sq\text{-}sum}(\langle a\,(i, D(i))\rangle) \\
&\le (1/P)\,\mathrm{sq\text{-}sum}(\langle cT_1(i)\rangle) \\
&= c \cdot (1/P)\,\mathrm{sq\text{-}sum}(\langle T_1(i)\rangle) \\
&= c \cdot \mathrm{swa}\,(\mathcal{J}) \; .
\end{aligned}
$$

The fourth step of our analysis relates the total satisfied time to the aggregate critical-path length.

Lemma 11. *Suppose that a job set $\mathcal{J}$ is scheduled by AGDEQ, where ρ and δ are A-GREEDY's responsiveness and utilization parameters, respectively. The total satisfied time of $\mathcal{J}$ can be bounded as*

$$
\mathrm{sat}\,(\mathcal{J}) \le \frac{2}{1 - \delta} T_\infty(\mathcal{J}) + |\mathcal{J}|\,(L \log_\rho P + L) \; ,
$$

where $T_\infty(\mathcal{J})$ is the aggregate critical-path length of $\mathcal{J}$.

Proof. We bound the total satisfied time using Lemma 4:

$$
\begin{aligned}
\mathrm{sat}\,(\mathcal{J}) &= \sum_{J_i \in \mathcal{J}} |S(i)| \\
&\le \sum_{J_i \in \mathcal{J}} \left(\frac{2T_\infty(i)}{1 - \delta} + L \log_\rho P + L \right) \\
&= \frac{2}{1 - \delta} T_\infty(\mathcal{J}) + |\mathcal{J}|\,(L \log_\rho P + L) \; .
\end{aligned}
$$

We can now apply the results of our four-step analysis to obtain a bound on total response time.

Theorem 2. *Suppose that a job set $\mathcal{J}$ is scheduled by AGDEQ. Let ρ be A-GREEDY's responsiveness parameter, δ its utilization parameter, and L the quantum length. The total response time $R(\mathcal{J})$ of the schedule is at most*

$$
R(\mathcal{J}) \le \left(2 - \frac{2}{|\mathcal{J}| + 1} \right) \left(\frac{\rho + 1}{\delta} \mathrm{swa}\,(\mathcal{J}) + \frac{2}{1 - \delta} T_\infty(\mathcal{J}) + |\mathcal{J}|\,L(\log_\rho P + 1) \right) \; ,
$$

where $\mathrm{swa}\,(\mathcal{J})$ is the squashed work area of $\mathcal{J}$, and $T_\infty(\mathcal{J})$ is the aggregate critical-path length of $\mathcal{J}$.

Proof. Combine Lemmas 9, 10, and 11.

Since both swa $(\mathcal{J})/|\mathcal{J}|$ and $T_\infty(\mathcal{J})/|\mathcal{J}|$ are lower bounds on $\overline{R}(\mathcal{J})$, we obtain the following corollary.

Corollary 2. *Suppose that a job set $\mathcal{J}$ is scheduled by AGDEQ. Let ρ be A-GREEDY 's responsiveness parameter, δ its utilization parameter, and L the quantum length. The mean response time $\overline{R}(\mathcal{J})$ of the schedule satisfies*

$$\overline{R}(\mathcal{J}) \leq \left(2 - \frac{2}{|\mathcal{J}|+1}\right)\left(\left(\frac{\rho+1}{\delta} + \frac{2}{1-\delta}\right)\overline{R}^*(\mathcal{J}) + L\log_\rho P + L\right) ,$$

where $\overline{R}^*(\mathcal{J})$ denotes the mean response time of $\mathcal{J}$ scheduled by an optimal clairvoyant scheduler.

Proof. Combine Theorem 2 with Inequalities (3) and (4).

Since both the quantum length L and the processor number P are independent variables with respect to any job set $\mathcal{J}$, Corollary 2 shows that AGDEQ is $O(1)$-competitive with respect to mean response time for batched jobs. Specifically, when $\delta = 1/2$ and ρ approaches 1, AGDEQ's competitiveness ratio approaches the minimum value 16. Thus, AGDEQ is $(16 + \epsilon)$-competitive with respect to mean response time for any constant $\epsilon > 0$.

The competitive ratio of 16 for AGDEQ is a worst-case bound. We expect that in practice, however, AGDEQ should perform closer to optimal. In particular, when the job set $\mathcal{J}$ exhibits reasonably large total parallelism, we have swa $(\mathcal{J}) \gg T_\infty(\mathcal{J})$, and thus, the term involving swa $(\mathcal{J})$ in Theorem 2 dominates the total response time. More importantly, the job scheduler DEQ is not actually an adversary of A-GREEDY, and simulations of A-STEAL [2] suggest that in practice A-GREEDY should produce waste closer to $(1/\delta - 1)T_1(i)$. From the proof of Lemma 10, one can determine that the coefficient on the term swa $(\mathcal{J})$ becomes $(2 - 2/(|\mathcal{J}|+1))/\delta$ when a job's waste is no more than $(1/\delta-1)$ times its work. That is to say, in this scenario, the mean response time of a job set scheduled by AGDEQ is about $(2/\delta)$ swa $(\mathcal{J})$. Since δ is typically in the range of 0.5 to 1, if the job set has reasonably large total parallelism, AGDEQ is likely to achieve the mean response time of less than 4 times the optimal.

6   ASDEQ Algorithm and Performance

ASDEQ is a distributed two-level adaptive scheduler that uses the A-STEAL algorithm [2,3] as its thread scheduler and DEQ as its job scheduler. A-STEAL is a decentralized thread scheduler that employs randomized work stealing [16,31, 47,13,4] to schedule and execute a job without central knowledge of all available threads. The interactions between A-STEAL and DEQ follow the scheduling model described in Section 2. In this section, we briefly overview the A-STEAL algorithm. We show that ASDEQ is $O(1)$-competitive with respect to makespan for jobs with arbitrary release time and $O(1)$-competitive with respect to mean response time for batched jobs.

The Adaptive Stealing Thread Scheduler

The A-STEAL algorithm is a decentralized adaptive thread scheduler with parallelism feedback, and like A-GREEDY, A-STEAL performs two functions. Between quanta, it estimates its job's desire and requests processors from the job scheduler. A-STEAL applies the same desire-estimation algorithm as A-GREEDY to calculate its job's desire. During the quantum, A-STEAL schedules the ready threads of the job onto the allotted processors using an adaptive work-stealing algorithm.

Each processor allotted to a job whose threads are scheduled by A-STEAL maintains a **deque** (double-ended queue) of those threads that are ready to execute. To handle an increase in allotment, A-STEAL creates an empty deque for each newly allotted processor. When the allotment decreases, A-STEAL marks the deques from deallotted processors as **muggable deques**. An allotted processor works on only one ready thread at a time. When the current thread spawns a new thread, the processor pushes the current thread onto the top of the deque and begins working on the new thread. When the current thread completes or blocks, the processor pops the topmost thread off the deque and begins working on it. If the deque of a processor becomes empty, however, the processor becomes a **thief**. The thief first looks for a muggable deque. If one is found, the thief **mugs** the deque by taking over the entire deque as its own. Otherwise, it randomly picks a **victim** processor and **steals** work from the bottom of the victim's deque. If the victim has no available work, then the steal is **unsuccessful**, and the thief continues to steal at random from the other processors until it is **successful** and finds work. At all time steps, every processor is either working, stealing, or mugging.

Analysis

We now show that ASDEQ is $O(1)$-competitive with respect to both makespan and mean response time. The methods used to analyze ASDEQ are similar to those for AGDEQ. Since ASDEQ is a randomized scheduling algorithm, however, we show that its makespan (or its expected mean response time) is within a factor c of that incurred in an optimal clairvoyant algorithm in expectation, not in the worst case. Let $\chi = (\tau, \pi)$ be the schedule of a job set $\mathcal{J}$ produced by ASDEQ. For simplicity we shall use the notations $\mathrm{T}(\mathcal{J}) = \mathrm{T}_\chi(\mathcal{J})$ and $\mathrm{R}(\mathcal{J}) = \mathrm{R}_\chi(\mathcal{J})$.

The next two lemmas, proved in [3], bound the expected satisfied steps and the waste of any single job scheduled by A-STEAL. They provide a starting point for the analysis.

Lemma 12. *[3] Suppose that* A-STEAL *schedules a job* J_i *with critical path length* $T_\infty(i)$ *on a machine with* P *processors. Let* ρ *denote* A-STEAL*'s responsiveness parameter,* δ *its utilization parameter, and* L *the quantum length. Then,*

A-STEAL *produces at most* $48T_\infty(i)/(1-\delta) + L\log_\rho P + L$ *satisfied steps in expectation.* □

Lemma 13. *[3] Suppose that* A-STEAL *schedules a job* J_i *with work* $T_1(i)$ *on a machine with* P *processors. Let* ρ *denote* A-STEAL*'s responsiveness parameter,* δ *is its utilization parameter, and* L *is the quantum length. Then,* A-STEAL *wastes at most*

$$W \le \left(\frac{1+\rho-\delta}{\delta} + \frac{(1+\rho)^2}{\delta(L\delta-1-\rho)}\right) T_1(i) \tag{14}$$

processor cycles in the course of the computation. □

The next theorem shows that ASDEQ is $O(1)$-competitive with respect to makespan for a job set $\mathcal{J}$ with arbitrary release time. The following bound is based on the release time $r(i)$, critical-path length $T_\infty(i)$, and work $T_1(i)$ of an individual job $J_i \in \mathcal{J}$, as well as on the total work $T_1(\mathcal{J})$ of the job set $\mathcal{J}$.

Theorem 3. *Suppose that* ASDEQ *schedules a job set* $\mathcal{J}$ *on a machine with* P *processors. Let* ρ *denote* A-STEAL*'s responsiveness parameter,* δ *its utilization parameter, and* L *the quantum size. Then, we expect* ASDEQ *to complete* $\mathcal{J}$ *in*

$$E[T(\mathcal{J})] = \left(\frac{\rho+1}{\delta} + \frac{(1+\rho)^2}{\delta(L\delta-1-\rho)}\right)\frac{T_1(\mathcal{J})}{P}$$

$$+O\left(\frac{\max_{J_i \in \mathcal{J}}\{r(i)+T_\infty(i)\}}{1-\delta}\right) + L\log_\rho P + 2L \tag{15}$$

time steps.

Proof. The proof is similar to that of Theorem 1. Let job J_k be the last job to complete among the jobs in $\mathcal{J}$. Let $S(k)$ denote the set of satisfied steps for J_k, and let $D(k)$ denote the set of deprived steps for J_k. The earliest that the job J_k can start its execution is at the beginning of the quantum immediately after J_k's release, which is the quantum q satisfying $Lq < r(k) \le L(q+1)$. Therefore, we have

$$T(\mathcal{J}) < r(k) + L + |S(k)| + |D(k)| . \tag{16}$$

Since Lemma 12 bounds the number of J_k's satisfied steps, we focus on bounding the quantity the number $|D(k)|$ of J_k's deprived steps. DEQ must allot all processors to jobs on any deprived step, and hence we have $a(\mathcal{J}, D(k)) = \sum_{t \in D(k)} \sum_{J_i \in \mathcal{J}} a(i,t) = P|D(k)|$. The allotted processor cycles are either working or wasted. Define the constant c to be

$$c = \frac{\rho+1}{\delta} + \frac{(1+\rho)^2}{\delta(L\delta-1-\rho)} .$$

Lemma 13 shows that the waste $w(i)$ for any job J_i is at most $(c-1)T_1(i)$. Since the total allotment $a(\mathcal{J}, D(k))$ is at most the sum of the total work and total waste, we have $P|D(k)| = a(\mathcal{J}, D(k)) \le \sum_{J_i \in \mathcal{J}}(T_1(i)+w(i)) \le \sum_{J_i \in \mathcal{J}} cT_1(i) = cT_1(\mathcal{J})$, which gives us $|D(k)| \le cT_1(\mathcal{J})/P$.

Combining this bound, the bound $E\left[\|S(k)\|\right] \leq 48T_\infty(k)/(1-\delta) + L\log_\rho P + L$ from Lemma 12, and the bound $E\left[T(\mathcal{J})\right] < r(k) + L + E\left[\|S(k)\| + |D(k)|\right]$ from Inequality (16) completes the proof.

The next theorem shows that ASDEQ is $O(1)$-competitive with respect to mean response time for batched jobs.

Theorem 4. *Suppose that a job set $\mathcal{J}$ is scheduled by* ASDEQ*. Let ρ denote* A-STEAL*'s responsiveness parameter, δ its utilization parameter, and L the quantum length. Then, the expected response time of the schedule satisfies*

$$E\left[R(\mathcal{J})\right] = \left(2 - \frac{2}{|\mathcal{J}|+1}\right)\left(\frac{\rho+1}{\delta} + \frac{(1+\rho)^2}{\delta(L\delta-1-\rho)}\right)\mathrm{swa}\left(\mathcal{J}\right)$$
$$+ O\left(\frac{T_\infty(\mathcal{J})}{1-\delta}\right) + 2|\mathcal{J}|L(\log_\rho P + 1)\,,$$

where $\mathrm{swa}\left(\mathcal{J}\right)$ *is the squashed work area, and $T_\infty(\mathcal{J})$ is the aggregate critical-path length.*

Proof. The proof of the theorem follows closely on that of Theorem 2. It turns out that Lemma 9 holds for any two-level scheduler that uses DEQ, irrespective of the thread scheduler. Lemma 10 holds with the new constant

$$c = \frac{\rho+1}{\delta} + \frac{(1+\rho)^2}{\delta(L\delta-1-\rho)}\,.$$

Lemma 11 can be adapted by using Lemma 12 in place of Lemma 4 to produce the bound

$$E\left[\mathrm{sat}\left(\mathcal{J}\right)\right] = O\left(\frac{T_\infty(\mathcal{J})}{1-\delta}\right) + L\log_\rho P + L\,.$$

Combining these bounds yields the theorem.

Theorems 3 and 4 show that ASDEQ is $O(1)$-competitive for both makespan and, in the batch setting, mean response time. We anticipate that ASDEQ's competitive ratios would be small in practical settings, especially when many jobs have total work much larger than critical-path length and the machine is moderately or highly loaded. In this case, the term on $T_1(\mathcal{J})/P$ in Inequality (15) is much larger than the term $\max_{J_i \in \mathcal{J}} \{T_\infty(i) + r(i)\}$, which is to say, the term on $T_1(\mathcal{J})/P$ generally dominates the makespan bound. The proof of Theorem 3 calculates the coefficient of $T_1(\mathcal{J})/P$ in Inequality (15) as the ratio of the total allotment (total work plus total waste) versus the total work. When the job scheduler is DEQ, which is not a true adversary, empirical results [2] indicate that each job J_i only wastes about $(1/\delta - 1)T_1(i)$ processor cycles, which is not as large as the worst-case waste in Lemma 13. Therefore, when we use DEQ as the job scheduler, the coefficient of $T_1(\mathcal{J})/P$ seems more likely to approach $1/\delta$. In other words, the makespan of a job set $\mathcal{J}$ scheduled by ASDEQ might more typically be about $T_1(\mathcal{J})/\delta P$. Since δ is typically in the range of 0.5 to 1, ASDEQ may exhibit makespans that are only about 2 times optimal when the jobs have reasonably large parallelism and the machine is moderately or heavily loaded. Similarly, ASDEQ may exhibit only 4 times optimal with respect to mean response time for batched jobs under the same conditions.

7 Competitiveness of Mean Response Time for Nonbatched Jobs

This section studies the competitiveness of deterministic algorithms for minimizing mean response time for nonbatched job sets where jobs can be released at arbitrary times. Let $n = |\mathcal{J}|$ be the number of jobs in a job set $\mathcal{J}$, and let P be the number of processors on which the jobs are scheduled. For jobs with arbitrary release times, Motwani, Phillips, and Torng [42] study the scheduling of serial jobs on single processor, and show that every deterministic algorithm has competitiveness $\Omega(n^{1/3})$, and any randomized algorithm has competitiveness $\Omega(\log n)$ by implicitly assuming that $n > P$. We extend their result for deterministic scheduling of nonbatched jobs by showing that any deterministic algorithm is $\Omega(n^{1/3})$-competitive with respect to mean response time no matter what the relation between n and P. Thus, our results for batched job sets in Section 5 cannot be extended to yield strong results for nonbatched job sets, except possibly if randomization is employed.

The following theorem provides the lower bound.

Theorem 5. *Suppose that a nonbatched job set $\mathcal{J}$ is scheduled on P processors. Any deterministic nonclairvoyant algorithm has competitive ratio $\Omega\left(n^{1/3}\right)$ with respect to the mean response time.*

Proof. We exhibit a job set $\mathcal{J}$ on which any deterministic clairvoyant Algorithm A must perform poorly with respect to the optimal offline clairvoyant algorithm. We construct $\mathcal{J}$ with $n = m^3 - m^2 + m$ jobs in two phases as follows. In the first phase, we allow Algorithm A to execute on m jobs released at time 0 for $m(m-1)$ time steps during which no job completes no matter how Algorithm A allocates the P processors. We give each of the m jobs the work it has executed thus far plus P additional work. In the second phase, we release the remaining jobs at times $m(m-1), m(m-1)+1, m(m-1)+2, \ldots, m(m-1)+m^3-m^2-1$, each with work P. Every job $J_i \in \mathcal{J}$ has a critical-path length of $T_\infty(i) = 1$.

We now analyze the total response time for Algorithm A. For the m jobs released in the first phase, none completes within the $m(m-1)$ time steps. Immediately after time $m(m-1)$, we have $m+1$ jobs, each with P work remaining. To minimize total response time, the best that Algorithm A can do on time step $m(m-1)+1$ is to use all P processors to complete one job. At that point, however, another job is released, and we once again have $m+1$ jobs, each with P work remaining. This process continues until all $m^3 - m^2 + m$ jobs complete. Let χ denote the schedule of the job set $\mathcal{J}$ produced by the algorithm A. By

Definition 1 the total response time for Algorithm A is

$$
\begin{aligned}
R_X(\mathcal{J}) &= \sum_{J_i \in \mathcal{J}} (T_X(i) - r(i)) \\
&= \sum_{J_i \in \mathcal{J}} T_X(i) - \sum_{J_i \in \mathcal{J}} r(i)) \\
&= \sum_{k=m(m-1)+1}^{m^3-m^2+m} k - \sum_{k=m(m-1)}^{m^3-m^2-1} k \\
&= -m(m-1) + \sum_{k=m^3-m^2}^{m^3-m^2+m} k \\
&= -m(m-1) + \frac{1}{2}(2m^3 - 2m^2 + m)(m+1) \\
&= \Omega(m^4) \ .
\end{aligned}
$$

The optimal algorithm works differently, because it knows the future. During the first $m(m-1)$ time steps, the optimal algorithm ignores the largest of the m jobs released at time 0 and works on the other $m-1$ jobs. The total work that can be accomplished in the first $m(m-1)$ time steps is $Pm(m-1)$. Since the total work of the jobs released at time 0 is $Pm(m-1) + Pm = Pm^2$, the largest job must have at least Pm work, and thus the remaining $m-1$ jobs have at most $Pm^2 - Pm = Pm(m-1)$ work among them. Thus, by ignoring the largest jobs during the first phase, the optimal algorithm can complete all but the largest job. Immediately after time $m(m-1)$, we have 2 jobs, one with Pm work remaining, and one with P work remaining. The optimal algorithm completes the smaller job in 1 time step, at which point a new job with P work is released. The process repeats, and the optimal algorithm always schedules the newly released job on all processors, which completes in just 1 time step. Finally, at time $m(m-1) + m^3 - m^2 = m^3 - m$, only the large job remains, which completes at time $m^3 - m + (Pm)/P = m^3$, because the optimal algorithm schedules its Pm work on all P processors.

The optimal algorithm's response time for each of the $m-1$ smaller jobs released at time 0 is at most $m(m-1)$, for each of the $m^3 - m^2$ jobs released in the second phase is 1, and for the largest job is m^3. Thus, the total response time is

$$
\begin{aligned}
R^*(\mathcal{J}) &\leq (m-1) \cdot m(m-1) + (m^3 - m^2) \cdot 1 + 1 \cdot m^3 \\
&= O(m^3) \ .
\end{aligned}
$$

Hence, the competitive ratio is $R(\mathcal{J})/R^*(\mathcal{J}) = \Omega(m^4)/O(m^3) = \Omega(m) = \Omega(n^{1/3})$.

8   Related Work

This section discusses related work on the problem of scheduling to minimize makespan and mean response time. In the offline version of the problem, all the jobs' resource requirments and release times are known in advance. In the online clairvoyant version of the problem, the algorithm knows the resource requirements of a job when it is released, but it must base its decisions only on jobs that have been released. In this paper, we have studied the online nonclairvoyant version of the problem, where the resource requirements and release times are unknown to the scheduling algorithm.

Extensive research [38, 18, 43, 33, 34, 56, 48, 50, 57] has been conducted on both the offline and online clairvoyant versions of the problem. Since both adaptive and nonadaptive task scheduling is strongly NP-hard even for a fixed number (≥ 5) of processors [23], existing work has tended to focus either on finding polynomial-time approximation algorithms or on the optimality of special cases.

The online nonclairvoyant version of the problem includes the scheduling of a single parallel job, multiple serial jobs, and multiple parallel jobs.

Prior work on scheduling a single parallel job tends to focus on nonadaptive scheduling [13, 9, 28, 15, 10, 44] or adaptive scheduling without parallelism feedback [4]. For jobs whose parallelism is unknown in advance and which may change during execution, nonadaptive scheduling is known to waste processor cycles [53], because a job with low parallelism may be allotted more processors than it can productively use. Moreover, in a multiprogrammed environment, nonadaptive scheduling may not allow a new job to start, because existing jobs may already be using most of the processors. Although adaptive scheduling without parallelism feedback allows jobs to enter the system, jobs may still waste processor cycles if they are allotted more processors than they can use.

Adaptive thread scheduling with parallelism feedback has been studied empirically [54, 52, 49] and theoretically [1, 2, 3]. Using an adaptive thread scheduler with parallelism feedback, if a job cannot effectively use the allotted processors, the job scheduler can repurpose those processors to the other jobs that can use them. A-GREEDY and A-STEAL have been shown [1, 2] to achieve nearly linear speedup and waste a relatively small number of processor cycles for individual jobs. These algorithms model the job scheduler as the thread scheduler's adversary. An analytical technique called "trim analysis" shows that the thread scheduler can perform poorly on at most a small number of time steps while exhibiting near-optimal behavior on the vast majority. A-GREEDY and A-STEAL focus on scheduling individual jobs well with respect to both time and waste, but they do not offer any guarantee for the execution time of the overall job set.

Some researchers [17, 30, 35, 5, 7] have studied the online nonclairvoyant scheduling of serial jobs to minimize the mean response time on single or multiple processors. For jobs with arbitrary release times, Motwani, Phillips, and Torng [42] show that every deterministic algorithm has competitiveness $\Omega(n^{1/3})$ with respect to mean response time, implicitly assuming that $n > P$. Moreover, any randomized algorithm has competitiveness $\Omega(\log n)$, also assuming that $n > P$. They also show that round-robin is $(2 - 2P/(n + P))$-competitive. Becchetti and Leonardi [7] present a version of the randomized multilevel feedback algorithm (RMLF) and prove an $O(\log n \log(n/P))$-competitiveness result against any oblivious adversary on a machine with P processors. This RMLF algorithm achieves a tight $O(\log n)$ competitive ratio against an oblivious adversary on a machine with a single processor, thereby matching the lower bound for this case.

Shmoys, Wein and Williamson in [51] study the lower bounds of online non-clairvoyant scheduling of serial jobs with respect to makespan. They show that the competitive ratio is at least $(2-1/P)$ for any preemptive deterministic online algorithm, and at least $(2 - 1/\sqrt{P})$ for any nonpreemptive randomized online algorithm with an oblivious adversary.

Adaptive parallel job scheduling has been studied empirically [41,59,55,36,39] and theoretically [29,20,42,24,25,6]. McCann, Vaswani, and Zahorjan [41] study many different job schedulers and evaluated them on a set of benchmarks. They also introduce the notion of dynamic equipartitioning, which gives each job a fair allotment of processors based on the job's request, while allowing processors that cannot be used by a job to be reallocated to other jobs. Their studies indicate that dynamic equipartitioning may be an effective strategy for adaptive job scheduling. Brecht, Deng, and Gu [14] prove that dynamic equipartitioning with instantaneous parallelism as feedback is 2-competitive with respect to the makespan for jobs with multiple phases, where the parallelism of the job remains constant during the phase and the phases are relatively long compared to the length of a scheduling quantum. Their job execution model assumes that the scheduler can achieve linear speedup during each phase as long as the allotted processors are less than the instantaneous parallelism. With similar settings and assumptions, Deng and Dymond [22] prove that DEQ with instantaneous parallelism is 4-competitive for batched multiphase jobs with respect to the mean response time.

9   Conclusion

Although the results in this paper are entirely theoretical, we are optimistic that AGDEQ and ASDEQ will perform well in the real world. The original analyses of A-GREEDY [1] and A-STEAL [2,3] model the job scheduler as an adversary and thereby produce pessimistic bounds. A more friendly job scheduler, such as DEQ, should therefore allow jobs using A-GREEDY and A-STEAL to incur less waste and shorter execution time than predicted by the theoretical bounds. Since our analyses make use of these pessimistic bounds, we conjecture that in practice the observed makespan and mean response time will be much smaller than what the theoretical bounds predict. We are hopeful that our theoretical work will be complemented by empirical research that can shed additional light on the practicality of provably good two-level schedulers.

Acknowledgement

We would like to acknowledge Kunal Agrawal of MIT CSAIL for initiating the original work on the adaptive thread scheduler A-GREEDY, which has led to fruitful collaborations with her, as well as the independent work reported in this paper.

References

[1] Kunal Agrawal, Yuxiong He, Wen Jing Hsu, and Charles E. Leiserson. Adaptive task scheduling with parallelism feedback. In *PPoPP*, 2006.

[2] Kunal Agrawal, Yuxiong He, and Charles E. Leiserson. An empirical evaluation of work stealing with parallelism feedback. In *ICDCS*, 2006.

[3] Kunal Agrawal, Yuxiong He, and Charles E. Leiserson. Work stealing with parallelism feedback. Unpublished manuscripts, 2006.

[4] Nimar S. Arora, Robert. D. Blumofe, and C. Greg Plaxton. Thread scheduling for multiprogrammed multiprocessors. In *SPAA*, pages 119–129, Puerto Vallarta, Mexico, 1998.

[5] Nir Avrahami and Yossi Azar. Minimizing total flow time and total completion time with immediate dispatching. In *SPAA*, pages 11–18, New York, NY, USA, 2003. ACM Press.

[6] Nikhil Bansal, Kedar Dhamdhere, Jochen Konemann, and Amitabh Sinha. Nonclairvoyant scheduling for minimizing mean slowdown. *Algorithmica*, 40(4):305–318, 2004.

[7] Luca Becchetti and Stefano Leonardi. Nonclairvoyant scheduling to minimize the total flow time on single and parallel machines. *J. ACM*, 51(4):517–539, 2004.

[8] Guy Blelloch, Phil Gibbons, and Yossi Matias. Provably efficient scheduling for languages with fine-grained parallelism. *Journal of the ACM*, 46(2):281–321, 1999.

[9] Guy E. Blelloch, Phillip B. Gibbons, and Yossi Matias. Provably efficient scheduling for languages with fine-grained parallelism. In *SPAA*, pages 1–12, Santa Barbara, California, 1995.

[10] Guy E. Blelloch and John Greiner. A provable time and space efficient implementation of NESL. In *ICFP*, pages 213–225, 1996.

[11] Robert D. Blumofe. *Executing Multithreaded Programs Efficiently*. PhD thesis, Massachusetts Institute of Technology, Cambridge, MA, USA, 1995.

[12] Robert D. Blumofe and Charles E. Leiserson. Space-efficient scheduling of multithreaded computations. *SIAM Journal on Computing*, 27(1):202–229, February 1998.

[13] Robert D. Blumofe and Charles E. Leiserson. Scheduling multithreaded computations by work stealing. *Journal of the ACM*, 46(5):720–748, 1999.

[14] T. Brecht, Xiaotie Deng, and Nian Gu. Competitive dynamic multiprocessor allocation for parallel applications. In *Parallel and Distributed Processing*, pages 448 – 455. IEEE, 1995.

[15] R. P. Brent. The parallel evaluation of general arithmetic expressions. *Journal of the ACM*, pages 201–206, 1974.

[16] F. Warren Burton and M. Ronan Sleep. Executing functional programs on a virtual tree of processors. In *FPCA*, pages 187–194, Portsmouth, New Hampshire, October 1981.

[17] C. Chekuri, R. Motwani, B. Natarajan, and C. Stien. Approximation techniques for average completion time scheduling. In *SODA*, pages 609–618, Philadelphia, PA, USA, 1997. Society for Industrial and Applied Mathematics.

[18] Jianer Chen and Antonio Miranda. A polynomial time approximation scheme for general multiprocessor job scheduling (extended abstract). In *STOC*, pages 418–427, New York, NY, USA, 1999. ACM Press.

[19] Su-Hui Chiang and Mary K. Vernon. Dynamic vs. static quantum-based parallel processor allocation. In *JSSPP*, pages 200–223, Honolulu, Hawaii, United States, 1996.

[20] Xiaotie Deng and Patrick Dymond. On multiprocessor system scheduling. In *SPAA*, pages 82–88, 1996.

[21] Xiaotie Deng, Nian Gu, Tim Brecht, and KaiCheng Lu. Preemptive scheduling of parallel jobs on multiprocessors. In *SODA*, pages 159–167. Society for Industrial and Applied Mathematics, 1996.

[22] Xiaotie Deng, Nian Gu, Tim Brecht, and KaiCheng Lu. Preemptive scheduling of parallel jobs on multiprocessors. In *SODA*, pages 159–167, Philadelphia, PA, USA, 1996. Society for Industrial and Applied Mathematics.

[23] Jianzhong Du and Joseph Y.-T. Leung. Complexity of scheduling parallel task systems. *SIAM J. Discrete Math.*, 2(4):473–487, 1989.

[24] Jeff Edmonds. Scheduling in the dark. In *STOC*, pages 179–188, 1999.

[25] Jeff Edmonds, Donald D. Chinn, Timothy Brecht, and Xiaotie Deng. Non-clairvoyant multiprocessor scheduling of jobs with changing execution characteristics. *Journal of Scheduling*, 6(3):231–250, 2003.

[26] Zhixi Fang, Peiyi Tang, Pen-Chung Yew, and Chuan-Qi Zhu. Dynamic processor self-scheduling for general parallel nested loops. *IEEE Transactions on Computers*, 39(7):919–929, 1990.

[27] Dror G. Feitelson. Job scheduling in multiprogrammed parallel systems (extended version). Technical report, IBM Research Report RC 19790 (87657) 2nd Revision, 1997.

[28] R. L. Graham. Bounds on multiprocessing anomalies. *SIAM Journal on Applied Mathematics*, pages 17(2):416–429, 1969.

[29] Nian Gu. Competitive analysis of dynamic processor allocation strategies. Master's thesis, York University, 1995.

[30] Leslie A. Hall, David B. Shmoys, and Joel Wein. Scheduling to minimize average completion time: off-line and on-line algorithms. In *SODA*, pages 142–151, Philadelphia, PA, USA, 1996. Society for Industrial and Applied Mathematics.

[31] Robert H. Halstead, Jr. Implementation of Multilisp: Lisp on a multiprocessor. In *LFP*, pages 9–17, Austin, Texas, August 1984.

[32] S. F. Hummel and E. Schonberg. Low-overhead scheduling of nested parallelism. *IBM Journal of Research and Development*, 35(5-6):743–765, 1991.

[33] Klaus Jansen and Lorant Porkolab. Linear-time approximation schemes for scheduling malleable parallel tasks. In *SODA*, pages 490–498, Philadelphia, PA, USA, 1999. Society for Industrial and Applied Mathematics.

[34] Klaus Jansen and Hu Zhang. Scheduling malleable tasks with precedence constraints. In *SPAA*, pages 86–95, New York, NY, USA, 2005. ACM Press.

[35] Bala Kalyanasundaram and Kirk R. Pruhs. Minimizing flow time nonclairvoyantly. *J. ACM*, 50(4):551–567, 2003.

[36] Scott T. Leutenegger and Mary K. Vernon. The performance of multiprogrammed multiprocessor scheduling policies. In *SIGMETRICS*, pages 226–236, Boulder, Colorado, United States, 1990.

[37] Steven Lucco. A dynamic scheduling method for irregular parallel programs. In *PLDI*, pages 200–211, New York, NY, USA, 1992. ACM Press.

[38] Walter Ludwig and Prasoon Tiwari. Scheduling malleable and nonmalleable parallel tasks. In *SODA*, pages 167–176, Philadelphia, PA, USA, 1994. Society for Industrial and Applied Mathematics.

[39] Shikharesh Majumdar, Derek L. Eager, and Richard B. Bunt. Scheduling in multiprogrammed parallel systems. In *SIGMETRICS*, pages 104–113, Santa Fe, New Mexico, United States, 1988.

[40] Xavier Martorell, Julita Corbalán, Dimitrios S. Nikolopoulos, Nacho Navarro, Eleftherios D. Polychronopoulos, Theodore S. Papatheodorou, and Jesús Labarta. A tool to schedule parallel applications on multiprocessors: The NANOS CPU manager. In Dror G. Feitelson and Larry Rudolph, editors, *JSSPP*, pages 87–112, 2000.

[41] Cathy McCann, Raj Vaswani, and John Zahorjan. A dynamic processor allocation policy for multiprogrammed shared-memory multiprocessors. *ACM Transactions on Computer Systems*, 11(2):146–178, 1993.

[42] Rajeev Motwani, Steven Phillips, and Eric Torng. Non-clairvoyant scheduling. In *SODA*, pages 422–431, 1993.

[43] Gregory Mounie, Christophe Rapine, and Dennis Trystram. Efficient approximation algorithms for scheduling malleable tasks. In *SPAA*, pages 23–32, New York, NY, USA, 1999. ACM Press.

[44] Girija J. Narlikar and Guy E. Blelloch. Space-efficient scheduling of nested parallelism. *ACM Transactions on Programming Languages and Systems*, 21(1):138–173, 1999.

[45] Emilia Rosti, Evgenia Smirni, Lawrence W. Dowdy, Giuseppe Serazzi, and Brian M. Carlson. Robust partitioning schemes of multiprocessor systems. *Performance Evaluation*, 19(2-3):141–165, 1994.

[46] Emilia Rosti, Evgenia Smirni, Giuseppe Serazzi, and Lawrence W. Dowdy. Analysis of non-work-conserving processor partitioning policies. In *IPPS*, pages 165–181, 1995.

[47] Larry Rudolph, Miriam Slivkin-Allalouf, and Eli Upfal. A simple load balancing scheme for task allocation in parallel machines. In *SPAA*, pages 237–245, Hilton Head, South Carolina, July 1991.

[48] Uwe Schwiegelshohn, Walter Ludwig, Joel L. Wolf, John Turek, and Philip S. Yu. Smart smart bounds for weighted response time scheduling. *SIAM J. Comput.*, 28(1):237–253, 1998.

[49] Siddhartha Sen. Dynamic processor allocation for adaptively parallel jobs. Master's thesis, Massachusetts Institute of technology, 2004.

[50] Kenneth C. Sevcik. Application scheduling and processor allocation in multiprogrammed parallel processing systems. *Performance Evaluation*, 19(2-3):107–140, 1994.

[51] D. B. Shmoys, J. Wein, and D. P. Williamson. Scheduling parallel machines online. In *FOCS*, pages 131–140, 1991.

[52] B. Song. Scheduling adaptively parallel jobs. Master's thesis, Massachusetts Institute of Technology, 1998.

[53] Mark S. Squillante. On the benefits and limitations of dynamic partitioning in parallel computer systems. In *IPPS*, pages 219–238, 1995.

[54] Kaushik Guha Timothy B. Brecht. Using parallel program characteristics in dynamic processor allocation policies. *Performance Evaluation*, 27-28:519–539, 1996.

[55] Andrew Tucker and Anoop Gupta. Process control and scheduling issues for multiprogrammed shared-memory multiprocessors. In *SOSP*, pages 159–166, New York, NY, USA, 1989. ACM Press.

[56] John Turek, Walter Ludwig, Joel L. Wolf, Lisa Fleischer, Prasoon Tiwari, Jason Glasgow, Uwe Schwiegelshohn, and Philip S. Yu. Scheduling parallelizable tasks to minimize average response time. In *SPAA*, pages 200–209, 1994.

[57] John Turek, Uwe Schwiegelshohn, Joel L. Wolf, and Philip S. Yu. Scheduling parallel tasks to minimize average response time. In *SODA*, pages 112–121, Philadelphia, PA, USA, 1994. Society for Industrial and Applied Mathematics.

[58] Peng Yang, Dirk Desmet, Francky Catthoor, and Diederik Verkest. Dynamic scheduling of concurrent tasks with cost performance trade-off. In *CASES*, pages 103–109, New York, NY, USA, 2000. ACM Press.

[59] K. K. Yue and D. J. Lilja. Implementing a dynamic processor allocation policy for multiprogrammed parallel applications in the Solaris™ operating system. *Concurrency and Computation-Practice and Experience*, 13(6):449–464, 2001.

[60] John Zahorjan and Cathy McCann. Processor scheduling in shared memory multiprocessors. In *SIGMETRICS*, pages 214–225, Boulder, Colorado, United States, May 1990.

Scheduling Dynamically Spawned Processes in MPI-2

Márcia C. Cera[1], Guilherme P. Pezzi[1], Maurício L. Pilla[2],
Nicolas Maillard[1], and Philippe O.A. Navaux[1]

[1] Universidade Federal do Rio Grande do Sul, Porto Alegre, Brazil
{mccera, pezzi, pilla, nicolas, navaux}@inf.ufrgs.br
http://www.inf.ufrgs.br
[2] Universidade Católica de Pelotas, Pelotas, Brazil
http://esin.ucpel.tche.br/

Abstract. The Message Passing Interface is one of the most well known parallel programming libraries. Although the standard MPI-1.2 norm only deals with a fixed number of processes, determined at the beginning of the parallel execution, the recently implemented MPI-2 standard provides primitives to spawn processes during the execution, and to enable them to communicate together.

However, the MPI norm does not include any way to schedule the processes. This paper presents a scheduler module, that has been implemented with MPI-2, that determines, on-line (i.e. during the execution), on which processor a newly spawned process should be run, and with which priority. The scheduling is computed under the hypotheses that the MPI-2 program follows a Divide and Conquer model, for which well-known scheduling algorithms can be used. A detailed presentation of the implementation of the scheduler, as well as an experimental validation, are provided. A clear improvement in the balance of the load is shown by the experiments.

1 Introduction

The Message Passing Interface (MPI) [12] has imposed itself since 1996 as the library for parallel programming in High Performance Computing (HPC). MPI's clean definition of messages, as well as the natural and efficient extension that it provides to classical sequential languages (C/Fortran), make it the most encountered parallel programming interface for clusters and dedicated parallel machines. Virtually all the distributed benchmarks in HPC have been ported to MPI (*e.g.* Linpack [8], NAS [7]); and nowadays the most challenging HPC applications are programmed in MPI (*e.g.* weather forecast, astrophysics, quantum chemistry, earthquakes, nuclear simulations... [15]).

The MPI 1.2 norm builds upon PVM (Parallel Virtual Machine) [16] to define a SPMD (Single Program, Multiple Data) programming approach, based on a fixed number of processes that can communicate through messages. MPI 1.2 defines groups of processes, as well as a communication space (communicator) to isolate the communication within a group. In a group, each process is identified by a rank. Messages are defined by a source and destination process, a basic type and a number of elements of this type. The data is packed by the programmer into a buffer of appropriated size. Communication may be synchronous or not, blocking or not. For non-blocking communications, a set of primitives allows to test the completion and to wait for it.

E. Frachtenberg and U. Schwiegelshohn (Eds.): JSSPP 2006, LNCS 4376, pp. 33–46, 2007.
© Springer-Verlag Berlin Heidelberg 2007

In spite of the success of MPI 1.2, one of PVM's features, not implemented in MPI 1.2, has long been missed: the dynamic creation of processes. The success of Grid Computing and the necessity to adapt the behavior of the parallel program, during its execution, to changing hardware, encouraged the MPI committee to include the dynamic management of processes (creation, insertion in a communicator, communication with the newly created processes...) in the MPI-2 norm. Other features have also been added, such as Remote Memory Access - RMA (one-sided communication) and parallel I/O. Although it has been defined in 1998, MPI-2 has taken some time to be implemented, and was included in a few MPI distributions only recently.

Neither MPI 1.2 nor MPI-2 define a way to schedule the processes of a MPI program. The processor on which each process will be executed, and the order in which the processes could run, is left to the MPI runtime implementation and is not specified in the norm. In the static case, for a regular application on homogeneous platforms, the schedule is trivial, or can be guided by some information gathered on the program [14]. Yet, in the dynamic case, a scheduling module should be developed to help decide on which processor each process should be physically started, during the execution. Since MPI-2 implements the dynamic creation of processes, the scheduling decision has to be taken on-line. As will be shown in Sec. 5, the native LAM solution is far from being efficient and may lead to very poor run-times.

This paper presents an on-line scheduler which targets dedicated platforms and attempts to minimize the execution time, regardless of other criteria. This contribution is organized as follows: Section 2 presents the dynamic process creation part of the MPI-2 norm as well as the distributions of MPI that implement it, and how MPI-2 programs can scheduled. Section 3 details the implementation of a scheduler for MPI-2 programs. In Sec. 4, the programming model, used in our test-cases with MPI-2, is presented, and Sec. 5 shows how the scheduler manages the balance of the load among the processors, with two distinct benchmarks. Finally, Sec. 6 concludes this article and hints at the following work to be done.

2   Dynamic Creation of Processes in MPI

Since 1997, MPI-2 has provided an interface that allows the creation of processes during the execution of a MPI program, and the communication by message passing. Although MPI-2 provides more functionalities, this article is restricted to the dynamic creation of processes. Sec. 2.1 details the MPI_Comm_spawn primitive which creates new MPI processes, and show how they may exchange messages. Section 2.2 presents how to schedule such spawned processes.

There is an increasing number of distributions that implement MPI-2 functionalities. LAM-MPI is the first distribution of MPI to have implemented MPI-2. LAM also ships some tools to support the run-time in a dynamic platform: the lamgrow and lamshrink primitives allow to pass to the runtime information about newly entering or leaving processors in the MPI virtual parallel machine. MPI-CH is the most classical MPI distribution, yet its implementation of MPI-2 dates back only to January 2005 only. This distribution aims at high-performance and scaling up to tens or hundreds of thousands of processors. Open-MPI is a brand new MPI-2 implementation based on the experience gained from the developments of the LAM/MPI, LA-MPI, and FT-MPI projects [9]. HP-MPI is a high-performance MPI implementation delivered by Hewlett-Packard. It was announced in December, 2005, that it now implements MPI-2.

2.1 MPI-2

MPI_Comm_spawn is the newly introduced primitive that creates new processes after a MPI application has been started. It receives as arguments the name of an executable, that must have been compiled as a correct MPI program (thus, with the proper MPI_Init and MPI_Finalize instructions); the possible parameters that should be passed to the executable; the number of processes that should be created to run the program; a communicator, which is returned by MPI_Comm_spawn and contains an inter-communicator so that the newly created processes and the parent may communicate through classical MPI messages. Other parameters are included, but are not relevant to this work. MPI_Comm_spawn is a collective operation over all processes of the original communicator since it needs to be updated with the data about the children.

In the rest of this article, a process (or a group of processes) will be called *spawned* when it is created by a call to MPI_Comm_spawn, where the process that calls the primitive is the *parent* and the new processes are the *children*.

MPI_Comm_connect / MPI_Comm_accept. With MPI-2, it is possible to establish a connection among dynamically created processes to exchange information in a client/server model. To do this, a process (the server) creates a port with MPI_Open_port, to which another process can connect afterwards. After the creation, the port name is published by MPI_Publish_name. Once the port is open and its name is published, the process allows connections by MPI_Comm_accept which returns an inter-communicator. This primitive is blocking and each process in the input communicator (MPI_Comm_accept's fourth argument) will be connected to a specific process using the same port name.

On the other hand, the client process looks the name up of the port previously published with MPI_Lookup_name. Afterwards, the client establishes connection to the server through MPI_Comm_connect. The output of this primitive is an inter-communicator to communicate with the server. When all communications are done, the process can disconnect calling MPI_Comm_disconnect, and the server can close the port with MPI_Close_port. More details about these primitives can be found in [13].

2.2 On-Line Scheduling of Parallel Processes

The extensive work on scheduling of parallel programs has yielded relatively few results in the case where the scheduling decisions are taken on-line, *i.e.* during the execution. Yet, in the case of dynamically evolving programs such as those considered with MPI-2, the schedule must be computed on-line. The problem is crucial, since a good, on-line, schedule may grant both efficient run-time and portability.

The most used technique is to keep a list of ready tasks, and to allocate them to idle processors. Such an algorithm is called *list scheduling*. The description of the tasks must be such that it allows to compute, at runtime, which tasks are ready. Thus, the programming environment must enable the description of the tasks and of their dependencies, typically the input and output data for each task [10]. The theoretical grounds of list scheduling relies on Graham's analysis [11]. Let T_1 denote the total time of the computation related to a sequential schedule, and T_∞ the critical time on an unbounded number of identical processors. If the overhead O_S induced by the list scheduling (management of the list, process creation, communications) is not considered, then $T_p \leq T_1/p + t_\infty$, which is nearly optimal if $T_\infty \ll T_1$. This bound is extended to non identical processors by Bender and Rabin [1].

Workstealing is a distributed version of list scheduling that has been proven to be optimal for a class of programs called fully strict. In this case, with a high probability, each processor makes $O(T_\infty)$ steal attempts [4]. The total number of steal attempts made by p processors is bound by $O(p.T_\infty)$, which yields: $T_p \leq \frac{T_1}{p} + O(p.T_\infty)$. The fully strict model implies that a parent process be blocked until all of its spawned tasks return their results. It includes all Divide and Conquer parallel programs for example. Some parallel programming environment that implement a "Divide & Conquer" programming interface are for example Cilk [2,3] and Satin [17,18].

Three important characteristics motivate the use of this programming model:

1. some of the most rated parallel programming interfaces are based on this model;
2. its use allows to have some performance bounds on the schedules (using workstealing);
3. a large set of important applications can be efficiently programmed with such a model. The LU factorization, Branch and Bound search, or sorting are examples.

Workstealing (and list scheduling) only uses a basic information of "load" about the available processors in order to allocate tasks to them when they turn idle (or underloaded). Typically, workstealing uses the number of processes in the local waiting list of each processor to estimate its load.

Our scheduler is based on the assumption that the MPI-2 program is using a Divide and Conquer programming model: basically, the idea is to use a Cilk-like program, where the 'fork' construct would be substituted by the MPI_Comm_spawn, and the 'synch' by the MPI_Finalize. Processes migration is not allowed in this model, which is also non-preemptive.

3   A Scheduler for MPI-2 Programs

The scheduler is constituted of two main parts: a set of header files that re-define some of MPI-2's constructs at compile-time; and a scheduler daemon that runs during the execution of the application (the mpirun script has been tampered in order to run this extra process along with the "normal" application MPI processes). The overloaded primitives are used to enable the communication between the MPI processes and the scheduler, so that the latter may update its data-structure about the MPI computation and take the scheduling decisions.

The scheduler must maintain a task graph, in order to compute the best schedule of the processes. It is implemented in two modules: `sched` which is in charge of updating the task graph; and `libbetampi` which implements the internal routines corresponding to the overloaded MPI-2 routines.

3.1 The Scheduler

The task graph is maintained as a generalized tree, where a node may have p children, p being the number of processes spawned by a parent. The implementation is made in the `graph` module. Each node in the tree points to an internal data-structure, `struct process_desc`, that represents a MPI process. Each process has a state, which can be `Blocked`, `Ready` or `Running`. To control the states of processes, the scheduler maintains lists that represent each state; it moves the processes from one list to another when the parallel program executes. In the current version, the scheduler does not control the states of processes but this functionality will be included in a future version. The overloaded MPI-2 primitives send (MPI) messages to the scheduler process to notify it of each event regarding the program. The scheduler waits for these messages, and when it receives one, it proceeds with the necessary steps: update of the task graph; evolution of the state of the process that sent the message; possible scheduling decision.

The scheduling decisions are to be taken:

- At process creation (as a result of a `MPI_Comm_spawn` call): the newly created process(es) has to be assigned a processor where it will be physically forked;
- At process termination (`MPI_Finalize`), since an occupied processor will be freed; an already existing process may start running;
- When new processor(s) get(s) available. In the current version, this is not contemplated.

Since neither preemption nor migration are used, no other event may require a scheduling decision between the creation and the termination of a process.

3.2 The Overloaded Primitives

To be consistent with the scheduling decisions, the MPI-2 primitives that require overloading are:

- `MPI_Comm_spawn`: the overloaded version has the following action: the parent process first sends a MPI message to the scheduler, informing the number n of processes that it wants to spawn, and its own pid. It then waits (with a blocking `MPI_Recv`) for a return from the scheduler.

  At this point, there is an important issue about the physical creation of processes (physical spawn), that may be done either by the parent process or by the scheduler. In the first case, the scheduler will decide of the location of the children and return the information to the parent process. After the creation of the children, the parent process can determine their pids and send them back to the scheduler, so that it may, later on, issue remote system call in order do priorize them. Thus, in this approach there are two communications between the parent and the scheduler.

On the other hand, if the physical creation is done by the scheduler, it will decide the location of the children, physically create them, and use the inter-communicator returned by MPI_Comm_spawn to locally determine the children's pids. Thus, the scheduler can definitely update its task graph. But then, it has to send the MPI_Comm_spawn return code back to the parent process, as well as the inter-communicator. This second option needs only one communication between the scheduler and the parent.

The current version of the scheduler has been implemented with the first option, where the physical spawn is done by the parent process. Figure 1 shows the steps of the overloaded MPI_Comm_spawn. First, the parent process will create new processes (children) through the MPI_Comm_spawn primitive (step 1). The overloaded primitive will establish a communication (step 2) between the parent and the scheduler, to notify the creation of the processes and the number of children that will be created (in the diagram, only one process is created). The scheduler updates the task graph structure (step 3), decides on which node the children should physically be created, and returns this physical location of the new processes (step 4). The parent process, that had remained blocked in a MPI_Recv, receives the location and physically spawns the children (step 5). It then enters into a blocking receive of a message from the scheduler, until all his children complete, so that the computation may be fully strict.

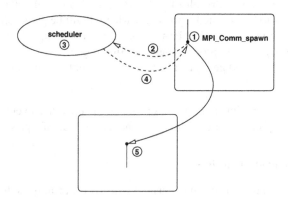

Fig. 1. MPI_Comm_spawn overload

Notice that the creation of new processes is delayed until the scheduler decides where to execute them. This enables the manipulation of the (light) process descriptor data-structure, until there is some idle processor. Then, the scheduler may decide to allocate the created processes to this processor, and only then will the physical creation occur. Thus, the overhead of the heavy process creation is delayed until an otherwise idle processor may do it.

- MPI_Finalize: this serves to notify the scheduler that a process has terminated, and therefore that a processor will be idle. The MPI_Finalize just sends a message to the scheduler.

Figure 2 shows the MPI_Finalize overload. Step 1 represents the call of MPI_Finalize, where is send a message to scheduler (step 2) notifying the scheduler of the process completion. The scheduler updates the task graph structure (step 3) and, if there are processes waiting for a processor, it will unblock a process (shows in step 4).

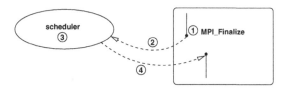

Fig. 2. MPI_Finalize overload

- MPI_Init: in order to know if a MPI program is called as an "entry point" of the computation, *i.e.* directly run by mpirun or mpiexec, or as a spawned program (*i.e.* through MPI_Comm_spawn calls), the MPI_Init function is overloaded and tests the size of the MPI_Parent_group. It is zero if and only if the program has been "mpirun". In the other case, this call serves to get the parent communicator and merge it together with the program's MPI_Comm_world, so that all processes may communicate through an unique communicator.

From the scheduler point of view, the decisions taken are:

- when it receives a message from a parent process, the scheduler updates its task graph, associating the parent's pid to n processes children (the pid and n are the information contained in the message). It then decides on which nodes the n children will be created (the heuristics are detailed in Sec. 3.4), and send their locations to the parent. Afterwards, the scheduler will receive another message from the parent, with the pids of the children that have been created, in order to store them in the task graph.
- when it receives a message from a terminating process, the scheduler updates its task graph to delete the terminated process, and can take the appropriate scheduling decision; for instance, it could remotely contact the source processor of the message, to notify the process with the new highest priority that it can use the processor. Finally, it sends a message to the parent process, that was blocked in a receive that would notify it that its children had completed their computation.

3.3   The Task Graph Structure of the Scheduler

The scheduler needs to update the task graph of the application dynamically. This graph must allow for an arbitrary number of children for each element that will be known at execution time. To support this feature, the scheduler uses a rooted tree data-structure, with left-child, right-selling representation [6]. Each graph node has a pointer that will cast to a process_desc structure with the information about the MPI processes.

3.4   Scheduling Heuristics

The scheduler can apply scheduling heuristics in two levels: to schedule processes into resources and to priorize the execution of the processes that are ready to run. In the first level the heuristics find a good distribution of processes among the available resources. In the other level it can change the processes priority to get a better resource utilization and performance.

The LAM MPI-2 implementation provides a Round-Robin mechanism to distribute processes on the nodes through a special key, `lam_spawn_sched_round_robin`, that can be set into `MPI_Comm_spawn`'s `MPI_Info` argument. In order to specify the value of this information, the `MPI_Info_set` primitive is used. But this mechanism is only efficient when more than one process are created by the same `MPI_Comm_spawn` call. If only one process is created by the call into a loop structure (for example into a while), all the children processes will be allocated in the same resource. To bypass this restriction, our scheduler implements its own Round-Robin mechanism that is able to distribute the processes in the available resources. With this mechanism, when only one process is spawned by the call, the scheduler maintains information about the last resource that has received a spawned process and allocates the new process to the next available resource in the process topology ($new\_resource = (last\_resource + 1)\%total\_resources$). If more than one process is spawned, then the MPI-2 standard solution is used. The advantage of this approach is that the distribution occurs transparently, without any change in the implementation of the application.

The second level of scheduling isn't implemented in the current version of the scheduler. The priority of the processes is left under the responsibility of the operating system's scheduler, on each node. But it is important to notice that it aims to execute fully strict applications. To make it possible to enforce a coherent execution, one has to provide a blocking mechanism to make the parent processes wait for the execution of their children. This is made through a blocking `MPI_Recv` into the overloaded `MPI_Comm_spawn`, that will wait until the scheduler sends a message (one by child), triggered by the children's `MPI_Finalize`. This approach guarantees a hierarchical execution where new processes have higher priority.

4   Programming with MPI-2: The Fibonacci Example

This section presents an example of how to program an MPI-2 application that dynamically spawns new processes. The example computes *Fibonacci* numbers and is programmed in a recursive way following this definition:

$$\text{fib}(n): \begin{cases} \text{if } n < 2 \rightarrow \text{fib}(n) = n \\ \text{else fib}(n) = \text{fib}(n-1) + \text{fib}(n-2) \end{cases}$$

Although the Fibonacci sequence may seem somewhat artificial, its main interest is in the recursive computational scheme. It is frequently used to test Divide and Conquer parallel programs. The recursive calls will be implemented, in MPI-2, with the `MPI_Comm_spawn` primitive. The most technical decision when programming this recursive application is about the synchronization at the start and the termination of the processes. The MPI-2 primitive that spawns new processes takes as argument, besides other information, the executable file name and the command line parameters. These parameters may be used to pass data to the starting process without exchanging additional messages, but this may not be convenient for complex data-types. In this case, the most portable way is to use normal message passing: the data is packed using a classical MPI data-type and sent as a message. On the Fibonacci example, the first method has been chosen, since only an integer has to be transmitted from the parent to the children.

The communication in MPI may be synchronous or not. In the contemplated case, if synchronous send or receives were used, deadlock could occur: for example, a synchronous send, in the parent, before spawning the children, would obviously prevent them from being created and therefore from receiving the data and match the parent's send. In the case of the receives in the parent from the children, one wants them to be synchronous, in order to implement a fully strict computation: the parent has to be blocked until all its children end up their computation and send their output back.

From the children's point of view, all they have to communicate is the result of their computation. They have to send it back to their parent, and this communication must be asynchronous in our implementation of the scheduler: remember that in order to block the parent process until the return of its children, the overloaded MPI_Comm_spawn blocks the parent into a receive. If the child process uses a synchronous send, it will never complete, since it would wait for the matching receive from the parent's side, who is busy waiting for a message from the scheduler.

Figure 3 presents the example code that shows how the synchronization was implemented, and this synchronization prevents any deadlock. MPI_Comm_spawn calls the executable Fibo, that includes the code segment of the figure 3. Notice that the MPI_Comm_spawn is a collective operation which imposes a synchronization among all processes in a same communicator (since the latter must be updated with the descriptors of the children processes). This feature does not influence the scheduling decisions, but may impact the overhead imposed by the scheduler. Yet, in the case of Divide and Conquer parallel programs, the children processes are recursively created from one unique parent an its communicator. Thus, in the context of this work, the synchronization occurs between one parent and each one of its children without any global synchronization.

5 Experimental Evaluation of the Scheduler

This section presents and analyzes the executions of two example programs with three different schedulers: the LAM scheduler, an scheduler directly embedded in the application and the proposed scheduler, discussed in Sec. 3. All tests have been made on a cluster of up to 20 Pentium-4 nodes dual, each one with 1 GB de RAM. The main purpose of these tests is to find out how the spawned processes are distributed on the processors, with each one of the three schedulers. Our claim is that the use of the proposed scheduler enables a good distribution of the spawned processes.

In the following, the section 5.1 presents a Fibonacci test-case designed with MPI-2 and some results and conclusions about this experiment. Afterwards, Sec. 5.2 shows a second benchmark that demonstrates the behavior of the schedulers in a situation that is more CPU-involved and which is highly irregular.

```
if (n < 2) {
   MPI_Isend (&n, 1, MPI_LONG, 0, 1, parent, &req);
}
else{
   sprintf (argv[0], "%ld", (n - 1));
   MPI_Comm_spawn ("Fibo", argv, 1, local_info, myrank,
                MPI_COMM_SELF, &children_comm[0], errcodes);
   sprintf (argv[0], "%ld", (n - 2));
   MPI_Comm_spawn ("Fibo", argv, 1, local_info, myrank,
                MPI_COMM_SELF, &children_comm[1], errcodes);
   MPI_Recv (&x, 1, MPI_LONG, MPI_ANY_SOURCE, 1,
                      children_comm[0], MPI_STATUS_IGNORE);
   MPI_Recv (&y, 1, MPI_LONG, MPI_ANY_SOURCE, 1,
                      children_comm[1], MPI_STATUS_IGNORE);
   fibn = x + y;
   MPI_Isend (&fibn, 1, MPI_LONG, 0, 1, parent, &req);
}
MPI_Finalize ();
```

Fig. 3. Part of MPI-2 code from the Fibonacci example

5.1   The Fibonacci Test-Case with MPI-2

This implementation of the Fibonacci program is not designed for speed measurements, since it implies two recursive calls (following the exact definition) and could be implemented using only one recursion. Thus, the number $N(p)$ of spawned processes to compute fib(p) is exponential (it is trivial to obtain that $N(p) = 1 + N(p-1) + N(p-2)$, with $N(2) = N(1) = 1$, and thus $N(p) \geq \text{fib}(p) = \lceil \frac{\Phi^p}{\sqrt{5}} \rceil, \Phi = \frac{1+\sqrt{5}}{2}$.

In all experiments have been used the LAM-MPI distribution. To run the Fibonacci test-case, three different configurations have been used:

1. Simple calls to MPI_Comm_Spawn were issued, using only LAM's embedded scheduling mechanism. With the default provided MPI_Info, LAM uses the Round-Robin policy.
2. The MPI_Info_Set primitive has been issued before each spawn, not with the lam_spawn_sched_round_robin key, but directly with the hard-coded ID of the node onto which should run the process. This is the internal mechanism directly written in the source code. The node ID is computed to implement a simple Round-Robin allocation to the nodes. Notice that each process that issued a spawn computes the round-robin allocation from the node ID on which it is executing.
3. A proposed scheduler has been used, with the scheduling heuristic as described in Sec. 3.4 (Round-Robin), yet this time the scheduling decision is external to the source application.

First, Table 1 presents the schedules obtained when computing the 6th Fibonacci number with the three configurations using 5 nodes.

Table 1. Comparing different schedules: number of processes spawned on each node

Environment	Node 1	Node 2	Node 3	Node 4	Node 5
fib(6) with LAM standard scheduler	25	0	0	0	0
fib(6) with embedded scheduler	8	4	8	2	3
fib(6) with proposed scheduler	5	5	5	5	5

In the first case (LAM's native schedule) all processes were spawned in the same node. The second case just changed the starting node and this is reflected by a non-constant number of processes allocated to each node. In the last case, our scheduler provides an effective Round-Robin distribution of processes among the nodes and a perfect load balance.

The question that remains is about the first case: if the LAM scheduler uses a Round Robin algorithm, should it not spawn processes on all nodes? The reason why this does not happen is that LAM does not keep scheduling information between two spawns. That means that LAM will always start spawning on the same node and only if multiple processes are spawned in the same call the processes will be balanced. This situation gets clearer observing Table 2 with an experiment that compares the result of spawning 20 processes in a single call, *vs.* in a loop of multiple, individual spawns (MPI_Comm_Spawn).

Table 2. Spawning 20 processes in 5 nodes using single and multiple spawn calls with LAM scheduler

Environment	Node 1	Node 2	Node 3	Node 4	Node 5
20 spawns of 1 process	20	0	0	0	0
1 spawn of 20 processes	4	4	4	4	4

In order to stress the scheduler with a higher number of spawned processes, the execution of the computation of fib(13) has been used. It results in 753 processes. Table 3 shows the distribution of the processes among 5 nodes, obtained with our scheduler.

Table 3. Computing the 13th Fibonacci number with the new scheduler

	Node 1	Node 2	Node 3	Node 4	Node 5	Total Number of Processes
fib(13)	151	151	151	150	150	753

Table 3 shows again the effect of our scheduler: besides the good load balance that has been reached, the proposed scheduler makes it possible to compute the 13th Fibonacci number, which is not practicable with the standard LAM mechanism: on our experimental platform, LAM tries to run all the processes on a single node, reaches an internal upper bound on the number of processes descriptors that it can handle, and fails.

5.2   Computing Prime Numbers in an Interval

In this test-case, the number of prime numbers in a given interval (between 1 and N) is computed by recursive search. As in the Fibonacci program, a new process is spawned for each recursive subdivision of the interval. Due to the irregular distribution of prime numbers and irregular workload to test a single number, the parallel program is natively unbalanced.

Table 4 presents the distribution of the processes among 5 nodes when executing the computation in an interval between 1 and 20 millions, using LAM's native scheduler and the proposed one.

Table 4. Comparing LAM's standard scheduler and the proposed one: number of processes spawned on each node

Environment	Node 1	Node 2	Node 3	Node 4	Node 5	Time (s)
LAM's standard scheduler	39	0	0	0	0	181.15
proposed scheduler	8	8	8	8	7	46.12

Table 4 shows, once more, the good load balance that has been reached with the proposed scheduler. Measuring the execution time, the average duration of the parallel program has been $181.15s$ using LAM's standard scheduler and $46.12s$ with the proposed scheduler. Clearly, the good load balance with our solution has a direct consequence about the performance of the application.

In this kind of application where the tasks are irregular, a solution that gathers information about the load on each node in order to decide where to run each process should be more efficient. Future work on the proposed scheduler should tackle this issue.

6   Conclusion and Future Work

The implementation of MPI-2 is a new reality in distributed programming, which permits the use of MPI's based HPC codes with new infrastructures such as computational grids. However, the diversity of programming models that can be supported by MPI-2 is difficult to match with efficient scheduling strategies. The approach presented in this paper is to restrict MPI-2 programs to fully strict computations, which enable the use of Workstealing.

This article has shown how MPI-2 can be used to program with such a model, and how it can be coupled with a central scheduler. Some preliminary tests have been presented, that show that LAM MPI's native scheduling functionalities are clearly outperformed by such a solution. Although a distributed solution would be much more scalable, this centralized prototype results in a simple implementation and already validates the interest in such a scheduler of dynamic spawned processes in MPI.

It is therefore interesting to continue the development of such a scheduler, to implement a real workstealing algorithm: an easy way to do it is to decide on which processor to execute the processes, based on information about their respective loads. The first effort in this perspective is shown in [5], where a better use of the available resources has been turned possible, through the information about the workload. Future work could also include altering the priority of the processes on each node, through remote system calls, to control the execution of the parallel, dynamic program.

Special thanks: this work has been partially supported by HP Brazil.

References

1. A. M. Bender, , and M. O. Rabin. Online scheduling of parallel programs on heterogeneous systems with applications to cilk. In *Theory of Computing Systems, Special Issue on SPAA '00*, volume 35, pages 289–304, 2002.
2. M. A. Bender and M. O. Rabin. Scheduling cilk multithreaded parallel programs on processors of different speeds. In *Twelfth annual ACM Symposium on Parallel Algorithms and Architectures - SPAA*, pages 13–21, Bar Harbor, Maine, USA, 2000.
3. R. D. Blumofe, C. F. Joerg, B. C. Kuszmaul, C. E. Leiserson, K. H. Randall, and Y. C. E. Zhou. Cilk: an efficient multithreaded runtime system. *ACM SIGPLAN Notices*, 30(8):207–216, Aug. 1995.
4. R. D. Blumofe and C. E. Leiserson. Space-efficient scheduling of multithreaded computations. *SIAM Journal on Computing*, 27(1):202–229, 1998.
5. M. C. Cera, G. P. Pezzi, E. N. Mathias, N. Maillard, and P. O. A. Navaux. Improving the dynamic creation of processes in mpi-2, 2006. accepted to 13th European PVMMPI Users Group Meeting, set, 2006, Bonn, Germany.
6. T. H. Cormen, C. E. Leiserson, and R. L. R. ans Clifford Stein. *Introduction to Algorithms.* The MIT Press, 2 edition, 2001.
7. D. Bailey et al. The NAS parallel benchmarks. Technical Report RNR-91-002, NAS Systems Division, Jan. 1991.
8. J. Dongarra, P. Luszczek, and A. Petitet. The LINPACK benchmark: past, present and future. *Concurrency and Computation: Practice and Experience*, 15(9):803–820, 2003.
9. E. Gabriel, G. E. Fagg, G. Bosilca, T. Angskun, J. J. Dongarra, J. M. Squyres, V. Sahay, P. Kambadur, B. Barrett, A. Lumsdaine, R. H. Castain, D. J. Daniel, R. L. Graham, and T. S. Woodall. Open MPI: Goals, concept, and design of a next generation MPI implementation. In *Proceedings, 11th European PVM/MPI Users' Group Meeting*, pages 97–104, Budapest, Hungary, September 2004.
10. F. Galilée, J.-L. Roch, G. Cavalheiro, and M. Doreille. Athapascan-1: On-line Building Data Flow Graph in a Parallel Language. In IEEE, editor, *International Conference on Parallel Architectures and Compilation Techniques, PACT'98*, pages 88–95, Paris, France, October 1998.
11. R. Graham. Bounds on multiprocessing timing anomalies. *SIAM J. Appl. Math.*, 17(2):416–426, 1969.
12. W. Gropp, E. Lusk, and A. Skjellum. *Using MPI: Portable Parallel Programming with the Message Passing Interface*. MIT Press, Cambridge, Massachusetts, USA, Oct. 1994.
13. W. Gropp, E. Lusk, and R. Thakur. *Using MPI-2 Advanced Features of the Message-Passing Interface*. The MIT Press, Cambridge, Massachusetts, USA, 1999.
14. N. Maillard, R. Ennes, and T. Divério. Automatic data-flow graph generation of mpi programs. In *SBAC'05*, Rio de Janeiro, Brazil, November 2005.
15. S. Moore, F. Wolf, J. Dongarra, S. Shende, A. D. Malony, and B. Mohr. A scalable approach to mpi application performance analysis. In *Recent Advances in Parallel Virtual Machine and Message Passing Interface, 12th European PVM/MPI Users' Group Meeting*, volume 3666 of *Lecture Notes in Computer Science*, pages 309–316. Springer, 2005.

16. V. S. Sunderam. PVM: A framework for parallel distributed computing. *Concurrency: practice and experience*, 2(4):315–339, Dec. 1990.
17. R. V. van Nieuwpoort, T. Kielmann, and H. E. Bal. Satin: Efficient Parallel Divide-and-Conquer in Java. In *Euro-Par 2000 Parallel Processing*, number 1900 in Lecture Notes in Computer Science, pages 690–699, Munich, Germany, Aug. 2000. Springer.
18. R. V. van Nieuwpoort, J. Maassen, R. Hofman, T. Kielmann, and H. E. Bal. Satin: Simple and efficient java-based grid programming. In *AGridM 2003 Workshop on Adaptive Grid Middleware*, New Orleans, Louisiana, USA, 2003.

Advance Reservation Policies for Workflows

Henan Zhao and Rizos Sakellariou

School of Computer Science, University of Manchester
Oxford Road, Manchester M13 9PL, UK
{hzhao,rizos}@cs.man.ac.uk

Abstract. Advance reservation of resources has been suggested as a means to provide a certain level of support that meets user expectations with respect to specific job start times in parallel systems. Those expectations may relate to a single job application or an application that consists of a collection of dependent jobs. In the context of Grid computing, applications consisting of dependent tasks become increasingly important, usually known as workflows. This paper focuses on the problem of planning advance reservations for individual tasks of workflow-type of applications when the user specifies a requirement only for the whole workflow application. Two policies to automate advance reservation planning for individual tasks efficiently are presented and evaluated.

1 Introduction

With the emergence of more and more sophisticated services, Grid computing is becoming rapidly a popular way of providing support for many data intensive, scientific applications that, among other, may have large computational resource requirements. Such applications, without being embarrassingly parallel, may demonstrate a reasonably large degree of task parallelism. The specific paradigm we consider in this paper concerns Grid workflow applications. These applications require the execution of a list of tasks in a specific order. Most often, tasks and their dependences can be represented by a Directed Acyclic Graph (DAG). Several studies [4,19,30] indicate that such DAG-like applications would constitute an important use case for emerging Grids.

DAG scheduling, as an optimization problem, has been well studied in the context of traditional homogeneous (and recently heterogeneous) parallel computing [12,23,29]. However, in the context of the Grid, the underlying environment is significantly different. Besides the heterogeneity and the possibly substantial communication overheads, there are issues related to the different administration domains that might be involved in providing resources for an application to run. All these issues may hinder the exploitation of parallelism. However, the most important characteristic of a Grid environment is that the traditional model of running on homogeneous parallel machines, where a single local scheduler would be in charge, is no longer the norm. The consequence is that it cannot be guaranteed that the attempt to exploit parallelism may result in any performance

E. Frachtenberg and U. Schwiegelshohn (Eds.): JSSPP 2006, LNCS 4376, pp. 47–67, 2007.

improvements. For example, the parallel tasks may not actually execute in parallel on different resources (belonging to different administration domains) simply because of different behaviours that the job queue of each resource may adopt. In principle, this is due to the limited level of service that most current systems can offer; essentially this is summarized to "run a job whenever it gets to the head of the job queue". From the user's point of view, this might be perceived as lack of acceptable quality in the service offered when running onto a large, distributed, multi-site platform.

Advance Reservation of resources has been suggested as a means to guarantee that tasks will run onto a resource when the user expects them to run [17,28]. Essentially, advance reservation specifies a precise time that jobs may start running. This allows the user to request resources from systems with different schedulers for a specific *time interval* (e.g., start time, finish time), thereby obtaining a sufficient number of resources for the time s(he) may need. Advance reservation has already received significant attention and has been considered an important requirement for future Grid resource management systems [25]. There has been already significant progress on supporting it by several projects and schedulers, such as the Load Sharing Facility platform (LSF) [16], Maui [10], COSY [6], and EASY [15,27]; still, there is some scepticism in the community, especially with respect to the degree to which advance reservations contribute to improving the overall performance of a scheduler [9]. Various techniques have also been proposed to solve a number of problems stemming from advance reservation, such as reservation planning [31], Quality of Service [18] and resource utilization issues [13,14,21].

All existing work on advance reservation assumes that the environment consists of independent jobs competing for resources. However, in the context of workflow applications, such as those considered in [4,19,30], the workflow consists of a set of tasks linked by precedence constraints to a DAG. Although one might consider the whole workflow as a single job for which resources are negotiated and reserved for its whole duration (that is, start of the entry task until the finish of the exit task), this solution may lead to a waste of resources and low utilization: this is because precedence constraints and a varying degree of parallelism may leave resources without work to do. In that case, one may want to reserve resources for specific tasks. However, the reservation of tasks cannot be done without taking into account all other tasks in the DAG and, in particular, precedence constraints as well as the time that each task may need in order to complete (clearly, a child node in the DAG cannot start execution when a parent node is still running).

This paper focuses on the problem of planning advance reservations for the individual tasks of a DAG on a heterogeneous platform taking into account a user constraint in terms of the latest possible time that the execution of the whole DAG needs to be completed. In other words, we assume that the user specifies a time interval for which resources for the whole DAG are required. This time interval is determined by the time that the application can start running and the latest possible time that it can finish. Given this time interval, the problem relates to how to reserve appropriate time intervals for each task taking also into account the overall user constraint about the latest possible time that the whole application (that is, the DAG) can finish.

This paper describes and evaluates two different strategies to solve the problem of finding individual task reservations. These strategies attempt to include sufficient 'extra time' to individual task reservations based on a user's request for the latest time that the whole execution of the DAG must finish. To the best of our knowledge, there has not been any prior work on this problem. The increasing interest in workflows in the context of the Grid requires studies to be undertaken at the level of finding appropriate strategies for planning reservations.

The remainder of the paper is organized as follows. Section 2 provides some background for the model used and the problem considered. Section 3 proposes two novel heuristics for task reservation in DAGs. Six different variants of the two heuristics have been implemented and are evaluated in Section 4. Finally, Section 5 concludes the paper.

2   Background

The model we use to represent the application, that is the DAG, and its associated information (e.g., estimated execution time of tasks and communication costs) is based on a model widely used in other heterogeneous computing scheduling studies [23,29,33]. A DAG consists of nodes and edges, where nodes (or tasks) represent computation and edges represent precedence constraints between nodes. The DAG has a single entry node and a single exit node. There is also a set of machines (resources) on which nodes can execute (usually, the execution time is different on each machine) and which need different time to transmit data. A machine can execute only one task at a time, and a task cannot start execution until all data from its parent nodes is available. An estimate for the execution time of each task on each machine is supposed to be known. Same, the amount of data that needs to be communicated between tasks is also known; along with an estimate for the communication cost between different machines, the last two values give the estimated data communication cost between two tasks that have a direct precedence constraint (that is, they are linked with an edge in the DAG) and they are running on specific (different) resources.

A number of papers have addressed the problem of minimizing the makespan when mapping the nodes of the DAG onto a set of heterogeneous machines; several algorithms, such as HEFT [29] or HBMCT [23], are known to provide good performance. It might be observed here that those algorithms could be used to provide an initial solution to the problem of planning advance reservations. In particular, these algorithms can provide a mapping of the tasks onto space and time (meaning on what machine a task will execute and what its starting time would be). As long as the overall makespan is smaller than the latest acceptable finish time for the whole application, one could plan reservations on the basis of this mapping.

However, there is one more subtle point to be made. The algorithms above provide a mapping on the basis of the estimated execution time of each task. In practice, the execution time of a task may differ significantly from the static estimate. Using advance reservation, if a job exceeds the time for which a resource has been reserved, it will, most likely, be killed (if re-negotiation is not possible). In the case of a DAG, killing one task would imply that all children tasks cannot start at their specified point in time (that is, the reservation slot for the resource); this may lead to an application failure, or, at best, the need to renegotiate the reservation of resources for the current task and all its descendants. If, for a moment, we consider advance reservation in the context of a single job rather than a DAG, it should be noted that, when making advance reservations, users are expected to reserve resources for a somewhat longer period of time than the time they predict their application will need. Certainly, performance prediction can never be perfect, however, adding some 'extra spare time' or 'slack' to the reservation will minimize the chances of their job getting killed (because it is still running at the end of the reservation slot). It would be against the whole concept of orchestrating and enacting workflows to expect that users would reserve resources separately for each task of their workflows; instead, it is anticipated that users would specify requirements (and hence add some 'slack') for the whole workflow.

In previous work [24,32], it has been observed that, after scheduling a DAG, individual tasks in a DAG might include some 'slack' anyway, as a result of precedence and resource constraints (for example, think of the parent of a task, which finishes much earlier than all other parents of the task). In [24], the notion of *spare time* is introduced to represent the maximal time that a task can afford to delay without affecting the start time of any of its dependent tasks (both on the DAG or on the same machine). Using this notion, assume a DAG, where the user has specified the latest acceptable finish time (or deadline) for the whole DAG, and an initial schedule has been constructed, using any conventional DAG scheduling algorithm, such as HEFT [29] or HBMCT [23]. Then, the problem becomes how to distribute fairly any extra time left between the finish time of the last task in the DAG and the latest acceptable finish time of the whole DAG, to the individual reservations of each task of the DAG, in such a way that each task gets the maximum possible amount of *spare time* comparing to the time it is predicted it will need [1]. Such a distribution would increase the *spare time* of each task (the spare time defined as above); it can be assumed safely that this would minimize the chances of an application failure due to the task still running at the end of its reservation slot.

To illustrate the above, consider the example schedule in Figure 1(a), where a simple DAG with 5 tasks has been mapped onto 3 machines. The problem is how to distribute to individual tasks the overall application spare time (that is, the user specified deadline for the overall application minus the finish

---

[1] Clearly, the assumption is that the maximum acceptable finish time for the whole application is greater than the finish time of the last task of the DAG as obtained by the initial schedule of the DAG.

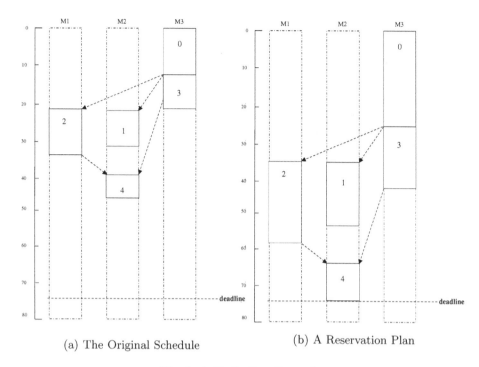

(a) The Original Schedule   (b) A Reservation Plan

Fig. 1. A Motivation Example

time of Task 4). A possible distribution that provides to each task an amount of spare time approximately equal to its original execution time estimate is shown in Figure 1(b).

It should be mentioned that in several cases, the initial allocation of the tasks may give some spare time to some tasks as a result of parent-children relationships (for example, where one parent with a single child task finishes much earlier than the other parent) [24].

3   Towards a Solution of the Problem

3.1   Input and Notation

The input and the notation used is as follows:

- A workflow application is given; this is represented by a Directed Acyclic Graph (DAG) $G = (V, E)$, where V is a set of n tasks, and E is the set of edges representing flow of data between tasks.
- A set of (heterogeneous) resources is given. We assume that each resource in this set qualifies to run any task of the DAG.

(1) Phase 1: Obtain initial assignment by allocating each task in the
given workflow (DAG) to a resource using a DAG scheduling algorithm.
(2) Phase 2:
Repeat
Compute the Application Spare Time
Obtain a new allocation by selecting a policy for allocating
this Application Spare Time to each task
Until the Application Spare Time is zero or reaches a pre-defined value.
The last allocation provides the final reservation plan.

Fig. 2. Advance Reservation Planning for DAG applications

- For each task of the DAG, an estimated execution time on each machine
  is known. In addition, the amount of data that needs to be communicated
  between tasks is known, as well as the communication cost per data unit
  between different machines.
- An algorithm, alg, can be used to schedule the DAG onto the set of heterogeneous resources. This algorithm produces an initial mapping (or allocation)
  of tasks onto machines. This allocation is denoted by $alct$; the finish time of
  this allocation is $FinishTime_{alct}$. As noticed in the motivating example in
  the previous section, the initial allocation can be used to specify a reservation
  slot for each task (for example, see the slots for each task in Figure 1.a).
- A user specified maximum acceptable time by which the whole application
  (DAG) must finish is given by the user; this is denoted by $Deadline_G$. Note,
  that in real practice, users are expected to specify an earliest possible start
  time as well as a latest acceptable finish time. Without loss of generality, we
  consider the earliest possible start time to be equivalent to time zero in our
  setting.
- Finally, we define *Application Spare Time (AST)* to be the difference between $Deadline_G$ and $FinishTime_{alct}$, that is, $AST_{alct} = Deadline_G - FinishTime_{alct}$.

The purpose of this paper is to come up with an efficient strategy that would
distribute the AST_{alct} to individual tasks, thereby extending their reservation
slots (in a way similar to what we did in Figure 1(b) for the original schedule
in Figure 1(a)) and making them more resilient to unexpected delays in their
execution. This would minimize the chances that the application will need to
re-negotiate resources (or even fail), because the execution of a task exceeds the
time for which the resource has been reserved.

3.2   Outline of the Solution

Our strategy to come up with reservations for each task of the DAG consists
of two phases as shown in Figure 2. In the first phase, an initial allocation of a
given DAG application is constructed. Given a set of (heterogeneous) resources,

the initial allocation is obtained using any algorithm for scheduling DAGs onto those resources in a way that minimizes the makespan (such as, [23,29]). This allocation is constructed by taking into account estimated execution times for the tasks and for the communication. The initial allocation provides a start time and a finish time for each task assigned to a particular resource. If the makespan of this initial schedule exceeds the user deadline, this allocation is rejected and the user can be informed that the DAG cannot be scheduled within the required time.[2] If the makespan is less than the user deadline, the next phase is invoked.

In the second phase, the problem becomes how to distribute the *application spare time* to individual tasks in a way that each task has a sufficient spare time of its own, and, ideally, the application finish time becomes equal to the deadline specified by the user. Two strategies are used for this purpose — they are explained below.

3.3   Recursive Spare Time Allocation

The key idea of the first strategy is to use a formula to compute an amount of spare time to be added to each task on the basis of the overall application spare time. After such an amount of extra spare time is added to each task, the reservation slot of each task is appropriately extended and a new overall application spare time (smaller than the original, because of the extended reservation slots) is computed. This procedure is applied repeatedly until the overall application spare time becomes smaller than a threshold. The strategy is illustrated in Figure 3.

Four different formulae have been used to compute the amount of spare time to be added to each task:

1. The application spare time is divided evenly amongst all the tasks (this is the approach used in the description of the strategy in the Figure 3).
2. The application spare time is divided amongst tasks in such a way that each task gets the same percentage of spare time as a proportion to its estimated execution time (equivalent to the initially estimated reservation slot).
3. The application spare time is divided amongst tasks in such a way that each task gets the same percentage of spare time as a proportion to its estimated execution time, but, in the first iteration, spare time is given only to the tasks in the critical path of the allocation.
4. The application spare time is divided amongst tasks in such a way that each task gets the same percentage of spare time as a proportion to its estimated execution time. As opposed to the number 2 approach above, this approach takes into account, each time, the spare time that a current task may exhibit as a result of successor tasks starting not immediately after the end of the current task.

---

[2] This case, however, is beyond the scope of this paper. As already mentioned, we assume that the deadline specified by the user is always greater than the makespan achieved by the DAG scheduling algorithm.

Input:
>   An application (workflow) represented by a DAG G with n tasks
>   A set of machines
>   A user defined deadline for the execution of the DAG, $Deadline_G$
>   An initial schedule, S, built using any DAG scheduling algorithm (e.g., HBMCT),
>   making use of estimates for the task execution time and the communication
>   The initial schedule is used to generate for each task, i, a $ReservationSlot(i)$,
>   which contains $task\_start\_time$, $task\_finish\_time$, $machine\_id$

Algorithm:
$totalST = 0$
$AST = Deadline_G - FinishTime_S$
repeat
>   for each task $i = 1$ to n do
>   compute the Spare Time for i, $SpareTime(i)$
>   end for
>   //compute an amount of spare time to add to each task
>   //for example, allocating the same amount of spare time to each task, as below
> $task\_spare\_time = AST \ / \ n$
>   for each task $i = 1$ to n do
> $totalST \mathrel{+}= task\_spare\_time$
>   if($SpareTime(i) < totalST$)
>   extend $ReservationSlot(i)$ by ($totalST - SpareTime(i)$)
>   end if
>   end for
>   update Schedule S with the new (extended) reservation slots
>   (for each $ReservationSlot(i)$, $task\_start\_time$ and $task\_finish\_time$ are shifted
>   to a later time that depends on the extension of the $ReservationSlot$ of
>   the parents)
> $AST = Deadline_G - FinishTime_S$
>   //threshold is the criterion to exit the loop
>   //its value can be 5% of the deadline for example
until ($AST < threshold$)

Fig. 3. The Recursive Spare Time Allocation Approach

3.4   The Critical Path Based Allocation

The critical path based policy tries to distribute the application spare time to the tasks on the critical path first (since those tasks determine the finish time of the application), and then it tries to balance the spare time of tasks in the remaining execution paths. The critical path based approach is shown in Figure 4. Same as before, two different formulae are used to compute the amount of spare time to be added to each task on the critical path:

1. The application spare time is divided evenly amongst the tasks in the critical path (this is the approach used in the description of the strategy in the figure).

Input:
   An application (workflow) represented by a DAG G with n tasks
   A set of machines
   A user defined deadline for the execution of the DAG, $Deadline_G$
   An initial schedule, S, built using any DAG scheduling algorithm (e.g., HBMCT),
       making use of estimates for the task execution time and the communication
   The initial schedule is used to generate for each task, i, a $ReservationSlot(i)$,
       which contains $task\_start\_time$, $task\_finish\_time$, $machine\_id$

Algorithm:
$AST = Deadline_G - FinishTime_S$
for each task $i = 1$ to n do
  $MinSpareTime(i) = AST$
end for
Find all paths $Paths$ in the initial schedule S from the entry task in G to the exit task
Find the critical path in the initial schedule S and its tasks, $critical\_path\_tasks$
$num\_of\_cp\_tasks$ = number of $critical\_path\_tasks$
$cp\_spare\_time = AST$ / $num\_of\_cp\_tasks$
for each task i in $critical\_path\_tasks$
  $MinSpareTime(i) = cp\_spare\_time$
end for
for each other path p in $Paths$ do // not the critical path
  $num\_of\_cp\_task\_this\_path$ = the number of critical path tasks on the path p
  $remain\_spare\_time = AST - num\_of\_cp\_task\_this\_path * cp\_spare\_time$
  $num\_of\_task\_this\_path$ = the number of tasks on p
  $remain\_tasks = num\_of\_task\_this\_path - num\_of\_cp\_task\_this\_path$
  $remain\_spare\_time\_each\_task = remain\_spare\_time/remain\_tasks$
  for each task i in this path
    if $(MinSpareTime(i) > remain\_spare\_time\_each\_task)$ then
       $MinSpareTime(i) = remain\_spare\_time\_each\_task$
    end if
  end for
end for
for each task $i = 1$ to n do
    extend $ReservationSlot(i)$ by $MinSpareTime(i)$
end for
update Schedule S with the new (extended) reservation slots
  (for each $ReservationSlot(i)$, $task\_start\_time$ and $task\_finish\_time$ are shifted to
  a later time that depends on the extension of the $ReservationSlot$ of the parents)

Fig. 4. The Critical Path Based Allocation Approach

2. The application spare time is divided amongst tasks in the critical path in such a way that each task gets the same percentage of spare time as a proportion to its current execution time.

3.5   An Example

An example workflow with 10 tasks is used here to illustrate the two proposed approaches. The example is shown in Figure 5(a); (b) gives the estimated

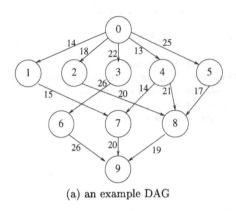

(a) an example DAG

task	M0	M1	M2	task	M0	M1	M2
0	17	19	21	5	30	27	18
1	22	27	23	6	17	16	15
2	15	15	9	7	49	49	46
3	4	8	9	8	25	22	16
4	17	14	20	9	23	27	19

(b) the computation cost of nodes on
three different machines

processors	time for a data unit
m0 - m1	0.9
m1 - m2	1.0
m0 - m2	1.4

(c) the communication cost table for
interconnected machines

(d) the initial schedule derived by the
HBMCT algorithm

	Reservation Slot			Reservation Slot	
task	start	finish	task	start	finish
0	0	17	5	17	47
1	36.6	59.6	6	51	68
2	42.7	57.7	7	59.6	105.6
3	47	51	8	62.3	84.3
4	28.7	42.7	9	105.6	124.6

(e) Reservation Slot of each task in the initial
schedule on three different machines

Fig. 5. An example of reserving slots using a schedule generated by the HBMCT
algorithm

computation cost of each task on 3 different machines, and (c) gives the comm-
munication costs between machines. Using the HBMCT DAG scheduling algorithm [23], the schedule is shown in Figure 5(d) with a makespan of 124.6; an
initial reservation for each task of the workflow is built from this schedule with
the starting time and finishing time of each task shown in Figure 5(e).

Assume a deadline of 200 to finish the whole workflow is requested from the
user. Then, using the schedule above, the initial Application Spare Time (AST)
to be distributed to tasks is equal to $200 - 124.6 = 75.4$. Figure 6 shows the
first iteration of the Recursive Spare Time Allocation approach. The approach
computes the spare time of each task and allocates the same amount of spare

	task	spare time	allocated spare time	Slot (start)	Slot (finish)
	0	0	7.54	0	24.54
	1	0	7.54	44.14	74.68
	2	4.6	2.94	57.78	75.72
	3	0	7.54	62.08	73.62
Iteration 1	4	0	7.54	36.24	57.78
AST = 75.4	5	0	7.54	24.54	62.08
	6	1.2	6.34	73.62	96.96
	7	0	7.54	74.68	128.22
	8	2.3	5.24	77.38	104.62
	9	0	7.54	133.36	159.90

Fig. 6. An example to illustrate the steps of the Recursive Spare Time Allocation Approach using the workflow in Figure 5

path	num_cp_tasks	remaining ST	allocated spare time
0→1→7→9 (cp)	4	75.4	{(0, 18.85), (1, 18.85),(7, 18.85),(9, 18.85)}
0→5→3→6→9	2	37.7	{(0, 18.85), (5, 12.56),(3,12.56), (6, 12.56), (9, 18.85)}
0→4→2→8→9	2	37.7	{(0, 18.85), (4, 12.56),(2,12.56), (8, 12.56), (9, 18.85)}
0→4→7→9	3	18.85	{(0, 18.85), (4, 12.56), (6, 12.56), (9, 18.85)}
0→5→8→9	2	37.7	{(0, 18.85), (5, 12.56), (8, 12.56), (9,18.85)}

(a) reservation steps

task	Slot (start)	Slot (finish)	task	Slot (start)	Slot (finish)
0	0	35.85	5	35.85	78.41
1	55.45	97.30	6	94.97	124.53
2	74.11	101.67	7	97.30	162.15
3	78.41	94.97	8	101.67	136.23
4	47.55	74.11	9	162.15	200

(b) The final reservation slot of each task

Fig. 7. An example to illustrate the steps of the Critical Path Based Allocation Approach using the workflow in Figure 5

time to each task apart from the ones already having some spare time. Those tasks will be allocated the difference only. For instance, task 2 had spare time of 4.6 from the initial schedule, therefore, another 2.94(= 7.54 − 4.6) is allocated to it in the new reservation slot. After two more iterations, where additional spare time is added to each task, the reservation slots for each task and the final schedule are shown in Figure 8(a).

Figure 7 shows the reservation steps using the Critical Path Based Allocation approach. All paths in the initial schedule are found, and the tasks which are in the critical path (which is {0, 1, 7, 9}) obtain the same amount of time by dividing the AST evenly. The spare time for the remaining tasks is computed by dividing the remaining amount of AST in the path. Only the smallest amount of spare time that each task may obtain from different paths will count. For instance, the spare time of task 5 on the (scheduled) path {0, 5, 3, 6, 9} is

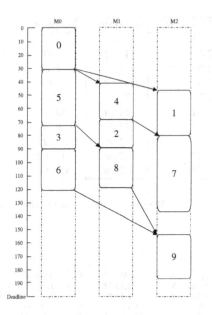
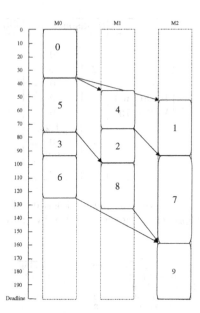

(a) reservation slots for each task using the Recursive Spare Time Allocation Approach (the threshold is 5%)

(b) reservation slots for each task using the Critical Path Based Allocation Approach

Fig. 8. The final reservation of each task of the workflow in Figure 5(a) using the proposed two approaches

12.56, and on the other path {0, 5, 8, 9}, the amount for task 5 is 18.85; however, only the smallest amount, 12.56, counts to the final reservation slot. The reservation slots for each task and the final schedule are shown in Figure 8(b).

4   Experimental Results

4.1   The Setting

We evaluated the performance of the proposed strategies in terms of their ability to distribute the application spare time to the individual tasks as well as their behavior with respect to possible failures at run-time due to differences from the predicted task execution times. For the evaluation we used simulation.

Both strategies described above (and all their variants, that is, a total of six variants) are implemented. The six variants are denoted by r_even_time, $r\_even\_percent1$, r_cp_first, $r\_even\_percent2$, for the recursive spare time allocation strategy (in the order they were presented in Section 3.3), and cp_even_time, and $cp\_even\_percent$ for the critical path based strategy (again, in the order they were presented in Section 3.4).

Four different DAG scheduling algorithms have been used to obtain the initial allocation: HBMCT [23], FCP [22], DLS [26] and HEFT [29].

Five different types of DAGs have been used for the evaluation. The first corresponds to a real-world workflow application, Montage [3,4]. The second corresponds to generic Fork&Join DAGs; the structure can be seen an abstraction of Montage. It consists of repetitive layers where in each layer a number of tasks are spawned to be joined again in the next layer. The number of tasks that are spawned each time is decreased by 1. The third and fourth types of DAGs correspond to Fast-Fourier-Transform (FFT) and Laplace operations [11]; comparing to the previous DAGs their structure is fully symmetric. These two graphs have been extensively used in several studies related to DAG scheduling [2,22,23,24]. Finally, the fifth type aims to provide a more unstructured type of DAGs and is randomly generated as follows. Each graph has a single entry and a single exit node; all other nodes are divided into levels, with each level having at least two nodes. Levels are created progressively; the numbers of nodes at each level is randomly selected up to half the number of the remaining (to be generated) nodes. Care is taken so that each node at a given level is connected to at least one node of the successor level and *vice versa*.

All five types of DAGs have been used by a plethora of studies related to DAG and workflow scheduling in the literature [4,19,2,22,24,23,30,33]. In our experiments, we used DAGs of about 60 tasks each (this is approximately 60, because some types of DAG cannot generate DAGs of exactly 60 tasks). We always assumed that 5 machines were available. Regarding the estimated execution time of each task on each different machine: this is randomly generated from a uniform distribution in the interval [10,100], for the last 4 types and the interval [50,100] for Montage, while the communication-to-computation ratio (CCR) is randomly chosen from the interval [0.1, 1].

Two sets of experiments were carried out. The first set evaluates the performance of each variant in terms of the spare time assigned to each task. For the comparison, we assume a fixed deadline. However, given that each algorithm may generate a different schedule, the makespan of the initial allocation is expected to differ; this means that the application spare time to be distributed to tasks may be different (since the deadline is always the same) depending on the original DAG scheduling algorithm used. Thus, we present the application spare time as a percentage ratio of the corresponding makespan (i.e., the $FinishTime_{alct}$), as follows:

$$\alpha = (AST_{alct}/FinishTime_{alct}) \times 100.$$

In general, the smaller the value of α is, the tighter the required deadline would be, comparing to the makespan of the initial schedule; consequently, the less the spare time that can be distributed to each task (although, as a result of a seemingly inefficient schedule in terms of the overall makespan, tasks may have already a high spare time inherent in the schedule).

The second experiment considers run-time execution time deviations from the estimated execution time of each task (that was used to plan their reservations) and evaluates how well the strategies can accommodate those deviations.

Finally, we also evaluate the running time of each variant.

4.2 Performance Results

Distribution of Spare Time. Using a common deadline in all cases (which we assume it is at time 1500 after the start of the first task of the DAG), the six variants are evaluated using four different DAG scheduling algorithms for the initial allocation and five different types of DAGs. In each case, we are interested to find out how well each variant distributes the application spare time to individual tasks. Thus, for all tasks of the DAG, we find the minimum, average, and maximum spare time for a task (denoted by Min, Avg, Max) as a percentage of the task's estimated execution time. The minimum spare time percentage is the most important indicator, since it shows the highest percentage of deviation from the estimated execution time of a task that can be afforded by any task without exceeding the reserved timeslot.

The results, averaged over 100 runs, are shown in Table 1. Several observations can be made:

- It appears that all six different variants manage to achieve a reasonable distribution of the spare time to each task as can be seen by observing the minimum spare time percentage (which is for each task analogous to what the value of α is for the whole DAG). In most cases, this seems to be close to or higher than the corresponding value of α. It also appears that the critical path based approaches (cp_even_time and cp_even_percent) lead to slightly higher values for the minimum spare time percentage. It is interesting to notice that, for the Montage workflow, HBMCT manages to guarantee a minimum spare time percentage of 47.8% for each task, even though the value of α is only 34.
- On the DAG scheduling algorithm front, it is interesting to notice that HBMCT generally shows the highest minimal spare time percentage (the only exception being FFT graphs, where the DLS algorithm performs better, by about 5%, in 4 out of the 6 variants). It is worth to notice also that, even though it has a lower α value (that is, a longer makespan) the FCP algorithm outperforms HEFT (which has a higher α value and hence more application spare time to distribute to individual tasks) in terms of the spare time percentage, for all types of DAG except Montage. This can be attributed to the inefficient initial schedule that FCP builds, which already gives a rather large amount of spare time to each task. Still, however, FCP is outperformed by HBMCT.
- The different types of DAGs, although they generate different results, still exhibit a consistent behaviour. The only exception arises for the Montage workflow and in relation to the FCP algorithm. It can be speculated that, although an originally inefficient schedule (as the one produced by the FCP algorithm) may have some inherent spare time, this is not necessarily fairly distributed amongst tasks. There might be an argument here in favour of algorithms where a carefully produced original schedule (not necessarily optimized for minimum makespan) already includes some spare time carefully distributed among tasks, but this remains to be investigated.

Table 1. Minimum, maximum, and average spare time as a percentage of the estimated execution time of each task using: 6 approaches to distribute spare time to tasks; 4 different DAG scheduling algorithms to obtain the initial schedule; 5 different types of DAGs of about 60 tasks on average; and scheduling on 5 machines. In all cases, the user specified deadline is 1500.

Montage		HBMCT α=34			FCP α=7			DLS α=32			HEFT α=24		
		Min	Max	Avg	Min	Max	Avg	Min	Max	Avg	Min	Max	Avg
	r_even_time	38.3	110.2	66.5	20.4	157.7	48.2	36.7	108.6	62.7	26.8	140.4	56.9
	r_even_percent1	40.8	107.5	69.8	22.3	146.8	45.8	34.1	108.0	68.4	27.5	132.0	58.3
	r_cp_first	40.0	102.9	70.2	23.1	135.8	44.4	35.4	111.6	65.9	32.7	134.5	59.9
	r_even_percent2	42.6	108.3	72.5	22.7	149.5	46.8	35.4	115.7	67.9	28.4	131.7	60.5
	cp_even_time	43.9	111.6	78.7	24.4	159.6	50.5	35.7	122.7	70.2	30.7	148.2	62.5
	cp_even_percent	47.8	98.7	78.8	23.9	160.6	55.1	40.1	115.9	68.4	34.9	145.1	61.6
Random		HBMCT α=24			FCP α=9			DLS α=23			HEFT α=16		
		Min	Max	Avg	Min	Max	Avg	Min	Max	Avg	Min	Max	Avg
	r_even_time	21.2	200.6	55.3	18.3	186.4	47.6	18.2	193.2	46.9	15.6	172.7	42.6
	r_even_percent1	25.9	178.6	60.4	19.9	179.0	48.2	17.5	187.9	44.1	15.0	160.6	41.1
	r_cp_first	24.0	203.8	55.4	19.2	180.9	46.8	19.6	192.6	44.6	15.9	172.2	44.0
	r_even_percent2	23.6	168.4	56.6	19.2	178.3	48.9	17.5	182.6	42.8	15.2	154.5	35.6
	cp_even_time	27.6	194.7	58.3	20.8	177.1	48.7	20.2	184.4	48.4	16.5	169.9	37.2
	cp_even_percent	25.6	172.2	55.3	19.6	178.2	49.9	22.0	170.4	50.7	16.6	155.4	40.1
Laplace		HBMCT α=28			FCP α=11			DLS α=28			HEFT α=18		
		Min	Max	Avg	Min	Max	Avg	Min	Max	Avg	Min	Max	Avg
	r_even_time	25.4	205.7	62.3	23.0	188.1	55.5	24.3	208.4	66.2	18.7	175.4	56.9
	r_even_percent1	23.3	187.7	70.4	21.6	166.0	62.4	21.7	182.1	64.9	18.7	168.4	57.1
	r_cp_first	26.8	215.5	70.5	23.1	182.4	56.9	23.7	198.5	66.5	20.4	177.5	54.8
	r_even_percent2	26.0	185.7	72.3	19.2	173.8	59.3	25.5	190.8	73.8	20.0	172.5	60.5
	cp_even_time	27.1	206.4	66.9	23.0	178.2	55.5	24.1	197.4	67.4	23.8	189.4	56.9
	cp_even_percent	28.4	196.9	68.6	24.6	171.7	56.6	25.9	192.7	67.3	21.2	172.6	58.8
F&J		HBMCT α=19			FCP α=7			DLS α=18			HEFT α=12		
		Min	Max	Avg	Min	Max	Avg	Min	Max	Avg	Min	Max	Avg
	r_even_time	19.3	165.2	50.5	17.5	156.6	52.7	18.7	151.7	52.9	15.2	140.9	50.5
	r_even_percent1	18.5	156.8	51.6	17.3	154.3	54.9	19.7	139.5	55.5	14.9	142.4	48.4
	r_cp_first	20.2	161.8	55.8	19.5	163.9	56.8	21.0	158.7	55.0	18.4	151.6	50.6
	r_even_percent2	18.9	150.5	53.0	18.2	159.8	59.3	20.3	145.1	57.9	17.0	151.4	50.7
	cp_even_time	19.6	160.3	57.7	17.7	164.8	60.6	19.1	167.6	58.9	17.8	151.9	54.8
	cp_even_percent	19.5	155.4	60.3	18.8	151.7	60.1	20.7	160.6	70.2	17.6	146.3	57.3
FFT		HBMCT α=21			FCP α=8			DLS α=21			HEFT α=15		
		Min	Max	Avg	Min	Max	Avg	Min	Max	Avg	Min	Max	Avg
	r_even_time	21.6	198.7	56.7	17.9	170.6	54.0	22.3	193.7	57.5	18.2	180.6	55.7
	r_even_percent1	23.6	185.3	58.3	16.7	165.6	57.4	22.2	176.6	60.9	20.2	164.9	58.6
	r_cp_first	20.7	192.9	60.6	18.2	171.8	57.0	23.1	203.0	62.5	21.6	200.4	60.8
	r_even_percent2	24.1	182.4	60.4	20.2	159.8	58.2	23.7	179.0	61.9	23.6	196.9	60.5
	cp_even_time	23.2	191.9	60.6	21.9	181.6	59.1	25.7	190.4	62.4	24.6	199.8	62.0
	cp_even_percent	24.6	187.1	61.8	20.4	176.6	60.2	24.9	195.1	65.8	23.9	191.7	62.5

Evaluation of the behaviour of our approach with run-time changes.
The second set of experiments examines how well the proposed approaches behave in a realistic environment, where they need to accommodate deviations from the estimated execution time of each task at run-time. In order to emulate run-time changes (in relation to the estimated execution times) we adopt the notion of *Quality of Information* (QoI) [24]. This represents an upper bound on the percentage of error that the statically estimated execution time may have with respect to the actual execution time. So, for example, a percentage error of 10% would indicate that the actual run-time execution time of a task will be within 10% (plus or minus) of the static estimate for the task. Clearly, in this

case, if the planned reservations for each task have a spare time higher than 10% (as a percentage of the task's estimated execution time), the actual execution time of a task cannot exceed its reservation slot.

In this set of experiments, we used only the HBMCT algorithm, since it appears to perform generally better than the other algorithms considered earlier. We also consider only the Montage workflow. We consider different values for α (20, 50, 100, 150) and QoI (equal to 20%, 50%, 100%, 150% of the estimated execution time). Our aim is to evaluate the number of failures (a failure means that one task of the DAG could not complete its execution within its reserved slot) as well as the utilization of the reserved slots (this is the average utilization of the reserved slots for each machine). For comparison purposes, the six variants proposed in this paper are compared against an approach which reserves all resources that might be needed for the entire execution of the DAG ($DAG\_Reserve$). The results are shown in Table 2. Same as before, the experiment is repeated 100 times and 5 machines are considered.

The main observation is that, generally, if the value of the QoI is less than the value of α it is unlikely to have failures (the only exception seems to arise for the largest value of QoI, 150%). This can be justified using the results in the previous set of experiments, where it was observed that, generally, the minimum spare time percentage that can be added to each task is close to the value of α. This means that for deviations in the task execution time that are up to about α%, the reservation plan is quite resilient and no (or very few) failures are expected. The main lesson from this observation is that all that users need to do when asking for resources for a workflow is to specify the amount of 'slack' that they would be prepared to afford for the execution of the whole workflow: this should be roughly related to the maximum deviation that they expect from the estimated execution time of each task in the workflow. Individual reservation slots for each task can then be derived automatically using appropriate heuristics.

Comparing the variants proposed in this paper with the approach that reserves all resources throughout the entire DAG's execution, it can be seen that the former is more robust to failures (not surprising, given that in our variants the spare time of the whole DAG is distributed to individual tasks) but it suffers from low utilization within the reserved slots. It should be noted here that these values do not take into account the fact that our variants, which are based on individual task reservations, leave 'gaps' in the resources while the DAG is being executed. Thus, our variants allow to regain unused resource time after a job has been completed by *backfilling* [21] other, independent jobs that do not have advance reservation. This creates a better potential to increase overall resource utilization. Instead, in the case where the resources are reserved for the entire DAG, backfilling would not be desirable until the exit task of the DAG has been completed.

Running Time. Although the two strategies that were compared in the previous section perform similarly, the variants based on the recursive based strategy achieve the same result at a significantly reduced cost. Figure 9 shows how the running time varies for each variant considered. The experiment was carried out

Table 2. Number of failures (reservation slot exceeded) and average reserved slot utilization for each of 6 task reservation approaches and DAG reservation approach with different QoI and α values. Results obtained over 100 runs using Montage workflows each with 57 tasks and scheduling on 5 machines with HBMCT algorithm.

α	QoI	Number of Failures				Reserved Slot Utilization				
		20%	*50%*	*100%*	*150%*	*0%*	*20%*	*50%*	*100%*	*150%*
20	r_even_time	0	22	85	100	60.1	66.2	75.7	82.8	92.5
	r_even_percent1	0	20	84	100	59.4	65.6	74.3	81.3	90.3
	r_cp_first	0	22	84	100	59.3	66.8	76.0	81.9	92.0
	r_even_percent2	0	21	80	100	58.7	65.4	76.1	81.5	91.1
	cp_even_time	0	21	83	100	60.4	67.0	77.1	82.4	91.7
	cp_even_percent	0	21	82	100	60.6	66.6	75.9	82.1	91.9
	DAG_Reserve	0	8	59	100	44.7	46.4	49.5	53.5	58.8
50	r_even_time	0	0	19	46	52.5	59.4	70.2	82.6	91.9
	r_even_percent1	0	0	17	45	51.4	58.0	68.9	80.4	90.1
	r_cp_first	0	0	17	44	52.7	58.5	68.7	80.8	90.2
	r_even_percent2	0	0	17	44	52.4	58.7	69.3	81.0	90.4
	cp_even_time	0	0	16	44	52.1	59.0	69.5	80.9	89.8
	cp_even_percent	0	0	16	45	51.9	58.7	69.1	80.4	89.4
	DAG_Reserve	0	0	7	29	35.4	36.7	38.7	40.4	43.8
100	r_even_time	0	0	0	13	27.4	33.1	40.4	64.4	78.0
	r_even_percent1	0	0	0	10	26.3	31.4	38.8	63.1	77.9
	r_cp_first	0	0	0	11	25.9	32.0	38.7	63.2	77.0
	r_even_percent2	0	0	0	10	26.4	32.7	39.0	63.7	76.6
	cp_even_time	0	0	0	11	26.4	31.8	39.2	63.0	76.9
	cp_even_percent	0	0	0	11	26.2	31.6	39.0	63.2	77.3
	DAG_Reserve	0	0	0	5	20.3	21.5	25.0	27.9	31.3
150	r_even_time	0	0	0	7	21.7	25.8	35.5	46.4	61.2
	r_even_percent1	0	0	0	4	21.5	24.6	34.8	45.5	59.6
	r_cp_first	0	0	0	5	21.2	24.8	34.6	46.0	59.8
	r_even_percent2	0	0	0	5	20.9	24.7	34.0	46.0	60.5
	cp_even_time	0	0	0	5	21.2	24.4	34.0	46.4	60.7
	cp_even_percent	0	0	0	5	21.2	24.4	33.6	46.1	60.9
	DAG_Reserve	0	0	0	0	14.9	16.7	19.6	22.6	26.8

with random DAGs (since they provide us with more flexibility in specifying a different number of tasks for the DAG) having 20 to 100 nodes each; the reservation plans considered an alpha value of 50. It can been seen that the critical path based policies lead to faster increases in the running time than the recursive based ones as the number of nodes in the DAG increases. This is because finding every path from the entry node to the exit node in the allocated schedule takes a significant amount of time. This may indicate that the critical path based variants, although they have the potential to perform slightly better, they come with an extra cost.

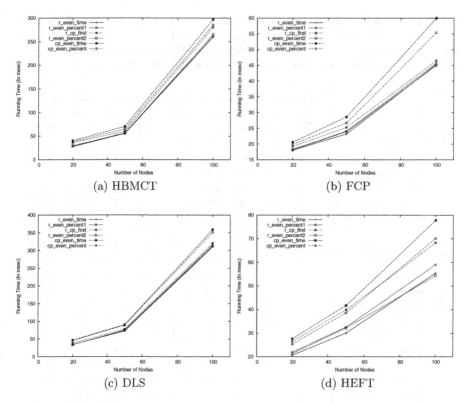

Fig. 9. Average running time (over 100 runs on randomly generated DAGs) of six different reservation planning variants and four different DAG scheduling algorithms

5   Conclusion

This paper presented two novel advance reservation policies for workflows, which attempt to distribute the spare time between an initial schedule (obtained by any DAG scheduling algorithm) and the deadline for the execution of the workflow gracefully to each task, in order to cope with run time execution time changes for each task. The approaches are based on either recursively allocating the time to each task or optimizing the critical path tasks. The strategies were designed to be usable by any DAG scheduling algorithm.

The main outcome of this work has been the proposal of efficient heuristics that can automate the process of coming up with reservation slots for scheduling individual tasks of a workflow (DAG), in the context of a system allowing advance reservations, without user intervention. In line with the philosophy for workflow automation in current research, all that the user needs to specify is the latest acceptable finish time for the whole workflow. As illustrated in the paper, the rest can be automated using a combination of appropriate heuristics.

Further evaluation could consider the heuristics presented in this paper in conjunction with a more dynamic environment, where DAGs as well as other jobs, not necessarily having advance reservations, co-exist. Such an environment could allow more complete analysis of resource utilization and performance by applying backfilling and/or techniques for dynamic re-planning advanced reservations based on run-time information.

Acknowledgements

We are grateful to the anonymous referees whose comments helped improve the paper. The work carried out in this paper has been funded by EPSRC, UK (grant reference GR/S67654/01) whose support we are pleased to acknowledge.

References

1. A. H. Alhusaini, V. K. Prasanna, and C. S. Raghavendra. A Unified Resource Scheduling Framework for Heterogeneous Computing Environments. In *8th Heterogeneous Computing Workshop (HCW)*, 1999.
2. O. Beaumont, V. Boudet, and Y. Robert. The Iso-Level Scheduling Heuristic for Heterogeneous Processors. *Proceedings of the 10th Euromicro Workshop on Parallel, Distributed and Network-Based Processing (PDP2002)*, 2002 (extended version available as Research Report RR2001-22, LIP, ENS Lyon, France).
3. G. B. Berriman, J. C. Good, A. C. Laity, A. Bergou, J. Jacob, D. S. Katz, E. Deelman, C. Kesselman, G. Singh, M. Su and R. Williams. Montage: A Grid Enabled Image Mosaic Service for the National Virtual Observatory. In the Conference Series of *Astronomical Data Analysis Software and Systems XIII (ADASS XIII)*, Volume 314, 2004.
4. J. Blythe, S. Jain, E. Deelman, Y. Gil, K. Vahi, A. Mandal, and K. Kennedy. Resource Allocation Strategies for Workflows in Grids. In *IEEE International Symposium on Cluster Computing and the Grid (CCGrid 2005)*.
5. L. Boloni, and D. C. Marinescu. Robust scheduling of metaprograms. *Journal of Scheduling*, 5, pp. 395-412, 2002.
6. J. Cao and F. Zimmermann. Queue Scheduling and Advance Reservation with COSY. In *Proceedings of 18th IEEE International Parallel and Distributed Processing Symposium (IPDPS)*, Santa Fe, USA, April 2004.
7. H. Casanova, A. Legrand, D. Zagorodnov and F. Berman. Heuristics for scheduling parameter sweep applications in Grid environments. In *9th Heterogeneous Computing Workshop (HCW'00)*, 2000.
8. I. Foster, C. Kesselman, C. Lee, B. Lindell, K. Nahrstedt, and A. Roy. A Distributed Resource Management Architecture that Supports Advance Reservations and Co-Allocation. In *Proceedings of the International Workshop on Quality of Service*, 1999.
9. D. G. Feitelson, L. Rudolph, and U. Schwiegelshohn. Parallel Job Scheduling — A Status Report. In *10th Workshop on Job Scheduling Strategies for Parallel Processing*, 2004.
10. D. Jackson, Q. Snell, and M. Clement. Core Algorithms of the Maui Scheduler. In *Job Scheduling Strategies for Parallel Processing (JSSPP)*, Springer-Verlag, Lect. Notes Comput. Sci. Vol. 2221, pp. 87-102, 2001.

11. Y.-K. Kwok and I. Ahmad. Dynamic Critical-Path Scheduling: An Effective Technique for Allocating Task Graphs to Multiprocessors. *IEEE Transactions on Parallel and Distributed Systems*, Vol. 7(5):506-521, 1996.

12. Y.-K. Kwok and I. Ahmad. Static Scheduling Algorithms for Allocating Directed Task Graphs. *ACM Computing Surveys*, 31(4):406-471, 1999.

13. B. Lawson and E. Smirni. Multiple-Queue Backfilling Scheduling with Priorities and Reservations for Parallel Systems. In *Job Scheduling Strategies for Parallel Processing*, Springer-Verlag, Lecture Notes in Computer Science, Vol. 2537, pp. 72-87, 2002.

14. B. Lawson, E. Smirni, and D. Puiu. Self-adapting Backfilling Scheduling for Parallel Systems. In *Proceedings of the 2002 International Conference on Parallel Processing (ICPP 2002)*, pages 583-592, Vancouver, B.C., August 2002.

15. D. A. Lifka, M. W. Henderson, and K. Rayl. Users Guide to the Argonne SP Scheduling System. Technique Report ANL/MCS-TM-201, Argonne National Laboratory.

16. Load Sharing Facility platform. *http://www.platform.com/products/LSF/*.

17. J. MacLaren. Advance Reservations: State of the Art. In Global Grid Forum 9 (GGF9), Scheduling and Resource Management Workshop, Chicago, USA, October 2003.

18. J. MacLaren, R. Sakellariou, K. T. Krishnakumar, J. Garibaldi, and D. Ouelhadj. Towards Service Level Agreement Based Scheduling on the Grid. In *Workshop on Planning and Scheduling for Web and Grid Services* (in conjunction with ICAPS-04), June 3-7, 2004, pp. 100-102.

19. A. Mandal, K. Kennedy, C. Koelbel, G. Marin, J. Mellor-Crummey, B. Liu and L. Johnsson. Scheduling Strategies for Mapping Application Workflows onto the Grid. In *IEEE International Symposium on High Performance Distributed Computing (HPDC 2005)*, 2005.

20. R. Min and M. Maheswaran. Scheduling Co-Reservations with Priorities in Grid Computing Systems. In *IEEE/ACM International Symposium on Cluster Computing and the Grid (CCGRID)*, 2002.

21. A. W. Mu'alem and D. G. Feitelson. Utilization, Predictability, Workloads, and User Runtime Estimates in Scheduling the IBM SP2 with Backfilling. *IEEE Transactions on Parallel and Distributed Systems*, 12(6):529-543, 2001.

22. A. Radulescu and A.J.C. van Gemund. Low-Cost Task Scheduling for Distributed-Memory Machines. *IEEE Transactions on Parallel and Distributed Systems*, 13(6):648-658, June 2002.

23. R. Sakellariou and H. Zhao. A Hybrid Heuristic for DAG Scheduling on Heterogeneous Systems. In *Proceedings of 13th Heterogeneous Computing Workshop (HCW 2004)*, 26-30 April 2004, Santa Fe, New Mexico, USA.

24. R. Sakellariou and H. Zhao. A low-cost rescheduling policy for efficient mapping of workflows on grid systems. *Scientific Programming*, 12(4):253-262, Dec. 2004.

25. U. Schwiegelshohn, P. Wieder and R. Yahyapour. Resource Management for Future Generation Grids. In *Future Generation Grids*, V. Getov, D. Laforenza, A. Reinefeld (Eds.), Springer, CoreGrid Series, 2005.

26. G. C. Sih and E. A. Lee. A compile-time scheduling heuristic for interconnection-constrained heterogeneous processor architecture. *IEEE Transactions on Parallel and Distributed Systems*, 4(2):175–187, February 1993.

27. J. Skonira, W. Chan, H. Zhou, and D. Lifka. The EASY - LoadLeveler API Project. In *Proceedings of the Workshop on Job Scheduling Strategies for Parallel Processing*, Springer-Verlag Lecture Notes In Computer Science, Vol. 1162, pp. 41-47, 1996.

28. W. Smith, I. Foster, and V. Taylor. Scheduling with Advanced Reservations. In *Proceedings of International Parallel and Distributed Processing Symposium (IPDPS)*, pages 127-132, May 2000.

29. H. Topcuoglu, S. Hariri, and M. Wu. Performance-effective and low-complexity task scheduling for heterogeneous computing. *IEEE Transactions on Parallel and Distributed Systems*, 13(3):260–274, March 2002.

30. M. Wieczorek, R. Prodan and T. Fahringer. Scheduling of Scientific Workflows in the ASKALON Grid Environment. In *SIGMOD Record*, volume 34(3), September 2005.

31. V. Yarmolenko and R. Sakellariou. An Evaluation of Heuristics for SLA Based Parallel Job Scheduling. In *3rd High Performance Grid Computing Workshop* (in conjunction with IPDPS 2006), IEEE Computer Society, 2006.

32. H. Zhao and R. Sakellariou. A Low-Cost Rescheduling Policy for Dependent Tasks on Grid Computing Systems. In *Proceedings of the 2nd AcrossGrids*, Lecture Notes in Computer Science, Vol. 3165, pages 21-31, Springer, 2004.

33. H. Zhao and R. Sakellariou. An Experimental Investigation into the Rank Function of the Heterogeneous Earliest Finish Time Scheduling Algorithm. In *Proceedings of 9th International Euro-Par Conference*, Lecture Notes in Computer Science, Vol. 2790, Springer, 2003.

On Advantages of Scheduling Using Genetic Fuzzy Systems

Carsten Franke*, Joachim Lepping, and Uwe Schwiegelshohn

Robotics Research Institute, Dortmund University, 44221 Dortmund, Germany
{carsten.franke, joachim.lepping, uwe.schwiegelshohn}@udo.edu

Abstract. In this paper, we present a methodology for automatically generating online scheduling strategies for a complex scheduling objective with the help of real life workload data. The scheduling problem includes independent parallel jobs and multiple identical machines. The objective is defined by the machine provider and considers different priorities of user groups. In order to allow a wide range of objective functions, we use a rule based scheduling strategy. There, a rule system classifies all possible scheduling states and assigns an appropriate scheduling strategy based on the actual state. The rule bases are developed with the help of a Genetic Fuzzy System that uses workload data obtained from real system installations. We evaluate our new scheduling strategies again on real workload data in comparison to a probability based scheduling strategy and the EASY standard scheduling algorithm. To this end, we select an exemplary objective function that prioritizes some user groups over others.

1 Introduction

In this paper, we address the development of a methodology to automatically generate scheduling strategies for Massively Parallel Processing (MPP) systems that consider the providers' preferences. The scheduling problem consists of n independent non-clairvoyant jobs that are submitted by different users over time. The scheduling strategy is responsible to assign the available processors of the MPP system to those jobs. However, the machine providers in real scenarios have different relationships to the various users or user groups. Those different relationships lead to different prioritizations of the users and their corresponding jobs. Consequently, the scheduling strategy needs to incorporate those priorities during the scheduling process.

Many installations use partitions [14] or quotas [31] to implement this kind of prioritizations of different user groups. However, those attempts result in a low system utilization in most of the cases [14]. Hence, we present the development of a rule based scheduling system that is able to generate schedules with a higher quality in terms of the provider preferences while not decreasing system utilization. To our knowledge, there is no similar work that is able to incorporate the user group prioritizations in a similar way.

---

* Born Carsten Ernemann.

E. Frachtenberg and U. Schwiegelshohn (Eds.): JSSPP 2006, LNCS 4376, pp. 68–93, 2007.

The development of scheduling strategies for MPP systems is based on work-load traces originating from real installations, see for example Heine et al. [16]. Such workload data include all hidden job dependencies, patterns and feedback mechanisms. For MPP systems several workloads are available, see the standard workload archive maintained by Feitelson [13], that are for instance described by Chapin [5]. Although those data are rather old they suffice for our purpose. So far, workload models are rarely used to develop scheduling algorithms as they are not able to describe workload traces with an acceptable accuracy, see Song et al. [28] and the given references there.

The online job scheduling on MPPs is usually non-clairvoyant as the processing time p_j of job j is not available at its release date r_j. However, users are often required to provide estimates $\bar{p}_j$ of the processing time that are mainly used to determine faulty jobs whose processing time exceeds the estimate. Further, parallel jobs on MPPs are typically not moldable or malleable, that is, they need concurrent and exclusive access to $m_j \leq m$ machines during the whole execution phase. The value m_j is provided at the release date r_j by the user. Finally, the completion time of job j in a schedule S is denoted by $C_j(S)$. As preemption is not allowed in many MPPs, each job starts its execution at time $(C_j(S) - p_j)$. Unfortunately, the available workload data do not provide any user group information nor define any complex scheduling objective. To address the user group problem, we are using the work of Song et al. [29], who have shown that users can be reasonably well partitioned into 5 groups for all available MPP workload traces. Those groups are differentiated with respect to job characteristics and frequency of job submissions. Within this work, we will also use 5 different user groups. However, we will use the user's resource consumption as the differentiation criterion. The binary function $\varrho_i(j)$ is used to state whether job j belongs to user group i ($\varrho_i(j) = 1$) or not ($\varrho_i(j) = 0$).

We present a methodology to automatically generate a rule based scheduling system that is able to produce good quality schedules with respect to a given complex provider objective. Note that our methodology is not restricted to a specific user group selection.

The individual preferences of the machine providers are expressed using a complex objective function that is generated by combining well known simple basic objectives. Even if different providers use the same objective functions for the various groups, the transformation of a generic multi-objective scenario into a specific scheduling problem with a single objective depends on the actual priorities assigned to the user groups and is likely to be individual. Hence, we focus on the development of a suitable methodology and do not generate a single scheduling strategy. Without loss of generality, we exemplarily select a complex objective function to demonstrate the feasibility of our approach. Here, we present a rule based scheduling that is able to adapt to various scenarios. So far, the use of rule based systems in scheduling environments is rare. Nevertheless, first attempts [10,4] have shown the feasibility of such an approach. However, those scheduling systems are all based on single simple objective evaluation functions that are not optimized.

The proposed scheduling process is divided into two steps. In the first step, the queue of waiting jobs is reordered according to a sorting criterion. Then an algorithm uses this order to schedule the jobs onto the available machines in the second step. Based on the present scheduling state, the rules determine the sorting criterion and the scheduling algorithm. In order to guarantee general applicability, the system classifies all possible scheduling states. This classification considers the scheduling decisions in the past, the actual schedule, and the current waiting queue. Note that we have chosen some classification features exemplarily. Other possible features can be used as well for this task. Our feature selection only serves the purpose to illustrate our methodology.

As already stated in many other publications, see for example Ernemann et al. [6,7], a local scheduling decision influences the allocation of future jobs. Hence, the effect of a single decision cannot be determined individually. Therefore, the whole rule base is only evaluated after the complete scheduling of all jobs belonging to a workload trace. This has a significant influence on the learning method to generate this rule base as this type of evaluation prevents the application of a supervised learning algorithm, see Hoffmann [17]. Instead, the reward of a decision is delayed and determined by a critic. Furthermore, the generation of an appropriate situation classification is not known in advance and must be generated implicitly while constructing the rule based scheduling system.

The various design concepts for Fuzzy logic controllers often use Evolutionary Algorithms to adjust the membership function as well as to define the output behavior of individual rules, see, for example, Hoffmann [17]. Especially Genetic Fuzzy Systems have been proven to deal with such classification and automatic rule base generation problems in a suitable way. All those Genetic Fuzzy Systems either encode single rules (*Michigan approach*, Bonarini [3]) or complete rule bases (*Pittsburgh approach*, Smith [27]).

Within this work, the determination of a Genetic Fuzzy System is realized using the Pittsburgh approach. In this case, each individual represents a whole rule base. During the evolution, the individual rules are adjusted in order to better fit to the given situations. Furthermore, we will present a Coevolutionary approach that uses two rule bases, one for the determination of the sorting criterion and one for the scheduling algorithm that is applied. Both rule bases evolve independently with the only exception that during the quality assignment one individual from each rule base must be selected.

We use an Evolution Strategies for the optimization of the rule based scheduling system. This is in contrast to the majority of Genetic Fuzzy Systems, see Hoffmann [17]. As our membership functions include real valued parameters, Evolution Strategies are superior to Genetic Algorithms in this case, see Bäck and Schwefel [1].

To finally show the results of our approach, we use a linear priority function which favors user group 1 over user group 2 over all other user groups. The choice of another priority function may lead to different results but does not affect the feasibility of our methodology. Due to the lack of a scheduling strategy supporting priority functions, no priority functions are available in practice. Therefore, we had to define one.

For the evaluation of the derived scheduling strategy we present the distance of this schedule from the Pareto front of all feasible schedules for this workload, as generated by Ernemann et al. [8]. Although the generation of an approximate Pareto front is not subject of this paper, two restrictions must be noted:

1. For real workloads, we are only able to generate approximate Pareto fronts. Therefore, schedules of this front are not guaranteed to be lower bounds.
2. The schedules are generated off-line. On-line methods may not be able to achieve as good results due to the on-line constraints.

On purpose, we selected a criterion where user groups with a high computing demand are preferred over user groups with a low demand. Then classical scheduling algorithms will typically generate acceptable results. This is not true for a prioritization of a user group with a low resource demand. Moreover, we also show the results of the best conventional strategy that does not support priorities.

The remainder of this paper is organized as follows. In Section 2, we introduce the underlying scheduling system, Evolutionary Algorithms, and Genetic Fuzzy Systems in more detail. The scheduling objectives and features are presented in Section 3. Then the model of our approach is described in Section 4. This is followed by a detailed analysis of the system behavior and an evaluation of the results. The paper ends with a brief conclusion.

2   Background

This section introduces the main scheduling algorithms and their application within our rule based scheduling system. Furthermore, the concept of Evolution Strategies is presented. Those strategies are used to optimize the rule based scheduling system.

2.1   Scheduling Concepts

As already mentioned, scheduling strategies of high performance parallel computers need to pay more attention to certain users or user groups in order to achieve a higher degree of satisfaction for them. Priority or membership information are not available in the workloads. Hence, we use the resource consumption as a grouping criterion such that user group 1 represents all users with a higher resource consumption whereas all users in group 5 have a very low resource demand. Details of the user group definitions are provided by Ernemann et al. [8].

As already introduced, a state of a scheduling system mainly consists of the current schedule, that describes the actual allocation of processor nodes to certain jobs, the scheduling results achieved so far, and the queue of waiting jobs. This waiting queue is typically ordered.

In most cases, a static ordering like sorting by submission time or sorting by estimated runtime is applied. In some other cases, the waiting queue is dynamically reordered depending on the system state by using a more complex sorting criterion that may for instance consider limits of the waiting time.

The various scheduling algorithms mainly differ in the way they select the next job from the sorted waiting queue to insert it into the existing schedule, that is, they obey different restrictions when choosing the next job. This results in different algorithmic complexities and correspondingly different execution times for the scheduling algorithms.

In the following, we present four selected scheduling algorithms in increasing order of algorithmic complexity. Note that the first three algorithms use a statically sorted waiting queue while the last algorithm dynamically reorders this queue.

- *First Come First Serve (FCFS)* starts the first job of the waiting queue whenever enough idle resources are available. Thus, this algorithm has a constant complexity as the scheduler always only tests whether the first job can be started immediately if a job in the schedule has completed its execution or a new job has risen to the top of the waiting queue.
- *List Scheduling* as introduced by Graham [15] is not applied in this work. However, it serves as the basic template for the two backfilling variants. By applying List Scheduling, the scheduler tries to find the first job within the queue of waiting jobs, that can be started on the currently idle resources. Again, the algorithm uses the sorted queue. The complexity is higher than in the case of FCFS as in the worst case, the whole queue is tested each time the scheduling procedure is initiated.
  - *EASY Backfilling (EASY)* is similar to the original List Scheduling. However, if the first job within the waiting queue cannot be started immediately the algorithm estimates the completion time of this job. To this end, a runtime estimation provided by the user is needed. Then EASY tries to find an allocation for the following jobs of the waiting queue on the currently idle resources while ensuring that the *first job* is not further delayed. This algorithm requires more time than List Scheduling, as the scheduler needs to estimate the processing of the first job in case that it cannot be started directly.
  - *Conservative Backfilling (CONS)* extends the concept of EASY. Here, the scheduler tries to find the next job within the waiting queue, that can be started immediately while ensuring that *no previous job* within the queue is further delayed. This results in a much higher complexity of the scheduling algorithm as in the worst case, the completion time of all jobs within the waiting queue except of the last job must be estimated each time the scheduling process is initiated.
- *Greedy Scheduling (Greedy)* uses a dynamically sorted waiting queue contrary to the already introduced scheduling algorithms. To this end, the algorithm defines a complex sorting criterion. Each time, the Greedy scheduling process in started, the queue is sorted according to this criterion. Then, a simple

FCFS is applied. The complexity of this algorithm is potentially high as the execution of the sorting function for each job within the waiting queue may be computationally expensive. Furthermore, the necessary sorting of all jobs must be taken into account. Greedy has the advantage to specify user or user group dependent preferences within the complex sorting criterion. In our case, the complex sorting function within the Greedy algorithm tries to schedule jobs of the user groups 1 and 2 earlier unless jobs from other user groups are already waiting for a very long time. This sorting criterion is modeled according to our scheduling objective. For more details on the used sorting criterion, see Ernemann et al. [8].

2.2 Evolution Strategies

To integrate those scheduling algorithms into an appropriate rule base system, we use Evolution Strategies, see Beyer and Schwefel [2], which are a subclass of Evolutionary Algorithms. Those algorithms are stochastic search methods that mimic the behavior of natural biological evolution. They operate on a population of μ individuals and apply genetic operators like selection, mutation and recombination to breed λ offspring individuals from those μ parent individuals. Within this paper, we do not provide a deeper insight into Evolution Strategies. Furthermore, for all details about specific genetic operators, we simply refer to references in the remainder of this paper.

2.3 Fuzzy Systems

Within this work, we aim to generate rule based scheduling systems. To this end, several approaches can be used. On the one hand, a static approach of defining strict boundaries for certain features and assigning a corresponding combination of sorting criteria and scheduling algorithm is possible. On the other hand, one may apply the more flexible approach of generating a Genetic Fuzzy System.

In our case, neither precise knowledge about the assignment of certain scheduling strategies to certain situations nor training data are available. Furthermore, individual scheduling decisions cannot be evaluated directly, but only after all jobs have been assigned to resources, see Section 1. Hence, the award for the assignment of scheduling strategies to situations is given by a critic only at the end of scheduling a whole workload trace. Furthermore, the generation of an appropriate situation classification is not known in advance and has to be generated implicitly during the generation of the rule based scheduling system.

3 Scheduling Objectives and Features

Within this section, we will introduce several simple scheduling objectives, which have been used to construct more complex evaluation functions for the whole scheduling procedure. However, our methodology is not limited to the presented objective and can be extended to any other criteria.

Furthermore, we apply several features to classify possible scheduling situations within our rule based scheduling system. The concept of this work can be extended to other features as well. Note that objectives evaluate the whole scheduling process at the end of a simulation while features only describe the current state of the system.

As mentioned in Section 1, the complex objective function of a machine provider in our case is based on individual properties of users or user groups. Therefore, both the objective and the feature set refer to those properties and to the overall performance of the whole system.

First, we introduce some definitions and notations.

- $(p_j \cdot m_j)$ as the Resource Consumption of a single job j,
- τ the set of all n jobs within our scheduling system,
- $\xi(t)$ the set of already finished jobs at time t,
- $\pi(t)$ the set of running jobs at time t, and
- $\nu(t)$ the set of waiting jobs at time t.

3.1   Scheduling Objectives

During the development of scheduling systems, an evaluation function is needed in order to describe the achieved quality. We generate our evaluation function by combining simple, commonly used scheduling objectives. Within this work, we exemplarily use 7 of those simple objectives.

Overall Utilization (U):

$$U = \frac{\sum\limits_{j \in \tau} p_j \cdot m_j}{m \cdot \left(\max\limits_{j \in \tau} \{C_j(S)\} - \min\limits_{j \in \tau} \{C_j(S) - p_j\} \right)} \tag{1}$$

Average Weighted Response Time (AWRT) over all jobs of all users:

$$\text{AWRT} = \frac{\sum\limits_{j \in \tau} p_j \cdot m_j \cdot (C_j(S) - r_j)}{\sum\limits_{j \in \tau} p_j \cdot m_j} \tag{2}$$

AWRT objective for user groups 1 to 5:

$$\text{AWRT}_i = \frac{\sum\limits_{j \in \tau} p_j \cdot m_j \cdot (C_j(S) - r_j) \cdot \varrho_i(j)}{\sum\limits_{j \in \tau} p_j \cdot m_j \cdot \varrho_i(j)} \;,\; i \in \{1, 2, \ldots 5\} \tag{3}$$

As we have the AWRT$_i$ for the 5 user groups, the AWRT for all users, and the utilization U the complex objective function in our system can be defined by using those 7 simple objectives.

3.2   Feature Definitions

Next, we present 7 features that are used for classification of system states within our rule base scheduling system.

In order to define our first feature, the Average Weighted Slowdown, we need to introduce the *Slowdown* (SD_j) for a single job j within schedule S:

$$SD_j = \frac{C_j(S) - r_j}{p_j} \tag{4}$$

SD_j will reach its minimum value of 1 if job j does not wait before it starts execution. Then the release date is identical with the job's start time. Normally, the range of this feature can be limited to the interval of $[1,100]$ as values greater than 10 occur very rarely in practice.

The feature *Average Weighted Slowdown* (SD) for all already processed jobs $j \in \xi(t)$ uses the same weighting as defined for the AWRT.

$$SD = \frac{\sum\limits_{j \in \xi(t)} p_j \cdot m_j \cdot (C_j(S) - r_j)}{\sum\limits_{j \in \xi(t)} p_j^2 \cdot m_j} \tag{5}$$

This measure indicates the average delay of jobs between their release and start time for the past. Further, this feature represents the scheduling decisions in the past as only already finished jobs are used to calculate this feature. Here, we have not limited the window for SD. In practical cases, a limitation to, for instance, the last month may be appropriate.

The *Momentary Utilization* (U_m) of the whole parallel computer at time t:

$$U_m = \frac{\sum\limits_{j \in \pi(t)} m_j}{m} \tag{6}$$

The *Proportional Resource Consumption of the Waiting Queue for User Group i* ($PRCWQ_i$):

$$PRCWQ_i = \frac{\sum\limits_{j \in \nu(t)} \bar{p}_j \cdot m_j \cdot \varrho_i(j)}{\sum\limits_{j \in \nu(t)} \bar{p}_j \cdot m_j} \tag{7}$$

Note that the real processing time p_j is unknown for the jobs in the waiting queue. Therefore, we use the estimated processing time $\bar{p}_j$ instead. $PRCWQ_i$ represents the relative part of the estimated resources consumption of user group i to all jobs within the waiting queue. Remember, we are using 5 user groups within our system. Hence, those five feature values represent the expected future of the system. Using these features, the scheduling system is enabled to react on a changed demand of the various user groups.

4   Rule Based Scheduling Systems

As stated in Section 1, local scheduling decisions influence the allocation of future jobs. Hence, the effect of a single decision cannot be determined individually. Therefore, the whole rule base is only evaluated after the complete scheduling of all jobs belonging to a workload trace. This has a significant influence on the learning method to generate this rule base as the evaluation prevents the application of a supervised learning algorithm. Instead, the reward of a decision is delayed and determined by a critic. Furthermore, the generation of an appropriate scheduling situation classification is not known in advance and has to be generated implicitly during the generation of the rule base scheduling system.

For a rule based scheduling approach, every possible scheduling state must be assigned to a corresponding situation class that is described using the already introduced features. A complete rule base RB consists of a set of rules R_i. Each rule R_i contains a conditional and a consequence part. The conditional part describes the conditions for the activation of the rule using the defined features. The consequence part represents the corresponding scheduling strategy recommendation.

In order to specify all scheduling states in an appropriate fashion each rule defines certain partitions of the feature space within the conditional part. The rule base system must contain at least one activated rule for each possible system state.

As already mentioned, the scheduling strategy specifies

1. a *sorting criterion* for the waiting queue $\nu(t)$ and
2. a *scheduling algorithm* that uses the order of $\nu(t)$ to schedule one or more jobs.

We use the term *strategy* to describe the whole scheduling process that consists of both steps. An *algorithm* only describes the procedure of the second step that uses the already sorted waiting queue.

First, the chosen sorting criterion is used to determine the sequence of jobs within the waiting queue. Second, the selected scheduling algorithm is used to find a processor allocation for at least one job of the sorted waiting queue. We have chosen four different sorting criteria. Those sorting criteria are only examples that are used to demonstrate our rule based scheduling approach. Other sorting criteria are possible and could easily be incorporate into the system. Our four sorting criteria are:

- *Increasing Number of Requested Processors:* Preference of jobs with little parallelism and therefore higher utilization. This sorting provides the potential gain of being able to insert many jobs into the current schedule as jobs with a smaller amount of requested processors are often easier to schedule.
- *Increasing Estimated Run Time:* Preference of short jobs and therefore higher job throughput.
- *Decreasing Waiting Time:* Preference of long waiting jobs. This sorting criterion provides a higher fairness as the jobs are processed according to their submission. Jobs with a higher waiting time are selected first.

– *Decreasing User Group Priority:* Preference of jobs from users with a higher resource demand. The sorting by user groups provides a higher ranking for all jobs of users with a higher overall resource demand according to their user group assignment. This criterion reflects our objective function.

The selected scheduling algorithm is one of the four methods presented in Section 2.1. Note that Greedy is already a complete scheduling strategy while the other scheduling algorithms of Section 2 must be supplement with a sorting criterion of $\nu(t)$. Again, the set of scheduling algorithm can be extended for other rule base systems. The general concept of the rule based scheduling approach is depicted in Figure 1.

As 4 different sorting criteria with 3 possible scheduling algorithms and the combined Greedy strategy are available, we have to chose one of 13 strategies for each possible system state. However, it is not practicable to test all possible assignments in all possible states. For example, lets assume a very coarse division of each feature into only 2 partitions. Then 13 possible strategies and 7 features result in $13^{2^7} \approx 3.84 \cdot 10^{142}$ simulations if all combinations in all possible situation states are tested. Additional problems occur during the generation of a rule based scheduling system as the number and reasonable partitions of features, that are required to describe the situation classes in an appropriate way, are generally unknown in advance.

Hence, we introduce three possible approaches to derive a rule based scheduling system using only a limited number of simulations.

4.1   Probability Driven Rule Base Development

A rigid rule base system uses N_F features with a fixed number of intervals for each feature ω. That is, each feature ω has $(N_{part,\omega} - 1)$ static bounds, that divide the possible value range of ω into $N_{part,\omega}$ partitions. The static bounds are specified before the assignment of sorting criteria and scheduling algorithms to the various situation classes are extracted. The concept of such fixed partitions is shown in Figure 2.

Generally, a larger number of partitions $N_{part,\omega}$ of a feature ω potentially leads to a more accurate rule set while more situation classes must be optimized. Overall, this results in N_r situation classes that must be provided to cover all possible system states with

$$N_r = \prod_{\omega=1}^{N_F} N_{part,\omega} \; .$$

The described rigid rule based system activates only a single rule in any system state. Hence, the output recommendation of this single activated rule is the output of the whole scheduling system.

In this work, we assume one division of the intervals of SD and $PRCWQ_1$ to $PRCWQ_5$ respectively. This leads to two partitions in each case. Further, we use two divisions for the U_m feature, resulting in three partitions. Overall, this

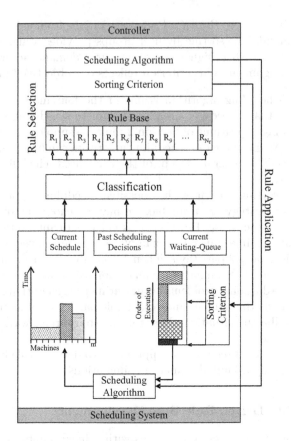

Fig. 1. General Concept of the Rule Based Scheduling Approach

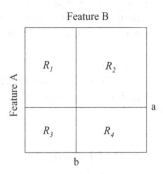

Fig. 2. Example partitioning of the feature space and the resulting set of rules $R_1 \ldots R_4$

produces ($N_r = 2^6 \cdot 3 = 192$) different situation classes that are needed to build a complete rule base.

Furthermore, we have evaluated several different division values for the situation class features. The partitions which achieved the best results are used for the rigid rule base system development,see Table 1.

Table 1. Feature Partitions for the Rigid Rule Based Scheduling Systems

Feature	Intervals
SD	[1-2],]2-100]
$U_{m[\%]}$	[0-75],]75-85],]85-100]
$PRCWQ_{1[\%]}$	[0-20],]20-100]
$PRCWQ_{2[\%]}$	[0-20],]20-100]
$PRCWQ_{3[\%]}$	[0-25],]25-100]
$PRCWQ_{4[\%]}$	[0-25],]25-100]
$PRCWQ_{5[\%]}$	[0-25],]25-100]

Such a rigid rule based scheduling system has the advantage of a simple implementation and easy interpretation. Future scheduling development may benefit from knowledge gained through this kind of interpretation. The selected scheduling algorithms and sorting criteria for a certain scheduling situation can directly be extracted from the corresponding rules without further computation.

Rule bases are generated by assigning potential scheduling strategies to rules in a random fashion such that each scheduling strategy is assigned to each rule the same number of times. Hence, not all rule bases are generated in a completely random way. Remember that the conditional part is rigid and does not vary. Thus, a single rule describes a single scheduling situation class completely.

Then we use those rule bases to produce schedules for the given workload data and evaluate those schedules with the help of the complex scheduling objective. Thus, each schedule results in a scalar objective value. The assignment of a special scheduling strategy to a rule is evaluated by adding the scalar objective values of all schedules that were generated using this assignment. Finally, we build the resulting rule base by assigning the scheduling strategies with the smallest sum of the objective values to the individual rule as we assume a minimization of the objective function. This approach is able to reduce the number of required simulations significantly as we only approximate the optimal assignments. In general, the performance can be increased by generating more rule bases. However, the trade-off between a better performance and more required simulations should be kept in mind.

A parameter p describes how often a scheduling strategy is assigned to a single rule. This parameter p influences the number of required simulations that is given by the product of the number of possible scheduling strategies (N_Ω) and the parameter p. In our simulations $p = 50$ turned out to be a good compromise between the required number of simulations and the scheduling quality. This results in our case in ($13 \cdot 50 = 650$) simulations which is significantly less than the required number of simulation for all possible assignments.

Unfortunately, the fixed division of the whole feature space has a critical influence on the performance of the scheduling system. At the moment, no mechanism is available that automatically adjusts the defined partitions.

Using this approach, we avoid the excessive amount of simulations that must be performed in order to generate the rule base. Further, our approach pays attention to the cooperation aspect of the rules within the final rule base as the evaluation of the assignment of a special scheduling strategy to the consequence part of a rule is based on several simulations with varying strategy assignments for all other rules.

4.2   Scheduling Strategies Based on Genetic Fuzzy Systems

The previously presented scheduling system has several drawbacks regarding the generation of an appropriate rule based scheduling system. Mainly, the static number of feature partitions and the static pre-defined bounds for these partitions are not flexible enough and may lead to bad scheduling results. Furthermore, the whole feature space needs to be divided and appropriate scheduling strategies assigned to each individual partition. Hence, the number of rules cannot be varied.

Consequently, we need a method that automatically adjusts the partition of the feature space and assigns appropriate scheduling strategies to the resulting regions in parallel. *Genetic Fuzzy Systems*, see Hoffmann [17], provide the capabilities to solve those problems. As already mentioned within the introduction, our Genetic Fuzzy System uses the Pittsburgh approach to encode a whole rule base in a single individual. Further, we parameterize the resulting system with Evolution Strategies.

Before the different rule base encoding schemes are explained in detail, we introduce the encoding of individual rules and detail the computation of the final Fuzzy controller output.

Coding of Fuzzy Rules. Our Genetic Fuzzy Systems are based on the traditional Takagi-Sugeno-Kang (TSK) model [30] for Fuzzy systems. The used coding schemes and learning techniques are adapted and slightly modified from the work of Juang et al. [21] and Jin et al. [20].

For a single rule R_i, every feature ω of all N_F features is modeled from a Gaussian Membership Function, $(\mu_i^{(\omega)}, \sigma_i^{(\omega)})$-GMF

$$g_i^{(\omega)}(x) = \frac{1}{\sigma_i^{(\omega)}\sqrt{2\pi}} \exp\left\{\frac{-(x - \mu_i^{(\omega)})^2}{2\sigma_i^{(\omega)2}}\right\}.$$

In Figure 3 a sample (5,0.75)-GMF is depicted.

A feature is then represented by a pair of real values $\mu_i^{(\omega)}$ and $\sigma_i^{(\omega)}$. The $\mu_i^{(\omega)}$ value is the center of the feature GMF that is covered by the rule R_i. Therefore, this value defines a domain in the feature space where the influence of the rule is very high.

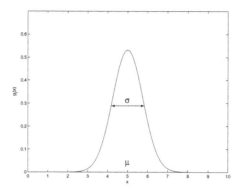

Fig. 3. Gaussian Membership Function with $\mu_i^{(\omega)} = 5$ and $\sigma_i^{(\omega)} = 0.75$

Note that, when using a so defined GMF as feature description, the condition

$$\int_{-\infty}^{\infty} g_i^{(\omega)}(z)dz = 1 \; \forall \; i \in \{1, \ldots N_r\} \wedge \; \omega \in \{1, \ldots N_F\}$$

always holds. In other words, for increasing $\sigma_i^{(\omega)}$ values, the peak value of the GMF decreases because the integral remains constant. Using this property of a GMF, we are able to reduce the influence of a rule for a certain feature completely by setting $\sigma_i^{(\omega)}$ to a very high value. Theoretically for $\sigma_i^{(\omega)} \to \infty$, a rule has no influence for this feature anymore. With this approach, it is also possible to establish a kind of default value that is used if no other peaks are defined in a feature domain. Based on this feature description, a single rule can be described by

$$R_i = \left\{ g_i^{(1)}(x), \; g_i^{(2)}(x), \; \ldots \; g_i^{(N_F)}(x), \boldsymbol{\Omega}_i(R_i) \right\}.$$

The consequence part $\boldsymbol{\Omega}_i$ of every rule R_i, $i \in \{1, \ldots N_r\}$, includes a weighted recommendation for all N_{Ω} possible outputs. Therefore, the consequence part of rule R_i is described by a vector

$$\boldsymbol{\Omega}(R_i) = \left(w_{i1} \; w_{i2} \ldots w_{iN_{\Omega}} \right).$$

We restrict the possible weight values to elements of the set $\{-5, -1, 0, 1, 5\}$. The value -5 represents a *particularly unfavorable* connection while 5 is *particularly favorable* one. The other possible weights can be interpreted accordingly. We use a non-linear weight scaling in order to force distinct recommendations. When considering the superposition of those weights similar weights may lead to almost indistinguishable recommendations. Furthermore, we also include 0 as possible weight to express that a rule behaves completely neutral with respect to the recommendation of a scheduling strategy for a given situation. This may also reduce the number of overall rules.

The main advantage of using several GMFs for describing a single rule is the automatic coverage of the possible feature space. In contrast to the rigid approach, even one rule gives a scheduling strategy for all possible system states. Hence, it is the focus of this approach to find a meaningful set of N_r rules that generates a good rule base system RB. Thus,

$$RB = \{R_1, R_2, \ldots R_{N_r}\}$$

is a complete rule base consisting of N_r rules.

Computation of the Controller Decision. For a given system state, we compute the superposition of the weighted output consequence parts of all rules. The system state is represented by the actual feature vector

$$\boldsymbol{x} = \left(x_1 \; x_2 \ldots x_\omega \ldots x_{N_F} \right)^T$$

of N_F feature values. Then we compute the degree of membership $\phi_i(x_\omega) = g_i^{(\omega)}(x_\omega)$ of the ω-th feature of rule R_i for all N_r rules and all N_F features. The multiplicative superposition of all these values as "AND"-operation leads to an overall degree of membership

$$\phi_i(\boldsymbol{x}) = \bigwedge_{\omega=1}^{N_F} g_i^{(\omega)}(x_\omega) = \prod_{\omega=1}^{N_F} \frac{1}{\sigma_i^{(\omega)} \sqrt{2\pi}} \exp\left\{ \frac{-(x_\omega - \mu_i^{(\omega)})^2}{2\sigma_i^{(\omega)2}} \right\}$$

for rule R_i. For all N_r rules together, the corresponding values $\phi_i(\boldsymbol{x})$ are collected in a membership vector

$$\phi(\boldsymbol{x}) = \left(\phi_1(\boldsymbol{x}) \; \phi_2(\boldsymbol{x}) \ldots \phi_{N_r}(\boldsymbol{x}) \right).$$

Next, we construct a matrix $\underline{C}^{N_F \times N_r}$ of the weighted consequences $\boldsymbol{\Omega}(R_i)$, $i \in \{1, \ldots N_r\}$ of all rules by using the weighted consequence vectors for all individual rules R_i. This yields

$$\underline{C}^{N_F \times N_r} = \left[\boldsymbol{\Omega}(R_1) \; \boldsymbol{\Omega}(R_2) \ldots \boldsymbol{\Omega}(R_{N_r}) \right].$$

Now, we can compute the weight vector $\boldsymbol{\Psi}$ by multiplying the membership vector $\phi(x)$ by the transposed matrix $\underline{C}^T$:

$$\boldsymbol{\Psi} = \phi(\boldsymbol{x}) \cdot \underline{C}^T = \left(\Psi_1 \; \Psi_2 \ldots \Psi_{N_\Omega} \right).$$

The vector $\boldsymbol{\Psi}$ contains the superpositioned weight values for all N_Ω possible scheduling strategy recommendations, that is, $\boldsymbol{\Psi}$ contains 13 elements.

Finally, we choose the scheduling strategy with the highest overall value as the output of the rule base system, that is

$$\arg\max_{1 \leq h \leq N_\Omega} \{\Psi_h\}.$$

As already mentioned, within the Pittsburgh approach, each individual represents a complete rule base. We construct such a complete rule base RB with a fixed number of rules N_r. A single rule consists of $(2 \cdot N_F)$ elements per rule within the conditional part. Furthermore, we include the vector $\Omega(R_i)$ for the consequence part, which consists of $N_\Omega = 13$ elements. Thus, a rule based scheduling system with constant number of rules can also be modeled using the following encoding. As such,

$$o_k = \{\underbrace{\overbrace{\mu_1^{(1)} \sigma_1^{(1)}, \ldots, \mu_1^{(N_F)} \sigma_1^{(N_F)}}^{R_1}, \underbrace{\Omega(R_1)}_{\Omega_1 \ldots \Omega_{N_\Omega}}}_{\text{GMF}}, \overbrace{\mu_2^{(1)} \sigma_2^{(1)}, \ldots, \mu_{N_r}^{(N_F)} \sigma_{N_r}^{(N_F)}, \Omega(R_{N_r})}^{R_2 \ldots R_{N_r}}\}$$

is the coding scheme of the object parameter vector o_k of individual a_k which is a complete rule base. Hence, the number of elements u within the object parameter vector o_k of the individual a_k can be computed by

$$u = N_r \cdot (2 \cdot N_F + N_\Omega).$$

We have chosen a non-isotropic mutation, see Bäck and Schwefel [2], as this allows the individual adaptation of the mutation for the different dimensions. Therefore, each object parameter of the individuals consists of a corresponding strategy parameter that specifies its mutation strength. Further, we apply a standard Evolution Strategy with $\mu = 3$ parent and $\lambda = 21$ offspring individuals. The ratio of $1/7$ is suggested by Schwefel [26]. Further, we do not use any recombination.

Within our Evolution Strategy, we used 40 generations with a randomly initialized first generation. Our (3+21)-Evolution Strategy leads to $3 + (40 \cdot 21) = 843$ evaluations for the development of a single rule base.

We use a constant number of rules $N_r = 10$ for each rule base. This results in a constant number of object and strategy parameters within each individual. Hence, $u = N_r \cdot (2 \cdot N_F + N_\Omega) = 10 \cdot (2 \cdot 7 + 13) = 270$ parameters must be determined. Thus, the two exogenous learning rates for the non-isotropic mutation are defined as:

$$\tau_0 = \frac{1}{\sqrt{2 \cdot u}} = 0.043, \text{ and } \tau_1 = \frac{1}{\sqrt{2\sqrt{u}}} = 0.174,$$

see Bäck and Schwefel [2].

Coevolutionary Genetic Fuzzy System Development. As presented in Section 4, the rule based scheduling system needs to determine for each scheduling state a corresponding sorting criterion and a scheduling algorithm. In the previously introduced rule based scheduling systems, a whole scheduling strategy, consisting of both, a sorting criterion and a scheduling algorithm, was assigned to the different scheduling states. However, this combined assignment is not necessary. Moreover, the assignment of the same sorting criterion to two scheduling states within the features space does not always lead to the assignment of the same scheduling algorithm. This motivates the usage of a Coevolutionary Algorithm as the assignment problem can easily be decomposed into two subproblems.

Concept of Cooperative Coevolutionary Algorithms. Coevolutionary Algorithms potentially lead to better solutions compared with standard Evolutionary Algorithms, if the problem can be decomposed into two subproblems, see for example Jansen et. al [19]. Furthermore, Potter and De Jong [25] have proven that Coevolutionary Algorithms achieve better results with fewer generations compared with standard Evolutionary optimization techniques.

In this work, we apply the commonly called Cooperative Coevolutionary Algorithm (CCA), see Paredis [24]. This model uses two distinct species. Both species are genetically isolated. Hence, the genetic operations are only applied to individuals of the same species. The two different species are evolved in two different populations in parallel by using standard Evolution Strategies. However, during the fitness evaluation, two individuals of each species must cooperate. In general, this concept allows a larger number of species.

First, two species with μ individuals each are randomly generated. Then, the individuals of both species are evaluated by randomly combining two individuals, one from each species. Note that other selection schemes are also possible and discussed in the literature, see for example Panait et al. [22]. However, those methods need more evaluations and additional simulations in our case. In order to avoid this effort, we use our simple heuristic. After evaluation, the genetic operators produce λ offsprings for each species separately. Then, the resulting offspring individuals are again evaluated by a randomly chosen cooperation. Finally, normal evolutionary selection determines the next parent generation.

Rule Based Scheduling Development by applying Coevolutionary Algorithms. As already mentioned, our scheduling problem can be decomposed into two separate subproblems. This concept is shown in Figure 4. Contrary to the general rule based scheduling, see Figure 1, we use two separate rule bases within the same feature space. One determines the sorting criterion depending on the system state and the other calculates the scheduling algorithm. However, the partitioning of this feature space differs between the two species. To this end, the different GMF-$\mu_i^{(\omega)}$ and GMF-$\sigma_i^{(\omega)}$ values are determined separately for the two species. The resulting scheduling system is expected to react on certain system states very accurately.

Such a coevolutionary approach yields several potential advantages for the resulting scheduling system and for the extraction process of appropriate rule bases.

First, each of the two separate rule bases has fewer output recommendations. In detail, for the sorting criterion as well as for the scheduling algorithm, we have only $N_\Omega = 4$ possible output recommendations instead of 13 as in the combined scenario. This reduces the length of the individuals within the populations and

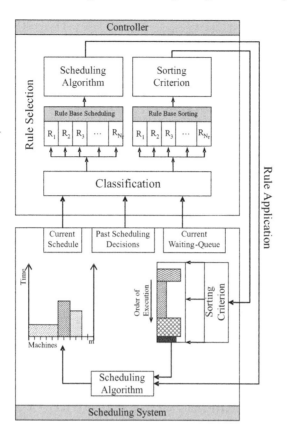

Fig. 4. General Concept of the Rule Based Scheduling Approach with Dedicated Rule Bases for Scheduling and Sorting

enables a better and faster adaptation. However, note that the sorting criterion is redundant if the Greedy scheduling algorithm is selected since Greedy includes its own sorting. Second, as the feature space partition can be optimized for both species separately, fewer rules might be required for each species.

The Evolution Strategies for both populations are identical. We apply the Pittsburgh approach with the same genetic operators and no recombination for both populations. In detail, we use a constant number of rules $N_r = 10$ and a $(3+21)$-Evolution Strategy for both populations. The optimization is limited to 40 generations. Consequently, each individual within the populations consists of

$$u = N_r \cdot (2 \cdot N_F + N_\Omega) = 10 \cdot (2 \cdot 7 + 4) = 180$$

object parameters. Hence, we adapt the learning rates for the non-isotropic mutation to

$$\tau_0 = \frac{1}{\sqrt{2 \cdot u}} = 0.053, \text{ and } \tau_1 = \frac{1}{\sqrt{2\sqrt{u}}} = 0.193,$$

see Bäck and Schwefel [2].

5   Evaluation

For the evaluation, we execute various discrete event simulations with real parallel computer workload traces. To this end, six well known workloads are selected. They were recorded at the Cornell Theory Center (CTC) [18], the Royal Institute of Technology (KTH) [23] in Sweden, the Los Alamos National Lab (LANL) [11] and the San Diego Supercomputer Center (SDSC 00/ SDSC 95/ SDSC 96) [12,32]. Each of these workloads provides information about the job requests for the computational resources. In order to make those workloads comparable they are scaled to a standard machine configuration with 1024 processors as described by Ernemann et al. [9]. The characteristics of the used workloads are presented in Table 2.

Table 2. Scaled Workload Traces from Standard Workload Archive [13] using the Scaling Procedure by Ernemann et al. [9]

Identifier	CTC	KTH	LANL	SDSC 00	SDSC 95	SDSC 96
Machine	SP2	SP2	CM-5	SP2	SP2	SP2
Period	06/26/96 - 05/31/97	09/23/96 - 08/29/97	04/10/94 - 09/24/96	04/28/98 - 04/30/00	12/29/94 - 12/30/95	12/27/95 - 12/31/96
Processors (m)	1024	1024	1024	1024	1024	1024
Jobs (n)	136471	167375	201378	310745	131762	66185

As no real life objective functions are available from the workload traces, we exemplarily use the objective function $(f_{obj} = 10 \cdot \text{AWRT}_1 + 4 \cdot \text{AWRT}_2)$. Clearly, this objective prioritizes user groups 1 and 2, with user group 1 having a higher priority than user group 2.

As already mentioned, we present our achieved results relative to the Pareto front (PF) of all feasible schedules for the simulated workloads. Noteworthy, the Pareto front was generated off-line and it cannot be taken for granted that this front can be reached by our proposed online scheduling systems at all. Therefore, we refer to this front as a reference for the best achievable solution. Note that our Pareto front is only an approximation as it is derived by heuristics. Although we do not know the real Pareto front, the high density of our approximation indicates that the quality of the approximation is very good, see Figure 7.

In Table 3, the absolute results are presented. We show the AWRT values for the user groups, the objective and the overall Utilization. It is obvious that all proposed concepts achieve better results than the EASY standard algorithm. We restricted the comparison to EASY as this is in most cases the best scheduling algorithm for the examined workloads with respect to the AWRT objective. Note that U remains constant and is not affected by the rule based scheduling concept although it is not explicitly included in the objective. As such we are able to prioritize different user groups without any reduction of the system utilization. Further, the results show that we are very close to the off-line generated Pareto front, see Figure 7.

Table 3. AWRT, f_{obj} (in Seconds), and U (in %) of the Pareto Front (PF), EASY Scheduling, the Pittsburgh Approach (PITTS), the Cooperative Coevolutionary Algorithm (CCA), and the Probability Procedure (PROB) for the CTC Workload

Approach	AWRT₁	AWRT₂	AWRT₃	AWRT₄	AWRT₅	U	f_{obj}
PF	49652.04	56330.98	60691.71	59698.30	32726.87	66.99	721844.268
EASY	59681.28	64976.07	50317.47	46120.02	31855.68	66.99	856717.0
PITTS	49639.195	56722.796	49541.757	59212.093	81268.331	66.99	723283.134
CCA	49676.087	56522.699	48723.312	57488.074	74983.133	66.99	722851.666
PROB	53780.183	59448.484	53185.9	53417.769	45390.11	66.99	775595.766

In Figure 5 we presents the results for all six examined workloads. The very simple and rigid probability driven procedure is already able to improve the objective significantly. Apart from the KTH workload the rule system improves the objective value by 10 % on average compared to EASY scheduling.

However, the two Genetic Fuzzy Systems outperform this procedure. It is noteworthy that the on-line rule based scheduling systems produce schedules almost as good as those achieved in the off-line case. Despite the approximative character of the Pareto front, one can reasonably say that the results are quite close to the fronts of all workloads.

The results listed in Table 4 demonstrate that the objective improvements really result in a shorter AWRT for the desired user groups. As we have already shown that the results are close to the Pareto front we now compare the Genetic Fuzzy System, created regarding to the Pittsburgh approach, with the EASY standard algorithm. The improvements of the AWRT in the gray shaded columns show that it is possible to shorten AWRT₁ and AWRT₂ significantely compared to EASY for most workloads. Apart from the SDSC 00 workload this prioritization is realized without deterioration of the utilization.

Table 4. AWRT and Utilization Improvements Achieved with the Genetic Fuzzy System in Comparison to the EASY Scheduling Algorithm (in Percent)

Workload	AWRT₁	AWRT₂	AWRT₃	AWRT₄	AWRT₅	U	f_{obj}
CTC	16.83	12.7	1.54	-28.39	-155.11	0	15.58
KTH	25.35	8.44	-57.64	-199.49	-744.53	0	19.82
LANL	19.75	14.84	-24.09	-47.2	-269.06	0	18.24
SDSC 00	60.83	42.37	-12.72	-3234.66	-14360.76	-5.57	55.79
SDSC 95	9.05	0.08	-20.7	-43.56	-38.55	0	6.37
SDSC 96	1.35	1.2	-20.03	-26.15	-4.09	0	1.31

In Figure 6, we exemplarily show the achieved AWRT improvements for all 3 approaches for the CTC workload. We can realize the desired group prioritization with all proposed approaches. Note that we limited this chart at the y-axis as the AWRT values for user group 5 are extremely large. As the utilization remains constant these user groups have to pay the price for the short AWRT of the favored user groups. This is acceptable as we did not take these user groups into account for our objective formulation.

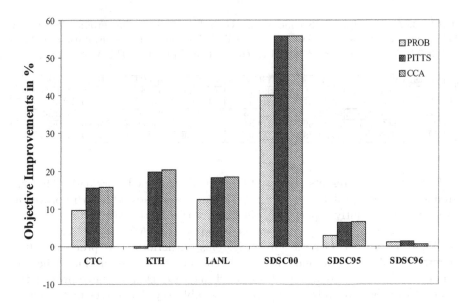

Fig. 5. Objective Improvements of all 3 Approaches in Comparison to EASY Scheduling

Finally, we show in Figure 7 the AWRT values of the two user groups to prioritize. This chart also depicts the Pareto front of all feasible schedules. Remember that we have 7 simple objectives. Each point within this chart represents a feasible schedule that is not dominated by any other generated feasible solution within the 7-dimensional objective space. As we show only a projection of the actual 7-dimensional Pareto front approximation, the elements cover an area in this 2-dimensional chart.

As the EASY standard algorithm does not favor any user groups, the achieved AWRT values are located in the mid of the projected front area. With the probability driven procedure, it is already possible to move the AWRT values towards the actual front. Obviously, this approach is capable to improve $AWRT_2$ significantly but it does only slightly improve $AWRT_1$. However, the two proposed Genetic Fuzzy Systems almost reach the front in our example. Thereby, the CCA leads to a little bit better results than the classic Pittsburgh approach.

5.1   Estimation of Computational Effort to Establish the Rule Based Scheduling System

Our chosen objective is just an example and the proposed methods can be used with any other objective as well. However, we restricted our analysis to these example as this already required a high computational effort. For the probability driven procedure, we simulated $(50 \cdot 13 = 650)$ rule systems per workload. Of course this value is scalable by choosing a smaller number of guaranteed

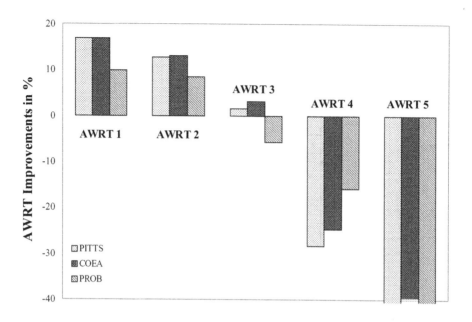

Fig. 6. AWRT Improvements of all 3 Approaches in Comparison to EASY Scheduling and the CTC Workload.

participations, but values smaller 50 did not yield good results. Nevertheless, this procedure established the rule bases with a comparatively small number of simulations.

The Genetic Fuzzy Systems are realized by an (3+21)-Evolution Strategy. In order to obtain good results, we simulated 40 evolutionary generations. Therefore, $(3 + 21 \cdot 40 = 843)$ objective evaluations per workload were necessary. Further, a single simulation of a complete workload takes about 4 hours computing time on average. For the Genetic Fuzzy System this resulted in 4 months computing time per workload and objective assuming only one available machine for the scheduling strategy generation.

Obviously, we are only able to present our results here because we used a compute cluster with 120 processors. With this installation, we can simulate all objective evaluations in parallel as they are completely independent from each other. Therefore, the simulation of one objective and one workload takes approximately one week. Furthermore, the parallel computation of the six workloads can also be realized. Despite the highly parallel execution of our simulations it still took more than 4 months to obtain the results presented in this paper.

Nevertheless, the presented effort estimates are only related to the generation of the rule bases. But remember that the execution of our scheduling algorithm in the runtime environment is not slower than the execution of a conventional scheduling algorithm.

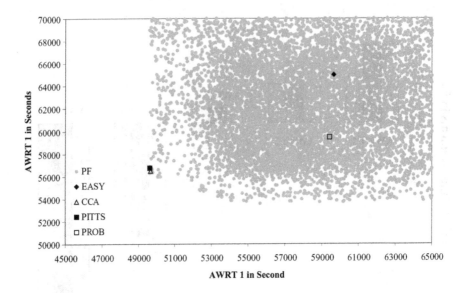

Fig. 7. $AWRT_1$ versus $AWRT_2$ of all 3 Approaches, the EASY Standard Algorithm, and the Pareto Front of all Feasible Schedules for the CTC Workload

6   Conclusion

In this paper, we have presented a novel approach to automatically generating online scheduling systems for a complex provider defined objective. The scheduling systems are based on rules that include standard scheduling algorithms. We used simulations with workload traces from existing installations during the development of the systems and during the evaluation process.

Even for a rather simple scheduling objective that prioritizes some user groups over others, we have demonstrated that a probability driven assignment procedure already leads to rule bases that typically produce better scheduling results than existing standard algorithms. The more sophisticated approaches using Genetic Fuzzy Systems significantly improve the achieved quality of the schedules. First, we compared our achieved results with the EASY standard scheduling algorithm. We achieved an improvement of about 10 % for our objective function with the adopted rule based scheduling system. Second, we compared our approaches with the off-line generated Pareto front of all feasible schedules. Here, we are even able to almost reach this front with the proposed Genetic Fuzzy Systems.

Acknowledgement

All authors are members of the Collaborative Research Center 531, "Computational Intelligence", at the Dortmund University with financial support of the Deutsche Forschungsgemeinschaft (DFG).

References

1. T. Bäck and H.-P. Schwefel. An Overview of Evolutionary Algorithms for Parameter Optimization. *Evolutionary Computation*, 1(1):1–23, 1993.
2. H.-G. Beyer and H.-P. Schwefel. Evolution Strategies – A Comprehensive Introduction. *Natural Computing*, 1(1):3–52, 2002.
3. A. Bonarini. Evolutionary Learning of Fuzzy rules: competition and cooperation. In W. Pedrycz, editor, *Fuzzy Modelling: Paradigms and Practice*, pages 265–284. Kluwer Academic Press, 1996.
4. R. Buyya, D. Abramson, and S. Venugopal. The Grid Economy. *Special Issue on Grid Computing, Proceedings of the IEEE*, 93(3):698–714, 2005.
5. S. J. Chapin, W. Cirne, D. G. Feitelson, J. P. Jones, S. T. Leutenegger, U. Schwiegelshohn, W. Smith, and D. Talby. Benchmarks and standards for the evaluation of parallel job schedulers. In D. G. Feitelson and L. Rudolph, editors, *Proceedings of the 5th Job Scheduling Strategies for Parallel Processing*, volume 1659 of *Lecture Notes in Computer Science (LNCS)*, pages 67–90. Springer, 1999.
6. C. Ernemann, V. Hamscher, U. Schwiegelshohn, A. Streit, and R. Yahyapour. On Advantages of Grid Computing for Parallel Job Scheduling. In *Proceedings of the 2nd IEEE/ACM International Symposium on Cluster Computing and the Grid (CCGRID2002)*, pages 39–46, Berlin, 2002. IEEE Computer Society Press.
7. C. Ernemann, V. Hamscher, and R. Yahyapour. Economic Scheduling in Grid Computing. In D. G. Feitelson, L. Rudolph, and U. Schwiegelshohn, editors, *Proceedings of the 8th Job Scheduling Strategies for Parallel Processing*, volume 2537 of *Lecture Notes in Computer Science (LNCS)*, pages 128–152. Springer, 2002.
8. C. Ernemann, U. Schwiegelshohn, N. Beume, M. Emmerich, and L. Schönemann. Scheduling Algorithm Development based on Complex Owner Defined Objectives. Technical Report CI-190/05, Dortmund University, Germany, 2005. http://sfbci.uni-dortmund.de/Publications/Reference/Downloads/19005.pdf.
9. C. Ernemann, B. Song, and R. Yahyapour. Scaling of Workload Traces. In D. G. Feitelson, L. Rudolph, and U. Schwiegelshohn, editors, *Proceedings of the 9th Job Scheduling Strategies for Parallel Processing*, volume 2862 of *Lecture Notes in Computer Science (LNCS)*, pages 166–183. Springer, 2003.
10. C. Ernemann and R. Yahyapour. *Grid Resource Management - State of the Art and Future Trends*, chapter Applying Economic Scheduling Methods to Grid Environments, pages 491–506. Kluwer Academic Publishers, 2003.
11. D. G. Feitelson. Memory usage in the LANL CM-5 workload. In D. G. Feitelson and L. Rudolph, editors, *Proceedings of the 3rd Job Scheduling Strategies for Parallel Processing*, volume 1291 of *Lecture Notes in Computer Science (LNCS)*, pages 78–94. Springer, 1997.
12. D. G. Feitelson. Metric and Workload Effects on Computer Systems Evaluation. *Computer*, 36(9):18–25, 2003.
13. D. G. Feitelson. Parallel Workload Archive. http://www.cs.huji.ac.il/labs/parallel/workload/, March 2006.
14. D. G. Feitelson and M. A. Jette. Improved Utilization and Responsiveness with Gang Scheduling. In D. G. Feitelson and L. Rudolph, editors, *Proceedings of the 3rd Job Scheduling Strategies for Parallel Processing*, volume 1291 of *Lecture Notes in Computer Science (LNCS)*, pages 238–261. Springer, 1997.

15. R. L. Graham. Bounds for certain multiprocessor anomalies. *Bell System Technical Journal*, 45:1563–1581, 1966.
16. F. Heine, M. Hovestadt, O. Kao, and A. Streit. On the Impact of Reservations from the Grid on Planning-Based Resource Management Computational Science. In V. S. Sunderam et al., editor, *Proceedings of the 5th International Conference on Computational Science (ICCS 2005)*, volume 3516 of *Lecture Notes in Computer Science (LNCS)*, pages 155–162. Springer, 2005.
17. F. Hoffmann. Evolutionary Algorithms for Fuzzy Control System Design. *Proceedings of the IEEE*, 89(9):1318–1333, 2001.
18. S. Hotovy. Workload Evolution on the Cornell Theory Center IBM SP2. In D. G. Feitelson and L. Rudolph, editors, *Proceedings of the 2nd Job Scheduling Strategies for Parallel Processing*, volume 1162 of *Lecture Notes in Computer Science (LNCS)*, pages 27–40. Springer, 1996.
19. T. Jansen and R. P. Wiegand. Exploring the Explorative Advantage of the Cooperative Coevolutionary (1+1) EA. In E. Cantú-Paz et al., editor, *Proceedings of the Genetic and Evolutionary Computation Conference (GECCO 2003)*, volume 2723 of *Lecture Notes in Computer Science (LNCS)*, pages 310–321. Springer, 2003.
20. Y. Jin, W. von Seelen, and B. Sendhoff. On Generating FC^3 Fuzzy Rule Systems from Data Using Evolution Strategies. *IEEE Transactions on System, Man and Cybernetics*, 29(6):829–845, 1999.
21. C.-F. Juang, J.-Y. Lin, and C.-T. Lin. Genetic Reinforcement Learning through Symbiotic Evolution for Fuzzy Controller Design. *IEEE Transactions on System, Man and Cybernetics*, 30(2):290–302, 2000.
22. L.Panait, R.-P. Wiegand, and S. Luke. A Sensitivity Analysis of a Cooperative Coevolutionary Algorithm Biased for Optimization. In K. Deb and R. Poli et al., editors, *Genetic and Evolutionary Computation - GECCO 2004*, volume 3102 of *Lecture Notes in Computer Science (LNCS)*, pages 573–584. Springer, 2004.
23. A. W. Mu'alem and D. G. Feitelson. Utilization, Predictability, Workloads, and User Runtime Estimates in Scheduling the IBM SP2 with Backfilling. *IEEE Transanctions on Parallel & Distributed Systems*, 12(6):529–543, 2001.
24. J. Paredis. Coevolutionary Computation. *Artificial Life*, 2(4):355–375, 1995.
25. M. A. Potter and K. De Jong. A Cooperative Coevolutionary Approach to Function Optimization. In Y. Davidor, H.-P. Schwefel, and R. Männer, editors, *Parallel Problem Solving from Nature – PPSN III*, volume 866 of *Lecture Notes in Computer Science (LNCS)*, pages 249–257. Springer, 1994.
26. H.-P. Schwefel. *Numerical Optimization of Computer Models*. John Wiley & Sons, Chichester, 1981.
27. S. F. Smith. *A Learning System Based on Genetic Adaptive Algorithms*. PhD thesis, Department of Computer Science, University of Pittsburgh, 1980.
28. B. Song, C. Ernemann, and R. Yahyapour. Parallel Computer Workload Modeling with Markov Chains. In D. G. Feitelson, L. Rudolph, and U. Schwiegelshohn, editors, *Proceedings of the 10th Job Scheduling Strategies for Parallel Processing*, volume 3277 of *Lecture Notes in Computer Science (LNCS)*, pages 47–62. Springer, 2004.
29. B. Song, C. Ernemann, and R. Yahyapour. User Group-based Workload Analysis and Modeling. In *Proceedings of the International Symposium on Cluster Computing and the Grid (CCGRID2005)*. IEEE Computer Society Press, 2005. CD-ROM.

30. T. Takagi and M. Sugeno. Fuzzy Identification of Systems and Its Applications to Modeling and Control. *IEEE Transactions on Systems, Man, and Cybernetics*, SMC-15(1):116–132, 1985.
31. D. Talby and D. G. Feitelson. Supporting Priorities and Improving Utilization of the IBM SP Scheduler Using Slack-Based Backfilling. In *Proceedings of the 13th International Parallel Processing Symposium and 10th Symposium on Parallel and Distributed Processing*, pages 513–517. IEEE Computer Society, 1999.
32. K. Windisch, V. Lo, R. Moore, D. G. Feitelson, and B. Nitzberg. A comparison of workload traces from two production parallel machines. In *6th Symp. Frontiers Massively Parallel Computing*, pages 319–326. IEEE Computer Society Press, 1996.

Moldable Parallel Job Scheduling Using Job Efficiency: An Iterative Approach

Gerald Sabin, Matthew Lang, and P. Sadayappan

Dept. of Computer Science and Engineering, The Ohio State University, Columbus
OH 43201, USA
{sabin, langma, saday}@cse.ohio-state.edu

Abstract. Currently, job schedulers require "rigid" job submissions from users, who must specify a particular number of processors for each parallel job. Most parallel jobs can be run on different processor partition sizes, but there is often a trade-off between wait-time and run-time — asking for many processors reduces run-time but may require a protracted wait. With moldable scheduling, the choice of job partition size is determined by the scheduler, using information about job scalability characteristics. We explore the role of job efficiency in moldable scheduling, through the development of a scheduling scheme that utilizes job efficiency information. The algorithm is able to improve the average turnaround time, but requires tuning of parameters. Using this exploration as motivation, we then develop an iterative scheme that avoids the need for any parameter tuning. The iterative scheme performs an intelligent, heuristic based search for a schedule that minimizes average turnaround time. It is shown to perform better than other recently proposed moldable job scheduling schemes, with good response times for both the small and large jobs, when evaluated with different workloads.

1 Introduction

Parallel job scheduling in a space-shared environment[1,2,3,4,5] is a research topic that has received a large amount of attention. Traditional approaches to job scheduling operate under the principle that jobs are *rigid* — that they are submitted to run on a certain number of processors, and that number is inflexible. Previously considered rigid scheduling schemes range from an early and simple first-come-first-serve (FCFS) strategy, which suffers from severe fragmentation and leads to poor utilization, to current backfilling policies which attempt to reduce the number of wasted cycles. Backfilling creates reservations for N jobs from a sorted queue (often based on arrival time, job size, or current wait time), and then allow jobs to start "out of order" provided that no reservations are violated. Variations of N, such as $N = 1$ (aggressive or EASY backfilling) or $N = \infty$ (conservative backfilling) exhibit different behaviors and have been studied in detail. The vast majority of this work assumes that the user provides the number of nodes the job must run on as well as the job's estimated runtime.

E. Frachtenberg and U. Schwiegelshohn (Eds.): JSSPP 2006, LNCS 4376, pp. 94–114, 2007.

However, many jobs do not actually require a specific number of processors; they can run on a range of processors. This range may be limited by constraints due to the nature of the job. For example, a job may require a minimum number of processors (possibly for memory or other hardware constraints), or it may not be able to effectively use a large number of processors. Thus, the user must balance these factors when determining the number of processors to request from the scheduler. In addition, in order to achieve a satisfactory wait time, the user must also consider the state of the job queue, the running jobs, and the scheduling policy in place.

In recent work, there has been interest in moldable scheduling, an alternative model to the traditional rigid scheme. In a moldable scheme, a job is submitted by the user accompanied by a range of processor choices and run times or the speedup characteristics and constraints of the job. In this way, the scheduler is given the ability to make the final decision regarding the size of the partition the job is given. In such a scheme, the increased flexibility the scheduler is afforded allows it to not only provide the user with a better response time than the rigid case but also be better suited to adapt to changes of job mix and load.

A fundamental issue in moldable job scheduling is the determination of the partition size for each job. Cirne [6,7] proposed and evaluated a moldable scheduling strategy using a greedy submit-time determination of each job's partition size. Later studies [8] showed that under a number of circumstances, a greedy strategy was problematic. Improved schemes were proposed and evaluated [9], but a shortcoming of previously proposed approaches is that the scalability of jobs is not taken into consideration. Given two similarly sized jobs with different scalabilities that are submitted at the same time, clearly it would be desirable to preferentially allocate more processors to the more scalable job. However, job mixes typically contain jobs with very different sizes. This paper addresses the issue of incorporating consideration of job scalability into a moldable scheduling strategy and demonstrates that the the importance of efficiency varies with respect to the characteristics of the workload a scheduler encounters. With this knowledge in hand, an iterative scheduling scheme is introduced which eliminates the need for scheduler parameterization based on workload characteristics and implicitly considers efficiency.

The remainder of the paper is organized as follows: Section 2 discusses related moldable job scheduling work. Section 3 describes the event-based simulator as well as the workloads used. Section 4 discusses the effects of "overbooking" introduced in previous work in a moldable scheduling model. Section 5 explores a scheme which uses efficiency and overbooking to outperform schemes which ignore job scalability. Section 6 introduces an iterative scheduling strategy which eliminates the need for tunable parameters. Finally, section 7 concludes the paper.

2   Related Work

There has been extensive research on parallel job scheduling in a non-preemptive space shared environment [1,2,4,10,11,12]. Much of the recent work focuses on scheduling "rigid" jobs, even though jobs may be able to run on a range of partition sizes. Previous work that focuses on moldable job scheduling aims primarily to minimize makespan or is set in the context of offline scheduling. Further, the realistic workloads [13] available today were not available when previous research into moldable scheduling was undertaken. This paper focuses on minimizing average turnaround time in an online scenario using realistic workloads.

Du and Leung [14] introduce a "Parallel Task System" (PST) for moldable jobs. The system is comprised of m processors, and n moldable jobs, whose speedups are assumed to be non-decreasing functions. They show that finding the minimal completion time for a PST is NP-hard. Krishnamurti and Ma [15] develop an offline approximation algorithm that attempts to minimize the makespan of a set of moldable tasks. The number of tasks is defined to be less than the number of partitions and the number of partitions is bounded. They propose an algorithm that incrementally reduces the execution time of the longest job. Other work studied the problem of reducing the makespan in an offline, multi-resource context [16,17] while others assumed processor subset constraints [18,19].

Eager, Zahorjanm, and Lazowska [20] suggest using the average parallelism of each task as a basis for processor allocation. They do not propose detailed scheduling algorithms. Ghosal, Serazzi, and Tripathi [21] extend the Eager et. al. work by introducing the concept of the processor working set (PWS). The PWS maximizes the number of processors that a job can efficiently use. The scheduling algorithms developed increase the average "power" [20] of the schedule. They develop online algorithms based on PWS for a setting similar to that of this paper.

Kleinrock and Huang [22] determine the number of processors to allocate in a parallel system where only one job can be executing at any given time. Again, the goal is to maximize power. This system is clearly not ideal for minimizing average turnaround time, as jobs are run sequentially in an FCFS manner.

Mccann, Vaswani, and Zahorjan [23] present a policy for a multi-processor system where jobs which can be resized dynamically (malleable). The scheduling policy transfers processors between running jobs based on the current parallelism of a job.

Sevick [24] provides a generic scheduling algorithm designed to reduce the average turnaround time in a wide range of environments (e.g., preemptive, non-preemptive, online, offline). The algorithm, based on Least Work First, determines a number of tasks to start simultaneously and then uses heuristics to assign each of the chosen tasks a set of processors.

Rosti et. al. [25] perform an analysis of non-work conserving scheduling algorithms. The analysis highlights the importance of realistic workload models when evaluating moldable schedulers. The non-work conserving algorithms are effective when there is large variance in the workload trace (as seen in real workloads) and with varying job types (as seen in real workloads). Non-work conserving algorithms outperform work conserving algorithms for the realistic workloads considered.

Downey [26,27] presents a careful analysis of job characteristics and mix in real traces; this analysis [26] is used to create predictors for the queue time of jobs in synthetic workloads. Downey describes a moldable scheduling scheme which aims to optimize the performance of each job by determining a partition size n such that the run time on n processors plus the predicted queue time on n processors is minimized. However, jobs are scheduled in a strict first-come-first-serve order which, again, hinders the ability of the system in improve average user metrics. Also, the greedy selection of partition size for individual jobs may harm the performance of other jobs in the system.

Downey [27] examines the performance of existing algorithms [28,29] under his workload model. He defines two variations of moldable schemes—those that make greedy decisions for individual jobs, resulting in smaller partition sizes, and those that schedule jobs on only the "ideal" number of processors that each algorithm chooses. Both variations suffers from the issue described above and from the strict first-come-first-serve order imposed on the scheduler.

Cirne et. al. [6,7] proposed a submit-time-based algorithm for moldable scheduling, where the desired processor allocation is decided upon submission to the scheduler in order to minimize response time. Once the desired allocation is determined the scheduler functions essentially the same as in the rigid case. As such, the scheduler is not able to take into account the inherently dynamic information about jobs and new job arrivals. Also, each job makes a greedy decision, which may not be a wise global decision [8]. However, using simulations and moldable traces based on real rigid traces, Cirne et. al. were able to show that their moldable scheduler can outperform a standard rigid parallel job scheduler.

Srinivasan et. al. [9,8] use lazy processor allocation, delaying this allocation decision until schedule time. This allows the scheduler to obtain more information regarding job runtimes and job arrivals before finalizing the number of processors a job will run on. In this context, an unbounded greedy choice will not lead to a good schedule. Therefore, techniques to limit the number of processors a job can take are developed. The authors are able to show that their new methods can improve the schedule for many moldable workloads.

3 Simulation Setup

This work uses an event based simulator in which we are able to evaluate proposed scheduling policies using varying workload characteristics. The simulator uses workload traces in the Standard Workload Format [13], which can be obtained from Dror Feitelson's publicly available Parallel Workload Archive [13]. This allows us to perform multiple simulations on identical workloads in order to achieve comparable results across proposed scheduling policies.

3.1 Workload Generation

The simulations were run with workloads based on a trace from a 512-node IBM SP2 system at the Cornell Theory Center (CTC) obtained from Feitelson's workload archive. The trace, supplied in the Standard Workload Format, contains the submit time, number of processors, actual runtime, and user estimated runtime of each job. To generate different offered workloads we multiply both the user supplied runtime estimate and the actual runtime by a suitable factor to achieve the desired offered load. As an example, assume that the original trace had a utilization of 65%. To achieve an offered utilization of 90%, the actual runtime and the estimated runtime are multiplied by a factor of 0.9/0.65. We use this method in lieu of shrinking the inter-arrival time between jobs to keep the duration of the trace consistent. In all simulations, the scheduler uses the runtime estimates provided by the user for scheduling purposes.

The data presented in the paper shows effective load, which is the load after adjusting for the scalability of the jobs. For instance, assume a job originally ran for 1000 seconds on 5 processors and had an efficiency of 50% (using our scalability model). Then the job contributes 2500 processor seconds to the effective load. In other words, the effective load represents the load for all jobs assuming the scheduler is able to run the jobs with ideal efficiency.

The trace used, as well as every other trace that we are aware of, does not contain any information regarding the scalability of the jobs. Therefore, we use the Downey model [30] of speedup for parallel programs and assign speedup characteristics to a job either by using fixed values or a random distribution.

3.2   The Downey Model

Downey's work [30] describes a model of speedup for parallel jobs. Speedup is defined as the ratio of the job's runtime on a single processor to the job's runtime on n processors. If L is the sequential runtime of the job and $T(n)$ is the runtime of the job on n processors, then $S(n) = L/T(n)$ where $S(n)$ is the speedup of the job. Downey's model is a non-linear function of two parameters:

- A denotes the average parallelism of a job and is a measure of the maximum speedup that the job can achieve.
- σ (*sigma*) is an approximation of the coefficient of variance in parallelism within a job. It determines how close to linear the speedup is. A value of 0 indicates linear speedup and higher values indicate greater deviation from the linear case. Previous work has shown that a sigma between 0 and 2 can be expected for many workloads [27].

Downey's speedup function is defined as follows:

For low variance ($\sigma \leq 1$)

$$S(n) = \begin{cases} \dfrac{An}{A + \sigma(n-1)/2} & 1 \leq n \leq A \\[2ex] \dfrac{An}{\sigma(A - 1/2) + n(1 - \sigma/2)} & A \leq n \leq 2A - 1 \\[2ex] A & n \geq 2A - 1 \end{cases}$$

and for high variance ($\sigma \geq 1$)

$$S(n) = \begin{cases} \dfrac{nA(\sigma+1)}{\sigma(n+A-1)+A} & 1 \leq n \leq A + A\sigma - \sigma \\ A & n \geq A + A\sigma - \sigma \end{cases}$$

4   Fair-Share Allocation and Overbooking

In this section, we review the fair-share strategy proposed in [8] along with an examination of the effect of varying the "weight factor" used in the fair-share schemes and how it affects jobs with different speedup characteristics.

4.1   Fair-Share Based Allocation

The fundamental problem with using an unrestricted greedy approach to choose partition sizes for jobs is that most jobs tend to choose very large partition sizes. In the extreme case, this degenerates to a scenario where each job chooses a partition size equal to the number of processors in the system, with jobs being run in FIFO order. In order to rectify this problem, fair-share-based limits were introduced [8]. Fair-share-based schemes impose an upper bound on a job's allocation based on its fractional weight (resource requirement in processor-seconds) in the mix of jobs. The partition size for each job is then chosen to optimize its turnaround time, subject to its fair-share upper bound. A proportional-share limit was first evaluated [8], where the upper-bound for a job's partition size was set in direct proportion to the job's weight. A later study [9] showed that better turnaround times were achieved by using a "square-root" based fair-share limit, where the bound was set in proportion to the square root of job's weight:

$$Weight\ fraction\ of\ job\ i = \frac{\sqrt{Weight\ of\ job\ i}}{\sum_{j \in jobs} \sqrt{Weight\ of\ job\ j}}.$$

We restrict our discussion of the fair-share moldable scheduling schemes to the schedule-time aggressive scheme, where the backfilling policy allows for $N = 1$ reservations from the queue and the decision of partition size is delayed until reservation time.

Srinivasan et. al. [8,9] use an additional system-wide "weight factor" which is multiplied with the weight fraction to raise the limit on the number of processors allocated for all jobs. Rajan [31] further examined the use of a system-wide weight factor. We will call this the *overbooking factor* and it will be the focus of our examination. Specifically, we describe how changes in the overbooking factor can benefit or harm jobs with different speedup characteristics and weight fractions.

4.2   Perfect Scalability

The "overbooking factor" (ObF) is a multiplicative factor used to scale up the weight-fraction of a job in determining the upper bound on partition size. With an overbooking factor of one (i.e., no overbooking), the sum of fair-share based partition limits of all jobs add up to the total number of available processors.

With an overbooking factor of two, the sum of upper bounds add up to twice the number of processors, etc. As ObF increases, average turnaround time improves at low load, but worsens at high load. An increase in ObF has several effects:

- It tends to increase the average number of waiting jobs in the queue; since each job's maximum partition size is increased, the number of jobs that can concurrently run decreases. This causes the average turnaround time of light jobs to increase, since turn-around of these jobs is dominated by queue time.
- The average run-time of heavy jobs tends to decrease, causing the average response time to also decrease, since it is dominated by the run-time and not queue time.
- When several similarly sized jobs are present, where as with ObF of one, they could all run concurrently, with higher ObF their execution gets serialized, but lowers average response time. For example, with two identically sized jobs, with ObF of one, they both could run concurrently using half the processors each. With ObF of two, each job would run using all the processors for one half the time, giving an average response time that is $(T/2 + T)/2$, i.e., 75% of that with ObF=1.

As the system approached saturation, the queue size increases rapidly with high ObF, causing the deterioration of performance of light jobs to overshadow the benefits of high ObF for the heavy jobs.

4.3   Non-ideal Job Scalability

The effect of the overbooking factor on performance changes under non-ideal scalability conditions [31]. Unlike the case where all jobs share a value of $\sigma = 0$ (perfect scalability), when σ is higher (poorer job scalability), it can be seen that increasing ObF causes an increase in average response time, even at low loads. This is because a higher ObF causes jobs to receive wider partition choices, and therefore uses more processor cycles for job execution than narrower partition choices. The detrimental effect of increasing ObF is more pronounced at high loads, where the waste of processor cycles by inefficient wide jobs causes an increase in queuing delays. This points to a need to take job scalability into consideration when performing moldable job scheduling.

5   Efficiency Considerations

In the previous section, we considered how overbooking, by itself, can either be helpful or harmful to the average response time of jobs within the fair-share scheme and that a job's efficiency needs to be taken into consideration when computing its processor allocation. In this section, we describe a scheduling policy that corrects for this oversight by optimizing for efficiency.

We must be careful when discussing "optimal efficiency," though. A schedule that is optimally efficient for the whole would be a schedule where every job is simply allocated a single processor. This schedule, while maximizing efficiency and throughput, obviously falls short of providing users with adequate response times.

Therefore we choose to maximize the "instantaneous" effective utilization. This is the sum of the number of processors a job runs on N_i multiplied by the efficiency of that job on that number of processors $e(N_i)$. for all jobs. We can see that maximizing the effective utilization is then the same as maximizing the speedup $s(N_i)$ of all jobs ($\sum[N_i * e(N_i)] = \sum[N_i * \frac{s(N_i)}{N_i}] = \sum[s(N_i)]$). In situations where there are less jobs than processors, each job's partition size will be computed such that processors are being used in a locally optimal manner.

5.1   Incorporating Efficiency into Fairshare

An optimally efficient schedule is one that makes the most efficient use of available cycles. However, response time is an important metric, so we still need to incorporate job size. Thus the thrust of this scheme is to close the gap between the weight-based allocation of the fair-share scheme, where jobs receive a proportion of the system ignoring how well they scale to fit their allocation, and an efficiency-based allocation, where the relative sizes of the jobs are ignored and the effective utilization is optimized.

In order to maintain this balance, we define a system-wide *efficiency factor* (EF). The efficiency factor limits how much a job's maximum allocation can change from its fair-share limit:

$$\max(1, FairshareLimit * (1 + EF)) \le$$
$$EfficiencyLimit \le min(SystemSize, FairshareLimit * (1 - EF))$$

In order to maximize the "instantaneous" effective utilization, or the sum of the speedups of all jobs, we take processors away from the fair share limit of the job with the smallest slope of its speedup curve for its current allocated limit and give processors to the job with the highest slope of its speedup curve, this leads towards equivalent derivatives of the speedup.

The algorithm for determining a job's maximum processor allocation is shown in Figure 1.

By including a job's speedup characteristics in its allocation we are able to take advantage of the benefits of overbooking for jobs that scale well enough to efficiently use additional processors without wasting processors on jobs that cannot efficiently use them.

5.2   Experimental Results

We evaluated our algorithm over a set of input traces, varying the efficiency and overbooking parameters of the scheduler. Traces were modified to contain speedup characteristics of jobs subject to the Downey model. For the sake of brevity we limit our discussion to overbooking factors of 1 and 4 and efficiency factors of 0, 0.5, and 1. We show two sets of results — one which assumes that each job can scale to the size of the system (A = system size) and another

```
void selectMaxProcessorLimit(){
    OrderedList jobs;
    /** All jobs start with the
    original fair share limit **/
    foreach j in jobs{
        j.nodeLimit = getFairshare(j);
        j.maxNodesLimit =
            min(SYS_SIZE, (1+EF)*j.nodeLimit);
        j.minNodeLimit =
            max(1,(1-EF)*j.nodeLimit);
    }

    /**Transfer processors from jobs with a small
       speedup slope to jobs with a high speedup
       slope, to optimize instantaneous effective
       utilization **/
    while(!complete){
        complete=true;
        sortBySlope(jobs);
        while(!canMove(sJob=jobs.getFirst()))
                jobs.removeFirst();
        while(!canMove(lJob=jobs.getLast()))
                jobs.removeLast();
        if(sJob.getSlope()<lJob.getSlope()){
                sJob.nodeLimit--;
                lJob.nodeLimit++;
                sortBySlope(jobs);
                complete=false;
        }
    }
}


/** Each job's original limit is between the max and
    the min.  During each call to selectMaxProcessorLimit
    each job will either gain or lose processor (not both). **/
boolean canMove(Job j){
  if(j.nodeLimit >= j.maxNodeLimit ||
        j.nodeLimit <=j.minNodeLimit){
      return false;
  }
  return true;
}
```

Fig. 1. The efficiency based moldable scheduling algorithm

that assigns each job a random value of A from a random uniform distribution between 1 and 2 times the number processors the job requests in the unmodified trace. In both sets of results, we chose the value of σ for each job from a uniform distribution between 0 and 2.

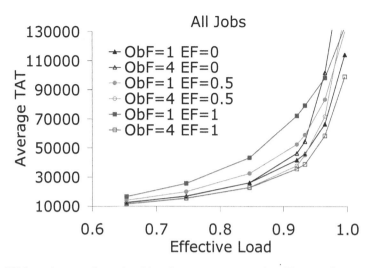

Fig. 2. With an increased overbooking factor, increasing the efficiency factor improves average turnaround time

Figure 2 shows that in the first scalability scenario (A = system size), a high overbooking factor and an efficiency sensitive strategy (EF=1.0) outperforms other scheduling strategies; the overall average turnaround time (TAT) is better than when using the fair-share alone (EF=0). We also note that increasing the efficiency factor in low overbooking hurts the average turnaround time due to poor utilization and a negative effect on large jobs (shown below).

In Figure 3 we examine the effects of overbooking on various job sizes. In general, we see that small jobs (200-3,200 processor seconds and 3,200 to 100,000 processor seconds) benefit from a low overbooking factor. When overbooking is low, large jobs (greater than 2,000,000 processor seconds) have limited partition sizes and processors remain free for small jobs. As the turnaround time of small jobs is dominated largely by time spent waiting in the queue, any increase in their runtime due to a smaller maximum partition size is negligible. We also see that a high efficiency factor boosts the performance of small jobs; they are able to gain processors at the expense of larger and more inefficient jobs.

As a job's size grows, its turnaround time becomes less dominated by the time it spends waiting in the queue and more dominated by its run time. The medium sized jobs illustrate the point where this transition begins to occur; the effect of a low overbooking factor and high efficiency factor becomes less pronounced. Allowing large jobs to claim more processors is the dominating factor in their turnaround time, as they can afford to wait in the queue to reduce runtime. A high overbooking factor plays the biggest role with these large jobs and the efficiency factor has little effect on their performance. However, when a *low* overbooking factor is used, a high efficiency factor becomes detrimental to large jobs — precisely for the same reason this scenario was beneficial for small jobs.

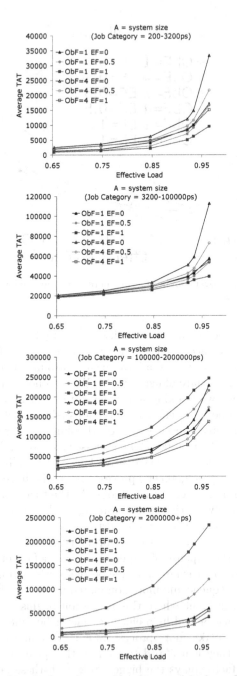

Fig. 3. Small jobs benefit from low overbooking and higher efficiency consideration, as their turnaround time is dominated by wait time. As job size grows, the benefit of efficiency consideration is diminished and eventually becomes detrimental to large jobs. However, in order for the larger jobs to perform well, a large overbooking factor is required.

The extreme end of the spectrum illustrates this clearly; efficiency plays almost no role when combined with a high overbooking factor for the largest jobs in the system.

To provide further contrast from the scenario presented in Figure 2, Figure 4 presents the situation where jobs do not all share a uniform maximum partition size. In this perhaps more realistic situation, each job's value of A is chosen randomly between 1 and 2 times the partition size requested in the original trace. Now that jobs do not all scale to the size of the system, we notice that the scheme which performs the best uses the plain fair-share scheme with no overbooking (ObF=1) and doesn't take efficiency into consideration at all (EF=0)! With overbooking, jobs can no longer effectively use the once-helpful large partitions given to them in the fair-share scheme and essentially waste machine cycles. The effects of this wastage become even more pronounced in higher load. Taking efficiency into account can reduce the detrimental effect of high overbooking, but at the cost of severely reducing the allocation of all but the most scalable jobs.

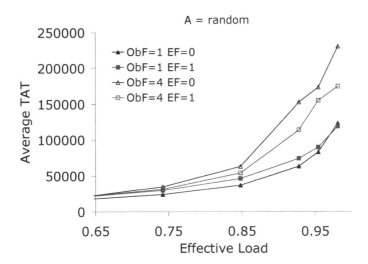

Fig. 4. With more variably scaling jobs, neither efficiency nor overbooking achieve better performance

Figure 5 shows category based results for this scalability scenario. Here it can be seen that taking efficiency into account is helpful for all job sizes. Due to the poor scalability, overbooking is detrimental to all job categories.

The results here make it clear that the choice of an effective overbooking factor and efficiency factor not only depend on the relative size of jobs in the system, but also their relative scalabilities and overall system load. With good overall scalability, using a high overbooking factor in combination with the efficiency based scheme provides the best results. However, with poorer scalability, a higher overbooking factor is very detrimental.

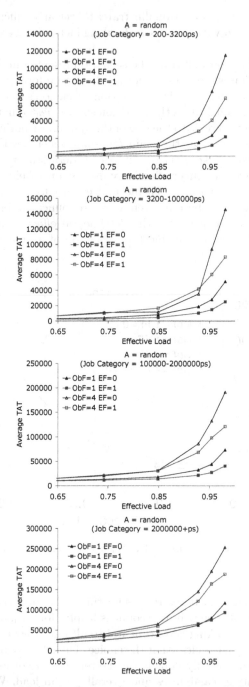

Fig. 5. With more variability in the speedup characteristics of jobs, overbooking is no longer helpful. Using the efficiency-based scheme is helpful for most jobs.

6   An Iterative Approach for Moldable Scheduling

The efficiency-sensitive moldable scheduling approach presented in the previous section was seen to provide benefits over the base fair-share strategy (EF=0). However, a difficulty with the approach is the need to choose appropriate parameters — the choice of the best overbooking factor and efficiency factor are dependent on the overall scalability characteristics of the job mix. If a job mix were to contain jobs of relatively uniform weight and similar maximum partition size, a high overbooking factor produces the best response times. However, if jobs differ considerably in their maximum partition size, a high overbooking factor leads to poor performance. It is equally problematic to choose the efficiency factor. Small jobs benefit from efficiency-based schemes but large jobs suffer under the same schemes.

A desirable moldable scheduling strategy would inherently take into account the efficiency, job size, system load and job mix without the need to "tune" parameters. In this section, we develop an iterative backfilling approach that does so.

Before describing the algorithm, we first provide a high level contrast of this approach with the previous section's strategy. The previous section's moldable scheduler associates a maximum allowable partition size with each job and uses a greedy scheduling strategy to choose an actual partition size (subject to a job's upper limit) in order to minimize response time. A job's size limit was determined using a fair-share proportion adjusted via the overbooking and efficiency factors. Although the idea of incorporating efficiency was effective, the problem with the approach was that the best choice for the overbooking factor and efficiency factor was dependent on the job mix. In order to avoid this problem, we consider a completely different approach to moldable scheduling — instead of simply setting an upper bound on job partition sizes, generate schedules incrementally and iteratively using global information.

6.1   The Iterative Algorithm

Our iterative algorithm begins by giving each job an initial minimal partition of one processor. A conservative backfilling schedule is generated; this schedule is then iteratively modified by giving a processor to the "most worthy" job — the job that, if given an additional processor, has the greatest decrease in runtime. If the addition of a processor to the most worthy job decreased the *average* response time of the schedule, the addition is accepted, otherwise not. Note that a job given an additional processor may have a start time *later* than previously reserved if its "waiting" allows it to improve the average turnaround time of the schedule.

Fig. 6 shows pseudocode for the iterative algorithm. Initially, each job is assigned one node. This allocation results in optimal per job efficiency, but may result in poor average turnaround and/or system utilization.

The next step (lines 3 to 12) searches for a schedule with an improved average turnaround time. Step 4 chooses the job which will benefit the most from

```
1.    void iterativeNodeAssignment(OrderedList reservedJobs){
2.        unmark all jobs in the reservedJobs list and
              set partition sizes to 1
3.        while(unmarked jobs exist)
4.            find unmarked candidate job j (see line 15)
5.            add one to partition size of job j
6.            create a conservative schedule for all jobs
7.            if(average turnaround time did not improve)
8.                mark job j
9.                decrement partition size of candidate job j
10.               create a conservative schedule for all jobs
11.           end if
12.       end while
13.   }
14.
15.   Job findUnmarkedCandidate(OrderedList reservedJobs){
16.       set bestImprovement to zero
17.       for each unmarked job j in the reserved job list
18.           let n be the current node assignment of job j
19.           let i be the expected runtime on n processors
20.           let i' be the expected runtime on n+1 processors
21.           if(i - i' > bestImprovement)
22.               set bestImprovement to i - i'
23.               set bestJob to j
24.       end for
25.       return bestJob
26.   }
```

Fig. 6. The iterative moldable scheduling algorithm

receiving an extra processor. This job is a "good" candidate to try increasing its processor allocation. Steps 5 to 11 determine if the increased allocation results in a better schedule. If the increase produces a worse schedule, the job is marked as a "bad" choice and the remaining jobs are considered.

This approach takes all the aspects discussed previously into account: load, scalability, job size, and utilization. If a job is small, the improvement from adding a processor will be minimal, and thus it will be less likely to receive an increased allocation. Likewise, if a job scales poorly, it will benefit less from receiving more processors, and will be less likely to be chosen as the candidate. If the load is low, "wider" jobs will result in a better average turnaround time, and wider allocations will be given. If the load is high, increasing the allocation of poorly scalable jobs will increase average turnaround time, and such jobs will be left "narrow". Finally, the system achieves good utilization, as processors will not be wasted unless there is no work to be done or using the processor reduces the average turnaround time.

Using turnaround time as the scheduling metric, selecting the job with the best absolute improvement in expected runtime, and iteratively searching and marking jobs provides a flexible, adaptable algorithm that is able to handle a diverse set of job scalability characteristics. This flexibility and adaptivity present here is not achievable with other algorithms without the addition of a complicated and dynamic tuning system, which while plausible, would not have the elegance of the simple iterative scheme.

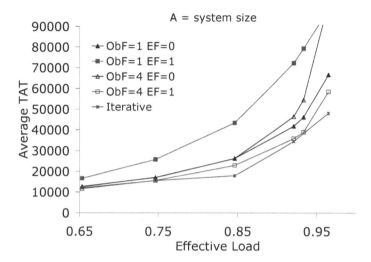

Fig. 7. In the situation where jobs scale to the size of the system, the iterative scheme outperforms even the best previous scheme

6.2   Results

In this section we compare the iterative algorithm described in Figure 6 to schemes which have been shown to be effective in certain contexts. The results show that the iterative algorithm is indeed able to perform very well in a variety of contexts and is competitive with the best previous algorithm (which varies when the scalability varies).

Figure 7 is the case where jobs scale to the size of the system (A = system size). As discussed previously, overbooking alone is not helpful as its generous allocation of processors leads to "wastage" of resources. Explicitly taking efficiency into account when choosing job widths allows more scalable jobs to receive more processors than non-scalable jobs, proving a better average turnaround time. In contrast, the iterative scheme is able to choose the "correct" job sizes, implicitly considering job size and scalability, and is better than even with the best of the previous scheduling scheme (ObF = 4, EF = 1). This search does come at a small cost: the scheduling time increases to a few hundred milliseconds. However, this cost is much lower than the time between useful scheduling events.

Figure 8 shows the iterative scheme's performance within job size categories. We can see that small jobs actually receive better performance in the iterative scheme than in other schemes, which was a major issues with earlier moldable

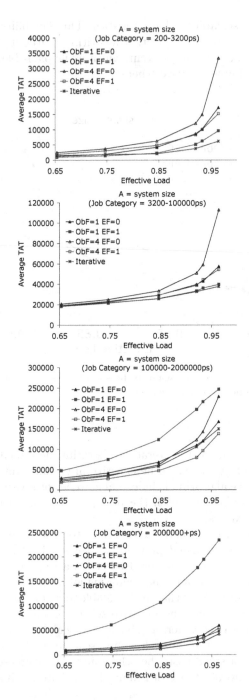

Fig. 8. The iterative scheme is able to mirror the performance of the best overbooking efficiency choices for different job categories

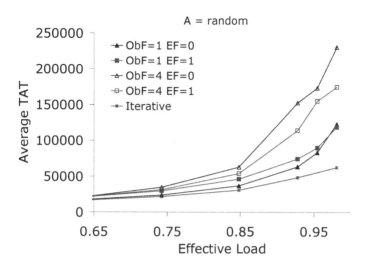

Fig. 9. When jobs vary more videly in scalability, the interactive scheme performs better than all previous schemes, especially as load increases

·scheduling strategies. Further, this improvement does not coincide with a deterioration in performance for the largest jobs. This is because the larger jobs are more likely to receive more processors — but this allocation is limited by a large job's effect on the other jobs in the queue. The iterative scheme is able to balance the needs of both small and large jobs.

Finally, Figure 9 shows the situation where each job's A value varies, as previously described. Recall that in this situation, the poor scalability becomes a problem for the schemes discussed. Increasing the overbooking factor was not helpful, nor was explicitly considering efficiency. Therefore, it was beneficial to use an efficiency factor of 0 or 1 and no overbooking. However, the iterative scheme outperforms all schemes previously considered — without having to "tune" any parameters. Figure 10 illustrates that the improvement in performance carries across all job size categories as well.

7   Conclusions

Current schedulers require users to examine the set of queued and running jobs when deciding upon a partition size for a job. It is left up to them to decide whether to request few resources and reduce the wait time of their job or request more resources and reduce the job's run time. A moldable scheduler shifts this responsibility from the user to the scheduler.

The work presented in this paper examines the effects of the overbooking factor introduced in previous work and demonstrates that overbooking in workloads consisting of jobs which scale well is beneficial, while overbooking can have a negative affect in workloads consisting of jobs of varying scalability.

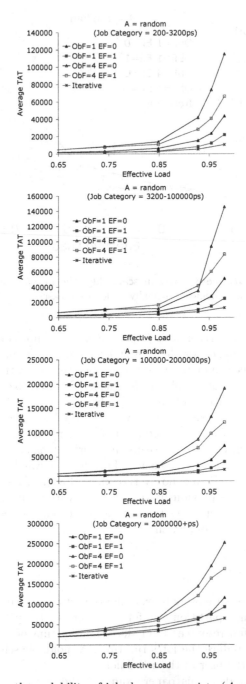

Fig. 10. Even when the scalability of jobs has more variety (A random), the iterative scheme is able to match the performance of the best overbooking and efficiency choices

Additionally, we explore the role efficiency can play in the selection of partition size and how the explicit consideration of job scalability can either reduce or increase the response time of a system, depending on job mix and scalability. Additionally, the "best" scheme for a particular job depends on the job's size. The results show that in order to achieve good performance, parameters must be heavily tuned according to expected job characteristics.

The iterative scheme eliminates the need for fine grained performance tuning. The approach provides a flexible, robust moldable scheduling policy that provides good performance in all situation studied. Without requiring tuning, the scheme achieves average response times comparable or better than the best of efficiency/overbooking schemes, across differing scalability scenarios.

References

1. Feitelson, D.: Workshops on job scheduling strategies for parallel processing. (www.cs.huji.ac.il/ feit/parsched/)
2. Feitelson, D.G., Rudolph, L., Schwiegelshohn, U., Sevcik, K.C., Wong, P.: Theory and practice in parallel job scheduling. In Feitelson, D.G., Rudolph, L., eds.: JSSPP. Volume 1291 of Lecture Notes in Computer Science., Springer (1997) 1–34
3. Weil, A.M., Feitelson, D.G.: Utilization, predictability, workloads, and user runtime estimates in scheduling the ibm sp2 with backfilling. IEEE Trans. Parallel Distrib. Syst. **12**(6) (2001) 529–543
4. Skovira, J., Chan, W., Zhou, H., Lifka, D.A.: The easy - loadleveler api project. In Feitelson, D.G., Rudolph, L., eds.: JSSPP. Volume 1162 of Lecture Notes in Computer Science., Springer (1996) 41–47
5. Frachtenberg, E., Feitelson, D.G., Petrini, F., Fernandez, J.: Flexible CoScheduling: Mitigating load imbalance and improving utilization of heterogeneous resources. In: IPDPS. Number 17 (2003)
6. Cirne, W., Berman, F.: Adaptive selection of partition size for supercomputer requests. In Feitelson, D.G., Rudolph, L., eds.: JSSPP. Volume 1911 of Lecture Notes in Computer Science., Springer (2000) 187–208
7. Cirne, W., Berman, F.: Using moldability to improve the performance of supercomputer jobs. J. Parallel Distrib. Comput. **62**(10) (2002) 1571–1601
8. Srinivasan, S., Subramani, V., Kettimuthu, R., Holenarsipur, P., Sadayappan, P.: Effective selection of partition sizes for moldable scheduling of parallel jobs. In Sahni, S., Prasanna, V.K., Shukla, U., eds.: HiPC. Volume 2552 of Lecture Notes in Computer Science., Springer (2002) 174–183
9. Srinivasan, S., Krishnamoorthy, S., Sadayappan, P.: A robust scheduling strategy for moldable scheduling of parallel jobs. In: CLUSTER, IEEE Computer Society (2003) 92–99
10. Srinivasan, S., Kettimuthu, R., Subramani, V., Sadayappan, P.: Characterization of backfilling strategies for parallel job scheduling. In: ICPP Workshops, IEEE Computer Society (2002) 514–522
11. Frachtenberg, E., Feitelson, D.G.: Pitfalls in parallel job scheduling evaluation. In Feitelson, D.G., Frachtenberg, E., Rudolph, L., Schwiegelshohn, U., eds.: JSSPP. Volume 3834 of Lecture Notes in Computer Science., Springer (2005) 257–282
12. Feitelson, D.G., Rudolph, L., Schwiegelshohn, U.: Parallel job scheduling - a status report. In Feitelson, D.G., Rudolph, L., Schwiegelshohn, U., eds.: JSSPP. Volume 3277 of Lecture Notes in Computer Science., Springer (2004) 1–16

13. Feitelson, D.G.: Logs of real parallel workloads from production systems. (URL: http://www.cs.huji.ac.il/labs/parallel/workload/)
14. Du, J., Leung, J.Y.T.: Complexity of scheduling parallel task systems. SIAM J. Discret. Math. **2**(4) (1989) 473–487
15. Krishnamurti, R., Ma, E.: An approximation algorithm for scheduling tasks on varying partition sizes in partitionable multiprocessor systems. IEEE Transactions on Computers **41**(12) (1992) 1572–1579
16. Garey, M.R., Graham, R.L.: Bounds for multiprocessor scheduling with resource constraints. SIAM J. Comput. **4**(2) (1975) 187–200
17. Garey, M.R., Johnson, D.S.: Complexity results for multiprocessor scheduling under resource constraints. SIAM J. Comput. **4**(4) (1975) 397–411
18. Li, K., Cheng, K.H.: Job scheduling in partitionable mesh connected systems. In: ICPP (2). (1989) 65–72
19. Tuomenoksa, D.L., Siegel, H.J.: Task scheduling on the pasm parallel processing system. IEEE Trans. Software Eng. **11**(2) (1985) 145–157
20. Eager, D.L., Zahorjan, J., Lazowska, E.D.: Speedup versus efficiency in parallel systems. (1995) 76–91
21. Ghosal, D., Serazzi, G., Tripathi, S.K.: The processor working set and its use in scheduling multiprocessor systems. IEEE Trans. Softw. Eng. **17**(5) (1991) 443–453
22. Kleinrock, L., Huang, J.H.: On parallel processing systems: Amdahl's law generalized and some results on optimal design. IEEE Trans. Softw. Eng. **18**(5) (1992) 434–447
23. McCann, C., Vaswani, R., Zahorjan, J.: A dynamic processor allocation policy for multiprogrammed shared-memory multiprocessors. ACM Trans. Comput. Syst. **11**(2) (1993) 146–178
24. Sevcik, K.C.: Application scheduling and processor allocation in multiprogrammed parallel processing systems. Technical Report CSRI-282, Computer Systems Research Institute, University of Toronto, Toronto, Canada, M5S 1A1 (1993)
25. Rosti, E., Smirni, E., Serazzi, G., Dowdy, L.W.: Analysis of non-work-conserving processor partitioning policies. In Feitelson, D.G., Rudolph, L., eds.: JSSPP. Volume 949 of Lecture Notes in Computer Science., Springer (1995) 165–181
26. Downey, A.B.: Using queue time predictions for processor allocation. In Feitelson, D.G., Rudolph, L., eds.: Job Scheduling Strategies for Parallel Processing. Springer Verlag (1997) 35–57
27. Downey, A.B.: A parallel workload model and its implications for processor allocation. Cluster Computing **1**(1) (1998) 133–145
28. Sevcik, K.C.: Characterizations of parallelism in applications and their use in scheduling. SIGMETRICS Perform. Eval. Rev. **17**(1) (1989) 171–180
29. Chiang, S.H., Mansharamani, R.K., Vernon, M.K.: Use of application characteristics and limited preemption for run-to-completion parallel processor scheduling policies. In: SIGMETRICS. (1994) 33–44
30. Downey, A.B.: A model for speedup of parallel programs. Technical Report CSD-97-933 (1997)
31. Rajan, A.: Evaluation of scheduling strategies for moldable parallel jobs. Master's thesis, The Ohio State University (2004)

Adaptive Job Scheduling Via Predictive Job Resource Allocation

Lawrence Barsanti and Angela C. Sodan

University of Windsor, Windsor ON N9B 3P4, Canada
barsant@uwindsor.ca, acsodan@uwindsor.ca

Abstract. Standard job scheduling uses static job sizes which lacks flexibility regarding changing load in the system and fragmentation handling. Adaptive resource allocation is known to provide the flexibility needed to obtain better response times under such conditions. We present a scheduling approach (SCOJO-P) which decides resource allocation, i.e. the number of processors, at job start time and then keeps the allocation fixed throughout the execution (i.e. molds the jobs). SCOJO-P uses a heuristic to predict the average load on the system over the runtime of a job and then uses that information to determine the number of processors to allocate to the job. When determining how many processors to allocate to a job, our algorithm attempts to balance the interests of the job with the interests of jobs that are currently waiting in the system and jobs that are expected to arrive in the near future. We compare our approach with traditional fixed-size scheduling and with the Cirne-Berman approach which decides job sizes at job submission time by simulating the scheduling of the jobs currently running or waiting. Our results show that SCOJO-P improves mean response times by approximately 70% vs. traditional fixed-size scheduling while the Cirne-Berman approach only improves it 30% (which means SCOJO-P improves mean response time by 59% vs. Cirne-Berman).

Keywords: adaptive job scheduling, molding, prediction.

1 Introduction

Most job-scheduling approaches for parallel machines apply space sharing which means allocating CPUs/nodes to jobs in a dedicated manner and sharing the machine among multiple jobs by allocation on different subsets of nodes. Some approaches apply time sharing (or better to say a combination of time and space sharing), i.e. use multiple time slices per CPU/node [23]. This is typically done via so-called gang scheduling which explicitly synchronizes the time slices over all nodes. Such time sharing creates multiple virtual machines which offers more flexibility for scheduling. Consequently, gang scheduling is shown in several studies to provide better response times and higher machine utilization (see, e.g., [9][10]). On the downside, gang scheduling involves process-switching overhead and increases the memory pressure.

E. Frachtenberg and U. Schwiegelshohn (Eds.): JSSPP 2006, LNCS 4376, pp. 115–140, 2007.

A different option of flexible scheduling that avoids additional memory pressure is adaptive CPU/node-resource allocation. The standard resource-allocation approach in job schedulers uses static job sizes: jobs request a certain number of CPUs/nodes to run (therefore, called rigid). Adaptive resource allocation means that the number of resources can be decided dynamically by the system. The precondition is that the jobs can deal with this dynamic resource allocation: either being moldable, i.e. able to adjust to the resource allocation at job start time, or being malleable, i.e. able to adjust to changes in the resource allocation during the job's execution. Then, adaptation may be used 1) to reduce fragmentation by adjusting the jobs' sizes to better fit into the available space, and 2) to adapt to varying system loads by reducing sizes if the system load is high and increasing sizes if the system load is low.

Malleability requires a special formulation of the program because the work to be performed per node changes dynamically–thus, we cannot expect every job to be malleable (though, in separate work, we address making applications malleable [22]). Moldability is easier to accomplish because often programs anyway initialize themselves according to the size with which they are invoked: a survey conducted among supercomputing-center users [5] found that most jobs (98%) were moldable, i.e. able to configure themselves as needed at start time. Based on the exploitation of moldability, Cirne-Berman [5] present a scheduler that employs an egoistic model and lets each job, after schedule simulation with different sizes, select the size which provides the best response time for the job. Response times are significantly improved by this approach which made molding a well-known alternative to standard space sharing. Indeed, results in [3][16] already found that molding provides good and sufficiently good results. However, our results with SCOJO [21] suggest that adaptation with runtime changes of job sizes performs clearly better.

Our SCOJO scheduler presented in [21] supports both start time adaptation for moldable and runtime adaptation for malleable jobs, while avoiding molding and only applying runtime adaptation if the jobs are long. In this paper, we present SCOJO-P, an extension of SCOJO that supports simpler workloads with only rigid and moldable jobs and also molds long jobs. To solve the problem of determining proper sizes, which is especially critical for long jobs, we employ a heuristic system-load prediction model.

In summary, SCOJO-P provides the following innovative contributions:

- employment of adaptation for both reduction of fragmentation and adjustment to differently high system load
- provision of heuristics for choosing job sizes under molding that are based on knowledge about the overall system load
- a solution with low time complexity
- consideration of the system load (including estimated future arrivals of jobs) over the whole runtime of the job

We compare SCOJO-P to a traditional non-adaptive scheduler and to the Cirne-Berman approach by evaluating all approaches in a simulation study. For both, the workload modeling and the prediction, we employ the Lublin-Feitelson model [13]. Our results show that SCOJO-P outperforms the other approaches.

2   Related Work

Almost all existing work on adaptive scheduling is done in the context of space sharing. A number of such approaches aim at minimizing the makespan, i.e. the overall runtime, for a static set of jobs, while focusing on the provision of tight worst-case bounds [8] [27]. These approaches apply a two-phase scheduling: they first determine the size for the jobs and then schedule the jobs. Realistic approaches need to consider dynamic job submission and they aim at a reduction of average response times and average slowdowns (response times in relation to runtimes). Furthermore, most adaptive approaches apply molding only. Mere molding of jobs bears the problem that a job might run earlier with fewer CPUs but get a better response time if started later with more CPUs/nodes. Thus, the prediction quality regarding what the best solution for the job is becomes critical. The approach of Cirne and Berman [5] molds jobs at the time of job submission without using any central control: predictions are based on simulating the schedule for different job sizes and then selecting the size for which the best response time is obtained. We discuss this approach in more detail below. This approach is modified in [25] by setting limits for the maximum size that depend on the current system load and on the job's size requests, by making decisions at job start time rather than submission time, and by using aggressive backfilling without any reservations. Though the results of the evaluations are presented with two below-average scalability factors (and one of them—scalability factor $\sigma = 0$—leading to an extreme curve which is linear for half of the relevant parameter range and then stays constant at maximum speedup), they suggest that the approach performs clearly better than Cirne-Berman. A few approaches are based on runtime adaptation for malleable jobs [6][15][17]. Most of these approaches exploit adaptation with the goal to adapt to varying system load. The approach by Naik et al. [15] adapts resource allocation only for medium- and long-running jobs. Short jobs are molded. The approach attempts to schedule all jobs from the queue but sets a limit for medium and long jobs to prevent starvation of short jobs. Dynamic adaptation for malleable jobs may keep jobs scheduled while adjusting the resource allocation [6][15] or checkpoint/preempt jobs and re-decide the job allocation [17].

The two basic approaches to decide about the job sizes are resource-based partitioning and efficiency-based partitioning [9]. Resource-based partitioning typically comes in the form of EQUI partitioning which means assigning the same number of resources to each job. This approach yields suboptimal performance in the general case as it does not consider how well the jobs use the resources [3][14]. However, resource-based allocation can be improved by defining different job-size classes like small, medium, large [15][2] and applying EQUI per job-size class-which comes close to efficiency-based partitioning. Efficiency-based partitioning exploits the efficiency characteristics of the applications and allocates more resources to jobs that make better use of them, which typically leads to the overall best results [3][14]. Similar to resource-based partitioning, efficiency-based partitioning may be applied in the form of providing equal efficiency to all jobs in the system (EQUI-EFF). In [12], the ratio of runtime to efficiency is used for efficiency-based partitioning. Job sizes may also be chosen to keep some CPUs/nodes idle in anticipation of future job arrivals. The work of Rosti et al. [18] combined this idea with EQUI partitioning and limiting the job sizes to a certain percentage of the machine size, either statically or in dependence of the waiting-queue length. In the approach of Parsons and Sevcik [17], first the minimum size is allocated and, then, any leftover resources are assigned to reduce fragmentation.

If exploiting the jobs' efficiency characteristics, speedup/efficiency functions are needed. Secvik's model presented in [19] addresses dynamically changing parallelism but the ideas are related to changing job sizes to obtain better efficiency: the model uses phase-wise linearly approximation for CPU/node allocations between minimum, average, and maximum parallelism. Downey [7] presents a more sophisticated model which also originally was meant to describe variations in parallelism and is adopted by the Cirne-Berman scheduler for speedup-curve modeling. It is briefly discussed in Section 4.6.

Furthermore, all partitioning approaches should consider minimum allocations (potentially defined by memory constraints), maximum allocations (beyond which speedup drops), and potential other job-size constraints like power-of-two [5][13][15].

3   The Cirne-Berman Scheduler

The scheduler presented by Cirne and Berman in [5] decides the best job size at job-submission time. The scheduler takes a list of different possible job sizes and corresponding runtimes. The number of different sizes is determined randomly as well as the probability that the sizes are power-of-two. The scheduler then simulates the scheduling of the job for each possible size separately, taking into account the current system load, i.e. the jobs currently in the waiting queue or running. After performing all simulations for all possible sizes, the size is chosen which provides the best response time for the job, and the job is submitted to the waiting queue with this size. This means that the approach can be set on top of an existing scheduler, provided that a simulator is available with the same scheduling algorithm as employed in the actual job scheduler. The scheduler uses conservative backfilling with best-fit selection. The scheme used for priority assignment and aging is not specified. The approach was evaluated with traces from supercomputer centers (considering all jobs to be moldable), combined with Downey's speedup model which we briefly discuss in Section 4.6. When comparing to our SCOJO-P scheduler, we employ, however, EASY backfilling. This appears to be no major disadvantage for the Cirne-Berman approach as molding can anyway more easily fit jobs into the schedule and, therefore, makes reservations less critical. As another consideration, conservative backfilling may preserve the original schedule more closely because no additional delays are allowed to be created. However, whichever backfilling approach is used, the problem vs. the simulated schedule is that new jobs with higher priority may arrive—especially under high load—and that job runtimes may have been overestimated. In both cases, the original schedule is changed. Furthermore, in our implementation of Cirne-Berman, we also have given no special consideration for power-of-two sizes and try all sizes in the range between minimum and maximum rather than generating certain limited sets of possible sizes. Otherwise, we are following the implementation as described in [5].

4   The SCOJO-P Space Sharing Scheduler

4.1   The Original SCOJO Scheduler

SCOJO [20][21] incorporates standard job-scheduling approaches like priority handling (classifying jobs into short, medium, and long and assigning higher priorities to shorter jobs), aging (to prevent starvation), and EASY backfilling. EASY backfilling means to permit jobs to be scheduled ahead of their normal priority order if not delaying the start time of the first job in the waiting queue.

The original SCOJO scheduler applies either standard space sharing or gang scheduling and can combine both with adaptive resource allocation. SCOJO can handle mixtures of rigid, moldable, and malleable jobs. SCOJO supports

- Adaptation to varying system load (jobs running and jobs in the waiting queue)
- Fragmentation reduction

The former exploits the fact that speedup curves are typically approximately concave (due to increasing relative overhead), i.e. if job sizes are reduced, the jobs run at higher levels of efficiency which improves the effective utilization of the system towards the progress of the jobs' execution. Then, running more jobs while reducing their sizes utilizes the resources better if the system load is high. Though the jobs run longer, in the end, all jobs (on average) benefit by shorter wait and shorter response times. If the system load is low, the jobs can use more resources to reduce their runtime up to their maximum size (N_{max}) beyond which the runtime would decline. Furthermore, SCOJO adjusts job sizes in certain situations to fit jobs into the machine that otherwise could not run, while leaving resources unused.

To implement system-load adaptation and fragmentation reduction, SCOJO divides into the following major steps (details can be found in [21]):

- Determine the job target sizes in dependence on the system load
- Shrinkage or expansion of running malleable jobs to their target sizes; allocation of all new malleable/moldable jobs with their target sizes

- During backfilling, potentially further shrinkage of new short or medium adaptable (moldable or malleable) jobs to fit them into the machine
- Potentially expansion of new moldable or malleable jobs to exploit any unused resources

The system load is estimated by calculating the needed number of nodes $N_{needed} = \sum_{i\ in\ running,waiting} N_{opt,i}$ which represents the sum of the optimum size requirements of all currently running and waiting jobs. We then classify the current resource needs into a) low, b) normal, and c) high according to whether all jobs in running and waiting queue with their optimum sizes N_{opt}: a) fit into the machine with a multiprogramming level of 1 while still leaving some space, b) fit with a potentially higher multiprogramming level, or c) do not fit with even the maximum multiprogramming level. This means we have either unused space, utilize the machine well, or have more jobs than fit without adaptation. If the system load is normal, optimum sizes are used. A high system load suggests to shrink sizes; and a low system load suggests to expand sizes. The exact factors for expanding and shrinking are calculated by trying to fit all jobs into the machine (high load) or utilize all resources (low load). This is done by decreasing or increasing all adaptable jobs' sizes relative to their optimum size, i.e. by the same percentage vs. their optimum size. This approximates an efficiency-based partitioning though it is EQUI-EFF only if all jobs have the same shape of speedup curves. At least, the proportional change in sizes makes sure that long jobs are not given any advantage if having high efficiency. In addition, the minimum job size considered during adaptation is set as the limit where further reduction in size does not provide much efficiency gain anymore, i.e. the curve is close to linear. Using sizes below this limit would not provide any benefit related to system load (though occasionally benefits in fragmentation reduction might be obtained).

To avoid configuration thrashing and adaptation with minor benefits, we consider reconfiguration only in certain time intervals and only if the change in the resource needs is relevant. Note that the system load is likely to change with day-night cycle as otherwise the machine would be overcommitted/saturated.

SCOJO does not apply any special measures to address power-of-two sizes as studies found the power-of-two sizes appear in most cases to be superficial, i.e. to stem more from standard practice rather than inherent properties of the applications [4].

Jobs are classified according to runtime. The original SCOJO takes long jobs as either rigid or malleable but does not mold them because the system load is likely to change over the runtime of long jobs. Then with a lack of prediction and consideration of details in the schedule, the initial size may prove to be disadvantageous to the job (if chosen smaller than desirable during a high-load phase) or disadvantageous to other jobs (if chosen too large during a low-load phase). Similarly, size reduction or size expansion to reduce fragmentation may especially be harmful regarding long jobs. Short jobs are not worth runtime adaptation and are treated as either rigid or moldable. Medium jobs can be rigid, moldable, or malleable.

The adaptive resource allocation of SCOJO was shown to improve response times and bounded slowdowns by up to 50% and to also tolerate reservations for local or grid jobs well [20][24]. These results were obtained with artificial workloads and the Lublin-Feitelson workload model, and combination with either space sharing or gang scheduling. Thus, for space sharing with the Lublin-Feitelson workload model and 60% moldable / 40% malleable jobs, we obtain 43% improvement in average response times and even 60.5% improvement in slowdowns [24].

4.2   The New SCOJO-P Scheduler

SCOJO-P [1] extends SCOJO in various ways, while restricting it regarding application characteristics. SCOJO-P is strictly space sharing and only handles rigid and moldable jobs. This makes SCOJO-P suitable for jobs which are not especially designed for adaptation and matches standard job mixes in super-computer centers as found by Cirne and Berman [5]. It also makes the results comparable to the Cirne/Berman approach.

The most important extensions of SCOJO-P are to consider the average load on the system over the runtime of a job when choosing a size for the job and to include the prediction of future job submissions. Moreover, SCOJO-P does not try to schedule all running and waiting jobs on the machine at the same time but rather aims at a long-term balanced high utilization of the machine. This is important if the load changes significantly over time. The overall algorithm includes the following steps:

- Adaptive target-size determination: selects a size (N_{target}) for the candidate job under concern for being scheduled (J_s) that will help the system maintain a consistent workload.
- Try to start J_s: if the target size of J_s is greater than the number of currently available processors (i.e. $N_{avail} < N_{target}$), then J_s can start with less than N_{target} processors if doing so provides a benefit (shorter response time) to J_s vs. being scheduled at a later time (when $N_{target} \leq N_{avail}$).
- Adaptive backfilling: adaptation is considered during backfilling in a simplified form.

Note that whereas SCOJO applies adaptation both at start time and, for malleable jobs, during their runtime, SCOJO-P only applies adaptation at start time as it exclusively supports molding. Fragmentation reduction is, however, considered when trying to fit a job into the system by shrinking its size below N_{target}. Below we describe the different steps in detail.

4.3   Adaptive Target-Size Determination

When determining the target size (N_{target}) of a job (J_s), all jobs that are currently running, that are in the waiting queue, or that are expected to arrive during the execution of J_s, are considered (the latter considers the corresponding statistical distribution of runtimes/sizes and of the jobs' interarrival times).

The target size of J_s is calculated using the following heuristic. The Load (average load per processor) is estimated over the runtime of J_s, assuming that J_s, the waiting jobs, and future jobs will all run with their optimal size, whereas, for running jobs, their allocated size is taken, i.e. initially

$$Load(J_s) = \sum_{i\ in\ J_s,running,waiting,future} work(job_i, J_s)/(MN * J_s) \text{ with}$$

$$work(job_i, J_s) = \begin{cases} min(runtime_{remain,job_i}), J_s) * N_{alloc,job_i} & if\ running \\ min(runtime(N_{opt,job_i}), J_s) * N_{opt,job_i} & if\ waiting/future \end{cases}$$

with MN being the number of nodes in the machine. Since the load is calculated over the runtime of J_s, for all jobs, only the overlapped runtime is considered. For future jobs, average optimum sizes and corresponding optimum runtimes are used. For the prediction of future jobs, we employ statistics from the workload regarding how many short, medium, and long jobs arrive in certain 30-minute time intervals of the day. This permits to predict how many short, medium, and long jobs will arrive during the runtime of J_s. To determine their work, we use average runtimes and sizes for each of the three job classes. For a visualization, see Fig. 1.

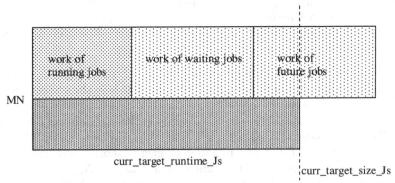

Fig. 1. Visualization of the load-estimation heuristic. The graphic shows a situation where not all jobs would fit into the machine with current size and corresponding runtime during the runtime of J_s. If relating the workload to the runtime of J_s, $Load > 1$. Whether the resulting load is considered ideal or not, depends on the setting of the parameters. However, with our settings, we would normally modify the job size to obtain a $Load < 1$.

If $Load$ is lower or higher than the ideal load per processor, a modifying factor (determined by the fail ratio of the ideal load vs. the resulting load) is calculated and used to resize all jobs proportionally, and the load is recalculated. This recalculation of modifying factor and load is done iteratively until a load close to the ideal load (or as close as possible) is obtained. Note that the load calculation has to be redone as the runtime of J_s and the overlaps change.

The ideal load cannot always be obtained because moldable jobs cannot expand/shrink beyond a maximum/minimum value and rigid jobs cannot be resized at all. If the ideal load is set $ideal\_avg\_load < 1$, it means that all waiting and future jobs should ideally be scheduled immediately (rather than being queued) by reducing their size. The load then corresponds to utilization. Since the algorithm does not consider packing but only the load, it may be the case that neither the currently considered job nor any of the waiting or future jobs can actually fit into the machine at the current point in time; even with ideal *Load*. If set near the expected utilization the ideal *Load* can take average fragmentation loss from packing problems into considerations. For the details of the algorithm, see Fig. 2.

Note that, though the calculation changes all sizes of the job considered for scheduling, waiting jobs, and future jobs proportionally, the target size is only determined for J_s. The other sizes are not recorded but are determined when the jobs are up for scheduling. Nevertheless the algorithm considers the global picture of the overall load.

Furthermore, by calculating the average load over the entire runtime of the job, the job gets a size which is appropriate for both potential high load and low load phases. This is important when scheduling long running moldable jobs because it prevents the jobs from starving the system in order to help themselves and from starving themselves to help the system.

The complexity of this algorithm depends on how quickly it converges to the ideal load. In the worst case, every size of the job being scheduled will be tested. Because the runtime changes with every iteration step, the load incurred by running, waiting, and future jobs also changes. Thus, using the modifier does not always provide better results and could even cause the algorithm to thrash. We prevent this from happening by comparing the load produced by each modifier to the best load obtained so far (i.e. the load that came closest to the ideal load). If after a couple iterations no new modifier has produced a load that is better than the current best load the algorithm terminates and uses the modifier that provided the current best load. In practice, we found only very few iteration steps to be needed.

4.4 Trying to Schedule the Job with Adaptive Target Size and Adaptive Backfilling

After determining the target size of the job, the scheduler tries to allocate the job to the machine. It is possible that, however, not enough nodes are currently available to schedule the job. Rather than considering the attempt of scheduling the job as failed, the scheduler decides whether to start the job right away with smaller than the target size (i.e. allocate fewer resources) or whether to start the job at a later point of time with more processors (up to the calculated target size).

To make this decision, the scheduling of all currently running jobs is simulated to determine the different times at which the job can be started with larger sizes. Note that this simulation is very simple as it only needs to check when currently

```
isOk_load = false;  sizeModifier = 1.0; best_avg_load = Max_Integer;
curr_target_size_Js = Js.optSize;
curr_target_runtime_Js = Js.runtime (curr_target_size_Js);

do {
// calculate the average system load via formula described in text
// but all size parameters (except for running and current) multiplied
// by sizeModifier
relevant_work = overlapSizeModified_work
   (running_jobs, waiting_jobs, future_jobs,Js);
available_workProcessing = n_machine * curr_target_runtime_Js;
avg_load = relevant_work / available_workProcessing;

// check whether sufficient approximation of ideal load
if ((avg_load >= ideal_avg_load-deltaSize) &&
    (avg_load <= ideal_avg_load+deltaSize))
   isOk_load = true;
else  {  // determine size modifier
   prev_sizeModifier = sizeModifier;
   sizeModifier = sizeModifier * ( ideal_avg_load / avg_load);
   if (prev_sizeModifier == sizeModifier) break;    // no change
   curr_target_size_Js = sizeModifier * Js.optSize;
   curr_target_runtime_Js = Js.runtime(curr_target_size_Js);
}

// check whether better approximation found
// if not, count bad trial to avoid endless search
if ( |avg_load - ideal_avg_load| < |best_avg_load - ideal_avg_load| ) {
   best_avg_load = avg_load;
   best_sizeModifier = prev_sizeModifier;    counter=0;
} else {
   counter++; if (counter == maxBadModifiers) break;
  }
} while (! isOk_load);
  // loop terminates if load o.k. or if no significant change anymore
```

Fig. 2. Algorithm applied when calculating target size N_{target} for job J_s

running jobs terminate. The latest possible start time would be when it can run with the calculated target size. Then, it is decided whether the current or any later start time with increased size ($N_{avail} < size \leq N_{target}$) provides a better response time for the job. If the current time provides the best response time, the job is started with that size. Otherwise, the size with the calculated best response time is memorized and guaranteed as the job's later minimum size (worst-case scenario) with which it will be run. If the job is started with $size < N_{target}$, this can be considered fragmentation reduction. For the algorithm, see Fig. 3.

SCOJO-P also considers size adaptation during backfilling, applying the same *sizeModifier* as calculated when attempting to schedule the first job in the

```
bestStartTime = currentTime; bestResponseTime = Js.runtime (freeProcs);
bestSize=Js.target_size;

while (freeProcs < Js.target_size) {
   startTime = sim.time (sim.nextJob_finished);
   size = min(target_size_Js,sim.freeProcs);
   responseTime = startTime - currentTime + Js.runtime (size);
   if (responseTime < bestResponseTime)
     {bestResponseTime=responseTime; bestStartTime=startTime;
      bestSize=size; }
}
if (bestStartTime == currentTime) schedule (Js, freeProcs);
else fixJobSize (bestSize);
```

Fig. 3. Finding the start time that delivers the best response time

queue. First, all jobs are uniformly resized by this same factor. Then, normal EASY backfilling applied.

4.5   Discussion of Expected Behavior and Benefits

The main benefits of the SCOJO-P algorithm as presented above are that the workload is estimated over the whole runtime of the job that is the candidate for scheduling. This estimation provides a good global picture, though it is heuristic. Thus jobs that encounter periods of both high and low usage can run with a size that is reasonable for the average load. This reduces the risk that sizes are chosen too high which would benefit the candidate job or too small which would benefit the other jobs. Moreover, Cirne-Berman is more likely to choose large partition sizes because the job tries to maximize its own benefit.

If comparing SCOJO-P to the Cirne-Berman approach, Cirne-Berman makes decisions per job at job submission time based on simulation of the schedule. However, new jobs with higher priorities can change the picture though the Cirne-Berman scheduler may still work well as long as only short jobs can get ahead. The approach in [25] has already shown that decisions at job start time work better than decisions at submission time. Furthermore, if priorities would be assigned with a different scheme such as giving long jobs higher priority, the Cirne-Berman approach is likely not to work well anymore whereas SCOJO-P considers them as part of the statistically based estimate. Furthermore, in SCOJO-P, prediction and runtime overestimates are easier to integrate. As shown above, predication only adds a term in the estimation of the load. Regarding overestimates, for future jobs, anyway statistics based on actual runtimes are used. For running and waiting jobs, the workload estimation from above can be refined by taking the runtimes as user-estimated runtimes and adding a statistical over-estimate model such as [26]. This may not correctly estimate the runtime per job but, at least with a large number of jobs in the system, provide a reasonable statistical approximation of the overall load in which we are interested only. Alternatively performance databases may be employed to obtain estimates of the actual runtimes [11] which would work well for Cirne-Berman, too.

Both approaches depend on reasonable estimates of the speedup curves as decisions about sizes and scheduling times take the changing job runtimes into consideration. However, SCOJO-P appears to be slightly less dependent on correct estimates of speedup curves as job sizes are changed proportionally for all jobs whereas Cirne-Berman depends more on detailed decisions in the simulation. Our evaluation below does not investigate dependence on correct estimates (nor does Cirne-Berman).

4.6   The Speedup Model Used

The implementation of the function $runtime(size)$ requires a speedup model. The Cirne-Berman approach [4] uses a statistical model to generate random min/max sizes and a random speedup curve for each job. The Cirne-Berman model is based on the Downey speedup model [7], originally meant to model parallelism behavior as does [19]. With adoption to speedup-up curves, this model defines the curve by the maximum speedup S_{max} a job can achieve (originally the average parallelism) and the scalability factor (originally the job's variance in parallelism) which determines how fast the job reaches its maximum speedup. Furthermore, the following relationship holds: $\sigma = (S_{max} - S_{opt})/(S_{opt} - 1)$. Cirne-Berman obtained distribution functions for these two parameters and coefficients' values fitting the observed data from their study and, based on the resulting statistical model, randomly generate speedup curves for the jobs. The moldability model is combined with the general workload by randomly generating the maximum speedup (independently from the runtime generated by the workload model) and mapping the generated runtime onto this curve. We implemented this model and found that the created speedup curves are not correlated with the runtimes/sizes produced by the Lublin-Feitelson model. Thus, the combined workload model often produces jobs with a maximum size far beyond the machine size. Furthermore, it can produce, for example, a job that runs in 20 seconds on 4 processors, while the Cirne-Berman speedup model could produce a speedup curve where the optimum job size is 32 processors yielding a runtime of 2 seconds. This would be similar to generating job runtimes and job sizes independently (though indeed they are correlated). Basically, the assumption of the the Cirne-Berman approach is that the user does not choose optimum sizes for submission, either because not knowing which they are or by e.g. choosing smaller than optimum sizes for strategic reasons (getting the job run earlier). This lack of correlation does not affect the Cirne-Berman scheduler as it simply chooses the size/runtime combination that produces the best simulation results. However, this approach does not work for a scheduler like SCOJO-P which considers relative efficiency, i.e. tries to run all jobs using their optimum size and only shrinks and expands when appropriate. Under the Cirne-Berman model, however, the optimum sizes are larger than the originally generated sizes in the workload which changes the target size of the workload. Larger sizes—as especially chosen under low load—are also harder to fit into the schedule, especially if not simulating possible fits. Furthermore, under high load, SCOJO-P tries to fit all jobs into the system which especially provides a benefit as long as jobs are in a range where the curve flattens. Since with the Cirne-Berman model the optimum sizes may be much larger than the submitted sizes, significant shrinking may be required into the range of closer-to-linear speedup.

Considering these problems with the lack of correlation between generated sizes and calculated optimum sizes, for our main tests, we have reverted back to a simpler model as used in [21]. This model assumes that the sizes produced by the workload model (or given by the user) represent a size for which a good cost/efficiency ratio is obtained. Though not required by the scheduler, this size is ideally the processor working set (PWS), i.e., the number of processors for which the ratio of runtime to efficiency is optimal [12]:

$$N_{PWS} = \{N \mid withT_N/E_N = T_1/N * 1/E_N^2) \text{ is minimal}\}$$

with T_N being the runtime and E_N the efficiency for a corresponding job size N. No larger size should be chosen unless otherwise resources are idle. Then, we calculate the speedup curve in the following way:

- We take the size created for the job by the statistical workload model as its optimum size N_{opt}. The assumption is that the user approximately knows which is the most meaningful size for the job. If the job is rigid, this will remain its size, if the job is moldable, this is the base size of the job. Though it is not necessarily N_{PWS}, we can perceive it as the size which makes sense under normal load conditions. Then, consequently, $runtime(N_{opt})$ is the time generated by the workload model. In the specific test setting which we use, $N_{opt} = N_{PWS}$.
- We define N_{max} and N_{min} relative to N_{opt} with always the same proportional factor, and interpolate the speedup curve between these points linearly (which is similar to [19]). N_{max} represents the size beyond which the speedup curve declines and N_{min} the minimum size needed by the job, e.g. because of memory constraints, or the size below which no further significant efficiency benefits can be obtained. Note, that typically $N_{min} > 1$.

The SCOJO-P algorithm always considers N_{max} and N_{min} as bounds when determining sizes (this consideration is omitted above in the pseudo code to keep it readable).

This model assumes the same shape of speedup curves for all jobs (though stretched according to where N_{opt}, N_{min}, and N_{max} lie). The scalability factor is $\sigma = 0.23$ for large numbers of nodes, $\sigma = 1$ for $N_{opt} = 2$, $\sigma = 0.46$ for $N_{opt} = 4$, and $\sigma = 0.29$ for $N_{opt} = 8$. This means scalability is worse for smaller N_{opt} and approaches $\sigma = 0.23$ quickly.

We also show results for using the Cirne-Berman adoption of Downey's model. Note that this model generates different scalability behavior randomly. To have a proper comparison to the Cirne-Berman implementation, we follow their approach in not correlating the generated speedup curve to the generated sizes/runtime though we agree with Downey's comment that user submissions are likely to be proportional to the maximum speedup [7]. (The latter means that a user is likely to choose a larger size—even if the machine is very busy—if the maximum speedup is very high.) Then, we calculate N_{opt} by finding N_{PWS} from the speedup formula. For predictions of speedup for future jobs, we use mean maximum speedups and mean variances. The σ values created by this model are random with a mean value of 1.2 which represents a rather poor scalability. Thus, significant benefits can be obtained if shrinking sizes in the range above N_{opt}. However, as we will detail in Section 5.4, the generated N_{opt} values are significantly higher with this model. Thus, if shrinking sizes under high load, they fall more likely in the range below N_{opt} where the curve is steeper and less likely a benefit can be obtained from shrinking job sizes (if the curve is close to linear, little efficiency gain is possible). If load is low, less benefit can be obtained from expanding sizes. Note that with the Cirne-Berman model, the relative size modification of SCOJO-P is only a heuristic regarding efficiency but no exact EQUI-EFF.

By testing our approach with both models, we cover the two extremes of, on one hand, the user having a good idea about the speedup curves and choosing the size according to what is optimum and, on the other hand, the user not knowing or not caring about the optimum at all when choosing the job size.

5   Experimental Evaluation

5.1   Test Environment and Measured Metrics

We evaluate utilization, wait times, response times (elapsed runtimes plus waiting times), and bounded slowdowns (response times in relation to runtimes with adjustment to a minimum runtime bound). The bounded slowdown (BSl), however, needs to be redefined for moldable jobs. We relate the slowdown to $runtime(N_{opt})$ as N_{opt} represents the standard size as it would be used without molding:

$$runtime(N_{opt}) < bound \rightarrow$$
$$BSl = max(T_{response}/max(runtime(N_{opt}), bound), 1)$$
$$runtime(N_{opt}) \geq bound \rightarrow BSl = T_{response}/runtime(N_{opt})$$

We have set the bound to 30 seconds. Rather than using the geometric mean like Cirne-Berman [5] to avoid too much influence from long jobs, we not only calculate the overall arithmetic mean, but also perform separate evaluations for short jobs, medium jobs, and long jobs.

5.2   Workload Model

We evaluate SCOJO-P via simulation. As already mentioned above, we apply the Lublin/Feitelson statistical model for the workload generation [13], including runtimes, sizes, and interarrival times. This model is derived from existing workload traces and incorporates correlations between job runtimes and job sizes and daytime cycles in job-interarrival times. We cut off the head and the tail of the created schedule (the first and last 5% of the jobs in the schedule) to avoid that the fill and drain phase influence the results. We test two different variations of the Lublin-Feitelson workload: the basic one and a higher workload (one with shortened interarrival times).

Since there is no information yet about speedup curves from real application traces, we apply the model as described in Section 4.6. Regarding moldability, the study in [5] suggests that 98% of the jobs are moldable. The figure, however, sounds a bit too optimistic–if users say that they can submit jobs as moldable, it does not necessarily mean that, in practice, they would do so and that applications are moldable in such a high percentage of cases. Furthermore, these are so far results from a single study only. Thus, we test different percentages of moldable jobs, including 100%. If less than 100% jobs are moldable, moldability is distributed over the different job classes short, medium, long with equal probability.

We assume all generated runtimes to represent correct runtimes (i.e. we do not consider over-estimates as would be possible if adding the model presented in [26]) which is sufficient for our evaluation. For SCOJO-P, wrong estimates would actually be relatively easy to incorporate: only the average percentage of the overestimate would be needed to model the predictions for running, waiting, and future jobs as we consider averages of runtimes only. The Cirne-Berman approach is more heavily depending on estimates as the approach determines sizes by simulating the actual schedule. Since we apply the same workload model to all approaches, comparing to the Cirne-Berman approach on the bases of correct runtimes is a conservative comparison regarding SCOJO-P. In other words, if including wrong estimates into the model, we expect SCOJO-P to perform relatively even better.

For details of the workload parameters, see Table 1. We have set the efficiency values $E = speedup/MN$ such that, in our test cases, $N_{opt} = N_{PWS}$. Note that in addition, we model the Cirne-Berman-Downey speedup model as described above. For this model, the parameters for the statistical generation and calculation of the maximum speedup and the scalability factor are chosen according to [4]. This model creates σ via a standard distribution with $mean = 1.209$ and $deviation = 1.132$.

Future job submissions in different time intervals are determined by using 30-minute intervals as in the Lublin-Feitelson model and evaluating actual workload simulations to extract the numbers of short, medium, and long jobs submitted on average in each of 48 time intervals per day.

5.3   Approaches Tested

As mentioned above, SCOJO-P employs EASY backfilling and priority assignment according to runtime, giving highest priority to short jobs. Long and medium jobs are aged to prevent starvation; that is, their priority is increased after they have waited 5 times as long as their optimum runtime. We use the same basic approaches, including the priority handling and EASY backfilling, for

Table 1. Workload parameters used for basic and additional evaluation

Parameter	Value
Machine size MN	128
Number of jobs in workload	10,000
Cut-off for fill and drain phase	5% of overall jobs each
α parameter of Lublin/Feitelson	$\alpha = 10.23$ (basic Workload W1)
model with impact on system load	$\alpha = 9.83$ (heavier Workload W2)
Classification of short jobs	$runtime(N_{opt}) < 60sec$
Classification of medium jobs	$60sec \leq runtime(N_{opt}) < 1hour$
Classification of long jobs	$1hour \leq runtime(N_{opt})$
percentage moldable jobs	80% and 100%
N_{opt}	as created by Lublin-Feitelson model
N_{min}	$max\{1/2N_{opt}, 1\}$
N_{max}	$min\{2 * N_{opt}, MN\}$
$E(N_{opt})$	0.65
$E(N_{min})$	0.8
$E(N_{max})$	0.4
$runtime(N_{opt})$	as created by Lublin-Feitelson model
$runtime(N_{min})$	$runtime(N_{opt}) * 2 * E(N_{opt})/E(N_{min})$
$runtime(N_{max})$	$runtime(N_{Opt}) * 1/2 * E(N_{opt})/E(N_{max})$

all approaches used in our comparison to have a fair comparison. (Note that the original Cirne-Berman approach applied conservative backfilling.) We also do not impose any size constraints in neither of the approaches though the original Cirne-Berman approach generates only a certain number of sizes and imposes a certain probability that the jobs's sizes have power-of-two constraints. We compare the following approaches:

- Basic scheduler without any adaptation (traditional)
- SCOJO-P with adaptation with prediction (predictive) or without prediction (non-predictive)
- Cirne-Berman approach for adaptation

The non-predictive variant of SCOJO-P is introduced to investigate how much the prediction contributes to the final results. For SCOJO-P, we additionally tested different load values for the target utilization. The one that performed best is 90% utilization. This is not surprising as this value corresponds to the maximum utilization which typically can be achieved on a machine, considering that there is always some fragmentation.

5.4   Experimental Results

We ran all tests four times with different random seeds and use the average for our results. We first test the scheduling approaches using our simple speedup model. The results for Workload W1 and 100% moldable jobs are shown in Fig. 4 to Fig. 7.

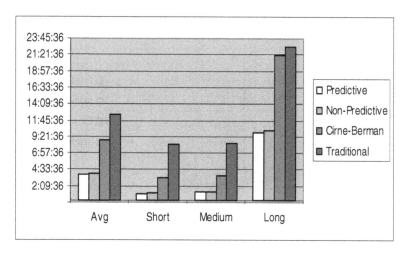

Fig. 4. Mean response times with basic Workload W1 (in hours), 100% moldable

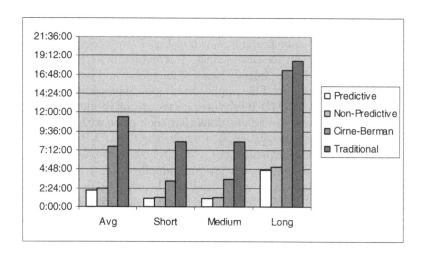

Fig. 5. Mean wait times for basic Workload W1 (in hours), 100% moldable

From Fig. 4, it can be seen that mean response times for jobs scheduled with SCOJO-P vs. Cirne-Berman are better for all job classes. Short and medium jobs are reduced to about 1/3 of their response times and long jobs to about 1/2. Regarding wait times, short and medium job again are cut to 1/3 but long jobs to 1/4, see Fig. 5. This suggests that SCOJO-P typically starts long jobs earlier, but with fewer processors than the Cirne-Berman approach does. Thus, runtime is increased but response time is actually decreased because of the earlier start time. Furthermore, using fewer processors for long jobs also leaves more room for short and medium jobs to squeeze through which explains their marginal improvement. To

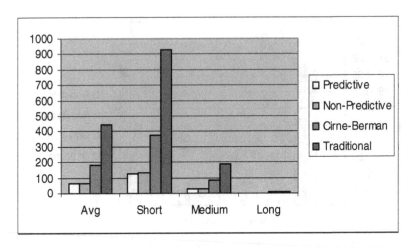

Fig. 6. Mean bounded slowdowns for basic Workload W1, 100% moldable

get a better insight into the behavior than the averages can provide for the highly varying result values and skewed distributions, we have calculated histograms. The corresponding response-time graph is shown in Fig. 7 (the other graphs are similar in their trend). We can see that SCOJO-P schedules more jobs with shorter response times (except for the initial classes of long jobs) and fewer jobs with excessively long response times. This applies to all job classes short, medium, and long, and supports that SCOJO-P produces better overall results.

Fig. 8 shows the number of adaptations that took place with each approach. Because it is considering the system as a whole, the SCOJO-P scheduler tends to shrink jobs rather than expand them; conversely, because the Cirne-Berman approach is trying to optimize each job individually it tends to expand jobs. The Cirne-Berman approach actually produced higher system utilization than SCOJO-P (89.69% vs 78.6%). The reason is most likely that SCOJO-P shrinks more jobs during phases with high load and may leave processors empty so they can service jobs in the near future. However, SCOJO-P still obtains better mean response times which makes sense if shrinking jobs to run with higher efficiency. Furthermore, we checked by how much jobs are shrunk or expanded and how the results distribute over the different job classes. On average, jobs are scaled by 0.4 to 0.5, i.e shrunk to 40% to 50% of their optimal size. Short and medium jobs are scaled by 0.44 to 0.58 (depending on the test run) and long jobs by 0.3 to 0.4. Without prediction, the factor for long jobs is 0.36 to 0.47 This shows that the classes are treated fairly equally though long jobs are shrunk a little more, especially if including predictions about future job arrivals. The Cirne-Berman approach shrinks jobs less: overall by about a factor of 0.8 and short jobs by about a factor of 0.72, i.e. short jobs are shrunk slightly more.

Looking at the results for the non-predictive SCOJO-P, we find them to be only a little worse. This means that the prediction-at least, in its current version-does not provide as much benefit as we had originally expected.

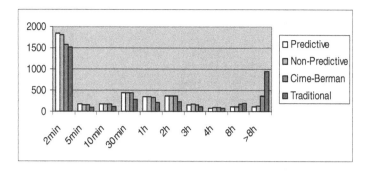

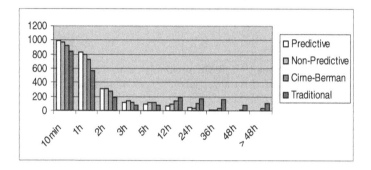

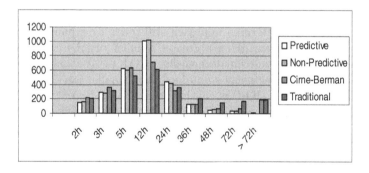

Fig. 7. Histograms for response times and short (top), medium (middle), and long (bottom) jobs. Note that the histogram categories are not equidistant to accommodate the skewed distributions. The labels mean: *label value of the preceding category < result values ≤ label valueof the current category*. The histogram shows the number of job results falling into each category.

Similar results were achieved with a workload where only 80% of the jobs were moldable. However, SCOJO-P actually performed slightly better (4%) with 80% moldable jobs, while Cirne-Berman performed a bit worse (-5%). This indicates that job shrinking in SCOJO-P might be a little too aggressive.

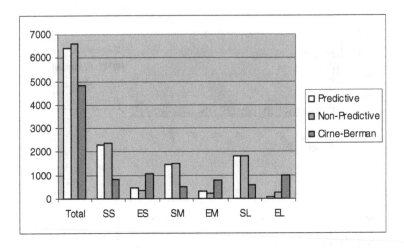

Fig. 8. Number of adaptations (W1, 100% moldable) that shrink (S*) or expand (E*) the job size vs. N_{opt}, calculated for short jobs (*S), medium jobs (*M), and long jobs (*L)

Fig. 9 to Fig. 12 show results for the higher Workload W2. As with the lower workload, SCOJO-P produces much better (67%) mean wait times for long jobs than the Cirne-Berman approach. This translates into a 48% improvement in the mean response time of long jobs which now benefit most. Looking at the adaptation statistics in Fig. 12, we see that even when there is a heavy workload on the system, the Cirne-Berman approach still tends to expand jobs. On the other hand, SCOJO-P is shrinking a greater number of jobs, thus allowing a greater number of jobs to run simultaneously. SCOJO-P is also benefiting from the increased processor effectiveness obtained from smaller job sizes.

We also found that SCOJO-P is consistently running faster (in our tests by more than a factor of 10 though the details depend on how many different sizes are tried with Cirne-Berman) confirms our claims regarding our algorithm being an efficient yet effective heuristic.

For comparison, we checked the results from the original SCOJO. Since our test environment and the generated random workloads are not exactly the same, a direct comparison is not possible. However, SCOJO reduces average response times by 50% if 80% of the long jobs are malleable (while 80% of the short and medium jobs are moldable). Adaptation with all classes being 80% moldable improves response times by approx. 35% vs. scheduling without adaptation. This means that the approx. 50% improvement which we get with SCOJO-P can in SCOJO only be accomplished with dynamic adaptation for malleable jobs.

Finally, we ran the tests (using two test runs) for W1 and 100% moldable again with the Cirne-Berman-Downey speedup model. The results for response times and bounded slowdowns are shown in Fig. 13 and Fig. 14. SCOJO-P still performs better: only slightly in average response times but clearly better in bounded slowdowns. However, also Cirne-Berman does not perform as well

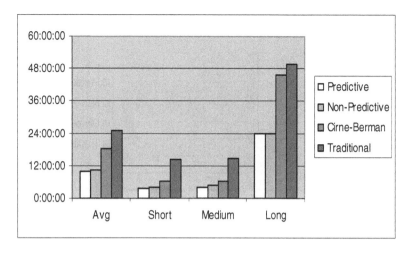

Fig. 9. Mean response times for Workload W2 (in hours), 100% moldable jobs

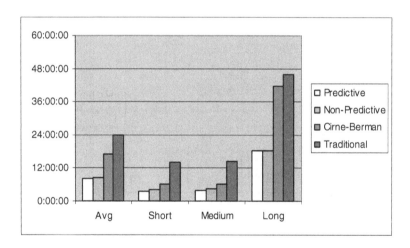

Fig. 10. Mean wait times for Workload W2 (in hours), 100% moldable jobs

anymore and is not much better in average response times than the traditional priority scheduler. We found that N_{max} and therefore N_{opt} are created very high. Thus, with our speedup model, the average N_{opt} is 12 (8 for short, 9 for medium, and 20 for long jobs) and with the Cirne-Berman-Downey model it is 69. There is not much difference for the different job classes with the latter (61 for short, 89 for medium, and 65 for long jobs). The high values of N_{opt} greatly reduce the benefit of shrinking job sizes. However, as discussed above, we consider the created sizes as too large and as not properly correlated to the submitted sizes. Note that the classification into short, medium, and long is based on the N_{opt} runtimes which changes the overall distribution of the jobs: if using for classification the N_{opt}

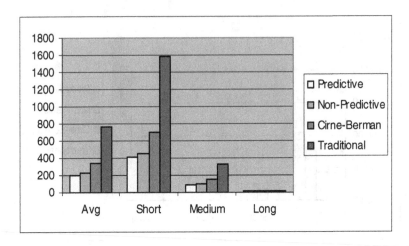

Fig. 11. Mean bounded slowdowns for Workload W2, 100% moldable jobs

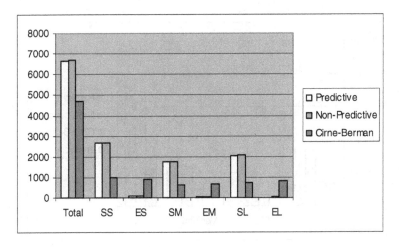

Fig. 12. Number of adaptations (W2, 100% moldable jobs) that shrink (S*) or expand (E*) the job size vs. N_{opt}, calculated for short jobs (*S), medium jobs (*M), and long jobs (*L)

runtimes derived by the Cirne-Berman-Downey model, the workload has 61% short jobs, 28% medium jobs, and 11% long jobs, whereas with the runtimes originally generated by Lublin-Feitelson, the percentages are 42.7% short jobs, 26.6% medium, and 30.7% long jobs. This underlines that the Cirne-Berman-Downey model significantly reshapes the jobs in the workload. Using this model, the non-predictive variant of SCOJO-P now performs better than the predictive variant. The reason is that the overly high N_{opt} values (which are far beyond the sizes with which the jobs are finally scheduled) negatively affect the predictions.

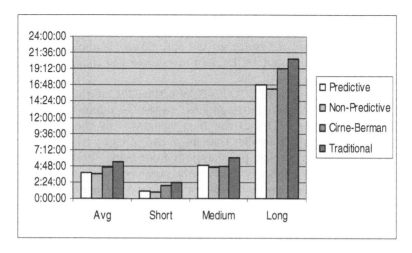

Fig. 13. Response times for W1 and 100% moldable jobs, using the Cirne-Berman-Downey speedup model

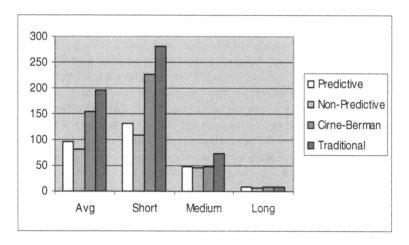

Fig. 14. Bounded slowdowns for W1 and 100% moldable jobs, using the Cirne-Berman-Downey speedup model

Regarding the size modification, we found that SCOJO-P now shrinks jobs significantly more vs. N_{opt} (certainly because N_{opt} is larger than in the simple model). The size modification factor is now around 0.1 with short jobs shrunk a little less (0.15), medium jobs shrunk more (0.07), and long jobs less (0.17). The latter is different from the simple model where long jobs are shrunk more. Without prediction, long jobs are shrunk relatively less (the factor is 0.23) as for the simple model. If comparing to the size generated by the Lublin-Feitelson model, the factors are about 3 for short jobs and about 5.5 for medium jobs, i.e. the job sizes are expanded significantly vs. the original size with which the jobs are submitted. Long jobs are still shrunk vs. the submit size (the factor is 0.62). For Cirne-Berman, the factor vs. the optimal size is about 0.22 for short and medium and 0.6 for long jobs, i.e. jobs are shrunk less than with SCOJO-P as found for the simple model.

We finally tried to improve SCOJO-P by artificially limiting the minimum size of the jobs: for medium and large jobs, we set the minimum to the point where $E \geq 0.9$ because we found the N_{min} generated by the Cirne-Berman-Downey model to be much smaller than N_{opt} and often to be close to 1. The limitation of the minimum size prevents jobs from being shrunk into a range where no or hardly any efficiency gain can be obtained. However, the modified version did not bring the expected benefits. We found the minimum now to be rather large; but small sizes apparently are important for increasing the chances to pack jobs into the schedule, especially with the large N_{opt} sizes generated by the Cirne-Berman-Downey model. However, these effects demonstrate that SCOJO-P works well as it is and exploits all–efficiency gain, better utilization, and better packing (fragmentation reduction)–when molding the jobs.

6   Summary and Conclusion

We have presented the SCOJO-P scheduler for adaptive resource allocation at job start time. SCOJO-P considers the estimated load of the machine over the whole runtime of the job to determine its ideal size. The load estimation includes an estimate about future job submissions. The Cirne-Berman approach for molding jobs, tries to maximize the benefits per jobs, which still converges to a situation where each job (on average) benefits. SCOJO-P directly considers the whole picture to balance the interests of the scheduled jobs with the interests of the other jobs. SCOJO-P also approximates an efficiency-based allocation by shrinking/expanding job sizes by certain factors and by using minimum sizes that keep the size adaptation in the range where efficiency gains can be obtained if choosing smaller sizes. SCOJO-P is an efficient yet effective approach which does not require any simulation of whole schedules. In the experimental study, SCOJO-P improves response times by 70% vs. traditional scheduling and by about 59% vs. the Cirne-Berman approach (which improves traditional scheduling by about 30%) if using a simple speedup model which takes the submission size as the optimal one. Investigating the effect of prediction, we found it contribute less to the good results than originally expected (though improvements are possible) and the main benefit stemming from considering the whole set of jobs on the system together. With the Cirne-Berman-Downey speedup model, optimal sizes for the generated curves are not correlated with the sizes originally generated in the workload and are much higher, leading to less efficiency gain if shrinking jobs and therefore to SCOJO-P only being slightly better than the Cirne-Berman scheduler but also Cirne-Berman not being much better in average response time than traditional non-adaptive scheduling. This appears to be less an argument against the schedulers but a call for further improvements in the statistical speedup/workload model.

Acknowledgements. This research was in part supported by NSERC and by CFI (Grant No. 6191) with contributions from OIT and IBM.

References

[1] Barsanti, L.: An Alternative Approach to Adaptive Space Sharing. Honors Thesis, University of Windsor, Computer Science (August 2005)

[2] Chiang, S.-H., Mansharamani, R.K., Vernon, M.K.: Use of Application Characteristics and Limited Preemption for Run-to-Completion Parallel Processor Scheduling Policies. Proc. ACM SIGMETRICS Conf. on Measurement and Modeling of Computer Systems (1994)

[3] Chiang, S.-H., Vernon, M.K.: Dynamic vs. Static Quantum-Based Parallel Processor Allocation. Proc. JSSPP Workshop on Job Scheduling Strategies for Parallel Processing, May 1996. Springer Verlag, Lecture Notes in Computer Science Vol. 1162 (1996) 200-223

[4] Cirne, W., Berman, F.: A Model for Moldable Supercomputer Jobs. Proc. IPDPS Int'l Parallel and Distributed Computing Symposium (April 2001)

[5] Cirne, W., Berman, F.: When the Herd is Smart–Aggregate Behavior in the Selection of Job Request. IEEE Trans. on Par. and Distr. Systems, Volume 14, Number 2 (Feb. 2003)

[6] Corbalan, J., Mortarell, X., Labarta, J.: Improving Gang Scheduling through Job Performance Analysis and Malleability. Proc. ICS (June 2001)

[7] Downey, A.: A Model for Speedup of Parallel Programs. Technical Report CSD-97-933, Univ. of California Berkeley (Jan. 1997)

[8] Dutot, P.-F., Trystram, D.: Scheduling on Hierarchical Clusters Using Malleable Tasks. Proc. SPAA Symp. on Parallel Algorithms and Architectures (July 2001)

[9] Feitelson, D.G., Rudolph, L., Schwiegelsohn, U., Sevcik, K.C., Parsons, W.: Theory and Practice in Parallel Job Scheduling. Proc. JSSPP Workshop on Job Scheduling Strategies for Parallel Processing, Springer Verlag, Lecture Notes in Computer Science, Vol. 1291 (1997)

[10] Franke, H., Jann, J., Moreira, J.E., Pattnik, P., Jette, M.A.: An Evaluation of Parallel Job Scheduling for ASCI Blue-Pacific. Proc. IEEE/ACM SC Supercomputing Conference (1999)

[11] Gibbons, R.A.: Historical Application Profiler for Use by Parallel Schedulers. Proc. JSSPP Workshop on Job Scheduling Strategies for Parallel Processing, April 1997, Lecture Notes in Computer Science 1291, Springer Verlag (1997)

[12] Ghosal, D., Serazzi, G., Tripathi, S.K.: The Processor Working Set and Its Use in Scheduling Multiprocessor Systems. IEEE Trans. Software Engineering, Volume 17, Number 5 (May 1991) 443-453

[13] Lublin, U., Feitelson, D.G.: The Workload on Parallel Supercomputers–Modeling the Characteristics of Rigid Jobs. Journal of Parallel and Distributed Computing, Volume 63, Number 11 (Nov. 2003) 1105-1122

[14] McCann, C., Zahorjan, J.: Processor Allocation Policies for Message Passing Parallel Computers. Proc. SIGMETRICS Conf. Measurement & Modeling of Computer Systems (May 1994) 208-219

[15] Naik, V.K., Setia, S.K., Squillante, M.K.: Processor Allocation in Multiprogrammed Distributed-Memory Parallel Computer Systems. Journal of Parallel and Distributed Computing, Volume 46, Number 1 (1997) 28-47

[16] Padhye, J.D., Dowdy, L.: Dynamic Versus Adaptive Processor Allocation Policies for Message Passing Parallel Computers: An Empirical Comparison. Proc. JSSPP Workshop on Job Scheduling Strategies for Parallel Processing, Springer Verlag, Lecture Notes in Computer Science Vol. 1162 (1996) 224-243

[17] Parsons, E.W., Sevcik, K.C.: Implementing Multiprocessor Scheduling Disciplines. Proc. JSSPP Workshop on Job Scheduling Strategies for Parallel Processing, Springer Verlag, Lecture Notes in Computer Science (1997)

[18] Rosti, E., Smirni, E., Serazzi, G., Dowdy, L.W.: Analysis of Non-Work-Conserving Processor Partitioning Policies. Proc. JSSPP Workshop on Job Scheduling Strategies for Parallel Processing (1995)

[19] Sevcik, K.C.: Characterization of Parallelism in Applications and Their Use in Scheduling. Performance Evaluation Review, Volume 17 (1989) 171-180

[20] Sodan, A.C., Huang, X.: SCOJO-Share-Based Job Coscheduling with Integrated Dynamic Resource Directory in Support of Grid Scheduling. Proc. HPCS Ann. Int. Symposium on High Performance Computing Systems, (May 2003) 213-221

[21] Sodan, A.C., Huang, X.: Adaptive Time/Space Scheduling with SCOJO. Proc. HPCS, Winnipeg (May 2004)

[22] Sodan, A.C., Han, L.: ATOP-Space and Time Adaptation for Parallel and Grid Applications via Flexible Data Partitioning. Proc. 3rd ACM/IFIP/USENIX Workshop on Reflective and Adaptive Middleware (Oct. 2004)

[23] Sodan, A.C.: Loosely Coordinated Coscheduling in the Context of Other Dynamic Approaches for Job Scheduling–A Survey. Concurrency & Computation: Practice & Experience, Volume 17, Number 15 (Dec. 2005) 1725-1781

[24] Sodan, A.C., Doshi, C., Barsanti, L., Taylor, D.: Gang Scheduling and Adaptive Resource Allocation to Mitigate Advance Reservation Impact. IEEE CCGrid, Singapore (May 2006)

[25] Srinivasan, S., Subramani, V., Kettimuthu, R., Holenarsipur, P., Sadayappan, P.: Effective Selection of Partition Sizes for Moldable Scheduling of Parallel Jobs. Proc. HiPC (2002)

[26] Tsafrir, D., Etsion, Y., Feitelson, D.G.: Modeling User Runtime Estimates: Proc. JSSPP Workshop on Job Scheduling Strategies for Parallel Processing, Lecture Notes in Computer Science, Vol. 3834 (2005) 1-35

[27] Turek, J., Wolf, J.L., Pattipati, K.L., Yu, P.S.: Scheduling Parallelizable Tasks: Putting it All on the Shelf. SIGMETRICS Performance Evaluation Review–Proc. SIGMETRICS Conf. on Measurement and Modeling of Computer Systems, Volume 20, Number 1 (June 1982)

A Data Locality Aware Online Scheduling Approach for I/O-Intensive Jobs with File Sharing[*]

Gaurav Khanna[1], Umit Catalyurek[2],
Tahsin Kurc[2], P. Sadayappan[1], and Joel Saltz[2]

[1] Dept. of Computer Science and Engineering
{khannag, saday}@cse.ohio-state.edu
[2] Dept. of Biomedical Informatics
The Ohio State University
{umit,kurc}@bmi.osu.edu, Joel.Saltz@osumc.edu

Abstract. Many scientific investigations have to deal with large amounts of data from simulations and experiments. Data analysis in such investigations typically involves extraction of subsets of data, followed by computations performed on extracted data. Scheduling in this context requires efficient utilization of the computational, storage and network resources to optimize response time. The data-intensive nature of such applications necessitates data-locality aware job scheduling algorithms. This paper proposes a hypergraph based dynamic scheduling heuristic for a stream of independent I/O intensive jobs with file sharing behavior. The proposed heuristic is based on an event-driven, run-time hypergraph modeling of the file sharing characteristics among jobs. Our experiments on a coupled compute/storage cluster show it performs better compared to previously proposed strategies, under a varying set of parameters for workloads from the application domain of biomedical image analysis.

1 Introduction

Data-driven approaches that make use of large datasets to solve complex problems in science and engineering have become increasingly important. Data analysis is a key component in data-driven science and engineering, enabling a better understanding of the problem under study and more efficient refinement of the search space of solutions. Data analysis applications often involve access and processing of many subsets of a dataset. Most scientific datasets are stored in files. A request for the region of interest specifies a subset of data files and/or segments in data files – either directly as input parameters or after an index lookup that finds the files and file segments of interest.The data of interest is

---

[*] This research was supported in part by the National Science Foundation under Grants #CCF-0342615 and #CNS-0403342.

E. Frachtenberg and U. Schwiegelshohn (Eds.): JSSPP 2006, LNCS 4376, pp. 141–160, 2007.

retrieved from the storage system and transformed into a data product that is more suitable for examination by the scientist.

When several data-intensive jobs are submitted to a high-performance system, they have to be scheduled to compute nodes for execution. Unlike traditional compute intensive jobs, data analysis jobs may require access to a large number of files and high data volume. When mapping such data-intensive jobs to compute nodes, scheduling mechanisms need to take into account not only the computation time of the jobs, but also the overheads of retrieving files requested by those jobs. Moreover, the staging of files should be carefully coordinated to minimize I/O overheads. Traditional job schedulers for compute-intensive jobs running at supercomputer centers are not designed for data intensive jobs, since they take into account CPU related metrics (e.g. user estimated job run times) and system state (e.g. queue wait times) for making scheduling decisions, but they do not take into account data related metrics.

This paper addresses the efficient execution of a stream of dynamically arriving data-intensive jobs exhibiting file-shared I/O behavior [14]. In our model, the files required by the jobs are initially resident on a storage cluster. When a job is scheduled to a compute node, the files accessed by the job are staged from remote storage nodes to the compute node before the job is executed. Since disk space on compute nodes is limited, effective management of data on the local disk of compute nodes is also important. Obviously, by running jobs on the storage nodes the cost of data staging can be avoided; however, in real setups storage nodes are designed to maximize storage space and I/O bandwidth, and have only limited computation power[1]. Thus, we assume that jobs cannot be executed directly on storage nodes.

We propose a new algorithm to schedule a stream of dynamically arriving jobs that share input files. The algorithm is based on a hypergraph formulation of the workload and a K-way partitioning of the hypergraph to yield a locality aware and load-balanced allocation of jobs on the compute cluster. The proposed approach formulates the sharing of files among jobs as a hypergraph. The hypergraph representation also models the load on the compute nodes due to currently executing jobs. It also takes into account the fact that some files might already have been staged or are currently being staged to the compute nodes due to previously executed or currently running jobs. The experimental results show that when there is high degree of file sharing among jobs, our formulation results in much better schedules compared to the *JobDataPresent + DataLeastLoaded* algorithm [13] and the *Minimum Execution Time, Minimum Completion Time, Switching Algorithm* heuristics [10,2,3], modified to handle data intensive jobs. We have also observed that as the average job inter-arrival times decrease, the proposed approach outperforms the other heuristics.

---

[1] Even though per node storage nodes might have comparable power to compute nodes, generally the number of storage nodes are much less than the number of compute nodes. For example, at Ohio Supercomputer Center 0.5 Petabyte Mass Storage System is derived from 24 storage nodes, whereas they have thousands of compute nodes.

2   Problem Definition and Use-Case Applications

We target streams of dynamically arriving jobs which consist of independent sequential programs. Each job requests a subset of data files from a dataset and can be executed on any of the nodes in the compute cluster. The data files required by a job should be staged to the compute node where the job is allocated for the job to execute correctly; a data file is the unit of I/O transfer from the storage cluster to the compute cluster. The jobs may share a number of files with previously scheduled jobs or with jobs arriving in future.

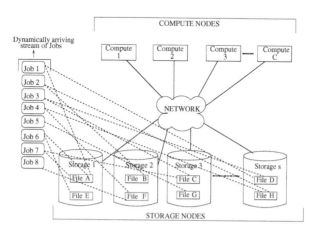

Fig. 1. Scheduling problem

Our objective is, given a stream of dynamically arriving jobs and a set of files required by these jobs, 1) to schedule the jobs in an efficient manner, 2) to decide which files need to be remotely transferred and their respective destination nodes, so as to minimize the average job response time. Figure 1 depicts an illustration of this problem. Each job in the job stream is represented by a computation weight, a list of input files, and their file sizes.

Formally, let $S = < j_1, j_2, \ldots, j_n >$ be a stream of n jobs arriving dynamically. Let $Arrival(j_i)$ be the arrival time of the job j_i and $Exec(j_i)$ be the total time the job j_i spends in execution. Some of the jobs will not be able start execution as soon as they have been submitted. Let $Start(j_i)$ be the time instant when the job j_i starts execution. In our case, this corresponds to the case when the first data transfer for the job j_i starts. If the job finds all its files locally, then it is the time when the job starts its computation. The wait time of a job $Wait(j_i)$ is the time it spends in the queue before it starts execution.

$$Wait(j_i) = Start(j_i) - Arrival(j_i) \qquad (1)$$

The response time $Response(j_i)$ of the job is the turnaround time which refers to the total time spent by job in the queue and in execution.

$$Response(j_i) = Wait(j_i) + Exec(j_i) \qquad (2)$$

$Completion(j_i)$ refers to the instant when the job finishes execution.

$$Completion(j_i) = Arrival(j_i) + Response(j_i) \tag{3}$$

And the $AverageResponseTime$ is defined as the overall average of response times of the jobs in the stream.

$$AverageResponseTime = \frac{\sum_{i=1}^{i=n} Response(j_i)}{n} \tag{4}$$

We have evaluated our approach using application scenarios from **Biomedical Image Analysis** application class. Biomedical imaging is a powerful method for disease diagnosis and for monitoring therapy. State-of-the-art studies make use of large datasets, which consist of time dependent sequences of 2D and 3D images from multiple imaging sessions. Systematic development and assessment of image analysis techniques requires an ability to efficiently invoke candidate image quantification methods on large collections of image data. A researcher may apply several different image analysis methods on image datasets containing thousands of 2D and 3D images to assess ability to predict outcome or effectiveness of a treatment across patient groups.

3   Related Work

Relatively little scheduling research so far has given importance to the issues of data locality and I/O contention. Ranganathan et. al. [13] proposed a decoupled approach to scheduling of computations and data for data-intensive applications in a grid environment, and evaluated its effectiveness via simulation studies. The algorithm combines a scheduling scheme, called *Job Data Present* with a replication heuristic, referred to as *Data Least Loaded* in a decoupled fashion. The algorithm incorporates a notion of eligible nodes for each job, which are the set of nodes that store the file required by the job. It works by picking a job from a FIFO queue and assigning it to the node that already has the required data. If more than one compute nodes are eligible candidates, then it chooses the least loaded node. The replication mechanism *Data Least Loaded* is decoupled from the scheduling policy. The replication mechanism keeps track of the popularity of files, and when the popularity of a file exceeds a threshold, then the file is replicated to the least loaded node in the compute cluster. As the replication threshold decreases, the number of dynamic data replications increases. This in turn increases the possibility of increased end-point contention on the storage cluster. Therefore, there is a tradeoff between the benefit of a low replication threshold and the increased contention. In our case, we allow multiple files per job which means that there may exist compute nodes which store subsets of the files required by a job. This essentially amounts to allocating a job to a node such that the expected data transfer time to stage in the set of files required by a job is minimized.

Casanova et al. [3] modified the MinMin, MaxMin, and Sufferage job scheduling heuristics to take into account the cost of inter-site file access, in the context of scheduling parameter sweep applications in a Grid environment. Jain et.al. [5] model scheduling of I/O operations (with certain assumptions) as a bipartite graph coloring problem with two separate sets of nodes namely, disks and processors. Our difference is that we consider grouping and mapping of jobs to compute nodes in tandem with ordering of jobs and scheduling of remote I/O operations for file transfers. Mohamed et al. [12] presented a Close-To-Files (CF) job placement algorithm which tries to place jobs on clusters with enough idle processors that are close to the storage sites where the files reside.

Multi-query workloads also arise in the context of database applications. The work of Mehta et al. [11] is one of the first to address the problem of scheduling queries in a parallel database by considering batches of queries. In [1], Andrade et.al. propose a dynamic scheduling model for multi-query workloads in data analysis applications. The goal is to maximize data and computation reuse and concurrent execution on SMP nodes through semantic caching and ordering of queries based on priority metric. These strategies mainly target efficient reuse of results from previously executed queries.

Kotz et al. [8] propose a technique called disk-directed I/O to organize multiple overlapping I/O operations with a view to optimize disk performance which is the bottleneck. The work of Kavas et al. [6] focusses on loading of executables on the compute nodes and not just data. They propose reliable multicast mechanisms to load a file to multiple nodes at once thereby reducing the storage node overheads.

In an earlier work [7], we looked at the problem of scheduling a batch of data-intensive jobs with batch-shared I/O behavior. We modeled the sharing of files among jobs as a hypergraph and employed hypergraph partitioning to obtain a partitioning of jobs onto compute nodes that computationally balanced the workload and reduced remote I/O operations for file transfers. In this paper, we are targeting an online scenario where a set of file-shared data-intensive jobs arrive over time. To accomplish this, we have extended our previous work [7] in such a way so as to dynamically model the state of the system at each scheduling instant which includes the content of disk caches at the compute nodes, the remaining execution time of the running jobs, and the pending jobs that are present in the system. Our approach for the batch mode case involves a one time hypergraph modeling and partitioning which looks at the entire set of jobs that have arrived together as a batch and the initial system state which is cold, to yield a load-balanced connectivity minimizing allocation of jobs. Whereas for this work, we propose repeated partitioning and remapping of jobs at each scheduling instant by taking into account the current state of the system at each scheduling instant.

4   Dynamic Job Scheduling

We propose an Online Hypergraph partitioning based scheduling (Online-HPS) heuristic, a two stage dynamic scheduling framework. In the first stage, jobs are mapped to compute nodes, and in the second stage, the order of the jobs in each compute node are determined. These two stages are then applied in a repeated fashion at certain scheduling events which may correspond to job arrivals or job completions.

For mapping jobs to compute nodes we employ a hypergraph-based formulation, hence we start with a brief description of hypergraphs and hypergraph partitioning followed by our proposed mapping technique. We will continue with a description of job ordering stage.

4.1 Hypergraph Partitioning

A hypergraph $\mathcal{H} = (\mathcal{V}, \mathcal{N})$ is defined as a set of vertices $\mathcal{V}$ and a set of nets (hyper-edges) $\mathcal{N}$ among those vertices. Every net $n_j \in \mathcal{N}$ is a subset of vertices, i.e., $n_j \subseteq \mathcal{V}$. The size of a net n_j is equal to the number of vertices it has, i.e., $s_j = |n_j|$. Weights (w_i) and costs (c_j) can be assigned to the vertices $(v_i \in \mathcal{V})$ and edges $(n_j \in \mathcal{N})$ of the hypergraph, respectively. $\mathcal{P} = \{V_1, V_2, \ldots, V_P\}$ is a P-way partition of $\mathcal{H}$ if 1) each part is a nonempty subset of $\mathcal{V}$, 2) parts are pairwise disjoint and 3) union of P parts is equal to $\mathcal{V}$.

In a partition $\mathcal{P}$ of $\mathcal{H}$, connectivity λ_j of a net n_j denotes the number of parts connected by n_j. A net n_j is said to be cut if it connects more than one part, i.e. $\lambda_j > 1$. The cost of a partition Π is computed as $\chi(\Pi) = \sum_{n_j \in \mathcal{N}_E} c_j(\lambda_j - 1)$, where $\mathcal{N}_E$ is the set of cut nets and each cut net n_j contributes $c_j(\lambda_j - 1)$ to the cutsize. This cost metric is also known as connectivity-1 metric. The hypergraph partitioning problem can be defined as the job of dividing a hypergraph into two or more parts such that the cutsize is minimized, while a given balance criterion among the part weights is maintained. Algorithms based on the multi-level paradigm, such as PaToH [4], have been shown to compute good partitions quickly for this NP-hard problem.

4.2 Runtime Hypergraph-Based Mapping of the System State

We develop a hypergraph formulation to model the sharing of files among the jobs present in the system. At each scheduling event, a new hypergraph is constructed which models 1) the current state of the system that includes the pending jobs and the files requested by them, 2) the currently executing jobs, and 3) the files already cached on the compute nodes due to previously executed jobs. This is followed by K-way partitioning of the hypergraph to obtain a load-balanced cut minimizing mapping of the pending jobs onto the compute nodes. The currently executing jobs are incorporated in the partitioner to take into account the current value of load on each of the compute nodes and thereby facilitate load balance as a result of the new partitioning.

Our hypergraph model consists of two sets of vertices, one set of vertices represents the pending jobs which are present in the system and the other set represents jobs currently in execution on the compute nodes. A particular job j_i is represented by a vertex v_i in the hypergraph. Each hyper-edge n_j represents a file f_j and connects to two different set of vertices, one set is the set of vertices corresponding to pending jobs that require this file as input, and the other is the vertices corresponding to running jobs which are running on a node already having a cached a copy of file f_j. This hypergraph is partitioned into P groups, where P is the number of compute nodes, and each group is mapped to a

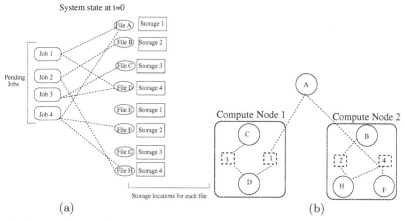

Fig. 2. a) A snapshot of the system at t=0. Jobs 1,2,3 and 4 have arrived into the system. Letters represent files and numbers represent the jobs. Lines connecting the jobs to files represent the associated file requests for each job. b) Hypergraph partitioning across two compute nodes at t=0.

compute node. The partitioning is done so that the compute and I/O weight of the clusters are balanced and the cost of transferring shared files across clusters is minimized. The partitioning should ensure that the vertices corresponding to running jobs are allocated to the same compute node on which they are already running. This is made sure by pinning the vertices corresponding to running jobs onto the nodes in which they are running.

Figure 2(a) illustrates the state of the system at time t=0. It shows the arrival of 4 jobs into the system and their associated file requests. The boxes next to each file represent the storage locations for each file at t=0. Figure 2(b) illustrates a partitioning of the hypergraph representation of the system state shown in Figure 2(a). The figure shows that the hypergraph partitioning tries to cluster jobs sharing files together. Figure 3(a) illustrates the state of the system at time t=10. The figure shows two sets of vertices corresponding to pending jobs and running jobs respectively. Job 1 and Job 2 have run to completion and hence the corresponding vertices are not present. Replicas of files (i.e., multiple copies of files on the compute nodes) have been created as files had been staged onto the compute cluster for previous jobs. The solid lines show the file requests by running jobs which can be served locally whereas the dotted lines represent the file requests which may or may not be served locally based on the result of the subsequent partitioning.

Figure 3(b) illustrates a partitioning of the hypergraph representation of the system state shown in Figure 3(a). The solid boxes represent the running jobs which have been mapped to the same nodes as in Figure 2(b). This is accomplished by pinning down the running jobs onto the nodes on which they are already running. The dotted boxes represent the pending jobs which have been been mapped to one of the compute nodes. The partitioning in Figure 3(b) shows that the jobs have been mapped to nodes with which they have strong affinity in

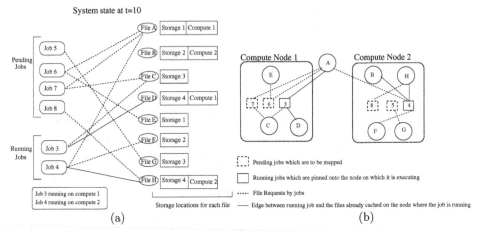

Fig. 3. a) A snapshot of the system at t=10. Jobs 5,6,7 and 8 have arrived into the system. Jobs 1 and 2 have finished execution. Jobs 3 and 4 are currently in execution on nodes 1 and 2 respectively. b) Hypergraph partitioning across two compute nodes at t=10.

terms of the files already cached on those nodes while maintaining load balance. The figure shows two sets of lines. The dotted lines represent the file requests associated with the jobs. The solid lines connect each running job to the files that are already cached on the node on which the job is running. These associations between a net representing a file already cached on a node with the vertex representing the job running on that node are done to exploit the file affinities of certain pending jobs to nodes which have copies of one or more files requested by these jobs. Any pending job which requests a lot of files already cached on a node will therefore have greater inter-job affinity with the running job on that node. Therefore, in essence, we have modeled both the inter-job file sharing affinities and the job-node affinity due to caching of files.

The weight of a vertex representing a pending job is equal to the estimated execution time of the corresponding job. The estimated execution time of a job is calculated as the sum of I/O overhead (the transfer time of files from storage nodes plus the I/O time to read files from local disk) and the computation cost of the job. The hypergraph based strategy globally partitions all the existing jobs into groups before any order for job execution is determined for a group. Hence it has to use a static vertex weights. The expected execution time of a job can possibly vary depending upon the node allocated to the job. This is because different nodes may have staged in different sets of files and therefore the job will have different locality of reference with each node. In other words, the execution times of jobs are not fixed but vary based on the allocation of the nodes and in time. In order to alleviate this issue and provide a better estimate of the execution time of a job, we compute the weight of a vertex as follows.

Let the set of files a job j_i needs be F_i. The cost of transferring one byte of file f_j, Tr_j, for job j_i is equal to

$$Tr(j_i) = \frac{Prob_{FNE}}{RBW} + (1 - Prob_{FNE}) \times \frac{(1 - Prob_{FE})}{RBW}. \qquad (5)$$

Here, RBW is the I/O bandwidth between a storage node and a compute node, $Prob_{FNE}$ is the probability that job j_i will be the first job to execute in its group that requires f_j, and $Prob_{FE}$ is the probability that j_i executes on a node, to which file f_j has already been transferred. In our current implementation, we assume uniform probability distribution. Hence, we have used $Prob_{FNE} = \frac{1}{s_j}$ and $Prob_{FE} = \frac{1}{P}$. Recall that s_j is the size of the hyper-edge n_j that represents file f_j. Hence it also denotes the number of jobs that shares the file f_j.

We assume that the computation time of a job is linear with the size of the input files it requires. This is a reasonable assumption since we assume that multiple instances of only a single application are being run on the system and there is no interference effect due to multiple different applications. With this assumption, the estimated execution time of job j_i is computed as

$$EstimatedExec(j_i) = \sum_{f_j \in F_i} filesize(f_j) \times (Tr_j + \frac{1}{LBW} + C) \qquad (6)$$

where LBW is the I/O bandwidth from local disk on a compute node and C is the compute cost of one byte. By assigning the files sizes as hyper-edge costs, the proposed method reduces the job mapping problem to the P-way hypergraph partitioning problem according to the *connectivity-1* cutsize definition [4]. Each and every file needed by the jobs in the job trace will be transfered to the compute system at least once. More specifically, if the jobs that share the file f_j is assigned to λ_j compute nodes, file f_j needs to transfered $\lambda_j - 1$ more times after its first transfer.

The weight of a vertex representing an already running job is equal to the remaining estimated execution time of the corresponding job. This is computed in a similar fashion as explained above except that it models the fact that some of the files required by a running job may already have been staged and therefore would not contribute to its remaining execution time.

By using expected execution times as vertex weights, the algorithm aims to balance computational load across the compute nodes. The expected execution time as calculated in equation 6 is based on a probabilistic model for estimating the cost of file transfer which assumes a uniform distribution. In scenarios where the data-staging costs are high and much more significant as compared to the computational costs, the impact of making such an assumption could affect load balance but the overall system performance would depend more on the connectivity metric. Therefore, the impact of the inaccuracy of this assumption would be lesser in such scenarios.

4.3   Job Ordering in a Compute Node and Scheduling of Remote File Transfers

Once the jobs have been mapped to a node, the local scheduling algorithm within each compute node decides the order in which to schedule the queued jobs and their associated file transfers. When a node becomes idle, the local scheduling algorithm running at the node decides the next job to execute on that node and also decides the schedule for its remote file transfers. Two jobs that are in different compute nodes may have their input files stored on the same set of nodes. Thus, ordering of jobs in each compute node and transfer of files should be done in a way to minimize end-point contention on the storage cluster.

We employ a strategy in which jobs within a group are scheduled based on their earliest completion time. Therefore, when a node becomes idle, the algorithm computes the completion time of each of the queued jobs present on that node and schedules the job with the earliest completion time. The earliest completion time of a job is computed iteratively and dynamically based on the availability of resources.

The algorithm maintains a *Gantt chart* for storage nodes. When a job in a group is scheduled for execution, time slots are reserved on storage nodes for file transfers required for this job. These time slots for a job are marked on the Gantt chart. In calculating the duration of time slots and marking them on the Gantt chart, we assume that multiple requests to the same storage node are serialized and that a compute node can receive a file after it has finished storing the previously received file on local disk.

The earliest completion time of a job j_i is estimated as the sum of time to stage its input files F_i and its execution time. The staging time is the time spent to make the input files ready in the compute node. If all of the input files are already in the compute node, the staging time will be zero. Otherwise, it will be the amount of time spent to transfer the last input file from the storage node. The transfer completion time for each file $f_j \in F_i$ (TCT_j) is estimated as the sum of the earliest time a transfer can start (first available slot in the Gantt chart after the time that the compute node becomes available) and the actual transfer time (size of f_j divided by the storage bandwidth; computed as the minimum of remote disk bandwidth and network bandwidth). The file f_j with the minimum TCT_j is picked and tentatively scheduled for transfer. TCTs of the rest of the input files are recomputed and the next file with the minimum TCT is picked and tentatively scheduled. This process is repeated until all of the input files are scheduled. TCT of the last file scheduled actually gives the staging time. Then the earliest estimated completion time for j_i is computed as the sum of 1) the completion time of file transfers from storage nodes, 2) I/O time to read the files on local disk, and 3) CPU time to process the files. The scheduling algorithm determines the job with the least completion time in each group, and the job j_i with the lowest *earliest completion time* out of these is scheduled first. Once j_i is scheduled, out of the other job groups (excluding the one containing j_i), the job with the minimum earliest completion time (taking into

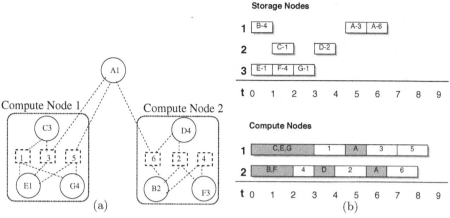

Fig. 4. a) Hypergraph representation of a queue of jobs at a certain point in execution. The numbers next to the alphabets representing the files are the storage node ids on which the corresponding files are resident. b) An illustration of the execution of the ordering algorithm on the set of queued jobs.

account the current reservations) is now picked and scheduled. When a running job completes, the job with earliest completion time from that group is scheduled.

Let us consider a hypergraph partitioning of a stream of six jobs which were submitted to a system of two compute nodes and 4 storage nodes. Figure 4(a) illustrates the corresponding hypergraph partitioning. Figure 4(b) illustrates the execution of the ordering algorithm on the set of mapped jobs shown in Figure 4(a) . In this figure transfer of each file takes 1 unit of time, and I/O and processing of a file takes 0.3 and 0.2 units of time, respectively. Since job 4 depends on two files, its earliest completion time is 3. Hence it has been scheduled first and 1 unit of time on storage node 1 and 1 unit of time on storage node 3 have been reserved. Since a job has been scheduled from group 2, next the job with the earliest completion time from group 1 is scheduled. Since all of the job in the group depends on 3 files, and they can be scheduled to transfer all of the files in 3 units, we pick one of them, say job 1. The algorithm continues by reserving the transfer of files for job 1, and another job from group 2 is picked.

4.4   File Eviction Policy

If the transfer of file for a particular job violates the disk space constraint on the compute cluster, a disk file eviction mechanism is invoked which deletes files in the increasing order of their value metric. The value of a file $Value_\ell$, is calculated as follows.

$$Value_\ell = \frac{AccessFreq(f_\ell) \times filesize(f_\ell)}{Numcopies(f_\ell)} \qquad (7)$$

$AccessFreq(f_\ell)$ represents the number of accesses to the file so far and is representative of its frequency of access. $filesize(f_\ell)$ represents the size of the file f_ℓ. $Numcopies(f_\ell)$ represents the number of copies of file f_ℓ in the compute cluster. If two files have the same frequency of access up to the current time in execution, and the same size, the file with fewer copies gets a higher popularity value as evicting that file is more likely to result in a remote file transfer when the file is again needed. The intuition behind including the file size in popularity computation is that greater the size of the file is, greater the cost of getting the file back to a node will be. The algorithm evicts smaller files, since the cost of staging such files again in future will be less.

We have integrated this file eviction mechanism into our proposed approach as well as MCT, MET, and SA approaches for the purpose of performance comparison. For the algorithm *Job Data Present* with *Data Least Loaded*, we employ an LRU based eviction mechanism as described in [13].

5   Existing Job Mapping Techniques

In this paper, we examine the *JobDataPresent* + *DataLeastLoaded* algorithm proposed in [13] in the context of data grids and the *Minimum Execution Time* (MET), *Minimum Completion Time* (MCT), *Switching Algorithm* (SA) heuristics, which were originally proposed for scheduling independent computational jobs to compute resources [10]. As in [2,3,7], we modify MET, MCT and SA to take into account 1) the time it takes to transfer input and output files to and from compute nodes in the environment, 2) files that have already been staged to a compute node in estimating the minimum completion time of a job and 3) in case of MCT and SA, also the files that are being staged to a compute node due to currently running job on that node. We also integrate the Gantt chart based explicit scheduling of remote file transfers as explained in Section 4.3 into the MET, MCT and SA algorithms.

JobDataPresent + DataLeastLoaded: The algorithm combines a scheduling scheme, called *Job Data Present* with a file replication heuristic, referred to as *Data Least Loaded* in a decoupled fashion. The details of the algorithm have been explained in Section 3.

Minimum Execution Time (MET): The MET heuristic assigns each job to a node that results in the least execution time ($Exec_i$) for that job. As a job arrives, all the compute nodes in the cluster are examined to determine the node that gives the best execution time for the job. When computing the expected execution time of a job on a node, MET takes into account the files already available on the node. If none of the files required by a job are found in any compute node, then the first available node is chosen to run the job. In other words, if the minimum execution time of a job an each node of the cluster is the same, then the first available node is chosen to execute the job. Therefore, MET heuristic inherently favors data locality since nodes which cache files required by a particular job are the ones which will get its best execution time.

Minimum Completion Time (MCT): The MCT heuristic assigns each job to a node that results in that job's earliest completion time ($Completion_i$). As a job arrives, all the compute nodes in the cluster are examined to determine the node that gives the earliest completion time for the job. When computing the expected completion time of a job on a node, MCT takes into account the files already available on the node and files which be available on the compute node in future due to staging of data caused by the currently executing job on the node, as well as the completion time of the currently assigned jobs to that node. Hence, MCT may discard data locality and assign a new job to node which does not have any of its files cached because the wait times on the nodes with which the job have very good file locality may be high.

Switching algorithm (SA): The MET heuristic has a potential drawback in that it can lead to load imbalance across nodes by assigning many more jobs to some node than to others since it blindly looks at data locality without considering possible load imbalance. The MCT heuristic assigns jobs to nodes to achieve earliest completion time thereby ensuring load balance but does not necessarily exploit data locality since it may not allocate a job to a node which already has its files cached due to excess waiting times on that node. SA heuristic is motivated by the fact that it is possible to use MET at the expense of load imbalance until a given threshold and then use MCT to smooth the load across the cluster. Similar to [10], let *ib* be the *load balance index* defined as $ib = load_{min}/load_{max}$ where $load_{min}$ and $load_{max}$ are the loads (completion time of the last job on that node) of minimum and maximum loaded nodes. We define two thresholds l and h. SA starts mapping jobs with MCT heuristic until the load balance index reaches to h, after that point it switches to MET and continues until load balance index decreases below l at that point it switches to MCT again and this cycle continues. In our experiments we have used $l = 0.3$ and $h = 0.7$. The goal of SA is to have a heuristic with the desirable properties of load balance as well as data locality optimization.

6   Experimental Results

We now present an experimental evaluation of the proposed strategies along with the MET, MCT, SA and JobDataPresent-DataLeastLoaded (JDPDLL) strategies. For evaluation, we used an application class: biomedical image analysis. We compared the performance of the various scheduling schemes under a varying set of scenarios covering multiple job-file sharing patterns and different distributions of job inter-arrival times.

6.1   Application Workloads

For the image analysis application, we implemented a program to emulate studies that involve analysis on images obtained from MRI and CT scans (captured on multiple days as follow-up studies). An image dataset consists of a series of 2D images obtained for a patient and is associated with meta-data describing patient and study related information (in our case, we used patient id and study id as the meta-data). Each image in a dataset is associated with an imaging modality and the date of image acquisition and stored in a separate file. An image analysis program can select a subset of images based on a set of patient ids and study ids, image modality, and a date range.

We evaluated the scheduling schemes using job traces where several aspects were varied: 1) job inter-arrival rate (to vary system load), 2) extent of file sharing among jobs, 3) temporal clustering characteristics of file-sharing behavior between jobs, and 4) burstiness of job arrivals.

We generated workloads with different degrees of file sharing among jobs: *high sharing*, *medium sharing*, and *low sharing*. The different degrees of sharing is achieved by varying the values of patient and time attributes across requests by different jobs. We generated workloads with 85%, 40%, and 10% overlap, on average, in terms of files requested by different jobs in the job trace for high, medium, and low overlap cases.

The dataset generated by the emulator corresponded to a dataset of 2000 patients and images acquired over several days from MRI and CT scans. Each job on an average accessed 6 files. The number of files accessed by a job varied from 4 to 10. The sizes of images were 4 MB and 64 MB for MRI and CT scans, respectively. The overall size of the dataset was around 2 Terabytes. Images for each patient were distributed among all the storage nodes in a round robin fashion.

The image analysis application typically involve computations equivalent of two floating point operations per word. We, therefore, emulated it with 2 FP operations per word and measured that this translates to a processing time of approximately 0.001s/MB of data in our test-bed[2].

6.2   Modeling the Load

In traditional compute-intensive job scheduling, the offered load on the system is calculated as:

$$OfferedLoad = \frac{\sum_{\forall i} Exec(j_i) \times n(j_i)}{P \times \max_{\forall i}(Arrival(j_i))} \tag{8}$$

where $n(j_i)$ represents the number of nodes allocated to a job j_i, P is the number of nodes in the system. In compute-intensive job scheduling, the *OfferedLoad* metric is entirely dependent on the job trace under consideration and is independent of the scheduling policy being employed. However, in the data-intensive scheduling scenario we are focusing on, the metric defined in

---

[2] It can be expected that when computation time dominates the overall execution time, the traditional job scheduling strategies would work well. The CPU power and memory bandwidth are increasing very rapidly and faster than the bandwidth of I/O devices. With such a trend, the I/O cost will become more pronounced thus entailing the need to develop scheduling algorithms which target data intensive applications.

Equation 8 is no longer dependent only on the job trace but is also a function of the scheduling policy. This is because in the data-intensive scenario, the job execution times are not fixed. Instead, they vary with time due to staging of files by previously run jobs and also vary based on the node allocated to the job because of varying degrees of locality. Therefore, the job execution times depend upon the scheduling policy. To address this issue, we propose the following new characterization of load which is dependent only on the characteristics of the job trace and is independent of the scheduling policy.

Let ArrivalRate be the job arrival rate in Jobs/sec. Let ServiceRate be the expected Job service rate in Jobs/sec. The expected load is defined as follows.

$$Load = \frac{ArrivalRate}{ServiceRate} \tag{9}$$

Let us consider a trace of N jobs, where each job has an associated set of file transfers. Let the set of files needed by job j_i be F_i.

Let $AvgExectime$ denote the average of the execution times over all the jobs.

$$AvgExecTime = \frac{1}{N} \times \sum_{\forall i} EstimatedExec(j_i) \tag{10}$$

The $EstimatedExec$ time is same as calculated based on the probabilistic model explained in Section 4.2. To achieve an overall load of 1, The time of arrival of the last arriving job $TLarrival$ in the system is calculated as follows.

$$TLarrival = AvgExectime \times \frac{N}{P} \tag{11}$$

To summarize, we first determine the arrival time of the last job by using the information about the files accessed by each job so as to achieve a load value of 1. We then generate job traces with different values of load by varying the number of jobs which arrive over a fixed period of time. The modeling of load is based on estimated execution times which are based on a probabilistic model as shown in equation 6. In reality, some jobs will require a lower actual execution time than their expected execution time if some needed files are locally available since they were staged by previously executed jobs. On the other hand, the execution time may be higher in reality, due to contention at the storage server node for file transfer.

6.3   Modeling the Arrival Process

We model the arrival process as a Poisson random process and evaluate it with two distributions corresponding to different job orderings - clustered distribution and random distribution. Clustered distribution refers to the case where jobs sharing files among themselves occur closer together in time. Random distribution refers to the case where jobs come in any random order. Here, the arrival times of file-sharing jobs may be widely separated from each other over time. We also model the arrival times using the model proposed by Lublin [9].

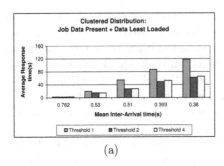
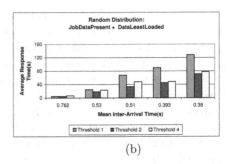

(a)   (b)

Fig. 5. Performance of *Job Data Present* coupled with *Data Least Loaded* under various replication thresholds

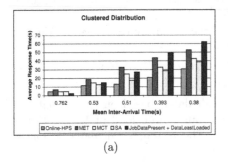
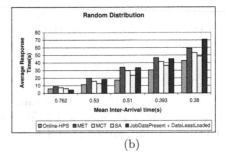

(a)   (b)

Fig. 6. Average Response time achieved by different algorithms for the (a) Clustered Distribution and (b) Random Distribution

The Lublin model is based on analysis of different production logs and uses statistical methods in order to achieve a good match of synthetic traces and actual trace data. The job arrival model takes into account both the stationary arrival process during peak hours and also the daily cycle. Since the model is based on long-running jobs from production supercomputer installations, we scaled down the arrival times to reduce the overall time to run our experiments.

6.4   Performance Evaluation on a Cluster

We conducted our experiments using a memory/storage cluster at the Department of Biomedical Informatics at the Ohio State University. The cluster consists of 64 nodes with an aggregate 0.5 TBytes of physical memory and 48TB of disk storage. These nodes are connected to each other through Infiniband.

One of the comparison schemes - JDPDLL - uses a critical "threshold" parameter to decide when a file should be replicated at another node. We first ran JDPDLL with different values of the replication threshold parameter. Figure 5 shows the variation in performance. The replication threshold represents the minimum number of references to a file by a compute node needed to trigger a replication of that file to a least-loaded node. Three different threshold

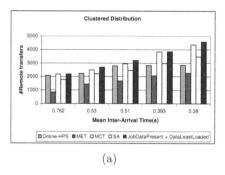 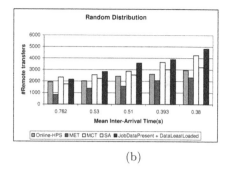

(a)   (b)

Fig. 7. Number of remote file transfers in different algorithms for the (a) Clustered Distribution and (b) Random Distribution

values were used: 1, 2 and 4. Figure 5 show that the choice of the threshold has a significant effect on the performance of this algorithm - there is a trade off between benefits of increased replication and the storage node end-point contention caused by an increasing number of dynamic data replications. In our experiments, we noted that a threshold value of 2 gave the best results and therefore this threshold is used for comparing the performance of this scheme against others.

Figure 6 shows the relative performance of the various scheduling schemes in terms of the average response time. These experiments were conducted using 4 compute nodes and 4 storage nodes. The number of jobs in the traces used for this experiment varied from 800 to 1600 and the time of arrival of the last job in each trace was around 600 secs. The value of load based on our characterization as explained in Section 6.2 varied from being around 1 for the 800 job trace to around 2 for the 1600 job trace. Each compute node used for this experiment had an available space of 15GB. The figures show that hypergraph-partitioning scheme (Online-HPS) performs better than the other schemes in most of the cases. This is because it models the inter-job affinity due to file-sharing and clusters jobs that share files transfers transfer of the same file multiple times. The benefit of the proposed scheme is higher as the inter-arrival times decrease since the partitioning scheme has information about more jobs at its disposal and it exploits this information to make more informed global decisions. The base schemes MCT, MET, SA, and JDPDLL consider one job at a time when making local greedy job mapping decisions and therefore do not take into account the implicit inter-job affinities due to file sharing.

At very low loads, JDPDLL performs the best since the average inter-arrival times are high and there are significant idle periods during which file replication occurs without interfering with other file transfers. of storage node end-point of both the job play a job-inter arrival time decreases, the performance of JDPDLL deteriorates compared to Online-HPS because the file replication activity causes contention with I/O from jobs reading input files from the storage nodes. The effect of end-point contention becomes more and more significant as the system load increases.

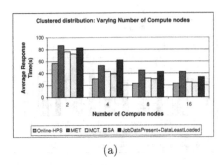
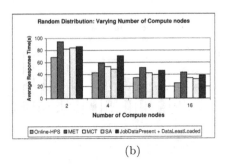

(a)   (b)

Fig. 8. (a) Average Response time achieved by the various algorithms with varying number of compute nodes for the (a) Clustered Distribution and (b) Random Distribution

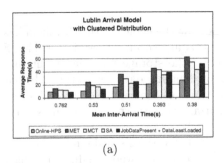
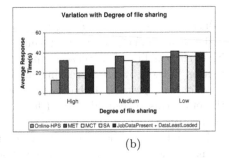

(a)   (b)

Fig. 9. (a) Performance of the various algorithms under the Lublin arrival model and (b) Performance of the different algorithms with variation in the degree of file sharing across jobs

Figure 7 shows the number of remote file transfers for all the algorithms for the same set of experiments as shown in Figure 6. As might be expected, Online-HPS causes fewer remote transfers compared to MCT, SA and JDPDLL. This is because it attempts to cluster together jobs that share files, thereby reducing the need for multiple transfers of the same file. The MET heuristic results in the least number of remote file transfers over all the schemes. This is because it maps each job to a node with which the job has maximum affinity in terms of the files already cached on it and required by the job. However, while doing so, it does not model the queue wait times at each node, thereby causing severe load imbalance across the nodes. Therefore, it gives the worst average response time in spite of being the best in terms of minimizing the remote file transfers.

To analyze the scalability of the proposed scheme with respect to the number of compute nodes, we ran experiments with the high overlap workload consisting of 1600 jobs. The number of compute nodes were varied from 2 to 16. These experiments were run using 4 storage nodes. Figure 8 shows the results with varying number of compute nodes. As is seen from the figure, Online-HPS achieves the best performance in terms of average response time in all the cases.

Figure 9(a) shows the relative performance of the various scheduling schemes in terms of the average response time by employing the Lublin arrival model to generate the job inter-arrival times. The results show that Online-HPS consistently performs well compared to the other schemes. The relative performance improvement under the Lublin model is higher compared to the traces modeling a Poisson arrival process. With the bursty nature of job arrival with the Lublin arrival process, the partitioning heuristic makes better job allocation decisions during bursts where a large number of queued jobs are available and inter-job file affinities can be exploited.

Figure 9(b) shows the relative performance of the various scheduling schemes on job traces with different degrees of shared I/O among jobs. These experiments were conducted using 4 compute nodes and 4 storage nodes. The high overlap job had 1200 jobs with an average inter-arrival time of 0.51. The medium and low overlap workloads had 800 and 400 jobs, respectively. These workloads were generated to have a uniform value of expected load. However, in reality, the medium and low overlap workloads took a longer time to execute since endpoint contention became more significant as the degree of file sharing decreased (due to increase in the number of remote file transfers). The results in Figure 9(b) show that the benefit of the Online-HPS scheme is greatest for the high overlap workload and reduces as the degree of overlap decreases.

7   Conclusions

This paper proposes a novel hypergraph based dynamic scheduling heuristic for a stream of dynamically arriving independent I/O intensive jobs. The approach is based on a run-time hypergraph based modeling of the system state, followed by locality-aware and load balanced mapping and scheduling of jobs onto the compute nodes. The performance results obtained on a coupled compute/storage cluster show that it achieves significant performance improvement over previously proposed heuristics - *MET*, *MCT*, *SA* and *JobDataPresent* with *Data Least Loaded* - when there is a high degree of file sharing among jobs. The previous schemes do not explicitly consider inter-job dependences arising out of file-sharing and thus make local decisions based on greedy heuristics. The choice of the best scheduling algorithm for a particular scenario depends upon parameters such as inter-arrival times and inter-job file sharing. Under very lightly loaded conditions, when the average job inter-arrival time is high, data replication proves to be more beneficial if a good choice of replication threshold is made. As inter-arrival times decrease, the proposed approach, which takes an integrated view of scheduling of computation and data placement, outperforms the other heuristics.

References

1. H. Andrade, T. Kurc, A. Sussman, and J. Saltz. Scheduling multiple data visualization query workloads on a shared memory machine. In *Proceedings of the 2002 IEEE International Parallel and Distributed Processing Symposium (IPDPS 2002)*, Fort Lauderdale, FL, April 2002.

2. H. Casanova, G. Obertelli, F. Berman, and R. Wolski. The AppLeS parameter sweep template: User-level middleware for the grid. In *Proceedings of the 2000 ACM/IEEE SC00 Conference*, pages 75–76, 2000.

3. H. Casanova, D. Zagorodnov, F. Berman, and A. Legrand. Heuristics for scheduling parameter sweep applications in grid environments. In *Proceedings of the 9th Heterogeneous Computing Workshop (HCW'00)*, pages 349–363, 2000.

4. U. V. Çatalyürek and C. Aykanat. Hypergraph-partitioning based decomposition for parallel sparse-matrix vector multiplication. *IEEE Transactions on Parallel and Distributed Systems*, 10(7):673–693, 1999.

5. R. Jain, K. Somalwar, J. Werth, and J. Browne. Heuristics for scheduling I/O operations. *IEEE Transactions on Parallel and Distributed Systems*, 8(3):310–320, Mar 1997.

6. A. Kavas, D. Er-El, and D. G. Feitelson. Using multicast to pre-load jobs on the parpar cluster. *Parallel Computing*, 27(3):315–327, 2001.

7. G. Khanna, N. Vydyanathan, T. Kurc, U. Catalyurek, P. Wyckoff, J. Saltz, and P. Sadayappan. A hypergraph partitioning based approach for scheduling of tasks with batch-shared I/O. In *Proceedings of the 5th IEEE/ACM International Symposium on Cluster Computing and the Grid (CCGrid 2005)*, May 2005.

8. D. Kotz. Disk-directed i/o for mimd multiprocessors. *ACM Transactions on Computer Systems*, 15(1):41–74, 1997.

9. U. Lublin and D. G. Feitelson. The workload on parallel supercomputers: modeling the characteristics of rigid jobs. *J. Parallel Distrib. Comput.*, 63(11):1105–1122, 2003.

10. M. Maheswaran, S. Ali, H. J. Siegel, D. A. Hensgen, and R. F. Freund. Dynamic matching and scheduling of a class of independent tasks onto heterogeneous computing systems. In *Heterogeneous Computing Workshop (HCW'99)*, pages 30–44, Apr. 1999.

11. M. Mehta, V. Soloviev, and D. J. DeWitt. Batch scheduling in parallel database systems. In *Proceedings of the 9th International Conference on Data Engineering (ICDE 1993)*, Vienna, Austria, 1993.

12. H. Mohamed and D. Epema. An evaluation of the close-to-files processor and data co-allocation policy in multiclusters. In *2004 IEEE International Conference on Cluster Computing*, pages 287–298. IEEE Society Press, 2004.

13. K. Ranganathan and I. Foster. Decoupling computation and data scheduling in distributed data-intensive applications. In *Proceedings of the Eleventh IEEE Symposium on High Performance Distributed Computing (HPDC)*, Edinburgh, Scotland, July 2002.

14. D. Thain, J. Bent, A. Arpaci-Dusseau, R. Arpaci-Dusseau, and M. Livny. Pipeline and batch sharing in grid workloads. In *Proceedings of High-Performance Distributed Computing (HPDC-12)*, pages 152–161, Seattle, Washington, June 2003.

Volunteer Computing on Clusters

Deepti Vyas and Jaspal Subhlok

Department of Computer Science, University of Houston, Houston, TX 77204

{dvyas,jaspal}@cs.uh.edu

Abstract. Clusters typically represent a homogeneous, well maintained pool of high-end computation resources. This makes them particularly attractive for volunteer computing, where unused compute cycles are utilized for scientific guest applications. Cluster nodes are not idle as often as public PCs, but they are frequently underutilized while actively executing parallel applications. Hence, fully exploiting clusters for volunteer computing requires the ability to efficiently and invisibly steal the unused cycles at a fine grain from the currently running host applications, without slowing them down. In this paper we present measurements on a production compute cluster that show long periods of CPU and memory underutilization patterns that could be used to execute guest applications. In our experiments with NAS benchmarks on a small Linux cluster, cycle stealing led to a 3.6% average slowdown of host applications in the best case. This was accompanied by an overall improvement in the system throughput of 38%, when progress of the guest applications was included. We introduce simple guidelines on using clusters for volunteer computing. We also argue for the support of "zero priority" processes in OS schedulers which could virtually eliminate the impact of volunteer computing on host applications.

1 Introduction

Volunteer computing, also referred to as public-resource computing or global computing, is based on exploiting unused cycles on ordinary desktop computers. The concept was pioneered by SETI@home [1], and is being increasingly employed to solve important real life problems. BOINC [2,3], a framework to support volunteer computing, is being used by a variety of scientific simulation projects such as protein folding, climate prediction, and biomedical computing. Condor [4] pioneered the employment of idle periods on organizational desktop systems for useful computing. We use the term volunteer computing for all scenarios where a low priority guest application can run on unused resources without significantly impacting high priority host applications. Examples of other projects with similar goals include Entropia [5], OpenMosix [6], and GridMP [7]. Availability of computation and storage resources that can be effectively employed for volunteer computing has been studied in [8,9].

A growing source of computation power today is compute clusters consisting of 10s to 1000s of processors. In addition to the high performance computing centers, it is becoming increasingly common for individual computational scientists and research groups to maintain their own clusters. In our estimate the combined compute power of all clusters on our campus (University of Houston) is comparable to the combined compute power of all desktops on campus, and we believe this is not uncommon.

E. Frachtenberg and U. Schwiegelshohn (Eds.): JSSPP 2006, LNCS 4376, pp. 161–175, 2007.

Computation clusters are particularly attractive for volunteer computing for a number of reasons.

- Clusters are typically built from high end computing and communication components.
- Clusters typically offer a homogeneous and well maintained pool of processors.
- While many supercomputing centers are heavily used, many clusters are also frequently idle, although the usage of a typical cluster node is certainly higher than a typical home PC. A recent study [10] of one group of clusters for scientific research found that their average usage varied between 7% and 22%.

In this paper we empirically demonstrate the following additional properties of cluster behavior that are relevant to volunteer computing.

1. CPU usage on clusters is frequently not close to the maximum while they are executing parallel scientific applications. The reason is that synchronization delays are fundamental to parallel processing, and increase as a fixed size problem is scaled up to a larger number of processors. For illustration, our experiments with NAS class B parallel benchmarks on 4 nodes show that their average CPU utilization varied from 53% to 100% as listed in Table 1. Further, the average speedup from 4 nodes (8 threads) to 8 nodes (16 threads) was 1.51 implying that the added 4 nodes were used only half as efficiently as the first 4 nodes. Other classes of applications, such as sparse matrix computations, are fundamentally more prone to synchronization delays due to load imbalance. We report on measured usage of a production cluster at the University of Houston that shows average CPU utilization of 64% even though applications are running on the nodes almost the entire time.
2. Usage of cluster nodes shows significant predictability, i.e., computation behavior in the recent past is a good predictor of the usage in the near future. The reason is that clusters are typically employed for long running scientific applications, and node usage for a single application is usually similar over the course of execution.

Table 1. Average CPU utilization of Class B NAS benchmarks on 4 cluster nodes

Benchmark	BT	CG	EP	FT	LU	MG	SP
CPU utilization (%)	90	65	100	53	94	73	81

Sometimes, techniques like backfilling [11,12] and interstitial computing [13] are used to increase the cluster utilization by scheduling small jobs on idle nodes. Since free cycles are available on many clusters only at a fine grain, a cluster is far more attractive for volunteer computing if guest applications can execute when CPU and memory are being underutilized, not just when the nodes are idle. Scheduling support for such fine-grained cycle stealing has been studied in [14,15,16]. However, the impact of resource sharing within a cluster node is difficult to predict although related research has addressed some aspects [17,18].

This paper focuses on fine-grained cycle stealing on Linux, which is the operating system of choice for cluster computing. We demonstrate that execution of low priority guest applications only have a small impact on regular host applications. We also discuss how various system and application factors affect the slowdown of host applications. This information, along with the fact that cluster usage shows significant predictability, helped us develop guidelines for employing volunteer computing on clusters that can minimize the impact on host applications while maximizing the benefit to guest applications. We argue that fine-grain cycle stealing on clusters with negligible impact on host applications is possible, but would require simple changes to the Linux scheduler.

The paper is organized as follows. Section 2 presents results on CPU and memory utilization of a production cluster. Section 3 presents results on cycle-stealing on a Linux cluster and its dependence on system and application factors. Section 4 outlines our approach to volunteer computing on clusters and recommends beneficial changes to OS schedulers, and section 5 contains conclusions.

2   Utilization of Clusters

The study presented in this section empirically measures the CPU and memory utilization on cluster nodes when they are busy executing scientific applications. Performance data was collected from a Beowulf cluster at the High Performance Computing Center at University of Houston, one of the most busy clusters on campus. The cluster consisted of 30 Intel Xeon dual processor nodes, running Linux (2.4.21 SMP kernel) with 2Gb RAM. The nodes were interconnected with a Gigabit ethernet network.

The data was collected over a period of 1 month and measurements were made at 5 minute intervals. The information was gathered from various files under the /proc file system of each node. CPU and memory utilization of representative nodes is plotted in Figure 1. Several small groups of nodes had very similar usage patterns. The nodes plotted in Figure 1 were not selected randomly, but chosen to represent different patterns. Figure 2 shows a zoomed in CPU utilization representing the first 12 hours of the periods covered in Figure 1 for two of the nodes. The graphs are in descending order of average CPU utilization within each figure.

Following are the main observations from this study of cluster utilization:

- The CPU utilization often shows fluctuation from point to point, as seen in Figure 2 which zooms in on the beginning part of the first two graphs in Figure 1. However, CPU utilization shows remarkable stability when it is considered over windows of several points. The average CPU utilization typically stays in a very narrow band from hours to days, and even weeks, in some cases, as seen in Figure 1. We presume this is a result of the same or similar applications running on the same group of nodes for extended periods of time.
- While nodes show long periods where CPU utilization is high, they also show long periods when CPU utilization is moderate or low. The average CPU utilization of a node varied between 25% to 85% with a mean around 64% and median around 65%.

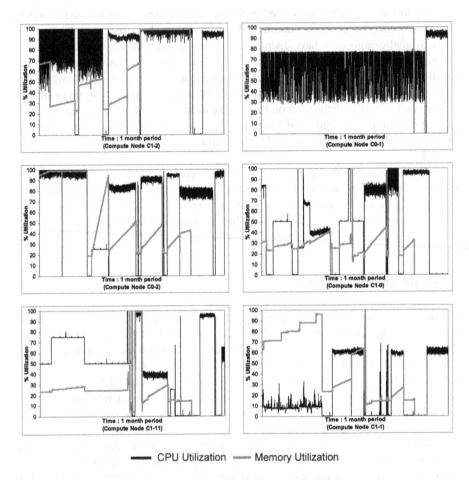

CPU Utilization ▬▬▬ Memory Utilization

Fig. 1. CPU and Memory utilization of sample nodes of a busy cluster plotted every 5 minutes over a period of 1 month (14 Jun 2005 to 16 Jul 2005)

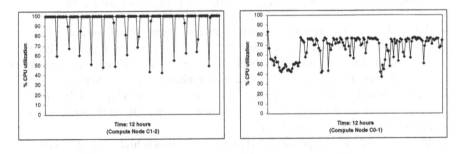

Fig. 2. CPU utilization for selected nodes plotted every 5 minutes over a period of 12 hours

- The memory utilization either stays steady or slowly increases linearly and then drops, over extended periods of time. The memory usage does not exhibit the short term fluctuations of CPU usage. However, we should point out that the reported memory utilization does not necessarily reflect the active set of pages and may include memory that has been released by the application, but is pending release at the system level.
- The average memory utilization can be close to 100% for a node for extended periods of time, but it is frequently around or well below 50% for extended periods of time. The average memory utilization of the nodes varied between 30% and 90% with a mean utilization around 52% and median utilization around 44%.

The main conclusion from this study, that is relevant to volunteer computing, is that cluster nodes show long and predictable periods of low CPU and memory utilization. The implication is that a substantial fraction of resources are available for volunteer computing, and when a scenario with good resource availability is identified, it is likely to continue for hours to days. The reason for such behavior is that clusters are typically employed for long running scientific applications. Hence, even though this study was limited, we expect the conclusions to be valid for other clusters employed for parallel scientific computing.

As pointed out earlier, the particular cluster that was monitored is known to be heavily utilized. The purpose was to investigate available resources while applications are running. Of course, if a cluster node is idle, it is an even more attractive option for volunteer computing (although perhaps not as predictable). The usage of clusters is likely to be higher than the average desktop, and indeed major supercomputing centers are known to be very busy. However, our observation is that smaller clusters often have considerable idle periods. A recent study of a 5 cluster research environment observed that the average time a system was busy ranged from 7.3% to 22% and a large fraction of jobs had a very small memory requirement [10].

We summarize this discussion as follows:

1. Many clusters nodes are idle and not running any applications a substantial fraction of the time. Of course, these can be directly exploited for volunteer computing.
2. When cluster nodes are busy running applications, a substantial fraction of the memory and CPU resources are often not utilized for extended periods of time. These idle resources can be exploited with fine-grain cycle stealing making clusters even more attractive for volunteer computing.

3   Fine Grain Cycle Stealing on Clusters

A critical consideration in making a cluster available for volunteer computing is how a high priority host application will be affected when a low priority guest application is stealing unused cycles for execution. Ideally, there should be no impact at all; the guest process should be scheduled only when the host process is blocked, and the guest process should be evicted as soon as the host process is ready to execute again. However, this is difficult to achieve for fine-grained cycle stealing when a host and guest application are executing concurrently because one of the goals of commercial operating system schedulers is to prevent starvation of low priority processes. Research has shown that it is possible to construct schedulers where the impact on the host application is negligible [14,16]. However, we are most interested in volunteer computing with mainstream operating systems since installing a new scheduler is not likely to be acceptable. All our experimentation is on Linux since that is the dominant cluster operating system.

The goal of the experiments was to see how to best run guest applications on Linux with minimum impact on host applications. Dependence on system factors such as priority mechanism and scheduler versions, as well as dependence on characteristics of host and guest applications, are also analyzed.

3.1   Experimental Setup

Our experimental environment consists of a ten-node cluster. Each node has 1GB of main memory and dual Pentium Xeon processors running at 1.8 GHz. The nodes are connected through a 1 Gbps ethernet switch. The cluster was running Rocks 4.0 Beta and a MPICH 1.2.6 version of MPI. This configuration is representative of small and midsize clusters employed for scientific computing.

To achieve fine-grained cycle stealing, the guest applications were run simultaneously with host applications, but at a lower priority using the UNIX *nice* mechanism. The execution times of the host and guest applications were measured when run individually (dedicated mode), and when run simultaneously (shared mode). Percentage *slowdown*, defined as the percentage increase in execution time when executing in shared mode as compared to dedicated mode, is used to quantify and compare the effect of sharing in different scenarios.

NAS Class B parallel benchmarks were used as host applications and guest applications. Unless otherwise noted, the experiments were run on 4 (dual processor) nodes, and each node ran 2 threads of the host application at normal priority (nice = 0) and 1 thread of the guest application at lowest priority (nice = 19). NAS benchmark EP (Embarrassingly Parallel) was used as the default guest application. The EP program has virtually no communication, and hence it represents a sequential compute intensive application.

3.2   Slowdown on Linux

We study the slowdown of host applications when running with a guest application on Linux, and examine how the slowdown can be minimized. The slowdown for the NAS benchmarks running as host applications, with the compute intensive EP benchmark as the guest application, is shown in Figure 3. Results are shown for Linux 2.4 and 2.6 kernels, as well as "2.6(tuned)", that will be explained later in this section.

The slowdown of the host application on Linux 2.4 kernel was relatively high when running concurrently with a minimum priority guest application, averaging 25% for the benchmark suite. This validates similar observations in [14,16]. As seen from Figure 3, the 2.6 kernel performs significantly better than the 2.4 kernel in this regard. The average slowdown is reduced from approximately 25% to 16%, but is still simply too large to be acceptable. This was surprising since the new O(1) scheduler in the 2.6 kernel was designed to respect the *nice* priorities more strictly.

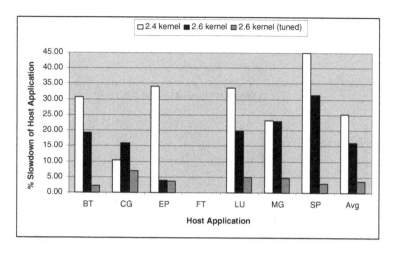

Fig. 3. Comparison of percent slowdown of the host application in shared mode when executing on different Linux kernels

Detailed investigation revealed the following. Unlike the 2.4 kernel, the 2.6 kernel has separate run queues for each of the two processors on a single node. In our scenario, one queue will have two processes, and the other queue will have one process, since there are 3 active processes (two host processes and one guest process). In some situations, both the host processes would get assigned to the same processor queue, with the one guest process assigned to the other processor's run queue. Clearly, this would lead to a nominal 50% slowdown of the host processes. The situation will eventually get corrected as the queues are periodically "load balanced". However, the default load balancing frequency is 200 milliseconds, implying that a phase of 50% slowdown could last for a significant amount of computing time. In order to mitigate this effect, we decreased the period between the invocation of the kernel load balancer to 10 milliseconds. Linux kernel 2.6 with this setting is referred to as "kernel 2.6 tuned" in Figure 3. We observe a dramatically reduced slowdown of the host application - down from an average of 16% to 3.6%. We believe that these are the lowest reported slowdowns for host applications when sharing the processors with a guest application on a widely deployed cluster operating system.

We would like to point out that "tuning" the Linux 2.6 kernel as discussed above technically contradicts our goal that an unmodified mainstream operating system should be employed. However, the tuning we have done is to mitigate the impact of an undesirable and unexpected side-effect of a new Linux feature. Hence we consider it to be a "performance bug fix" and expect that it will not be needed with continued development of Linux.

In the results discussed above, the host was assigned normal priority (nice = 0) while the guest was assigned the lowest priority available on the system (nice = 19). The lowest priority for the guest is expected to yield the least slowdown for the host, and this was validated. However, it would appear logical that the host application should be assigned the highest priority (nice = -20), rather than normal priority (nice = 0), to minimize the slowdown. The measured slowdown with normal and highest priority for the host is shown in Figure 4.

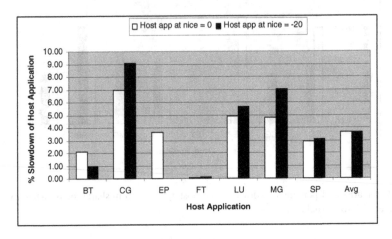

Fig. 4. Comparison of percent slowdown of the host application when running at normal priority (nice = 0) vs. when running at the highest priority (nice = -20) in shared mode

The slowdown was reduced dramatically with a higher priority when the host application was EP (the only application in the suite with no communication). Surprisingly the slowdown *increased* significantly for some of the communicating applications, in particular, CG (Conjugate Gradients) and MG (Multigrid). The average slowdown across the benchmark suite was virtually the same. The reasons for the higher slowdown for some applications are not understood and need to be investigated further. Related work has shown an increase in slowdown for some communicating applications when a larger time slice is given to all applications [18]. However, an increase in priority should result in a larger time slice only for the host application, so there is no apparent reason for its slowdown. Overall, there seems to be little benefit in raising the priority of the host applications.

Linux also supports a *realtime* priority level which appears attractive for host jobs for volunteer computing. However, this priority level blocks interrupts that are necessary for execution of parallel programs. Most applications in our benchmark were unable to complete execution with realtime priority.

3.3   Impact on Cluster Throughput

The goal in volunteer computing is for a guest application to make progress without any significant negative impact on the host application. Until now we have focused on analyzing the impact on the host application. We now study the progress of guest applications. However, instead of directly reporting on the performance of guest applications, we report on the increase in system throughput, which is a measure of the overall benefit of fine-grained cycle stealing, as a consequence of a guest application executing in addition to the host application. Any increase in throughput is due to the work that is accomplished by the guest application, after any negative impact on the host application has been accounted for.

We define *normalized throughput* as the number of units of work completed per unit time on the cluster. The normalized throughput when a cluster is executing a single application is always considered to be 1. In shared mode both the host application and the guest application run simultaneously. Depending on the rate at which the host and guest applications proceed while sharing nodes, the normalized throughput can be greater than or less than 1. The normalized throughput of the cluster in shared mode is represented as follows:

$$Normalized\ throughput = \frac{Th_D}{Th_S} + \frac{Tg_D}{Tg_S}$$

where

Th_D: Execution time of the host application in dedicated mode
Tg_D: Execution time of the guest application in dedicated mode
Th_S: Execution time of the host application in shared mode
Tg_S: Execution time of the guest application in shared mode

Figure 5 shows the percentage increase in the normalized throughput of the system when each host application is run in shared mode with EP as the guest application, as compared to dedicated execution of the host application.

We observe that there is a significant system throughput improvement that averages 38% for the benchmark suite. This comes at the cost of a relatively low 3.6% slowdown of the host applications. This demonstrates that a significant number of unused CPU cycles are available when the host application is executing in dedicated mode, and the guest application was able to utilize them successfully in shared mode.

The throughput improvement is the lowest for EP, LU (LU Matrix Factorization), and FT (Fast Fourier Transforms) benchmarks. We recall from Table 1 that these are the

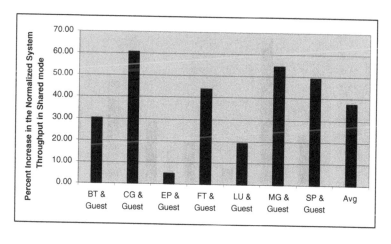

Fig. 5. Percent increase in the normalized system throughput with different benchmarks as host applications

benchmarks that show the highest CPU utilization in dedicated execution, all of them over 90%. Hence fewer CPU cycles were available for the guest application in these cases. If these applications were removed from the suite, the average increase in system throughput would be 52%. This is relevant, since execution of the guest applications can be managed to avoid periods of high CPU usage or other system activity.

3.4 Parallel Guest Applications

Volunteer computing with communicating parallel guest applications is an important challenge [19] that can be met more effectively with clusters. In order to investigate this possibility, we performed a set of experiments with the CG benchmark, which is the most communication intensive application in the NAS benchmark suite, as the guest application. This is in contrast to EP which has negligible communication. "Tuned" Linux 2.6 kernel, as discussed earlier, was employed in these experiments. Figure 6 presents a comparison of the slowdown of the host application with CG and EP as guest applications.

We observe that the slowdown for all host applications, with the exception of EP, is considerably higher when CG is the guest application. As seen in Figure 6, the average percentage slowdown of the host application when running with CG as guest, as compared to EP as guest, increases from 3.6% to 9%. One obvious reason is that EP being completely CPU bound just competes for CPU with the host application, while CG being communication intensive competes for CPU and network resources. However, a possibly more significant factor is the impact of the synchronization structure of the host and guest applications. CG being a communication intensive guest application is frequently blocked for communication, and hence cannot use the free CPU cycles when the host application itself is blocked for communication. As a result, the dynamic

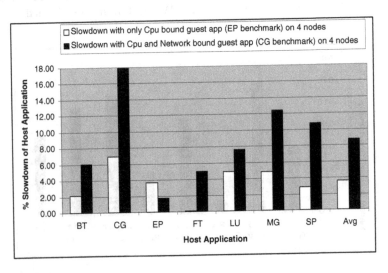

Fig. 6. Comparison of percent slowdown of the host application when running with the guest application EP vs. when running with the guest application CG

priority of the guest application rises and it is more likely to force an eviction of the host application later. We note that host application EP slows down less with CG as guest versus EP as guest. This is not surprising as they do not compete for communication resources. Further, unlike the case of EP as guest, CG as guest will sometimes not claim a proportional share of the CPU time since it can be blocked on communication.

The conclusion is that high communication parallel applications are not suitable for execution as guests on the current Linux operating system. However, parallel applications with moderate or low communication may be appropriate for volunteer computing.

3.5 Scalability

One of the factors that exacerbates the slowdown of a host application in shared execution is synchronization. When one node is slowed down due to sharing, it can have a cascading slowdown effect on the others. This effect is likely to be larger when the number of executing threads is higher. In order to investigate this, we compared the slowdown associated with execution on 4 nodes (8 threads) and 8 nodes (16 threads). The results are plotted in Figure 7.

The primary observation is that the the slowdown is slightly higher for a larger number of threads; the average slowdown was 3.6% for 8 threads and 4.5% for 16 threads. While this is encouraging, more experiments are needed to establish the impact of guest applications on large clusters.

4 Discussion

The following is a list of observations that are relevant for volunteer computing on clusters, based on the results in this paper and related research:

- Clusters show diverse usage patterns - many clusters are frequently idle.
- When a cluster is actively executing an application, a substantial fraction of the CPU and memory resources are often not used.
- The usage pattern of a cluster node can be similar for hours to days.
- If a host application uses most of the available CPU resources, there is little benefit from running a guest application simultaneously.
- Only guest applications that are sequential or have low communication requirements can generally execute with minimal effect on the host applications.
- We have shown in related work [18] that memory usage has little relation to performance with sharing, but when the combined memory requirement of all executing threads approaches the total system memory, the performance can deteriorate sharply. While these results were collected for applications with equal priority, it is reasonable to conclude that both host and guest applications will not be able to execute effectively when their combined memory requirement exceeds available memory.

Based on these observations we present a set of guidelines for volunteer computing on clusters. Note that the above observations are based on a recent Linux release.

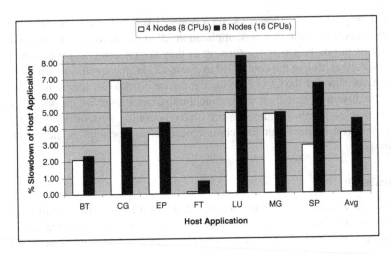

Fig. 7. Comparison of percent slowdown of the host application when running on 4 nodes vs. 8 nodes

Operating system support for zero priority processes that do not compete for resources can considerably ease the task of volunteer computing on clusters, and is discussed later in this section.

4.1 Guidelines for Volunteer Computing on Clusters

In the scenarios in which we performed our experiments, the slowdown of the host applications with a sequential guest application averages around 3.6% and the improvement in throughput (indicating the progress of the guest application) averages around 38%. However, in individual cases, the slowdown can be higher and improvement in throughput significantly lower. With the following basic considerations, we can limit the use of volunteer computing to scenarios where the cost is minimized and the benefit is maximized:

1. Only consider sequential applications and parallel applications with a low communication bandwidth as guest applications. While this condition cannot be enforced by a system, such applications will get very poor service and hence the procedure should be self correcting. Note that current volunteer computing frameworks are generally applicable only to "embarrassingly parallel" or "bag of tasks" applications.
2. Monitor the CPU, memory, and network usage on volunteered cluster nodes. Consider invoking a guest application only when a stable usage pattern emerges.
3. If the usage pattern shows CPU or network or memory usage above preset thresholds (say 85% for CPU) then do not invoke the guest application.
4. Before invocation, verify that the available memory exceeds the memory requirement of the guest application by a significant threshold.
5. If the resource usage pattern of the machine shows a significant change, suspend the guest application and restart after examining the criteria listed above.

Employing these guidelines will reduce the scenarios when volunteer computing can be applied on a cluster node, but also reduce the cost and increase the benefits when it is applied. Typically the resources available for volunteer computing exceed the demand, and the challenge is to exploit those resources effectively. Hence, eliminating potentially unattractive nodes is not a major concern.

4.2   Case for Zero Priority Processes

Ideally a guest application should only use idle resources and have no impact on the host applications. Our experiments demonstrate that the latest version of the Linux operating system allows the guest applications to execute with a small impact on executing the host applications, but it is not negligible. Volunteer computing on clusters will be considerably simplified with support for *zero priority* processes that would not consume any resources that other processes can potentially use. Such a zero priority process will never be scheduled so long as a higher priority process is able to execute, and would immediately relinquish the CPU when a higher priority process is ready to execute. Developing such schedulers is technically feasible and prototypes have been demonstrated in other research [14,16]. However, widely deployed operating systems have a concept of fairness that implies that even the lowest priority process must get a certain share of resources and should not starve. Support for zero priority processes, that never compete for resources, can be done without compromising other design goals of an operating system, although a detailed discussion is beyond the scope of this paper. Fairness and starvation are not issues if a process is explicitly designated as zero priority, except to ensure freedom from deadlocks and any other unintended consequences.

There will always be some performance impact due to guest jobs - some factors, e.g., the overhead of warming the cache after a context switch, cannot be eliminated. However, with a well designed implementation of zero priority processes and a good model for volunteer computing, we believe that the slowdown of host jobs can be made negligible, possibly well below 1%, which increases the appeal of volunteer computing dramatically.

5   Conclusions

Computation clusters present a vast and attractive resource of unused compute cycles that can be used for volunteer computing. Based on a study of a production cluster, we show that long periods of significant CPU and memory underutilization are common. However, utilizing these free cycles for guest applications, while other applications are executing, is a challenge. Based on our experiments on the most recent version of Linux, we show that these cycles can be exploited with only a small slowdown of the host applications. The contribution of this paper is to present evidence that clusters are attractive for volunteer computing and can be used efficiently for that purpose. The paper also offers guidelines on how slowdown of the host applications can be minimized and cluster throughput maximized for volunteer computing. Additional discussion emphasizes that simple support for zero priority processes will make the case of clusters for volunteer computing more compelling.

Acknowledgments

The staff at the High Performance Computing Center at University of Houston provided us with access to the computation clusters that made this project possible. We would like to thank all members of our research group, in particular, Tsung-I Huang and Qiang Xu, for their contributions to this work. We would also like to thank the Linux kernel developers and Rocks developers for their support. In particular, we want to thank Con Kolivas for providing and improving the smp nice patch. Finally, the anonymous referees made several suggestions that helped improve this paper.

This material is based upon work supported by the National Science Foundation under Grant No. ACI-0234328 and Grant No. CNS-0410797. Any opinions, findings, and conclusions or recommendations expressed in this material are those of the authors and do not necessarily reflect the views of the National Science Foundation. Support was also provided by University of Houston's Texas Learning and Computation Center.

References

1. Anderson, D., Cobb, J., Korpela, E., Lebofsky, M., Werthimer, D.: SETI@home: An experiment in public-resource computing. Communications of the ACM **45** (2002)
2. BOINC. (http://boinc.berkeley.edu/)
3. Anderson, D.: BOINC: A system for public-resource computing and storage. In: Fifth IEEE/ACM International Workshop on Grid Computing. (2004) 4–10
4. Litzkow, M., Livny, M., Mutka, M.: Condor - a hunter of idle workstations. In: 8th International Conference on Distributed Computing Systems. (1988) 104–111
5. Chien, A., Calder, B., Elbert, S., Bhatia, K.: Entropia: architecture and performance of an enterprise desktop grid system. Journal of Parallel and Distributed Computing **63** (2003) 597–610
6. OpenMosix. (http://openmosix.sourceforge.net/)
7. Grid MP. (http://ud.com/solutions/deploy/mp_enterprise.htm)
8. Anderson, D., Fedak, G.: The computation and storage potential of volunteer computing. In: Sixth IEEE International Symposium on Cluster Computing and the Grid. (2006)
9. Kondo, D., Taufer, M., Brooks, C., Casanova, H., Chien, A.: Characterizing and evaluating desktop grids: An empirical study. In: International Parallel and Distributed Processing Symposium (IPDPS'04). (2004)
10. Li, H., Groep, D., Wolters, L.: Workload characteristics of a multi-cluster supercomputer. In: 10th International Workshop on Job Scheduling Strategies for Parallel Processing. Springer Verlag (2004) 176–193
11. Zhang, Y., Franke, H., Moreira, J., Sivasubramaniam., A.: Improving parallel job scheduling by combining gang scheduling and backfilling techniques. In: 14th International Parallel and Distributed Processing Symposium. (2000)
12. Feitelson, D.G., Weil, A.M.: Utilization and predictability in scheduling the IBM SP2 with backfilling. In: 12th International Parallel Processing Symposium. (1998) 542–546
13. Kleban, S.D., Clearwater, S.H.: Interstitial computing: Utilizing spare cycles on supercomputers. In: IEEE International Conference on Cluster Computing. (2003)
14. Ryu, K., Hollingsworth, J.: Linger longer: fine-grain cycle stealing for networks of workstations. In: ACM/IEEE Conference on Supercomputing. (1998) 1–12
15. Ryu, K., Hollingsworth, J.: Resource policing to support fine-grain cycle stealing in networks of workstations. IEEE Transactions on Parallel and Distributed Systems **15** (2004) 878–892

16. Stiehr, G.: Using fine-grained cycle stealing to improve throughput, efficiency and response time on a dedicated cluster while maintaining quality of service. Master's thesis, Washington University (2004)
17. Weinberg, J., Snavely, A.: Symbiotic space-sharing on SDSC's DataStar system. In: 12th Workshop on Job Scheduling Strategies for Parallel Processing. (2006)
18. Ghanesh, M., Kumar, S., Subhlok, J.: Empirical evaluation of shared parallel execution on independently scheduled clusters. In: 1st International Workshop on Grid Performability. (2005)
19. Acharya, A., Edjlali, G., Saltz, J.: The Utility of Exploiting Idle Workstations for Parallel Computation. In: ACM SIGMETRICS International Conference on Measurement and Modeling of Computer Systems. (1997)

Load Balancing:
Toward the Infinite Network and Beyond

Javier Bustos-Jiménez[1,2,3], Denis Caromel[2], and José M. Piquer[1]

[1] Departamento de Ciencias de la Computación, Universidad de Chile. Blanco Encalada 2120,
Santiago, Chile
{jbustos,jpiquer}@dcc.uchile.cl
[2] INRIA Sophia-Antipolis, CNRS-I3S, UNSA. 2004, Route des Lucioles, BP 93, F-06902
Sophia-Antipolis Cedex, France
Denis.Caromel@sophia.inria.fr
[3] Escuela de Ingeniería Informática. Universidad Diego Portales Av. Ejercito 441, Santiago,
Chile

Abstract. We present a contribution on dynamic load balancing for distributed
and parallel object-oriented applications. We specially target peer-to-peer systems and their capability to distribute parallel computation. Using an algorithm
for active-object load balancing, we simulate the balance of a parallel application
over a peer-to-peer infrastructure. We tune the algorithm parameters in order to
obtain the best performance, concluding that our *IFL* algorithm behaves very well
and scales to large peer-to-peer networks (around 8,000 nodes).

1 Introduction

One of the most useful features of current distributed systems in the context of a desktop
Grid, is the ability to redistribute tasks among its processors. This requires a redistribution policy to gain in efficiency by dispatching the tasks in such a way that the resources
are used efficiently, i.e. minimising the average idle time of the processors and improving application performance. This technique is known as *load balancing* [1]. Moreover,
when the redistribution decisions are taken at runtime, it is called *dynamic load balancing*. With the objective of scaling up to very large scale Grid systems, we placed
ourselves in the context of using peer-to-peer (P2P) principles and frameworks. In this
work we use the definition of *Pure peer-to-peer (P2P)* [2]: each peer can be removed
from the network without any loss of network service.

In a previous work [3], we presented a P2P infrastructure developed within ProActive [4]. ProActive is an open-source Java middleware which aims to achieve seamless
programming for concurrent, parallel, distributed, and mobile computing, implementing the active-object programming model (see Section 2). In its P2P infrastructure, all
peers have to maintain a list of *"known nodes"* (also known as *acquaintances*). Initially,
when a fresh peer joins the network, it only knows peers from a list of potential network members. A peer inside the network will receive a fresh-peer request and it has
a certain probability of accepting the fresh peer as an acquaintance. If the fresh peer

E. Frachtenberg and U. Schwiegelshohn (Eds.): JSSPP 2006, LNCS 4376, pp. 176–191, 2007.

was accepted by the one inside the network, the latter forward the fresh-peer request to its own acquaintances. We exploited the P2P nature of this network in a randomised load-balancing algorithm and demonstrate that this approach performs better than a server-oriented scheme in a proprietary network [3].

Dynamic load balancing is a well-studied issue for distributed systems [5]. For instance, well-known load-balancing algorithms have been studied in the heterogeneous network context by Shivaratri, Krueger and Singhal [6] and in the P2P context by Roussopoulos and Baker [7]. However, these studies focus on balancing tasks (units of processing), while load-balancing of active objects is achieved by redistribution of queues.

Randomised load-balancing algorithms were popularised by work-stealing algorithms [8,9], where idle processors randomly choose another processor from which to "steal" work. A work-stealing algorithm aims to maintain all processors working, but its random nature causes the algorithm to respond slowly to overloading. Therefore, due to the fact that processors connected to a P2P network share their resources not only with the network but also with the processor owner, new constraints like reaction time against overloading and bandwidth usage become relevant [10].

Most of the research in load-balancing for P2P networks is based on a structured approach using a *distributed hash table* (DHT) [11], where each machine can be represented by several keys, and parallel applications are mapped into this DHT. As a consequence, load balancing becomes now a search problem on key/data spaces [12]. Our P2P infrastructure is unstructured and shared resource are computational nodes (JVMs). Therefore it is not necessary to identify resources uniquely as would be the case for P2P data. Another approach for load balancing on P2P environments is the use of *agents* which traverse the network equalising the load among them. The agents follow a model of an ant colony [13,14], *carrying* load among computers, and eventually making the system stable. Such a scheme focuses on load equalisation instead of the search of an optimal distribution. Our load balancing algorithm follows the same principles than MOSIX Distributed Operating System [15], but oriented to active objects, which are portable by definition and have no access to kernel calls. Moreover, information dissemination procedures are different: while MOSIX uses periodical randomised information sharing, we use on-demand information sharing because in [10] we demonstrate that no periodical information sharing provides scalability and updated load information [16] together.

In this paper we test this algorithm in a new setting: a simulated peer-to-peer network, trying to find its limits and analysing its behaviour. We show that the algorithm behaves very well but that some parameters need to be tuned for this kind of large networks.

This article is organised as follows. Section 2 presents ProActive as an implementation of *active-object programming model*. Section 3 explains the fundamentals of the randomised active-object load-balancing algorithm for P2P networks. Section 5 presents the simulated environment of our tests, the fine tuning of algorithm parameters, and the scalability tests. Finally, conclusions and future work are presented.

2   ProActive

The ProActive middleware is a Java library which aims to achieve seamless programming for concurrent, parallel, distributed and mobile computing. As it is built on top of the standard Java API, it does not require any modification of the standard Java execution environment, nor does it make use of a special compiler, pre-processor, or modified virtual machine.

The base model is a uniform *active-object* programming model. Each active object has its own control thread and can independently decide in which order to serve incoming method calls. Incoming method calls are automatically stored in a queue of pending requests (called a *service queue*). When the queue is empty, active objects wait for the arrival of a new request; this state is known as *wait-for-request*.

Active objects are accessible remotely via method invocation. Method calls with active objects are asynchronous with automatic synchronisation. This is provided by automatic *future objects* as a result of remote methods calls, and synchronisation is handled by a mechanism known as *wait-by-necessity* [17]. Another communication mechanism is the *group communication* model. Group communication allows triggering method calls on a distributed group of active objects with compatible type, dynamically generating a group of results [18].

ProActive provides a way to move any active object from any Java Virtual Machine (JVM) to another, called a *migration* mechanism [19]. An active object with its pending requests (method calls), futures, and passive (mandatory non-shared) objects may migrate from JVM to JVM through the *migrateTo(...)* primitive. The migration can be initiated from outside the active object through any public method, but it is the responsibility of the active object to execute the migration, this is known as *weak migration*. Automatic and transparent forwarding of requests and replies provide location transparency, as remote references toward active mobile objects remain valid.

3   IFL: A Randomised Load-Balancing of Active-Objects on P2P Networks

In a previous work [3] we exploited the results of Litzkow, Livny and Mutka, who reported that desktop processors are idle 80% of the time [20] (this value is reported up to 90% in 2005 [21,22]) and we followed the recommendations of [10] about minimisation of load-balancing messages to make a randomised algorithm of load-balancing. This algorithm, first called "Robin Hood" algorithm and later called "Inter-flops" (*IFL*) algorithm, is a sender-initiated scheme which use a minimal subset of the known peers to perform balance.

In this section we will present first the definitions used by the algorithm and then a description of original IFL algorithm and its extension for clustering of active objects.

3.1   Definitions

Assume $load_A$ is the usage percentage of processor A. Defining two thresholds, OT and UT ($OT > UT$), we say that a processor A is *overloaded* (resp. *underloaded*) if $load_A > OT$ (resp. $load_A < UT$). Additionally, aiming to minimise the number of migrations until a stable state in load-balancing, we use a *rank* value which gives the relative processing capacity of a node. Ranks and loads are stored locally by each node. The idea of using a *rank* to generate a total order relation among processors was popularised by the Matchmaking scheme [23] of *Condor* [20]. While Condor uses its rank to measure the desirability of a match, we used it to discard slow nodes at runtime.

3.2 Original Version of the IFL Algorithm

In a previous work [3], we have developed a load-balancing algorithm, which we called *IFL*. The *IFL* algorithm works as follows. Every time-step:

1. If a node (also known as *computation entity* or *processor*) is overloaded, it randomly chooses a minimal subset of (three, four or five of) its acquaintances. In Figure 1 (b) and (c), grey nodes represent the subset of acquaintances.
2. Only underloaded nodes who satisfy the rank criteria $requester\_rank < RB * my\_rank$ (where $RB \in [0,1]$ constant) will be able to reply the request. In Figure 1 (c), two nodes are discarded using this criteria (those marked by X).
3. Nodes that satisfy the criteria reply to the request. Then, the overloaded node will send an active object to the owner of the first received reply (Figure 1 (d)). We use this scheme because we want to maintain the active objects close to each other to avoid communication latency at runtime.
4. If no nodes satisfy the criteria, no balance is made during this time-step.

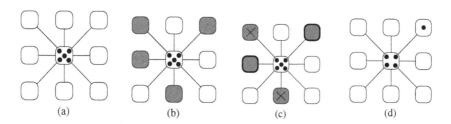

(a)   (b)   (c)   (d)

Fig. 1. Load-balancing algorithm for active-objects over Peer-to-Peer networks

This algorithm performs load balancing *only* until a stable state, reaching a local optimum of balance. If there are no overloaded nodes, no active object has incentive to migrate; thus, no incentive to search better machines (and increase speedup).

3.3 New Version of the IFL Algorithm

Considering that the communication scheme of ProActive is based in RMI that has a high-cost in bandwidth-usage and latency [24,25], we aimed to optimise the application performance by clustering active objects on the best qualified processors. Therefore, in this version of load balancing algorithm (the *IFL algorithm*), we add a work-stealing [1] step. Every time-step:

1. If a node is underloaded, it randomly chooses one of its acquaintances to which it sends a work-stealing request.
2. If the receiver satisfies the rank criteria $RS * requester\_rank > my\_rank$, it returns an active object to the caller.
3. If the node does not satisfy the criteria, no steal is made during this time-step.

Note that if we consider that each node made its first contact with a "near" peer (usually in the same physical network), it is more probable that stealing occurs between close nodes than remote ones.

4   Experimental Verification

To verify our theoretical reasoning, we experimented with a small-scale real laboratory environment. We tested the two versions of our algorithm (with and without work-stealing), we used Jacobi matrix calculus to solve a 3,600x3,600 matrix with 36 workers implemented as active objects (implementation details available in [3]). We run the test on a set of 25 of INRIA desktop computers, having 10 Pentium III 0.5 - 1.0 GHz, 9 Pentium IV 3.4GHz and 6 Pentium XEON 2.0GHz, all of them with a Linux operating system and connected by a 100 Mbps Ethernet switched network. Starting from random initial distributions, we measured the execution time of 1000 sequential calculus of Jacobi matrices.

For both versions we used as load index the CPU load and as rank the CPU speed. Also, using our knowledge of the lab networks, we experimentally defined the algorithm parameters as $OT = 0.8$ and $UT = 0.5$. We experimentally discovered that a value of RB between 0.5 and 0.9 produced similar performance. We explain this by the existence of a correlation between processing capacity and load state: it is highly probable to find a low capacity node overloaded than underloaded. Therefore, we fixed $RB = 0.7$. Also, given the primary results of Section 5.1, we experimentally defined $RS = 0.9$.

Figure 2 shows the mean execution time of the Jacobi application and the number of migrations. A low number of migrations corresponds to an initial distribution of active-objects near to an optimal state (local or global), and a high number of migrations corresponds to an initial distribution far from an optimal state. Also, the *mean time* performed by the Jacobi application *without* load balancing is represented by the horizontal line marked by (*), this value was obtained using a subset of the 10 best-ranked nodes, having the nodes full availability for Jacobi application. Note that this value is an approximation of the static optimal distribution, because all active objects have similar incoming service ratio.

Figure 2 shows that, for the first version of our algorithm, the presence of a local optimum attempts against a good performance of the application. For the second version, a performance near the global optimal state is reached for all migration counts.

In the next section we experiment *IFL* in the context of Desktop Grids to see if it can reach a near optimal state for a large number of nodes (around 8,000).

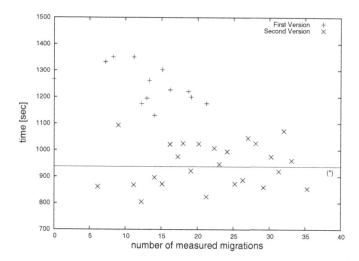

Fig. 2. Mean execution time for different number of migrations of the Jacobi Parallel Application, using the load balancing algorithm with and without work-stealing

5   Scaling Tests Using Simulation

In the study of Grids, one of the most important characteristics of nodes is its *processing capacity* [26,27]. In load-balancing, a function using both, processing capacity and amount of work that a node has to perform, determines if a node is on an overloaded or underloaded state. To have a reliable model of processing capacity, we made a statistical study of desktop computers registered at the Seti@home project [28]. This project aims to analyse the data obtained from the Arecibo Radio telescope, distributing units of data among personal computers and exploiting the processing capacity of up to 200, 000 processors distributed around the world to analyse the data [29]. We consider *Mflops* as a good metric to determine the processing capacity for parallel scientific calculus, because we are interested in processing balance, not data balance.

We grouped all desktop computers *Mflops* (d_r) in 30 clusters (C_t) using the following formula:

$$d_r \in C_t \; iif \; \lfloor \frac{r}{10^6} \rfloor = t$$

The resultant frequency histogram is shown in Figure 3.

Defining a normal distribution $nor(x)$ (equation (1)), we compared the real distribution against our $nor(x)$ model function using *Kolmogorov-Smirnov test statistics* (*KST*), giving us a value of $KST = 0.0605$. Therefore, we can deduce that using a level of significance 0.01, the capacity of processors in a Large-Scale network can be modelled by a normal distribution.

$$nor(x) = 16000 \times e^{\frac{(-(x-1300)^2}{2 \times 400^2}} \qquad (1)$$

We implemented in C a network simulator, using an $n \times n$ matrix for the nodes and an $n^2 \times n^2$ matrix for the edges. We assigned the nodes processing capacities (called μ)

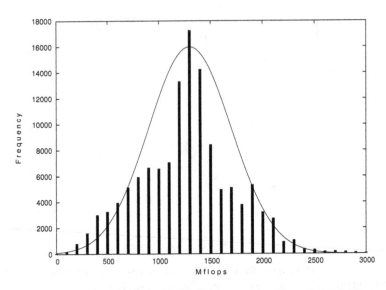

Fig. 3. Frequency distribution of Mflops for 200,000 processors registered at Seti@home and the normal distribution which model it

using a normal distribution $N(1, \frac{1}{9})$. Even thought this simple model seems to be naïve, it permits us to control the topology generated by the P2P Infrastructure of ProActive [3]. Simple models could be very powerfully as Kleinberg shows in his work about Small-world network algorithms [30].

In our simulations, we assume that all active objects are parts of a parallel application; therefore, we assume all service queues to have equal incoming message ratios λ. Clearly, real Grids run different parallel applications from different sources, having different service queue ratios and workloads. Nevertheless, from the point of view of a given parallel application, we consider other applications only as a reduction of processing capacity of network nodes.

Denoting by j the number of active objects in the node i at a given time, we say that the node i is overloaded if $j\lambda \geq \mu_i$ and underloaded if $j\lambda < T\mu_i$, where T is a given threshold between [0.5, 0.9]. The processor capacity μ_i is also used as the node rank. For consistency with the previous section, we use $UT = T \times \mu_i$ and $OT = \mu_i$. As in section 4, we use $RB = 0.7$.

We randomly placed m active objects in $(0 + x, 0 + y)$ (x and y defined on run-time) and tested the load-balancing algorithm, measuring the total number of migrations and the kind of processors used by the algorithm on each time-step. Each experimental sample is the mean number of 100 repetitions, fixing the parameter set $\{n, m, \lambda, T, RB, RS\}$ (see Table 1) and recalculating μ for all nodes in each repetition.

Our goals are first to perform a fine-tuning of the constant RS and second to determine whether our algorithm can reach a stable state near to the optimal on large-scale

P2P networks using a minimal subset of acquaintances. Even though migration cost seems to be a key issue for load balancing algorithms, the time spent in migration process is recuperated after a while because the increasing in service ratio of the active object in its new placement.

Table 1. Parameters and variables used in the simulation

Simulation parameters	Model parameters	Algorithm parameters
$n \times n$ Number of nodes	μ processor's capacity and ranking	UT threshold to determine an underloaded state
m Number of active objects	λ incoming ratio of an active object service queue	OT threshold to determine an overload state
x, y Initial deployment, length and high of nodes subset	T factor used to determine UT	RB Load-balancing similarity factor
		RS Work-stealing similarity factor

5.1 Fine-Tuning

We placed $m = 50$ active-objects in a simulated P2P network of 100 nodes, measuring the number of *accumulated* migrations performed by the algorithms until a given time-step (Figure 4a) and the mean number of overloaded nodes per time-step (Figure 4b), because it is imperative for all load-balancing algorithms to avoid increasing the number of overloaded nodes. As we expected, a lower value for RS generates a larger number of migrations: a low value of this factor will produce bad decisions of balance, migrating active objects to underloaded nodes with low processing capacity. Then, those active objects could cause overload in subsequent nodes, or an infinite migration among underloaded nodes.

Figure 5a presents the mean number of active-objects in nodes with capacity higher than one per total number of active objects during 100 repetitions, and Figure 5b presents the mean number of active objects in nodes with capacity higher than $1\frac{1}{3}$ by total number of active objects during 100 repetitions. Because we are using a normal distribution for the processor capacity μ, 50% of nodes will have $\mu \geq 1$ and 25% of nodes will have $\mu \geq 1\frac{1}{3}$.

Two behaviours are present in Figure 5 (a) and (b). First, because our algorithm aims to cluster active-objects on the best processors, for high values of RS, the number of active objects in the best quadrant of the processors increase. Second, for low values of RS, some active objects are stolen by worse processors. We can see from the plots that $RS \geq 0.9$ behaves very well, placing all of active objects in nodes with processing capacity greater than one. Therefore, in the following experiences we will use $RS \geq 0.9$.

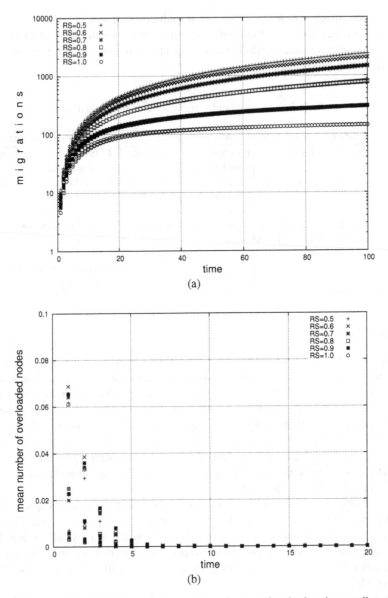

Fig. 4. Tuning for RS considering: a) mean number of accumulated migrations until each time-step; and b) mean number of overloaded nodes in each time-step. Using $RB = 0.7$, acquaintances subset size = 3, $|x - y| \leq 3$, $\lambda = 0.1, 0.2, 0.3$ and $T = 0.7$.

5.2   Scaling

As seen in the previous section, we aimed at optimising the application performance clustering active-objects on the best qualified processors. Therefore, using the values of μ, we sorted the nodes from higher to lower processing capacity and we defined the *optimal subset* as the first OPT nodes that satisfy the condition:

$$\sum_{i=1}^{OPT} \mu_i > m \times \lambda$$

Simulating an application of $m = 100$ active objects using different network size ($n \times n$), we have:

- $OPT(n = 10) = 13$,
- $OPT(n = 20, 30) = 11$,
- $OPT(n = 40) = 10$,
- $OPT(n \in [50, 90]) = 9$.

These results of the optimal subset size (OPT) are because we modelled processing capacity following a normal distribution. Therefore, larger the network size, higher the processing capacity of best nodes, then lower the number of nodes in the optimal subset.

In order to measure the performance of the *IFL* algorithm for large-scale networks, we define the "Algorithm Optimum" ($ALOP$) ratio as:

$$ALOP = \frac{Number\ of\ nodes\ used\ by\ IFL}{OPT}$$

At the same time, we calculate the mean number of accumulated migrations performed by all active objects from time-step 0 until time-step t.

An increase in the acquaintances subset size results in an increase in the probability to find a node to migrate, and hence an increase in the probability to reach the optimal state. Looking for the worst treatable scenario, and following the recommendations of [3], we only show the results for *subset size* = 3.

We measured scaling of the *IFL* algorithm in terms of $ALOP$ and the number of migrations, for networks of 100 (Figures 6 (a) and (b)) and 400 nodes(Figures 6 (c) and (d)). Even though in Section 5.1, a value of $RS = 0.9$ was promising, these plots show that the total number of migrations generated by this value makes the algorithm not scalable. Scalability in terms of migrations is presented in Figures 6 (b) and (d) only for values of $RS \geq 1.0$. The optimal scalability, in terms of $ALOP$, is presented in Figures 6 (a) and (c) for a value of $RS = 1.0$.

Considering that a $20x20$ network can be still considered as a small network, we test the scalability in terms of $ALOP$ and number of migrations over $n \times n$ P2P networks using $n = [10, 90]$, fixing the parameter RS in 1.0 and RB in 0.7. The results are shown in Figure 7 and Figure 8.

Figure 7 presents two behaviours at the same time:

1. **Number of nodes used by *IFL* algorithm through time**, because the number of optimal nodes used by a static distribution (OPT) is constant for each number of nodes ($n \times n$). We aim to cluster all active objects in a minimal set of nodes to avoid communication delays.
2. **ALOP ratio** (number of nodes used by *IFL* algorithm versus number of nodes used by an optimal statical distribution OPT), evaluating *"how good"* are the minimal subsets found by the *IFL* algorithm.

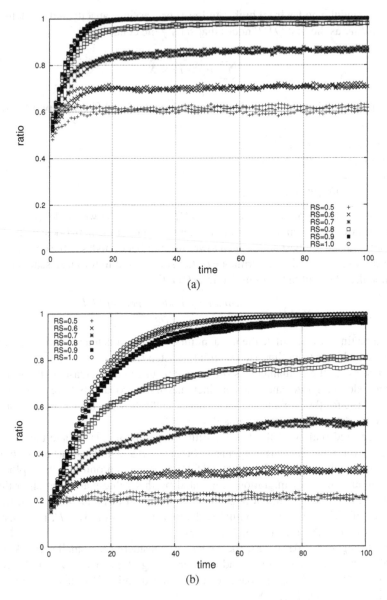

Fig. 5. Tuning the value of RS considering: a) mean number of active objects on a node with $\mu \geq 1$ per total number of active objects; and b) mean number of active objects on a node with $\mu > 1 + \frac{1}{3}$ per total number of active objects. Using $RB = 0.7$, acquaintances subset size = 3, $|x - y| \leq 3$, $\lambda = 0.1, 0.2, 0.3$ and $T = 0.7$.

In the beginning the *IFL* algorithm increases the number of nodes used, because active objects are first placed in a small subset of the network generating a high overload in this subset. Then, the algorithm quickly performs migrations to reduce the overload.

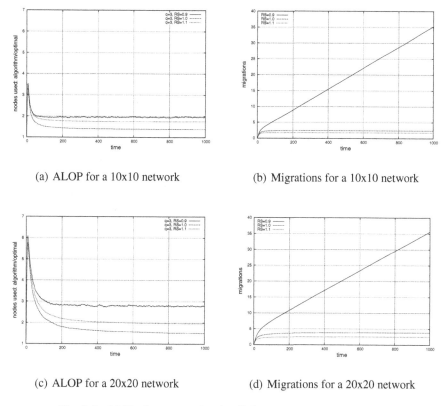

(a) ALOP for a 10x10 network   (b) Migrations for a 10x10 network

(c) ALOP for a 20x20 network   (d) Migrations for a 20x20 network

Fig. 6. Scalability for a network using $RS = 0.9, 1.0, 1.1, RB = 0.7$

Experiments report no overloaded nodes over 30 time-steps. After that, the *work-stealing* step of *IFL* algorithm works alone, clustering active-objects on the best nodes and thus, reducing the number of nodes used by the algorithm.

For networks of until 40×40 nodes, the *IFL* algorithm uses less than two times the optimal number of nodes. In other words, *IFL* algorithm uses less than 20 nodes from all the network until 1000 time-steps. For networks of 50×50 to 70×70 nodes, the algorithm uses less than three times the number of optimal nodes (i.e: 27). For larger networks, the algorithm uses more than three times the optimal number of nodes at time-step 1000; nevertheless, the curves seem to decrease before that value.

We expected the previous behaviour, because the distribution of processing capacity μ follows an exponential distribution; therefore, values of μ in the subset of the "best X nodes" will be higher for larger values of n (larger the network, smaller the subset size); and, because the *IFL* algorithm tries to use the nearest nodes while balancing an overloaded node. Therefore, as the network size increase, the probability of finding a node from the optimal subset decreases.

The plot in Figure 7 shows how at the first 10 time-steps the IFL algorithm reacts against an overloading distributing the active objects among the network and then, when a stable state is reached, it begins the clustering of active objects. Similar behaviour can

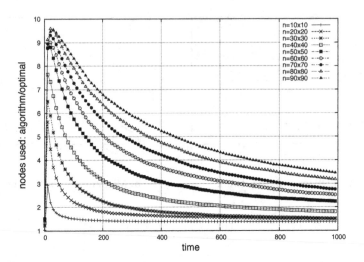

Fig. 7. Scalability in terms of number of processors used, having $RS = 1.0$

be seen in Figure 8, having a high number of *accumulated* migrations at the beginning and then the system becomes stable (for small-size networks) or there are some migrations in order to group the active objects on the "best processors" (large-size networks). Remember that plots present the *mean* number of *accumulated* migrations for m active objects; therefore, the contribution in plots of a each new migration is $1/m$.

For all studied network size, the curves remain under 6.5 migrations. Moreover, considering only the time-step 1000, we can see that the number of migrations is of order $O(\log(n))$. Both are promising results in terms of scalability of the *IFL* algorithm.

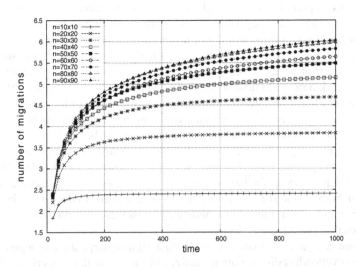

Fig. 8. Scalability in terms of number of accumulated migrations, having $RS = 1.0$

6   Conclusions

We studied the *IFL* load-balancing algorithm on P2P networks, aiming at reaching a near-optimal distribution of active objects using only local information provided by a P2P infrastructure. Using a simulated P2P network, we showed that, using only a low number of fixed links among nodes and a careful tuning of the algorithm parameters, a near-optimal distribution is reachable even for large-scale networks. We suggested to use a value near 1.0 for the stealing factor, which allows using around 1.7 times the optimal number of nodes for networks until 400 nodes, using less than 5.5 migrations per active object. Moreover, the number of migrations appears to be of order $O(\log(n))$ after the first optimal state (without overloaded nodes) is reached.

As seen in Section 5.1, the value of RS is a key factor for a low cost and efficient load balancing and we had many experimental tuning to find "optimal values" of it. RS seems to depend of network topology and we are studying its behaviour to calculate it automatically and dynamically.

As future work, we plan to test the algorithm using a large-scale P2P infrastructure deployed over real desktop computers, balancing a communication-intensive parallel application. It is the continued goal of this work to optimise this algorithm, looking for the best performance in migration decisions and the global distribution using only local information.

Acknowledgements

This work was supported by CoreGrid NoE.

The authors want to thank Satu Elisa Schaeffer for proofreading an earlier version of this paper and the anonymous reviewers for their helpful comments.

References

1. T. L. Casavant and J. G. Kuhl, "A taxonomy of scheduling in general-purpose distributed computing systems," *IEEE Transactions on Software Engineering*, vol. 14, no. 2, pp. 141–154, 1988.
2. R. Schollmeier, "A definition of peer-to-peer networking for the classification of peer-to-peer architectures and applications," in *2001 International Conference on Peer-to-Peer Computing (P2P2001)*, (Department of Computer and Information Science Linkopings Universitet, Sweden), IEEE Computer Society, August 2001.
3. J. Bustos-Jiménez, D. Caromel, A. di Costanzo, M. Leyton, and J. M. Piquer, "Balancing active objects on a peer to peer infrastructure," in *Proceedings of the XXV International Conference of the Chilean Computer Science Society (SCCC 2005)*, (Valdivia, Chile), pp. 109–115, IEEE Computer Society, November 2005.
4. Oasis Group at INRIA Sohpia-Antipolis, "Proactive, the java library for parallel, distributed, concurrent computing with security and mobility." http://proactive.objectweb.org, 2002.
5. L. P. P. dos Santos, "Load distribution: a survey." citeseer.ist.psu.edu/santos96load.html.
6. N. G. Shivaratri, P. Krueger, and M. Singhal, "Load distributing for locally distributed systems," *Computer*, vol. 25, no. 12, pp. 33–44, 1992.
7. M. Roussopoulos and M. Baker, "Practical load balancing for content requests in peer-to-peer networks," *The Computing Research Repository*, vol. cs.NI/0209023, 2002.

8. R. D. Blumofe and C. E. Leiserson, "Scheduling multithreaded computations by work stealing," *Journal of the ACM*, vol. 46, no. 5, pp. 720–748, 1999.

9. P. Berenbrink, T. Friedetzky, and L. A. Goldberg, "The natural work-stealing algorithm is stable," in *IEEE Symposium on Foundations of Computer Science*, (Washington, DC, USA), pp. 178–187, IEEE Computer Society, 2001.

10. J. Bustos-Jiménez, D. Caromel, M. Leyton, and J. M. Piquer, "Load information sharing policies in communication-intensive parallel applications," in *ISSADS* (F. F. R. Corchado, V. Larios-Rosillo, and H. Unger, eds.), Lecture Notes in Computer Science, Springer, 2006. To appear.

11. S. Ratnasamy, P. Francis, M. Handley, R. Karp, and S. Schenker, "A scalable content-addressable network," in *SIGCOMM '01: Proceedings of the 2001 conference on Applications, technologies, architectures, and protocols for computer communications*, (New York, NY, USA), pp. 161–172, ACM Press, 2001.

12. B. Godfrey, K. Lakshminarayanan, S. Surana, R. Karp, and I. Stoica, "Load balancing in structured p2p systems," *Lecture Notes in Computer Science*, vol. 2735, pp. 68–79, January 2003.

13. A. Montresor, H. Meling, and Ö. Babaoglu, "Messor: Load-balancing through a swarm of autonomous agents.," in *AP2PC*, vol. 2530 of *Lecture Notes in Computer Science*, pp. 125–137, Springer, 2002.

14. J. Cao, "Self-organizing agents for grid load balancing," in *GRID '04: Proceedings of the Fifth IEEE/ACM International Workshop on Grid Computing (GRID'04)*, (Washington, DC, USA), pp. 388–395, IEEE Computer Society, 2004.

15. A. Barak, S. Guday, and R. G. Wheeler, *The MOSIX Distributed Operating System: Load Balancing for UNIX*. Secaucus, NJ, USA: Springer-Verlag New York, Inc., 1993.

16. M. Mitzenmacher, "How useful is old information?," *IEEE Transactions on Parallel and Distributed Systems*, vol. 11, no. 1, pp. 6–20, 2000.

17. D. Caromel, "Toward a method of object-oriented concurrent programming," *Communications of the ACM*, vol. 36, no. 9, pp. 90–102, 1993.

18. L. Baduel, F. Baude, and D. Caromel, "Efficient, flexible, and typed group communications in java," in *Joint ACM Java Grande - ISCOPE 2002 Conference*, (Seattle), pp. 28–36, ACM Press, 2002. ISBN 1-58113-559-8.

19. F. Baude, D. Caromel, F. Huet, and J. Vayssiere, "Communicating mobile active objects in java," in *Proceedings of HPCN Europe 2000*, vol. 1823 of *LNCS*, pp. 633–643, Springer, May 2000.

20. M. L. Michael Litzkow and M. Mutka, "Condor - a hunter of idle workstations," in *Proc. of 8th International Conference on Distribuited Computing Systems*, pp. 104–111, 1998.

21. P. Domingues, P. Marques, and L. M. Silva, "Resource usage of windows computer laboratories.," in *34th International Conference on Parallel Processing Workshops (ICPP 2005 Workshops), 14-17 June 2005, Oslo, Norway*, pp. 469–476, IEEE Computer Society, 2005.

22. D. P. Anderson and G. Fedak, "The computational and storage potential of volunteer computing," in *CCGRID*, pp. 73–80, IEEE Computer Society, 2006.

23. R. Raman, M. Livny, and M. Solomon, "Matchmaking: Distributed resource management for high throughput computing," in *HPDC '98: Proceedings of the The Seventh IEEE International Symposium on High Performance Distributed Computing*, (Washington, DC, USA), p. 140, IEEE Computer Society, 1998.

24. Sun Microsystems, *RMI Architecture and Functional Specification*. http://java.sun.com/j2se/1.4.2/ docs/guide/rmi/spec/rmiTOC.html.

25. C. Nester, M. Philippsen, and B. Haumacher, "A more efficient RMI for Java," in *JAVA '99: Proceedings of the ACM 1999 conference on Java Grande*, (New York, NY, USA), pp. 152–159, ACM Press, 1999.

26. D. Vyas and J. Subhlok, "Volunteer computing on clusters," in *Proceedings of 12th Workshop on Job Scheduling Strategies for Parallel Processing (JSSPP)*, pp. 161–176, June 2006.

27. D. Epema, C. Franke, A. Iosup, A. Papaspyrou, L. Schley, B. Song, and R. Yahyapour, "On grid performance evaluation using synthetic workloads," in *Proceedings of 12th Workshop on Job Scheduling Strategies for Parallel Processing (JSSPP)*, pp. 227–247, June 2006.

28. P. Paul, "Seti @ home project and its website," *Crossroads*, vol. 8, no. 3, pp. 3–5, 2002.

29. D. P. Anderson, "Boinc: A system for public-resource computing and storage," in *GRID '04: Proceedings of the Fifth IEEE/ACM International Workshop on Grid Computing (GRID'04)*, (Washington, DC, USA), pp. 4–10, IEEE Computer Society, 2004.

30. J. M. Kleinberg, "The small-world phenomenon: an algorithm perspective," in *Proceedings of the Thirty Second Annual ACM Symposium on Theory of Computing*, (New York, NY, USA), pp. 163–170, ACM Press, 2000.

Symbiotic Space-Sharing on SDSC's DataStar System

Jonathan Weinberg and Allan Snavely

San Diego Supercomputer Center
University of California, San Diego
La Jolla, CA 92093-0505, USA
{jonw,allans}@sdsc.edu
http://www.sdsc.edu

Abstract. Using a large HPC platform, we investigate the effectiveness of "symbiotic space-sharing", a technique that improves system throughput by executing parallel applications in combinations and configurations that alleviate pressure on shared resources. We demonstrate that relevant benchmarks commonly suffer a 10-60% penalty in runtime efficiency due to memory resource bottlenecks and up to several orders of magnitude for I/O. We show that this penalty can be often mitigated, and sometimes virtually eliminated, by symbiotic space-sharing techniques and deploy a prototype scheduler that leverages these findings to improve system throughput by 20%.

1 Introduction

On SDSC's DataStar [3], as on all parallel systems, processes must share resources. Because the system does not time-share, each process receives its own processor with a dedicated level 1 cache. However, two processors must share a level two cache. The eight processors on each node must share a level 3 cache, main memory, an on-node file system, and bandwidth to off-node I/O.

Sharing, by its very nature, entails compromise. In the realm of parallel processing, that compromise may lead to performance degradation. The more heavily coexisting processes make use of a shared resource, the more likely it is that the performance of that resource will suffer. Heavy use of a shared cache might lead to lower hit rates, and consequently, lower per-processor throughput. As more processes make simultaneous use of a shared I/O system, blocking times increase and performance degrades.

Because the consequences of resource sharing are often ill-understood, scheduling policies on production space-shared systems avoid inter-job sharing wherever possible. On DataStar, for instance, nodes are never time-shared and parallel jobs have exclusive use of the nodes on which they run. Even then, the system's General Parallel File System (GPFS) remains a shared resource among all running jobs.

This is not an ideal policy in several circumstances. Resource utilization and throughput suffers when small jobs are forced to occupy an entire node while making use of only a few processors. The policy also encourages users to squeeze large parallel jobs onto the fewest number of nodes possible since doing otherwise is both costly and detrimental to system utilization. Such configurations are not always optimal;the processes

E. Frachtenberg and U. Schwiegelshohn (Eds.): JSSPP 2006, LNCS 4376, pp. 192–209, 2007.

of parallel jobs often perform similar computations, consequently stressing the same shared resources and exacerbating the slowdown due to resource contention.

In such situations, a more flexible and intelligent scheduler could increase the system's throughput by more tightly space-sharing *symbiotic*[1] combinations of jobs that interfere with each other minimally. Such a scheduler would need to recognize relevant job characteristics, understand job interactions, and identify opportunities for nondestructive space-sharing.

The purpose of this study is to investigate the feasibility of such an approach and quantify the extent to which it could improve throughput if implemented. To address these questions, we must determine:

* To what extent and why do jobs interfere with themselves and each other?
* If this interference exists, how effectively can it be reduced by alternative job mixes?
* Are these alternative job mixes feasible for parallel codes and what is the net gain?
* How can a job scheduler create symbiotic schedules?

We explore each of these questions in sections 3 through 5 respectively. This discussion is preceded by details of our hardware environment in section 2 and succeeded by comments on related and future work in sections 7 and 8.

2 Hardware Environment

The results described in this paper were derived from application runs on the San Diego Supercomputer Center's DataStar. The machine contains 272 IBM P655+ nodes, each consisting of 8 Power4 processors. Of those nodes, 171 are composed of 1.5 GHz processors while the others 1.7. Only the former were utilized for this study.

Each POWER4 processor contains a 32 KB L1 data cache. Two processors together comprise a *chip* and share a 1.5 MB L2 cache. The L3 cache on each chip is combined with that on the others to create a single node-wide, address-interleaved L3 cache of 128 MB.

Each node is also equipped with 16 GB of memory and a local scratch file system of approximately 64GB. Nodes are directly connected to the GPFS (IBM's parallel file system) through a Fibre Channel link and to each other by the Federation interconnect.

DataStar schedules jobs using a batch queueing model implemented by LoadLeveler [12]. Because the scheduler interface does not allow users to directly request that jobs be coscheduled, we achieved this effect when necessary by deploying MPI jobs that execute the desired sub-jobs on specified processors depending on rank.

3 The Effects of Sharing Resources

As an initial starting point, we can broadly divide the resources shared by processors on DataStar's nodes into two categories: memory and I/O. The memory resources consist

---

[1] *Symbiosis* is a term borrowed from Biology meaning the graceful coexistence of organisms in close proximity. We generalize the term to co-scheduled processes and emphasize the form in which neither does harm to the other.

of the three levels of cache along with the node's 16GB of main memory. The I/O resources consist of the on-node file system along with bandwidth to the system's GPFS.

To gauge the performance effects of resources sharing, we run a set of single-processor benchmarks meant to stress each resource. We then measure the slowdown incurred by each benchmark as we increase the number of its instances running concurrently on a single node. The maximum slowdown is displayed. When we refer to N concurrent instances of a benchmark, we refer to N independent, single-processor runs of some benchmark running concurrently on a single node. We calculate slowdown as $(T_N - T_1)/T_1$ where T_i is the runtime of the benchmark while i instances of it run concurrently on the node.

3.1 Memory Sharing

To test performance degradation of the memory subsystem, we choose the following three benchmarks, each meant to stress different sections of the system:

GUPS - Giga-Updates-Per-Second measures the time to perform a fixed number of updates to random locations in main memory [8,1]. We use it to investigate the effects of high demand on main memory bandwidth.

STREAM - A simple synthetic benchmark that measures sustainable memory bandwidth for vector compute kernels, commonly encountered in high-performance computing, by performing a long series of short, regularly-strided accesses through memory [8,2]. STREAM is highly cacheable and prefetchable and we therefore use it stress the machine's cache structure.

EP - Embarrassingly Parallel is one of the NAS Parallel Benchmarks [6]. It evaluates an integral by means of pseudorandom trials and is a compute-bound code. We use this as a control group to discern between performance degradation in the other benchmarks due to resource sharing and that attributable to other overheads.

Figure 1 shows the slowdown of each type of application. EP appears only slightly sensitive to the number of concurrent instances running on the node while GUPS and STREAM show a slowdown of up to 18% and 30% respectively.

Of note is the non-linear increase in slowdown. Since the majority of the slowdown is caused by the latter instances, we can speculate that running symbiotic jobs on those processors has the potential to eliminate a disproportionate share of the performance degradation.

The large jump in slowdown caused by adding a fifth instance of GUPS is particularly indicative of resource sharing. When fewer than five processes run on the node, DataStar is able to spread them onto separate chips and minimize resource sharing. Once a fifth instance of GUPS is added however, at least two processes must share one of the four chips and consequently an L2 cache. When sharing the L2 cache, each processes receives degraded service from it. Table 1 shows the L2 miss rates of each processor as more instances of GUPS are added. When two processes cohabitate a single chip, the miss rate increases from around .62 to .78, causing the sharp drop in performance.

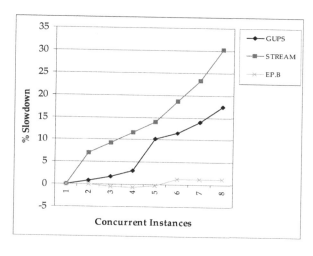

Fig. 1. Slowdown of memory intensive benchmarks as more instances of each run concurrently on a single node

Table 1. L2 miss rates as more processors of a node run GUPS concurrently

Chip 0		Chip 1		Chip 2		Chip 3	
P0	P4	P1	P5	P2	P6	P3	P7
61	-	-	-	-	-	-	-
.61	-	.61	-	-	-	-	-
.61	-	.61	-	.61	-	-	-
.62	-	.62	-	.62	-	.62	-
.76	.76	.60	-	.60	-	.60	-
.76	.76	.76	.76	.60	-	.60	-
.78	.78	.78	.78	.78	.78	.67	-
.78	.78	.78	.78	.78	.78	.78	.78

To verify that our observations from these benchmarks are representative of other applications and can be generalized, we repeat part of this experiment using single-processor runs of the NAS Parallel Benchmarks [6]. We use version 3.2 and problem sizes of class B. None of these benchmarks performs any significant I/O.

Table 2. Percent Slowdown of NPB while 4 and 8 instances of each run concurrently on a node

APP	BT	MG	FT	DT	SP	LU	CG	IS
4P	8	15	1	20	20	16	14	14
8P	12	48	30	38	33	41	54	58

The results in Table 2 confirm that slowdown from memory subsystem sharing tends to fall in the range of 10-60% and that the majority of performance degradation is often resultant of using the second half of a node. Further, we notice that the slowdown incurred by each benchmark due to the first four instances varies minimally, generally within 5%.

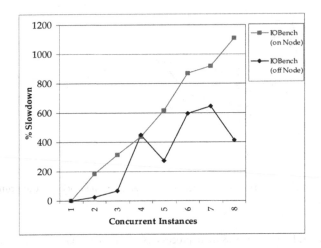

Fig. 2. Slowdown of I/O Bench as more instances run concurrently on a single node

3.2   I/O Sharing

To extend our investigation to shared I/O resources, we repeat the experiments from Section 3.1 using I/O Bench [4], a synthetic benchmark that measures the rate at which a machine can perform reads and writes to disk. The benchmark performs a series of sequential, backward, and random read and write tests.

We configure I/O Bench to use a file size of 600MB and block size of 4K. Each benchmark instance writes and reads its own set of three distinct files via sequential, backward, and random access. Concurrent processes never operate on the same files. We repeat the tests once for the on-node scratch file system and again for the off-node, shared, GPFS.

Figure 2 graphs the slowdown induced when concurrent, independent instances of I/O Bench run on a single node. The slowdown factors are far greater than those exhibited by the memory-intensive benchmarks, with the on-node numbers demonstrating super-linear slowdown. The off-node performance numbers, while not as egregious as their on-node counterparts, are nonetheless considerable. The erratic performance of the off-node measurements are likely an artifact of the varying demand placed on it by other applications concurrently executing on the system.

4   Mixing Jobs

Now that we have determined the ways in which resource sharing can degrade performance, we turn to investigate the extent to which this degradation can be mitigated by

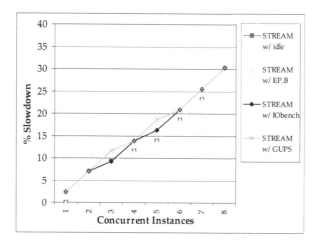

Fig. 3. STREAM

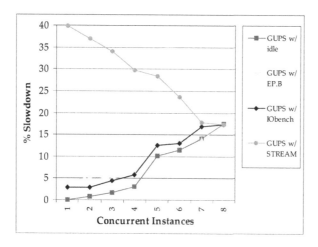

Fig. 4. GUPS

alternate job mixes. To gauge the performance effects of the benchmarks on each other, we repeat the experiments in Section 3, but utilize the unused processors in each experiment to concurrently execute other benchmarks instead of leaving those processors idle. We refer to the benchmark being tested as the *primary* benchmark and the one being executed by the spare processors as the *background* benchmark. To adjust for runtime discrepancies between primary and background benchmarks, the processors executing the background benchmark repeat execution until the primary benchmark completes.

Figures 3 through 6 graph these results. In each graph, the line labeled "[BENCH] w/ idle" is the performance curve as depicted in Figures 1 and 2, meaning that there is no background benchmark and consequently, the unused processors were idle

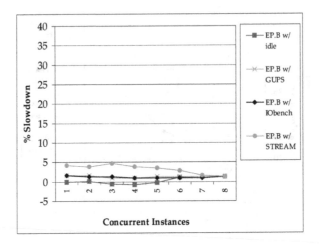

Fig. 5. EP.B

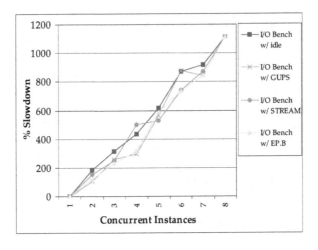

Fig. 6. I/O Bench

during the experiment. The other lines, labeled "[BENCH1] w/ [BENCH2]", indicate that instead of sitting idle, all unused processors were running the background benchmark BENCH2.

These graphs indicate that with only a single exception, utilizing unused processors to execute the other benchmarks has little to no effect on runtimes. These results clearly demonstrate that it is possible to mitigate resource-sharing slowdown by mixing memory, compute, and I/O intensive jobs.

The lone exception arises from combining the two memory-bound applications, STREAM and GUPS. Although GUPS has little effect on the performance of STREAM (Figure 3), the converse is untrue (Figure 4). This one-way interference is likely due to

Table 3. Percent slowdown of row application when all other processors on node execute column application

	Background Benchmark								
	BT	MG	FT	SP	LU	CG	IS	EP	I/O
BT	**12**	21	20	16	17	12	12	1	5
MG	11	**48**	25	25	25	11	11	1	4
FT	6	31	**30**	15	18	15	12	1	1
SP	21	48	36	**33**	31	23	19	2	5
LU	18	69	41	38	**41**	24	28	1	2
CG	26	82	64	42	55	**54**	36	3	7
IS	14	88	50	39	50	32	**58**	1	3
EP	2	4	4	4	4	3	2	**1**	2
I/O	-6	-2	2	-2	-6	-6	-2	-2	**1108**

STREAM's heavy cache use and the relatively low rate of memory operations achieved by GUPS. STREAM increases the L2 and L3 miss rates of GUPS by around .2 each while the presence of GUPS does not affect STREAM's cache miss rates.

To confirm that these results are generalizable, we repeat part of these experiments using the NAS Parallel Benchmarks. Again, we use EP as the compute-intensive code and I/O Bench as the I/O-intensive code. Table 3 lists the percentage slowdown incurred by each primary benchmark, listed on the vertical axis, when all the remaining processors on the node concurrently execute the background benchmarks listed on the horizontal axis.

The first item to note is that EP and I/O Bench are symbiotic with all of the NAS benchmarks. The degradation imposed by these benchmarks both to and by the others is negligible and appears to be within the margin of measurement error.

Secondly, the slowdown imposed by each benchmark on itself tends to be among the highest observed. This implies that opportunities for symbiotic combinations may be forthcoming in large enough application sets.

As we observed in Figure 4, the interactions between the NAS benchmarks can sometimes be one-sided when one benchmark makes heavier use of shared resources than another. The most flagrant example is MG, which causes the most performance degradation both to itself and to others.

Degenerate cases aside, ample opportunities exist for symbiotic sharing, even among those applications we consider memory-intensive. Pairing CG and IS, for example, would be substantially beneficial to both. BT appears to be another possible candidate.

5   Symbiotic Space-Sharing and Parallel Codes

In the previous two sections we have shown that resource-sharing among concurrent jobs can cause performance degradation and that this degradation can be effectively mitigated by symbiotic job mixes. This is sufficient motivation to begin sharing single nodes among two or more small jobs in a more intelligent way. However, the question still remains as to whether or not symbiotic job scheduling can help speed larger, parallel, multi-node applications. This section aims to address this question.

Generally, parallel codes employ every processor on each node. The scheduler's motivation to use fewer nodes is to minimize the occurrence of slower, inter-node communications and therefore, ostensibly reap performance benefits. The results presented in the previous two sections should give us pause as to whether this is a good scheduling strategy. Can the processor performance benefits of symbiotic space-sharing outweigh the penalty of additional inter-node communications?

To answer this question we again use the NAS Parallel Benchmarks, only this time, instead of using multiple single-processor runs, we employ a single 16-processor run for each benchmark. We execute each parallel benchmark first on 16 processors spread evenly across two 8-way nodes and then again on 16 processors spread evenly across four 8-way nodes, effectively utilizing only four processors per node.

To model the increased complexity of parallel I/O, we replace I/O Bench, which is a serial application, with BTIO [31], NPB's parallel I/O benchmark. BTIO is the same as the BT benchmark, but with frequent checkpointing to disk. There are several flavors of I/O that BTIO can utilize. We conduct our experiments using the following three:

MPI IO FULL - The full MPI-2 I/O implementation uses collective buffering, meaning that data scattered in memory among the processors is collected on a subset of the participating processors and rearranged before being written to file.

MPI IO SIMPLE - The simple MPI-2 I/O implementation does not leverage collective buffering, meaning that many seek operations may be required to write the data file.

EP IO - Using **E**mbarrassingly **P**arallel I/O, every processor writes its own file and files are not combined to create a single file.

Table 4. Speedup of 16-processor runs when executing across four nodes instead of two

Benchmark	Speedup
BT	1.13
MG	1.34
FT	1.27
LU	1.47
CG	1.55
IS	1.12
EP	1.00
BTIO EP	1.16
BTIO SIMPLE	4.97
BTIO FULL	1.16

The results in Table 4 were derived using the MPI implementation of the NPB version 3.2 with problem class C. Because we run these benchmarks across multiple nodes, the I/O tests cannot utilize the on-node I/O, but rather only the system's GPFS. Speedup is calculated using the traditional definition T_2/T_4 where T_N is the runtime of the benchmark on N nodes.

The results reveal that speedup from reduced resource contention in this benchmark set not only outweighs communication overheads, but does so significantly and consistently.

DataStar's current interface does indeed allow a user to request that his or her job be spread across more nodes than necessary and therefore attain these performance benefits. However, because the system does not node-share, such a request would be both a detriment to overall system utilization and costly to the user who is charged per node instead of per processor. Can a system-level, symbiotic space-sharing scheme help?

To find out, we re-run some of the 4-node tests, but allow two benchmarks to run on the nodes concurrently. For each result presented in Table 5, we execute two parallel benchmarks concurrently on four nodes with each benchmark using exactly half of each node.

Table 5. Speedup attained when parallel benchmarks share four nodes instead of running separately on two each

Bench A	Bench B	Speedup A	Speedup B
CG	IS	1.18	1.17
	BT	1.05	1.04
	EP	1.36	1.03
	BTIO(E)	1.38	1.07
	BTIO(S)	.55	1.03
	BTIO(F)	1.36	1.12
IS	BT	1.04	1.03
	EP	1.07	1.03
	BTIO(E)	1.11	1.07
	BTIO(S)	1.00	2.41
	BTIO(F)	1.13	1.13

These results show that speedup can be maintained even while no processors are idle. Speedup can be induced both by mixing categories of benchmarks and even by mixing some memory-bound codes. For the first time however, we observe some cross-category slowdown. CG and the BTIO benchmark with simple IO both slow considerably when paired. Nevertheless, these results demonstrate that executing parallel codes in symbiotic combination can indeed yield significant performance benefits. The average speedup increase is 15%, showing that for this set of benchmarks, the benefits of reduced resource sharing outweigh the increased cost of inter-node communications.

6   Towards a Symbiotic Scheduler

In the previous three sections, we have shown that symbiotic space-sharing can improve system throughput by reducing runtime inefficiencies while maintaining high system utilization. The most important question remaining is how to build schedulers that can leverage these concepts.

6.1 Identifying Symbiosis

The effectiveness of any symbiotic space-sharing scheduler is naturally contingent upon the level of symbiosis the scheduler can identify in a given job stream. In this section, we discuss some preliminary approaches for uncovering symbiotic space-sharing opportunities under various assumptions.

In the most restrictive input scenario, the scheduler has no history of the execution characteristics of jobs in the stream. In such circumstances, users could be asked to submit the application's bottleneck, if any, to the scheduler. It is not unreasonable to assume that a user might know that a certain application is I/O or compute intensive. These are the two categories in which we are most interested since they afford us the most likely opportunity for symbiotic job mixing. The scheduler would then pair I/O and compute intensive jobs to execute with memory-intensive ones. As we will see in Section 6.2, even this naive approach can reap significant benefits.

If a scheduler, however, were able to recognize and maintain statistics regarding jobs that commonly recur in the stream, then other techniques would be possible. Work-load traces have revealed that users tend to frequently resubmit similar or even identical jobs [9,10], a phenomenon that automated runtime predictors have leveraged in the past [11,22]. A symbiotic scheduler may utilize these same techniques to identify applications and associated resource bottlenecks. A user-supplied job category may be a good starting point, but the scheduler could improve on a strategy of random, cross-category pairing.

The most straight-forward approach is experimentation. The scheduler can be configured to space-share randomly selected cross-category pairs and learn the best combinations. *Better* combinations would be identified by metrics such as memory operations per second or floating point operations per second as reported by commonly available lightweight hardware counters. While sampling, the scheduler would exhibit a configurable bias towards choosing combinations known to be more efficient. This approach has been shown effective in multithreading scenarios [23,24].

A yet more intricate approach may be to deploy those hardware counters to collect statistics on applications as they run alone. The scheduler may subsequently use the results to predict optimal combinations, thereby decreasing its learning overhead. Figure 7 exemplifies one possible predictive strategy.

Figure 7 graphs the memory operations per second achieved by the single-processor NAS benchmarks while running alone versus the percentage slowdown incurred by each when four or eight concurrent instances of it run on a single node. For the full node runs, we can see a strong correlation between these two parameters. Among the NAS benchmarks, those able to perform memory operations at a faster rate are less likely to cause themselves slowdown. Since the slowdowns incurred by the half-node runs of all benchmarks are comparable, it is likely that applications with lower memory operations per second will benefit more from symbiotic scheduling. In this approach, the scheduler might increase utility by preferring to space-share applications that achieve a lower rate of memory operations per second.

Aided by the proper hardware counters, a scheduler could ideally discover symbiotic combinations relatively quickly. Given that, there is still a need for effective scheduling heuristics that can exploit these findings. We should keep in mind however that an

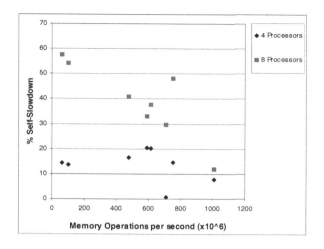

Fig. 7. Slowdown of NPB benchmarks as a function of memops/s

optimal symbiotic scheduler is not a necessary first step. The results presented hitherto suggest that much benefit would be achievable even by a naive implementation.

6.2 Prototype Symbiotic Scheduler

To test whether symbiotic space-sharing can indeed improve system throughput, we implemented a rudimentary symbiotic scheduler to compete against DataStar's production counterpart.

Experimental Setup. The scheduler was deployed on DataStar and given an ordered stream of one hundred randomly selected 4 and 16-processor jobs to execute using a total of 32 processors on four nodes. We refer to these job sizes simply as *small* and *large*. The jobs in the stream consisted of I/O Bench and variations of the NAS Parallel benchmarks from the following set: {EP.B.4, BT.B.4, MG.B.4, FT.B.4, DT.B.4, SP.B.4, LU.B.4, CG.B.4, IS.B.4, CG.C.16, IS.C.16, EP.C.16, BTIO_FULL.C.16}[2]. The job stream was generated by iteratively enqueueing jobs selected by weighted probability; small jobs were favored over large jobs in a 4:3 ratio and memory-intensive jobs were favored over compute and I/O intensive jobs in a 2:1:1 ratio.

Each job was submitted with an expected runtime that was used by the scheduler for backfilling. These runtime estimates were determined by executing each job using DataStar's default configuration. To constrain backfilling opportunities, at most twelve jobs occupied the queue at any given time.

The symbiotic scheduler mimics DataStar priorities by favoring large jobs and backfilling small ones whenever possible. The exact queueing algorithm is EASY backfilling [16] with the modification that large jobs are always moved ahead of small ones upon entering the queue.

---

[2] For small jobs, each of the 4 processors actually performs a full serial run of the benchmark at class B with collective communication at the beginning and end.

For each job, the processor allocation strategy employed by the symbiotic scheduler is the most simplistic of those we have previously discussed. The scheduler partitions each node evenly into *top* and *bottom* halves. It then executes jobs designated as memory-intensive on the top halves and all others on the bottom halves. The symbiotic scheduler spreads large jobs across all four nodes while the DataStar scheduler executes each on only two.

Scheduler Results. DataStar's makespan for the first eighty seven jobs was 5355s while the symbiotic scheduler completed the same jobs in 4451s, a speedup of 1.20. We ignore the final thirteen jobs because the eighty seventh job completed was the final memory-intensive job in the stream. The symbiotic scheduler's memory half was thereafter starved while the non-memory intensive half executed the final thirteen jobs, an artifact of the testing procedure.

The magnitude of speedup, however, is dependent on the runtime distribution of the jobs. Figure 8 provides a more insightful analysis. The figure illustrates the average *per-processor* speedup (across the entire workload) of applications executed by the symbiotic scheduler versus those executed using the default policies.

The 16-processor jobs each speed up where expected. The compute-bound EP code is unaffected while the I/O-bound BTIO benchmark and the memory-bound CG benchmark speed up by 11% and 25% respectively.

While the large jobs experience a decreased wallclock execution time, the small jobs, as expected, see an increase. This is because the symbiotic scheduler concurrently executes two small jobs on each node for 100% cpu utilization, while the DataStar scheduler executes only one. The symbiotic scheduler can only hope that by making intelligent choices it can mitigate this slowdown.

A perfect symbiotic schedule would therefore yield a per-processor speedup of 2. As expected, only EP achieves this, though the other slowdowns are relatively palatable, most often within 5-10%. Such modest runtime penalties are tenable tradeoffs for a doubling of system utilization.

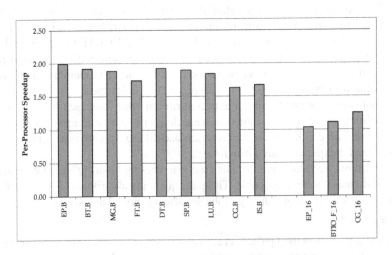

Fig. 8. Per-processors speedup of symbiotic schedule

7   Related Work

Many previous investigations of multi-resource aware job scheduling have been conducted, though none under assumptions applicable to today's scientific supercomputing installations. Our approach revisits the issue by starting with a modern production policy on a large MPP machine and relaxing some procedures to achieve higher performance and utilization. We assume rigid job sizes, FCFS-type queued space-sharing, and run-to-completion scheduling with no preemption.

We characterize previous related work into the following non-discrete categories:

7.1   Multithreading

Symbiotic job scheduling was originally proposed for machines utilizing Simultaneous Multithreading[23,24], later known as *Hyperthreading*, and was subsequently refined by McGregor et. al. [19]. Such examples are concerned with intimate, cycle-by-cycle resource sharing of multithreaded processors where sharing and contention involve functional units on the processor. Contrastingly, this work focuses on space-sharing contention for off-chip resources by multiple processors.

7.2   Paging

Some studies have sought to schedule job combinations that may limit the amount of paging induced by the workload. In 1994, Peris modelled the cost of paging behavior in parallel applications when working sets would not fit into local memory [21]. Batat and Feitelson suggest limiting the multiprogramming level of gang schedules in order to ensure that job combinations do not exceed a total memory limit [7]. Suh and Rudolf have proposed that if such a limit must be breached, then previously obtained application profile information can inform the scheduler of the best way to do so [26].

Though ensuring a job's ability to fit into memory is encompassed by this work, it is not the sole focus. We address contention for all resources on each node including caches, memory bus bandwidth, and local I/O in addition to global resources shared among multiple nodes. We also study the effects of allocating a job's processes across multiple nodes in order to compare slowdowns from resource contention and inter-node communications.

7.3   Time-Sharing

Application-aware job scheduling for time-sharing scenarios has also been studied. Many have proposed *affinity* techniques that mitigate cache perturbations by avoiding process migrations [25,29,28]. Such considerations are unique to time-sharing.

Wiseman and Feitelson have suggested that I/O and compute-intensive jobs can be symbiotically coallocated on the same processor set in a gang scheduled environment [30]. The focus of that work is on a relaxation of gang scheduling that allows two complementary jobs to cooperate via timely per-processor context switching. In contrast to this effort, our work targets resource sharing and contention in pure space-shared systems.

7.4 SMP Memory Bus Contention

It is well known that contention on the memory bus of an SMP is a scaling bottle-neck. Several studies have therefore investigated the possibility of relieving pressure on this bottleneck through appropriate job mixes. Liedtke introduced the topic in 2000 [15]. Both Antonopoulos [5] and Koukis [13] have built upon his work by proposing techniques for scheduling jobs on SMP nodes in a manner cognizant of memory bus contention.

These studies are similar to ours in spirit, but target different environments. Koukis, for instance, targets serial applications which are time-shared on a cluster of dual-way SMP servers running Linux. The possibility of parallel applications is addressed but not evaluated. Contrastingly, we are concerned with space-sharing parallel scientific applications in production supercomputing environments under the assumptions detailed at the start of this section. We also study the effects of the cache hierarchy and I/O.

7.5 Other Related Work

Some previous studies of multiple-resource allocation have also been conducted. Parsons and Sevcik investigated the coordinated allocation or processors and memory [20]; subsequently, Leinberger et. al generalized the problem to *k-resource scheduling* where the idea is to choose optimal job working sets when multiple resource requirements exist [14]. Unlike our study, this work assumes independently allocatable resources and well defined requirements for each job. On our target architecture, a predetermined bundle of resources is provided to a job along with each processor.

It has been observed that spacing I/O-intensive jobs in time on a parallel file system improves performance [18]. Our emphasis is primarily to spread these in space, and also to identify specific symbiotic partners for such jobs.

Mache and Garg have focused on finding a spatial layout for concurrent jobs in a parallel space-shared machine to minimize communication and maximize access to I/O nodes for I/O-intensive jobs [17]. We address a related but different problem in considering not only the physical layout but also the sets of jobs contending for resources.

Also described has been an approach for deriving beneficial symbiosis (i.e. commensalism), wherein one version of a program, executing concurrently with the main program, helps the main program resolve control-flow for instruction fetching [27]. Alternatively, we search the existing job-stream for sets to co-schedule that interfere as little as possible with each other. We expect the existence of commensal job combinations in realistic production environments to be unlikely.

8 Conclusions and Future Work

In this work, we have introduced symbiotic space-sharing as a promising technique for improving the performance efficiency of large-scale parallel machines. We have shown that a wide range of benchmarks commonly suffer between 10-60% slowdown due to memory resource contention and up to several orders of magnitude for I/O. We have shown that this effect can be mitigated by deploying alternate job mixes and have extended these results to parallel codes, demonstrating that node-sharing among parallel applications can increase throughput by increasing performance while maintaining high system utilization levels. We synthesized these findings by exhibiting a prototype scheduler that improves throughput by 20%.

Our results are derived from DataStar, a production machine at the San Diego Supercomputer Center, and the NAS Parallel Benchmarks, a widely used benchmark suite designed with the express purpose of evaluating the performance of parallel Supercomputers.

Through this work, we have explored the opportunity space for and confirmed the viability of symbiotic space-sharing. Future work may proceed in the following directions:

The confirmed promise of symbiotic space-sharing warrants the effort to conduct a study on its applicability to real-world production workloads. The effectiveness of our techniques remains to be seen for highly parallel, resource-intensive, scientific applications. Further, a study characterizing the job mixes in today's production queues would help us understand more extensively the opportunity for symbiotic job mixes and the heuristics that could exploit them.

The relationship between hardware counter statistics and symbiotic space-sharing should be further explored. Such efforts could help create automated algorithms to identify the limiting resource of applications. A more advanced result might be to use such counters to automatically identify symbiosis, even among applications bound by the same resource.

Research on production workloads and prediction of job interactions can facilitate the development of symbiotic scheduling heuristics. Particularly interesting would be a framework for evaluating tradeoffs between system throughput and fairness in queue times or between other policy objectives.

We are currently also extending this feasibility study onto grid schedulers in an attempt to understand the degree to which a grid-wide scheduler can improve the efficiency of its resource pool by scheduling symbiotic job combinations at each site. Through this approach, we also hope to study the degree to which a scheduler can increase throughput by lessening site load on resources such as a parallel I/O file system.

Acknowledgements

This work was supported in part by the DOE Office of Science through the award entitled HPCS Execution Time Evaluation, and by the SciDAC award entitled High-End Computer System Performance: Science and Engineering. This work was also supported in part by NSF NGS Award #0406312 entitled Performance Measurement & Modeling of Deep Hierarchy Systems.

References

1. http://icl.cs.utk.edu/projectsfiles/hpcc/RandomAccess/.
2. http://www.cs.virginia.edu/stream/.
3. http://www.npaci.edu/DataStar/guide/home.html.

4. http://www.sdsc.edu/pmac/Benchmark/iobench.
5. C. D. Antonopoulos, D. S. Nikolopoulos, and T. S. Papatheodorou. Scheduling Algorithms with Bus Bandwidth Considerations for SMPs. *icpp*, 00:547, 2003.
6. D. H. Bailey, E. Barszcz, J. T. Barton, D. S. Browning, R. L. Carter, D. Dagum, R. A. Fatoohi, P. O. Frederickson, T. A. Lasinski, R. S. Schreiber, H. D. Simon, V. Venkatakrishnan, and S. K. Weeratunga. The NAS Parallel Benchmarks. *The International Journal of Supercomputer Applications*, 5(3):63–73, Fall 1991.
7. A. Batat and D. G. Feitelson. Gang Scheduling with Memory Considerations. In *14th Intl. Parallel Distributed Processing Symp.*, pages 109–114, 2000.
8. J. Dongarra and P. Luszczek. Introduction to the HPCChallenge Benchmark Suite. Technical Report ICL-UT-05-01, ICL, 2005.
9. A. B. Downey and D. G. Feitelson. The elusive goal of workload characterization. *SIGMETRICS Perform. Eval. Rev.*, 26(4):14–29, 1999.
10. Feitelson and Nitzberg. Job Characteristics of a Production parallel scientific workload on the NASA Ames iPSC/860. In D. G. Feitelson and L. Rudolph, editors, *Job Scheduling Strategies for Parallel Processing – IPPS'95 Workshop*, volume 949, pages 337–360. Springer, 1995.
11. R. Gibbons. A Historical Application Profiler for Use by Parallel Schedulers. In *IPPS '97: Proceedings of the Job Scheduling Strategies for Parallel Processing*, pages 58–77, London, UK, 1997. Springer-Verlag.
12. S. Kannan, P. Mayes, M. Roberts, D. Brelsford, and J. Skovira. *Workload Management with LoadLeveler*. IBM, November 2001.
13. E. Koukis and N. Koziris. Memory Bandwidth Aware Scheduling for SMP Cluster Nodes. In *PDP '05: Proceedings of the 13th Euromicro Conference on Parallel, Distributed and Network-Based Processing (PDP'05)*, pages 187–196, Washington, DC, USA, 2005. IEEE Computer Society.
14. W. Leinberger, G. Karypis, and V. Kumar. Job scheduling in the presence of multiple resource requirements. In *Supercomputing '99: Proceedings of the 1999 ACM/IEEE conference on Supercomputing (CDROM)*, page 47, New York, NY, USA, 1999. ACM Press.
15. J. Liedtke, M. Volp, and K. Elphinstone. Preliminary thoughts on memory-bus scheduling. In *EW 9: Proceedings of the 9th workshop on ACM SIGOPS European workshop*, pages 207–210, New York, NY, USA, 2000. ACM Press.
16. D. A. Lifka. The ANL/IBM SP Scheduling System. In *IPPS 1995 Workshop on Job Scheduling Strategies for Parallel Processing*, volume 949, pages 295–303, 1995.
17. J. Mache, V. Lo, and S. Garg. Job Scheduling that Minimizes Network Contention due to both Communication and I/O. In *14th International Parallel and Distributed Processing Symposium*, page 457, Washington, DC, USA, 2000. IEEE Computer Society.
18. J. Mache, V. Lo, M. Livingston, and S. Garg. The impact of spatial layout of jobs on parallel I/O performance. In *IOPADS '99: Proceedings of the sixth workshop on I/O in parallel and distributed systems*, pages 45–56, New York, NY, USA, 1999. ACM Press.
19. R. L. McGregor, C. Antonopoulos, and D. Nikolopoulos. Scheduling Algorithms for Effective Thread Pairing on Hybrid Multiprocessors. In *Proceedings of the 19th IEEE International Parallel and Distributed Processing Symposium*, Denver, CO, April 2005. IEEE Computer Society Press.
20. E. W. Parsons and K. C. Sevcik. Coordinated allocation of memory and processors in multiprocessors. In *SIGMETRICS '96: Proceedings of the 1996 ACM SIGMETRICS international conference on Measurement and modeling of computer systems*, pages 57–67, New York, NY, USA, 1996. ACM Press.

21. V. G. J. Peris, M. S. Squillante, and V. K. Naik. Analysis of the impact of memory in distributed parallel processing systems. In *SIGMETRICS '94: Proceedings of the 1994 ACM SIGMETRICS conference on Measurement and modeling of computer systems*, pages 5–18, New York, NY, USA, 1994. ACM Press.

22. W. Smith, I. T. Foster, and V. E. Taylor. Predicting Application Run Times Using Historical Information. In *IPPS/SPDP '98: Proceedings of the Workshop on Job Scheduling Strategies for Parallel Processing*, pages 122–142, London, UK, 1998. Springer-Verlag.

23. A. Snavely and D. Tullsen. Symbiotic Job Scheduling for a Simultaneous Multithreading Processor. In *Proceedings of the Ninth International Conference on Architectural Support for Programming Languages and Operating Systems*, pages 234–244, November 2000.

24. A. Snavely, D. Tullsen, and G. Voelker. Symbiotic Jobscheduling for a Simultaneous Multithreading Processor. In *Proceedings of the ACM 2002 Joint International Conference on Measurement and Modeling of Computer Systems (SIGMETRICS. 2002)*, pages 66–76, Marina Del Rey, June 2002.

25. M. Squillante and E. Lazowska. Using Processor-Cache Affinity Information in Shared-Memory Multiprocessor Scheduling. *IEEE Transactions on Parallel and Distributed Systemse*, 4(2):131–143, February 1993.

26. G. E. Suh, L. Rudolph, and S. Devadas. Effects of Memory Performance on Parallel Job Scheduling. In *JSSPP '01: Revised Papers from the 7th International Workshop on Job Scheduling Strategies for Parallel Processing*, pages 116–132, London, UK, 2001. Springer-Verlag.

27. K. Sundaramoorthy, Z. Purser, and E. Rotenberg. Slipstream Processors: Improving both Performance and Fault Tolerance. In *Architectural Support for Programming Languages and Operating Systems*, pages 257–268, 2000.

28. J. Torrellas, A. Tucker, and A. Gupta. Evaluating the Performance of Cache-Affinity Scheduling in Shared-Memory Multiprocessors. *Journal of Parallel and Distributed Computing*, 24(2):139, February 1995.

29. R. Vaswani and J. Zahorjan. The Implications of Cache Affinity on Processor Scheduling for Multiprogrammed Shared Memory Multiprocessors. In *Proceedings of the 13th ACM Symposium on Operating System Principles*, pages 26–40, Pacific Grove, CA, October 1991.

30. Y. Wiseman and D. Feitelson. Paired Gang Scheduling. In *IEEE Transactions on Parallel and Distributed Systems*, volume 14, pages 581–592, 2003.

31. P. Wong and R. V. der Wijngaart. NAS Parallel Benchmarks I/O Version 2.4. Technical report, NASA Ames Research Center, Moffett Field, CA 94035-1000, January 2003. NAS Technical Report NAS-03-002.

Modeling Job Arrivals in a Data-Intensive Grid

Hui Li[1],[*], Michael Muskulus[2], and Lex Wolters[1]

[1] Leiden Institute of Advanced Computer Science (LIACS), Leiden University, Niels Bohrweg 1, 2333 CA Leiden, The Netherlands
hui.li@computer.org
[2] Mathematical Institute, Leiden University, Niels Bohrweg 1, 2333 CA Leiden, The Netherlands

Abstract. In this paper we present an initial analysis of job arrivals in a production data-intensive Grid and investigate several traffic models to characterize the interarrival time processes. Our analysis focuses on the heavy-tail behavior and autocorrelation structures, and the modeling is carried out at three different levels: *Grid*, *Virtual Organization (VO)*, and *region*. A set of *m-state Markov modulated Poisson processes (MMPP)* is investigated, while *Poisson processes* and *hyperexponential renewal processes* are evaluated for comparison studies. We apply the *transportation distance* metric from dynamical systems theory to further characterize the differences between the data trace and the simulated time series, and estimate errors by *bootstrapping*. The experimental results show that MMPPs with a certain number of states are successful to a certain extent in simulating the job traffic at different levels, fitting both the interarrival time distribution and the autocorrelation function. However, MMPPs are not able to match the autocorrelations for certain VOs, in which strong deterministic semi-periodic patterns are observed. These patterns are further characterized using different representations. Future work is needed to model both deterministic and stochastic components in order to better capture the correlation structure in the series.

1 Introduction

Performance evaluation of computer systems, such as comparing different scheduling strategies on parallel supercomputers, requires the use of representative workloads to produce dependable results [9,13]. On single parallel machines, a significant amount of workload data has been collected [33], characterized [23,27], and modeled [7,25,41]. Benchmarks and standards are also proposed for workloads in evaluations of parallel job schedulers [6].

In a production Grid environment, however, few work has been done because the Grid infrastructure is still emerging and it is difficult to collect traces at the Grid level. Let us take the LHC Computing Grid (LCG) [21] as an example. The LCG testbed currently has approximately 180 active sites with a total number of 24,515 CPUs and 3 Petabytes storage, which is primarily used for high-energy physics data processing. Resource brokering or superscheduling in such an environment is challenging given the fact that Grid schedulers do not have control over the participating resources. In

---

[*] Corresponding author.

E. Frachtenberg and U. Schwiegelshohn (Eds.): JSSPP 2006, LNCS 4376, pp. 210–231, 2007.

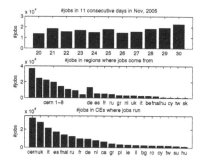

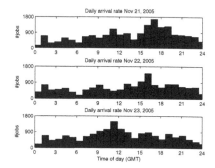

Fig. 1. Job distribution (cern - EU Center for Nuclear Research, fnal - Fermi Lab, the rest are country domain names)

Fig. 2. Daily arrival rate in three consecutive days in November, 2005. The time is in Greenwich Mean Time (GMT).

such contexts different scheduling and resource management systems have been proposed [31]. The current scheduling system deployed in LCG is a distributed version of the centralized resource broker, which originated in the EU DataGrid. It has multiple resource broker instances distributed in different regions/countries [11]. The Virtual Organization (VO) based scheduler with usage SLAs is proposed in a similar computing environment with similar workloads [10]. The evaluations of these different superscheduling architectures and strategies require proper workload models at different levels.

In this paper we present an initial analysis and modeling of Grid job arrival patterns. Our data is obtained via the Real Time Monitor [36] in the LCG production Grid. Our analysis focuses on the heavy-tail behavior and autocorrelations of job arrival processes. The modeling is carried out at the Grid, VO, and region level for facilitating evaluations of different scheduling strategies. A set of m-state Markov modulated Poisson processes (MMPP) is investigated for modeling, while Poisson processes and hyperexponential renewal processes are also evaluated for comparison. We apply the transportation distance metric from dynamical systems theory [28] to further characterize the differences between the data trace and the simulated time series.

The rest of the paper is organized as follows. Section 2 describes the workload, analyzes the daily arrival rate and summary statistics from different VOs and users, and presents the self-similarity measurements in terms of the Hurst parameter and the autocorrelation function (ACF). Section 3 introduces the selected traffic models and describes how to estimate parameters for each model. The transportation distance metric as an analysis tool is also presented. Section 4 presents the detailed modeling of job arrivals at the Grid, VO, and region level. The goodness of models are evaluated by the interarrival time distribution, the autocorrelation function and transportation distance of simulated traces. Section 5 discusses related work in the analysis and modeling of arrival processes in a broader perspective. Conclusions and future work are presented in Section 6.

2   Statistical Analysis

2.1   Workload Description

As mentioned above, LCG is a worldwide production Grid developed and operated for physics data processing. Almost all the jobs are trivially parallel tasks, requiring one CPU to process certain amount of data. Most of the jobs come from multiple large-scale physics experiments, such as *lhcb*, *cms*, *atlas* and *alice*. These experiments are also named as Virtual Organizations (VOs), in which users worldwide participate. The computing and storage resources define local sharing policies based on VOs and users. At the meta level workloads are managed and routed to resources via resource brokers (RBs), which do the matchmaking for jobs and try to balance the load at a global level.

There are resource brokers distributed over the Grid by regions, such as one in Germany, one in the UK, and so on. A majority of jobs come from CERN in Switzerland and there are around eight RB instances at CERN to share the workloads. The Real Time Monitor developed by Imperial College London [36] monitors jobs from all the major RBs in the LCG testbed, therefore the trace data it collects is representative at the Grid level. The job characteristics includes VO name, user DN (Distinguished Name), RB name, UI (User Interface), CE (Computing Element), submission time, run time and status. These attributes enable us to categorize, analyze and model job arrivals at different levels.

The LCG Real Time Monitor was in operation since October, 2005 and we use a period of eleven consecutive days (from Nov 20th to 30th, 2005) without missing data[1] in this study. Figure 1 shows the number of jobs in each day, number of jobs coming from different regions, and number of jobs in CEs where jobs get executed. We can see that a total number of 188,041 jobs distributed quite evenly over the period. More than 75% of jobs come from User Interfaces at CERN while the rest originated in around twenty different countries. The workloads are routed by resource brokers to computing resources in more than twenty countries, in which jobs are distributed in quite different orders than job origins. Job turnaround times are frequently used as the metric for the resource brokers to rank resources after matchmaking.

2.2   Job Arrival Analysis

Figure 2 shows the daily arrival rate in three consecutive days (GMT) on LCG in November, 2005. As we can see at the Grid level there are no clearly observable daily patterns, which are evident on single parallel machines [7,23,25]. Jobs are scattered in daily hours more evenly with peaks in the middle day or in the afternoon. The even distribution of jobs is explainable by the fact that users are simultaneously active across different time zones in the Grid. The peaks in the middle day or in the afternoon are mainly attributed to users at CERN, who submit a majority of jobs during the period under study.

Figure 3 and 4 show the number of jobs submitted by VOs and users. There is an interesting pattern that the job distribution for VOs can be fitted by an exponential

---

[1] Only jobs submitted to RBs are recorded and those who directly go to the Computing Elements are not available.

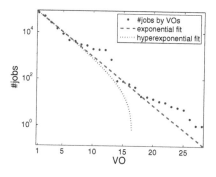

Fig. 3. Number of jobs submitted by VOs

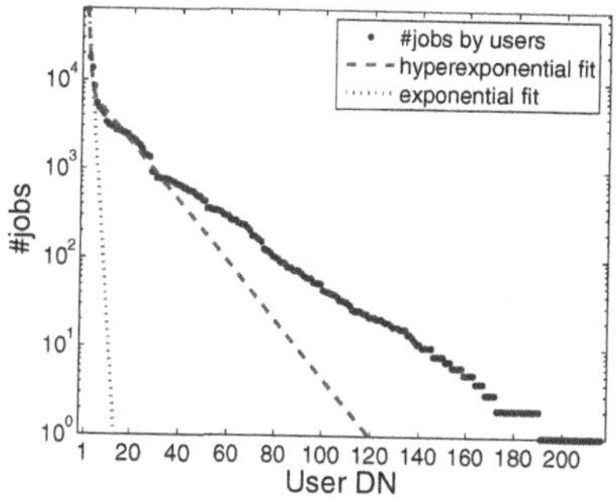

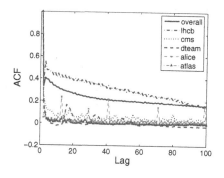

Fig. 4. Number of jobs submitted by users

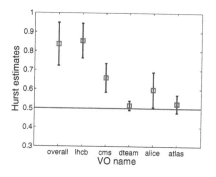

Fig. 5. Estimates of Hurst parameters for inter-arrival times

Fig. 6. Autocorrelation functions (ACFs) of interarrival times

function quite well. The top five VOs, namely *lhcb*, *cms*, *dteam*, *alice*, and *atlas*, submit almost 90% of the total number of jobs. The job distribution for users decreases even more sharply and a two-phase hyperexponential function has a better fit. The top 10% of users contribute to 90% of the whole workload and the top three account for 50%. This type of pattern is also observed in many social and physical phenomena, such as database transactions and Unix file sizes [13]. It is argued in [2] that it essentially originates in a priority selection mechanism between tasks and non-tasks waiting for execution. From a modeling perspective this pattern makes the VO an appropriate level for categorization since the limited number of main components represent most of the workloads.

2.3 Self-similarity

Self-similarity means that a process looks statistically the same over a wide range of different scales and is closely related to so-called "bursty" behavior and long range dependence [4]. The degree of the self-similarity of a stochastic process can be summarized by the Hurst parameter ($0 < H < 1$). A value of $H > 0.5$ indicates self-similarity with positive near neighbor correlation and the more H is close to 1, the more self-similar the process. As there is no consensus on how to best estimate the Hurst parameter, we use three estimation techniques, namely *R/S statistic, variance plot, Periodogram*, and try to find agreement among them[2]. Figure 5 shows the means and standard deviations of Hurst parameter estimates of the interarrival time processes for the Grid trace and different VOs. We can see that the overall Grid job arrivals are self-similar with $H \approx 0.84$. The VO *lhcb* is also strongly self-similar with the Hurst parameter reaching 0.85. The other VOs show moderate to weak self-similarity. These observations are also confirmed if we look at the autocorrelation function (ACF) of interarrival times, illustrated in Figure 6. Strongly self-similar processes (*overall, lhcb*) have a longer memory than the weakly self-similar counterparts (*dteam, atlas*), whose ACFs quickly approach zero as the lag increases. Autocorrelation is used as one of the statistical properties to measure the goodness of fit in the following sections.

3   Methodology

Job traffic can be mathematically described as a *point process*, which consists of a sequence of arrival instances. Two equivalent descriptions of point processes are *counting processes* and *interarrival time processes* [5,17]. In this paper we describe the traffic using the interarrival time process, sometimes also called the embedded process. Based on the analysis of job arrivals, several basic principles can be derived for model selection. Firstly, models should be parameterizable and flexible enough to represent the Grid job traffic at different levels. Secondly, models must be able to approximate both the interarrival time distribution (heavy-tail behavior) and the autocorrelation function. Thirdly, models should be analytically simple and there should exist proven methods to estimate their parameters from the data trace. Bearing these points in mind, we investigate a set of m-state Markov modulated Poisson processes to model job arrivals. Phase-type renewal processes and Poisson processes are also evaluated for comparison. We discuss the selected models and their corresponding parameter estimation methods in this section. The recently proposed transportation distance metric for the comparison of two time series is presented as a tool to further characterize the goodness of fit.

3.1   Markov Modulated Poisson Processes

A Markov modulated Poisson process (MMPP) is a doubly stochastic Poisson process whose intensity is controlled by a finite state continuous-time Markov chain (CTMC). Equivalently, an MMPP process can be regarded as a Poisson process varying its arrival rate according to an m-state irreducible continuous time Markov chain. Following the notations in [14], an MMPP parameterized by an m-state CTMC with infinitesimal generator Q and m Poisson arrival rates Λ can be described as

$$Q = \begin{bmatrix} -\sigma_1 & \sigma_{12} & \cdots & \sigma_{1m} \\ \sigma_{21} & -\sigma_2 & \cdots & \sigma_{2m} \\ \cdot & \cdot & \cdots & \cdot \\ \sigma_{m1} & \sigma_{m2} & \cdots & -\sigma_m \end{bmatrix}, \tag{1}$$

---

[2] Estimations of the Hurst parameters are calculated using a self-similarity analysis tool called SELFIS [19].

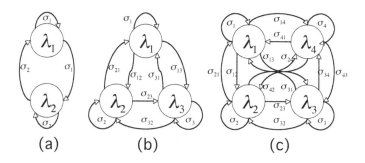

Fig. 7. MMPP models of state 2, 3, and 4, respectively

$$\sigma_i = \sum_{j=1, j \neq i}^{m} \sigma_{ij}, \tag{2}$$

$$\Lambda = diag(\lambda_1, \lambda_2, ..., \lambda_m). \tag{3}$$

MMPPs with state 2, 3, and 4 are illustrated in figure 7. The MMPP model is commonly used in telecommunication traffic modeling [16,17] and has several attractive properties, such as being able to capture correlations between interarrival times while still remaining analytically tractable. We refer to [14] for a thorough treatment of MMPP properties as well as its related queuing network models.

A natural problem which arises with the applications of MMPPs is how to estimate its parameters from the data trace. In [37] methods based on moment matching and maximum likelihood (MLE) are surveyed and it is proven that MLE methods are strongly consistent. In [38] Ryden proposed an EM algorithm to compute the MLE estimates of the parameters of a m-state MMPP. Recently, Roberts et al. improved Ryden's EM algorithm and extended its applicability in two important aspects [35]: firstly a scaling procedure is developed to circumvent the need for customized floating-point software, arising from the exponential increase of the likelihood function over time; secondly, evaluation of integrals of matrix exponentials is facilitated by a result of Van Loan, which achieves significant speedup. We implemented the improved version of Ryden's EM algorithm in Matlab and this is by far the best MLE estimator that we can find for m-state MMPPs. Given the difficult numerical issues involved, estimation errors could still be substantial, though. It should also be mentioned that the estimation for higher order MMPPs is increasingly difficult, since there are more parameters to take into account.

3.2 Hyperexponetial Renewal Processes

In a renewal process the interarrival times are independently and identically distributed but the distribution can be general. A Poisson process is characterized as a renewal process with exponentially distributed interarrival times. In phase-type renewal processes the interarrival times are distributed in so-called phase-type, e.g. as a n-phase hyperexponential distribution. In theory any interarrival distribution can be approximated by phase-type ones, including those which exhibit heavy-tail behavior [34].

However, a major modeling drawback of renewal processes is that the autocorrelation function (ACF) of the interarrival times vanishes for all non-zero lags so they cannot capture the temporal dependencies in time series. Unlike the renewal models, MMPPs introduce dependencies into the interarrival times so they can potentially simulate the traffic more realistically with non-zero autocorrelations.

There are special cases where an MMPP is a renewal process and the simplest one is the Interrupted Poisson Process (IPP). The IPP is defined as a 2-state MMPP with one arrival rate being zero. Stochastically, an IPP is equivalent to a 2-phase hyperexponential renewal process. Following the formulations in [14] the IPP can be described as

$$Q = \begin{bmatrix} -\sigma_1 & \sigma_1 \\ \sigma_2 & -\sigma_2 \end{bmatrix}, \quad \Lambda = \begin{bmatrix} \lambda & 0 \\ 0 & 0 \end{bmatrix}, \tag{4}$$

and the 2-phase hyperexponential distribution (H_2) has the density function

$$f_{H_2}(t) = p\mu_1 e^{-\mu_1 t} + (1-p)\mu_2 e^{-\mu_2 t}. \tag{5}$$

The parameters of H_2 can be transformed to parameters of IPP by

$$\lambda = p\mu_1 + (1-p)\mu_2, \tag{6}$$

$$\sigma_1 = \frac{p(1-p)(\mu_1 - \mu_2)^2}{\lambda}, \tag{7}$$

$$\sigma_2 = \frac{\mu_1 \mu_2}{\lambda}, \tag{8}$$

while the H_2 parameters (p, μ_1, μ_2) can be obtained from the data by applying an EM algorithm as described in [1], whose implementation is freely available [12].

3.3   Transportation Distance of Time Series

Coming from a dynamical systems theory background, Moeckel and Murray have given a measure of distance between two time series [28] that, from a time series perspective, excellently analyzes (short-time) correlations. It is based on recent research on nonlinear dynamics [18,3]. Given a time series, the data is first discretized, i.e. binned, with a certain resolution (a parameter of the method), and then transformed into points in a k–dimensional discrete space, referred to as the reconstruction space, using a unit-delay embedding. In dimension 2, for example, all $n-1$ consecutive pairs (x_i, x_{i+1}), $1 \leq i < n$, of n given data points thus constitute a point $y_i = (x_i, x_{i+1})$ in the reconstruction space. The idea is, that the essential dynamics of generic systems can usually be reconstructed sufficiently in a low dimensional space. The normalized k–dimensional probability distributions of these data points from the two series will then be considered as a transportation problem (also called a minimum cost flow problem): What is the optimal way, given the first probability distribution, to arrive at the second, just by transporting weight, i.e. probability, from some boxes to some others? With each movement a transportation cost is given, which is the normalized (by mass) taxi–cab distance from the first box to the second, measured in units of the discretization size[3], which is given by the resolution parameter of the method. The minimal such transportation cost can be computed by linear programming. We have written some code to generate a linear program from two time series which then will be fed into a specialized minimum-cost flow solver[4]. For details on linear programming, the transportation problem and algorithmic improvements, we refer to [39].

The transportation distance measures to which extent two given time series show the same k–correlation structure, and is thereby quite sensitive to (1) correlations, and (2) the underlying probability distributions. It is robust against small perturbations and outliers, too. A value of the transportation distance can be roughly interpreted as the average distance each data point of the first time series lies from a corresponding point in the second series.

Table 1. Transportation distances in dimension 1, i.e. for single interarrival times, between real data and simulated series of fitted Poisson, m-MMPP and IPP models. The time resolution is 10s intervals. All entries are normalized to mean taxi-cab distance (with a unit of 10s). Values depicted are bootstrap means and standard mean error, estimated by bootstrapping 50 times.

Level	Name	Poisson		IPP		MMPP2	
Grid	lcg	0.039	± 0.001	0.029	± 0.001	0.024	± 0.001
	lhcb	0.35	± 0.01	0.35	± 0.01	0.47	± 0.01
	cms	1.35	± 0.01	0.40	± 0.01	0.81	± 0.01
VO	dteam	4.57	± 0.02	1.03	± 0.02	17.07	± 0.05
	alice	1.57	± 0.02	0.98	± 0.02	1.21	± 0.02
	atlas	16.38	± 0.19	6.54	± 0.15	56.94	± 0.29
	cern	3.38	± 0.02	0.78	± 0.02	2.95	± 0.02
Region	de	9.60	± 0.09	3.77	± 0.06	35.97	± 0.14
	uk	28.91	± 0.16	7.58	± 0.10	95.83	± 0.51

Level	Name	MMPP3		MMPP4	
Grid	lcg	0.035	± 0.001	0.058	± 0.001
	lhcb	0.50	± 0.01	0.54	± 0.01
	cms	0.70	± 0.01	5.34	± 0.01
VO	dteam	21.65	± 0.06	N/A	
	alice	3.28	± 0.02	3.36	± 0.03
	atlas	47.70	± 0.50	5.49	± 0.19
	cern	2.53	± 0.03	25.17	± 0.08
Region	de	43.73	± 0.24	437.18	± 0.95
	uk	98.68	± 0.46	N/A	

---

[3] This is equivalent to considering all the points in each discrete box to be located at the center of their box.

[4] We use the *MCF* network simplex solver developed by Andreas Löbel [26], as well as the general purpose *lp_solve* linear programming solver [24] for comparing performance.

Table 2. Parameters of fitted Poisson, MMPP2 and IPP models as found by the EM algorithm

Level	Name	Poisson	MMPP2				IPP		
		λ	σ_1	σ_2	λ_1	λ_2	p	μ_1	μ_2
Grid	lcg	11.90	0.17	0.08	22.10	7.16	0.22	139.20	10.46
VO	lhcb	4.35	0.04	0.01	8.43	3.18	0.11	4.35	4.35
	cms	3.11	0.10	0.07	6.92	0.44	0.95	6.21	0.31
	dteam	1.64	0.83	0.08	17.86	0.10	0.91	18.31	0.17
	alice	2.38	0.16	0.06	6.67	0.73	0.78	6.79	0.71
	atlas	0.54	0.10	0.01	4.98	0.02	0.95	5.05	0.03
Region	cern	1.41	0.10	0.06	3.43	0.13	0.94	3.36	0.15
	de	0.83	0.17	0.03	4.98	0.03	0.94	5.08	0.06
	uk	0.19	0.36	0.01	4.93	0.03	0.75	5.82	0.05

Table 3. Transportation distances in dimension 2, i.e. comparing pairs of interarrival times, between real data and simulated series of fitted Poisson, m-MMPP and IPP models. The time resolution is 30 seconds. All entries are normalized to mean taxi-cab distance (with a unit of 30 seconds), and should therefore be about a factor of 3 smaller than the corresponding values in Table 1. Values depicted are bootstrap means and standard mean errors, estimated by bootstrapping 25 times.

Level	Name	Poisson		IPP		MMPP2	
Grid	lcg	0.0038	± 0.0001	0.0010	± 0.0001	0.0139	± 0.0001
VO	lhcb	0.179	± 0.001	0.182	± 0.001	0.244	± 0.001
	cms	0.747	± 0.004	0.394	± 0.003	0.500	± 0.004
	dteam	2.708	± 0.012	1.141	± 0.008	11.249	± 0.029
	alice	0.813	± 0.011	0.661	± 0.011	0.686	± 0.011
	atlas	11.041	± 0.123	5.601	± 0.084	37.764	± 0.175
Region	cern	2.174	± 0.012	0.818	± 0.010	1.917	± 0.016
	de	6.080	± 0.063	2.962	± 0.039	24.007	± 0.110
	uk	20.490	± 0.108	8.504	± 0.064	64.765	± 0.370

Level	Name	MMPP3		MMPP4	
Grid	lcg	0.0233	± 0.0002	0.0035	± 0.0001
VO	lhcb	0.274	± 0.001	0.295	± 0.001
	cms	0.458	± 0.004	3.279	± 0.008
	dteam	14.285	± 0.038	N/A	
	alice	1.936	± 0.022	1.963	± 0.018
	atlas	31.906	± 0.376	3.480	± 0.099
Region	cern	1.641	± 0.023	16.674	± 0.062
	de	28.786	± 0.196	290.859	± 0.618
	uk	65.414	± 0.429	N/A	

Unfortunately, the transportation distance is difficult to compute for higher lags, since the computational effort rises polynomially in the lag. We are working on approximation methods though, which might overcome this problem in the future [29].

Table 4. Error estimates for fitted MMPP2 model, standard mean errors have been estimated by bootstrapping 25 times with a geometrical blocksize distribution of mean length 100. Correlations between parameters have not been indicated.

Level	Name	MMPP2							
		σ_1		σ_2		λ_1		λ_2	
Grid	lcg	0.262	± 0.034	0.387	± 0.064	17.300	± 0.590	5.118	± 0.291
	lhcb	0.632	± 0.117	0.396	± 0.153	9.051	± 0.753	3.261	± 0.093
	cms	0.106	± 0.002	0.075	± 0.001	6.833	± 0.041	0.435	± 0.015
VO	dteam	0.824	± 0.016	0.079	± 0.001	17.651	± 0.211	0.100	± 0.003
	alice	0.172	± 0.004	0.069	± 0.004	6.692	± 0.022	0.728	± 0.023
	atlas	0.102	± 0.003	0.012	± 0.001	5.020	± 0.055	0.020	± 0.001
	cern	0.099	± 0.003	0.063	± 0.002	3.436	± 0.021	0.129	± 0.003
Region	de	0.174	± 0.006	0.035	± 0.002	5.095	± 0.064	0.032	± 0.002
	uk	2.279	± 0.261	0.128	± 0.033	4.925	± 0.530	0.054	± 0.006

Table 5. Bootstrapped rate parameters of fitted MMPP3 model, standard mean errors have been estimated by bootstrapping 25 times with a geometrical blocksize distribution of mean length 100. Correlations between rates have not been indicated.

Level	Name	MMPP3					
		λ_1		λ_2		λ_3	
Grid	lcg	1.979	± 0.205	2.290	± 0.209	13.812	± 0.210
	lhcb	1.913	± 0.135	2.092	± 0.162	5.087	± 0.150
	cms	0.257	± 0.032	0.672	± 0.099	7.098	± 0.098
VO	dteam	0.046	± 0.006	0.097	± 0.040	15.901	± 0.545
	alice	0.295	± 0.038	0.537	± 0.083	5.954	± 0.152
	atlas	0.001	± 0.054	0.163	± 0.091	4.839	± 0.174
	cern	0.094	± 0.014	0.284	± 0.052	4.050	± 0.077
Region	de	0.015	± 0.001	0.905	± 0.124	6.321	± 0.039
	uk	0.013	± 0.002	0.039	± 0.012	4.217	± 0.334

3.4 Bootstrapping

Error estimates for arbitrary functions of stochastic variables can be produced by *bootstraping/resampling* [8] techniques. The finite data trace is thereby assumed to be a *realization* of an underlying probabilistic process, i.e. data points are assumed to be drawn randomly from a (usually unknown) probability density. Each data value is sampled with an empirical probability that converges to this density, in the limit of an infinite data trace. The size of the variations in finite traces can be estimated by looking at additional data traces of the same length, sampled from the same distribution. Bootstrapping methods achieve this by resampling from the observed data trace itself, i.e. instead of choosing data points randomly from the unknown true density, points are chosen by its approximation, the known empirical density.

Since the transportation distance compares two probability densities, error estimates for this measure can be produced by the bootstrap method easily. We have implemented

Table 6. Bootstrapped transition parameters of fitted MMPP3 model, standard mean errors have been estimated by bootstrapping 25 times with a geometrical blocksize distribution of mean length 100. Correlations between parameters have not been indicated.

Level	Name	MMPP3					
		σ_{12}		σ_{13}		σ_{21}	
Grid	lcg	1.25	± 0.16	2.35	± 0.40	0.24	± 0.05
VO	lhcb	1.07	± 0.17	2.14	± 0.30	0.29	± 0.05
	cms	0.33	± 0.06	0.19	± 0.03	0.53	± 0.06
	dteam	0.35	± 0.05	0.13	± 0.03	0.57	± 0.07
	alice	0.50	± 0.06	0.27	± 0.04	0.48	± 0.05
	atlas	0.35	± 0.06	0.04	± 0.01	0.71	± 0.08
	cern	0.43	± 0.06	0.22	± 0.05	0.56	± 0.08
Region	de	0.011	± 0.001	0.016	± 0.001	0.089	± 0.006
	uk	0.42	± 0.05	0.10	± 0.02	0.74	± 0.08

Level	Name	MMPP3					
		σ_{23}		σ_{31}		σ_{32}	
Grid	lcg	0.72	± 0.10	0.06	± 0.01	0.10	± 0.02
VO	lhcb	1.07	± 0.17	0.12	± 0.02	0.17	± 0.03
	cms	0.31	± 0.06	0.13	± 0.02	0.15	± 0.02
	dteam	0.18	± 0.04	0.50	± 0.06	0.51	± 0.06
	alice	0.31	± 0.06	0.25	± 0.04	0.27	± 0.03
	atlas	0.19	± 0.05	0.22	± 0.05	0.24	± 0.03
	cern	0.34	± 0.06	0.19	± 0.03	0.29	± 0.04
Region	de	0.053	± 0.006	0.117	± 0.001	0.049	± 0.006
	uk	0.17	± 0.04	0.96	± 0.13	0.95	± 0.10

this method with 50 bootstraps of the same length in embedding dimension 1, and 25 in dimension 2, for each of the two time series fed into the distance algorithm. Results can be seen in Tables 1 and 3, where the bootstrap means and standard mean errors are shown. All of the results for the original series' distances lie scattered around the bootstrap means within one sampled standard deviation. This shows the appropriateness of the bootstrapping methodology, and we only give the bootstrap means in the tables for this reason.

For time series, where not only the distribution of values, but also the correlation structure is important, the simple bootstrap has to be replaced by more sophisticated methods. The block bootstrapping technique, developed by Künsch [20] and further analyzed in [32], instead of randomly choosing data points, randomly chooses sequences of consecutive points. The length of these *blocks* is again randomly chosen from a geometric distribution to smoothe boundary effects. We have applied this method with 25 bootstraps to the estimation of the MMPP model parameters by the EM algorithm. The mean block length has been chosen to be 100 interarrivals. Results can be seen in Table 4 for MMPP2, and Tables 5 and 6 for MMPP3, where we show bootstrap means and standard mean errors. Since there are strong correlations between parameters, these estimates have to be considered with some caution. This also explains the few discrepancies with the parameter estimation for the original data trace in Table 2.

4   Modeling

In a large-scale Grid environment different superscheduling architectures require modeling of job arrivals at different levels. By applying the methodology discussed above, we model the job traffic at the Grid, the Virtual Organization, and the region level, respectively in this section.

4.1   Grid Level

Figure 13 shows the fittings of the interarrival time in terms of complementary cumulative distribution function (CCDF) by five models, namely Poisson, IPP, MMPP2, MMPP3, and MMPP4. We can see that globally there is no heavy-tail behavior and all the models fit the job arrivals quite well. The transportation distances of dimension 1 given in Table 1 quantitatively measure the goodness of fit for interarrival time distributions. Since the values are all quite low, all models seem to reproduce correctly the probability distribution (1d), with MMPP2 being the best. The fittings of the autocorrelation function (ACF) of the interarrival time process are shown in Figure 14. As expected ACFs of Poisson and IPP vanish for all none-zero lags and they cannot capture the interdependencies of job arrivals. The MMPPs can introduce dependencies into the interarrival times, but they are not able to match the long memory of the original trace. By taking both CCDF and ACF into account we can conclude that MMPP2 is a better model for the Grid level job arrivals than the Poisson or IPP model. The transportation distances of dimension 2 given in Table 3 show the differences in pair correlations (2d), which are also quite small in value.

Figure 8 visually plots the sequences of interarrival times for the original trace and several models. We can see that both Poisson and IPP lack the kind of variability compared to the trace although their CCDFs fit quite well. MMPP2 looks more similar to the original data in terms of variability, therefore it can simulate the job traffic more realistically[5].

4.2   Virtual Organization Level

We model the five largest VOs, namely, *lhcb*, *cms*, *dteam*, *alice*, and *atlas*, in descendant order with respect to the number of jobs submitted. Figure 15 and 16 show the CCDFs and ACFs of the fitted models for the interarrival time process by *lhcb*. Being the largest VO in terms of the submitted jobs, *lhcb* has no heavy tail distribution of interarrivals and exhibits a long memory. It contributes significantly to the properties of overall Grid job arrivals shown in the last section. As to the models we can see that IPP produces identical fitting with Poisson. Both of them have slightly better results than MMPPs in terms of transportation distances of dimension 1 and 2. However, MMPP2 and MMPP3 have similar autocorrelations that come the closest to the original trace. Considering the tradeoffs, MMPP2 is selected as the best fit among the evaluated models. Clearly better

---

[5] This visual comparison should be replaced by objective, quantitative measures, of course, and this is exactly what the transportation distance achieves, when sufficiently high orders can be compared.

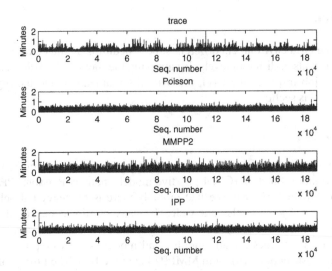

Fig. 8. Sequences of interarrival times of the Grid trace and the fitted models

models are needed to closely match the long memory in the series; we will elaborate why stochastic models fail to capture the autocorrelations in the coming sections, as well as indicate some future directions for research.

We observe that increasing the number of states in MMPPs would not necessarily improve the fitting. For instance, in the Grid and *lhcb* case MMPP4 is an overfitted model both in terms of CCDF and ACF. This phenomenon is seen with the transportation distance, too. It seems paradox at first, since MMPP4 is a more flexible model than MMPP3/MMPP2, but can be attributed to the following issues: (1) the parameter estimation by the EM algorithm does not easily give error estimates, so errors in the parameters could be substantial[6], (2) the data trace is finite, and actually rather small for fitting large interarrival times (which occur seldomly), (3) the compromise between fitting a lot of small interarrival times and some rarely occurring large events seems to favor the smaller times: there are too many large events generated by the higher order MMPPs, (4) there is a strong deterministic component in the *lhcb* data, as can be seen in Figure 9 and Figure 10 where we show the pair distribution for real data and simulated MMPP2 data. The large peak at about (24s, 24s) interarrival times is very difficult to model with a Poisson-based model, since waiting times in such models will always be from an exponential family, thereby monotonously decreasing with distance from the origin.

From Figure 17 to Figure 24 CCDF and ACF fittings are shown for the remaining four VOs. We can see that the less job submissions in the VO, the longer the tail the CCDF has. In those situations with heavy tails, the Poisson process fails to match the interarrival time distribution. For *cms* data with moderate interarrival time dependencies,

---

[6] In this respect, a Bayesian analysis by Monte-Carlo Markov Chain methods [40] would be desirable, since this would produce the *probability distribution* of the estimated parameters directly.

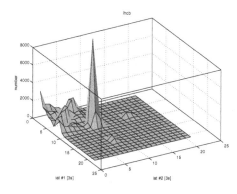

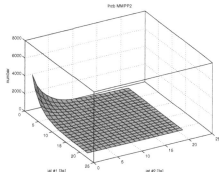

Fig. 9. Pairs of interarrival times for *lhcb*

Fig. 10. Pairs of interarrival times for MMPP2

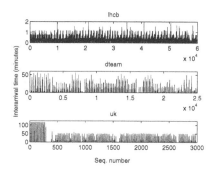

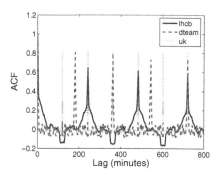

Fig. 11. Sequences of interarrival times for *lhcb*, *dteam*, and *uk*

Fig. 12. Autocorrelation functions for *lhcb*, *dteam*, and *uk* from the binned count processes

we can see that MMPP3 has very good fittings for both CCDF and ACF (Figure 17 and 18). For *dteam*, MMPPs exhibit longer memory which is not present in the data and IPP is shown to be the most suitable model (Figure 19 and 20). For *alice* both MMPP3 and MMPP4 can model the interarrival process better than others (Figure 21 and 22), although they tend to generate too many large times[7]. In the last VO we studied, namely *atlas*, MMPP4 is shown to be the best fitted model. MMPP2 and MMPP3 have too long memories and cannot fit the interarrival time distribution closely, while IPP has no memory and fails to match the heavy tail of the data (Figure 23 and 24).

Although no general conclusions can be reached, some observations are found to be very interesting. As the VO size decreases from *lhcb* to *cms*, then to *alice* and *atlas*, the models with the best fit are MMPPs with an increasing number of states, from 2 to 3 then to 4, although deterministic components can complicate this. This observation suggests that MMPPs have very attractive properties for modeling job traffic in the VO level, being general and analytically simple. With the VO size decreasing in an exponential

---

[7] This can be seen from their transportation distances, for example, which are more sensitive to large data values than to small ones.

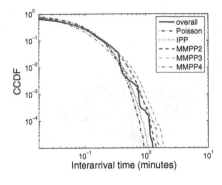

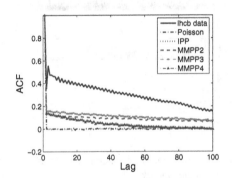

Fig. 13. Fitting the interarrival time distribution (CCDF) for the overall Grid job arrivals

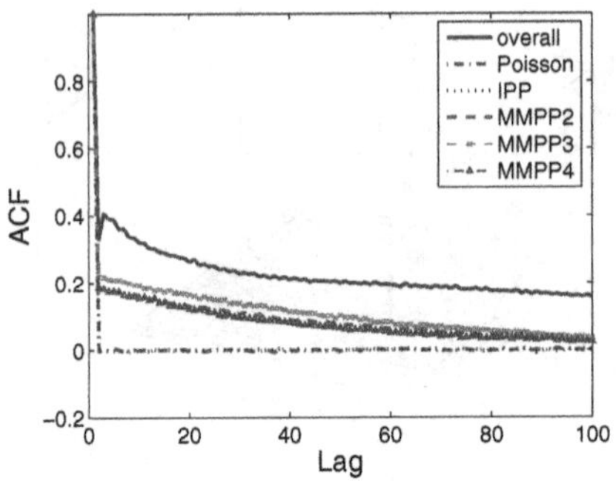

Fig. 14. Fitting the autocorrelation function (ACF) for the overall Grid job arrivals

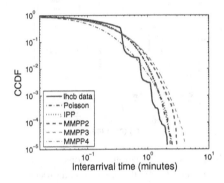

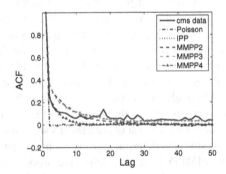

Fig. 15. Fitting the interarrival time distribution (CCDF) for job arrivals by VO *lhcb*

Fig. 16. Fitting the autocorrelation function (ACF) for job arrivals by VO *lhcb*

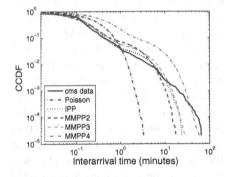

Fig. 17. Fitting the interarrival time distribution (CCDF) for job arrivals by VO *cms*

Fig. 18. Fitting the autocorrelation function (ACF) for job arrivals by VO *cms*

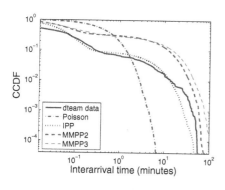

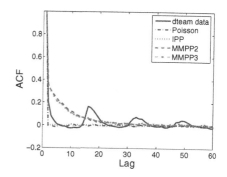

Fig. 19. Fitting the interarrival time distribution (CCDF) for job arrivals by VO *dteam*

Fig. 20. Fitting the autocorrelation function (ACF) for job arrivals by VO *dteam*

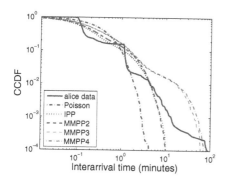

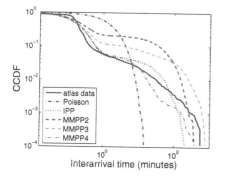

Fig. 21. Fitting the interarrival time distribution (CCDF) for job arrivals by VO *alice*

Fig. 22. Fitting the autocorrelation function (ACF) for job arrivals by VO *alice*

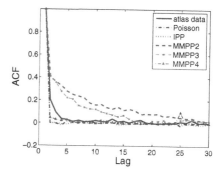

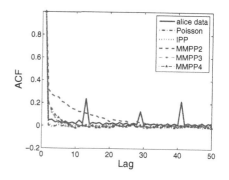

Fig. 23. Fitting the interarrival time distribution (CCDF) for job arrivals by VO *atlas*

Fig. 24. Fitting the autocorrelation function (ACF) for job arrivals by VO *atlas*

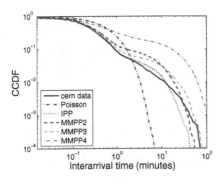

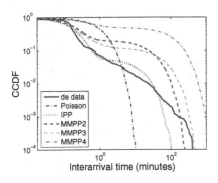

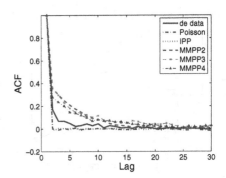

Fig. 25. Fitting the interarrival time distribution (CCDF) for job arrivals from *cern*

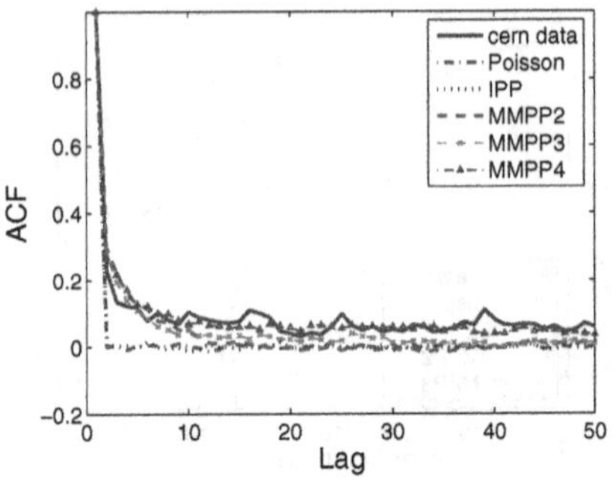

Fig. 26. Fitting the autocorrelation function (ACF) for job arrivals from *cern*

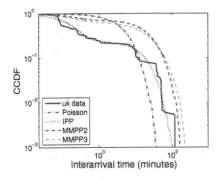

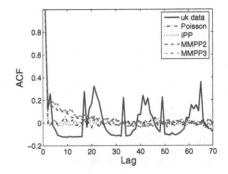

Fig. 27. Fitting the interarrival time distribution (CCDF) for job arrivals from *de*

Fig. 28. Fitting the autocorrelation function (ACF) for job arrivals from *de*

Fig. 29. Fitting the interarrival time distribution (CCDF) for job arrivals from *uk*

Fig. 30. Fitting the autocorrelation function (ACF) for job arrivals from *uk*

manner (see Figure 3), we can model the job arrivals of the corresponding VOs using MMPPs by increasing the number of states and/or further modeling of deterministic components. As a special case *dteam* will be discussed in detail in Section 4.4.

4.3 Region Level

Resource brokers in the current LCG testbed are distributed in regions, so it is important to model the job arrivals at the region level as well. Figure 25 to Figure 30 show the model fitting for *cern* (European Center for Nuclear Research), *de* (Germany), and *uk* (United Kingdom), respectively. Since a majority of jobs are originated in *cern* and routed by one of its eight resource broker instances, we use job arrivals by one randomly chosen resource broker in this study. From Figure 25 and 26 we can see that MMPP3 is the model with the best fit for *cern* data. MMPPs do not perform well for *de* and *uk*, introducing autocorrelations which are not observable in the real data. In these two cases IPP is shown to be the most suitable model, matching both the CCDFs and ACFs of the interarrival time processes.

4.4 Stochastic vs. Deterministic

In the modeling process, we find that for certain data such as *dteam* and *uk* the EM algorithm does not converge for estimating MMPP4 parameters (indicated by 'N/A' in the tables). This motivates us to plot the interarrival time sequences for all the data to see what kind of structures exist. The results are surprising: we find strong deterministic semi-periodic behavior for *lhcb*, *dteam* and *uk*. This is illustrated in Figure 11 and Figure 9. To further understand these patterns, we form a time series by counting number of jobs in intervals of 1 minute duration and plot the autocorrelation function (ACF) of this 'binned' counting process. Figure 12 shows these ACFs for the above mentioned data. The periodic behavior is clearly observed, with the period for *lhcb*, *dteam* and *uk* being 240 minutes, 180 minutes, and 120 minutes, respectively. For *dteam*, which stands for "deployment team", this pattern is explainable because jobs from this VO are mostly testing and monitoring jobs initiated by human or automatically by software. Jobs from *uk* during the period of study are mostly *dteam* jobs. It is interesting to see that the biggest VO *lhcb* also shows periodic behavior. If we take into account that close to 90% of *lhcb* jobs (around 60,000 jobs) are from one single user during the eleven days under study, we can assume that scripts are written to submit such production jobs, which are deterministic in nature.

We cannot say that the periodic behavior for large production VOs is a general feature and can be used in modeling. However, it is safe to assume that certain VOs are partly dedicated to testing and monitoring the Grid. In this case, for a realistic model to capture the behavior of such mixed deterministic (periodic) and stochastic components, we could follow the traditional route of time series analysis by either fitting and then subtracting the periodic components, or by introducing time-varying model parameters and change points [43].

5   Related Work

Traditionally, job arrivals have been analyzed and modeled on single parallel supercomputers. In [7] polynomials of degree from 8 to 13 are used to fit the daily arrival rates. In [25] a combined model is proposed where the interarrival times fit a hyper-Gamma distribution and the job arrival rates match the daily cycle. Time series models such as ARIMA are studied in [42], which try to capture the traffic trends and interdependencies. The impact of such models on the performance of parallel scheduling is also investigated.

The recent work by Medernach [27] is closely related to ours as he analyzes and models job arrivals on one cluster in LCG. The model developed is a ON-OFF Markov chain model, which essentially is a 2-phase hyperexponential renewal process (IPP). It is shown that for single users 2-phase hyperexponential distributions can fit the interarrival times well, although no analysis on dependencies of the series is available. As we model the job traffic at the VO and the Grid level, it can be regarded as a superposition of single user activities. It is well known that the superposition of individual renewal processes can be a correlated, nonrenewal stream [16,30], which justifies our choice of MMPPs as the candidate models. A further advantage of MMPPs is their stability in superposition: two or more superposed MMPPs are equivalent to some higher-order MMPP [14].

MMPPs have been very popular in modeling telecommunication traffic for more than twenty years. We refer to [17] for a comprehensive survey on stochastic modeling of traffic processes. Self-similarity based models have also been proposed in performance modeling of high-speed networks and we refer to [44] for a bibliographical guide.

6   Conclusions and Future Work

In this paper we present an initial analysis of job arrivals in a production data-intensive Grid, focusing on heavy-tail behavior and self-similarity of the interarrival time processes. Based on the analysis we investigate a set of m-state MMPPs to model the job traffic at different levels. Our conclusions can be summarized as follows:

1. There are no clearly observable daily patterns at the Grid level. Empirically, the number of jobs submitted by different VOs follows an exponential distribution.
2. The interarrival time process at the Grid level is distributed without a heavy tail and is strongly self-similar with $H \approx 0.84$. The best fitted model we find is MMPP2, but it still could not match the autocorrelation in the original trace.
3. The interarrival time processes of different VOs show strong, moderate, and weak self-similarity. The tail becomes longer as the number of jobs in the VO decreases. Experimental results suggest that with the VO size decreasing in an exponential manner, we can model the job arrivals of the corresponding VOs using MMPPs by increasing the number of its states.
4. At the region level, MMPPs are more suitable for processes with longer memories, while IPP can fit the interarrival time distributions very well, which is superior for those processes with very short memories.

5. The interarrival time processes for certain VOs show strong deterministic semi-periodic behavior. This explains the strong autocorrelations (long memory) of the data series. One source for such behavior is from large production VOs (e.g. *lhcb*), where scripts may be used for submitted production jobs. Others could be jobs for testing and monitoring purposes, which is essential for the operation and development of the Grid. Realistic modeling of job arrivals with mixed deterministic and stochastic components requires more future research.

We plan to release our Matlab programs developed for estimating and simulating MMPPs via [15]. Tools for calculating transportation distance are also available [29]. One interesting direction for further research is to correlate job arrivals with job run times to create a complete workload model for performance evaluation in a data-intensive Grid.

Acknowledgment

We are grateful to Gidon Moont, David Colling, and the e-Science group of HEP at Imperial College London who graciously provide us with the LCG Grid trace used in this study. M. Muskulus acknowledges support from NWO grant no. 635.100.006. We also want to thank all the reviewers for their many valuable suggestions that improve the quality of this paper.

References

1. S. Asmussen, O. Nerman and M. Olsson. Fitting phase-type distribution via the EM algorithm. *Scand. J. Statist.* 23:419–441, 1996.
2. A-L. Barabasi. The origin of bursts and heavy tails in human dynamics. *Nature*, 435:207–211, 2005.
3. S. Basu and E. Foufoula-Georgiou. Detection of nonlinearity and chaoticity in time series using the transportation distance function. *Physics Letters A*, 301:413–423, 2002.
4. J. Beran. Statistics for Long Memory Processes. Chapman and Hall, New York, 1994.
5. P. Brémaud. Markov Chains. Gibbs Fields, Monte Carlo Simulation, and Queues. Springer, New York, 2001.
6. S. J. Chapin, W. Cirne, D. G. Feitelson, J. P. Jones, S. T. Leutenegger, U. Schwiegelshohn, W. Smith, and D. Talby. Benchmarks and standards for the evaluation of parallel job schedulers. LNCS 1659:67–90. Springer-Verlag, 1999.
7. W. Cirne and F. Berman. A comprehensive model of the supercomputer workload. In *IEEE 4th Annual Workshop on Workload Characterization*, 2001.
8. A. C. Davison and D. V. Hinkley. Bootstrap Methods and Their Applications. Cambridge University Press, 1997.
9. A. B. Downey and D. G. Feitelson. The elusive goal of workload characterization. *Performance Evaluation Review*, 26(4): 14–29, 1999.
10. C. Dumitrescu, I. Raicu, and I. Foster. DI-GRUBER: A Distributed Approach to Grid Resource Brokering. In proceedings of *Supercomputing '05*, ACM, 2005.
11. Workload Management in EGEE and gLite. http://lxmi.mi.infn.it/egee-jra1-wm/.
12. EMpht program. http://home.imf.au.dk/asmus/.

13. D. G. Feitelson. Workload modeling for performance evaluation. LNCS 2459:114–141, 2002.
14. W. Fischer. and K. Meier-Hellstern. The Markov-modulated Poisson process (MMPP) cookbook. *Performance Evaluation*, 18(2):149–171, 1993.
15. Hui Li. Tools for Workload Modeling in the Grid. http://www.liacs.nl/home/hli/gwm/.
16. H. Heffes and D. M. Lucantoni. A Markov modulated characterization of packetized voice and data traffic and related statistical multiplexer performance. *IEEE J. on Sel. Areas in Comm.*, SAC-4(6):856–868, 1986.
17. D. L. Jagerman, B. Melamed, and W. Willinger. Stochastic modeling of traffic processes. *Frontiers in Queueing: Models, Methods and Problems*, CRC Press, 1996.
18. H. Kantz and T. Schreiber. Nonlinear Time Series Analysis. Cambridge University Press, 2003.
19. T. Karagiannis and M. Faloutsos. SELFIS: A Tool For Self-Similarity and Long-Range Dependence Analysis. In *1st Workshop on Fractals and Self-Similarity in Data Mining: Issues and Approaches*, Canada, 2002.
20. H. R. Künsch. The jackknife and bootstrap for general stationary observations. *The Annals of Statistics* 17, 1217–1241, 1989.
21. The Worldwide LHC Computing Grid project. http://lcg.web.cern.ch/LCG/.
22. W. Leland, M. Taqqu, W. Willinger, and D. Wilson. On the self-similar nature of ethernet traffic (extended version). *IEEE/ACM Trans. on Networking*, 2(1):1–15, 1994.
23. H. Li, D. Groep, and L. Wolters. Workload Characteristics of a Multi-cluster Supercomputer. LNCS 3277:176–193, Springer-Verlag, 2004.
24. lp_solve 5.5.0.7. http://lpsolve.sourceforge.net/5.5/.
25. U. Lublin and D. G. Feitelson. The workload on parallel supercomputers: modeling the characteristics of rigid jobs. *J. Para. and Dist. Comput.*, 63(11): 1105–1122, 2003.
26. A. Löbel. Solving large-scale real-world minimum-cost flow problems by a network simplex method. Technical Report SC 96-7, Konrad-Zuse-Zentrum für Informationstechnik Berlin (ZIB), February 1996. Software available at http://www.zib.de/Optimization/Software/Mcf/.
27. E. Medernach. Workload analysis of a cluster in a Grid environment. In *proceedings of 11th workshop on Job Scheduling Strategies for Parallel processing*, 2005.
28. R. Moeckel and B. Murray. Measuring the distance between timeseries. *Physica D*, 102:187–194, 1997.
29. M. Muskulus et. al. Estimating differences between probability densities and time series. In preparation. Software available at http://www.math.leidenuniv.nl/~muskulus/.
30. M. F. Neuts. Structured Stochastic Matrices of M/G/1-type and their Applications. Marcel Dekker, NY, 1989.
31. J. Nabrzyski, J. M. Schopf, and J. Weglarz (Editors). Grid Resource Management: State of the Art and Future Trends. ISBN: 1402075758, Springer, 2003.
32. D. N. Politis. The Impact of Bootstrap Methods on Time Series Analysis *Statistical Science* 18(2):219–230, 2003.
33. Parallel Workload Archive. http://www.cs.huji.ac.il /labs/parallel/workload/.
34. A. Riska. Aggregate Matrix-analytic Techniques and their Applications. PhD thesis, Department of Computer Science, College of William and Mary, 2002.
35. W. J. J. Roberts, Y. Ephraim, and E. Dieguez. On Ryden's EM algorithm for estimating MMPP's. *IEEE Sig. Proc. Let.*, to appear.
36. The LCG Real Time Monitor. http://gridportal.hep.ph .ic.ac.uk/rtm/.
37. T. Ryden. Parameter estimation for Markov modulated Poisson processes. *Communications in Statistics - Stochastic Models*, 10(4):795–829, 1994.
38. T. Ryden. An EM algorithm for estimation in Markov-modulated Poisson processes. *Comp. Stat. and Data Analysis*, 21:431–447, 1996.

39. A. Schrijver. Theory of Linear and Integer Programming. Wiley, Chichester, 1998.
40. S. L. Scott. Bayesian Methods for Hidden Markov Models: Recursive Computing in the 21st Century. *J. Am. Stat. Assoc.*, 97(457):337-351.
41. B. Song, C. Ernemann, and R. Yahyapour. Parallel Computer Workload Modeling with Markov Chains. LNCS 3277:47–62, Springer-Verlag, 2004.
42. M. S. Squillante, D. D. Yao, and L. Zhang. The impact of job arrival patterns on parallel scheduling. *ACM SIGMETRICS Performance Evaluation Review*, 26(4):52–59, 1999.
43. J. I. Takeuchi and K. Yamanishi. A Unified Framework for Detecting Outliers and Change Points from Time Series. *IEEE Transactions on Knowledge and Data Engineering*, 18(4):482–492, 2006.
44. W. Willinger, M. S. Taqqu, and A. Erramilli. A Bibliographical Guide to Self-Similar Traffic and Performance Modeling for Modern High-Speed Networks. In *Stochastic Networks: Theory and Applications*: 339–366, Oxford University Press, 1996.

On Grid Performance Evaluation
Using Synthetic Workloads

Alexandru Iosup[1], Dick H.J. Epema[1], Carsten Franke[2,*],
Alexander Papaspyrou[2], Lars Schley[2], Baiyi Song[2], and Ramin Yahyapour[2]

[1] Faculty of Electrical Engineering, Mathematics, and Computer Science
Delft University of Technology, The Netherlands
`{A.Iosup,D.H.J.Epema}@tudelft.nl`
[2] Information Technology Section, Robotics Research Institute
Dortmund University, Germany
`{Carsten.Franke,Alexander.Papaspyrou,`
`Lars.Schley,Song.Baiyi,Ramin.Yahyapour}@udo.edu`

Members of the CoreGRID European Virtual Institute on Grid Resource
Management and Scheduling

Abstract. Grid computing is becoming a common platform for solving large scale computing tasks. However, a number of major technical issues, including the lack of adequate performance evaluation approaches, hinder the grid computing's further development. The requirements herefore are manifold; adequate approaches must combine appropriate performance metrics, realistic workload models, and flexible tools for workload generation, submission, and analysis. In this paper we present an approach to tackle this complex problem. First, we introduce a set of grid performance objectives based on traditional and grid-specific performance metrics. Second, we synthesize the requirements for realistic grid workload modeling, e.g. co-allocation, data and network management, and failure modeling. Third, we show how GRENCHMARK, an existing framework for generating, running, and analyzing grid workloads, can be extended to implement the proposed modeling techniques. Our approach aims to be an initial and necessary step towards a common performance evaluation framework for grid environments.

1 Introduction

Grid computing facilitates the aggregation and sharing of large sets of heterogeneous resources spread over large geographical areas. This proves beneficial in many situations, for example when applications require more resources than locally available, or when work needs to be balanced across multiple computing facilities [16]. With the industrial and scientific communities tackling increasingly larger problems, grid computing is becoming a common infrastructural

---

* Born C. Ernemann.

E. Frachtenberg and U. Schwiegelshohn (Eds.): JSSPP 2006, LNCS 4376, pp. 232–255, 2007.

solution, and is starting to replace traditional parallel environments, at least in terms of offered computational power (see Appendix A).

However, key features of grids are still ardent research subjects, e.g., sophisticated resource planning strategies or the adaptation of existing applications to grids. Many of these features require in-depth knowledge of the behavior of grids, and realistic performance evaluation and comparison of existing and new approaches.

Grid performance evaluation raises very different challenges for the procedure and the adoption aspects. Also, the motivation of an evaluation may have a major impact on the approach that is taken during the evaluation itself. The various existing approaches to tackle the performance evaluation problem in the area of parallel environments [27,51] cannot be directly applied in grids, due to the grids' dynamic and large-scale nature. Other grid-oriented approaches, though valuable, either do not use realistic workloads [10] or use non-validated measurement data as input for the evaluation process [37], and cannot be used for reliable system comparisons and evaluations, cf. [8,24,12]. Furthermore, the actual adoption of an evaluation procedure as a benchmark is a community approach which requires the agreement of a sufficient number of grid stakeholders; this hinges on the existence of one or more established procedures, currently lacking in grids.

In addition, performance evaluation and comparison require the existence of workload traces within a grid, which at the moment simply do not exist. The main difficulty in obtaining such traces is not only one of obtaining access to data, but also that required data may not exist. In a recent analysis of (incomplete) traces obtained from grid environments [30], we observe that these traces log partially or even not at all information regarding the actual job origins (e.g., when users are mapped randomly to pools of usage certificates), the resource consumption (e.g., when the local resource managers do not log the actual CPU, I/O, and bandwidth consumptions, or when information about jobs running across grid sites cannot be correlated), job the coupling/dependencies (e.g., when job batches or jobs belonging to an organization are not recorded as such), or the failures. To ameliorate the lack of grid traces, synthetic, that is, generated on the foundation of an appropriate model, workloads are used for evaluation purposes. The main and, in fact, very hard problem is to create a good model without having any workload instances (i.e., real system traces). While there exist good models in the parallel processing community, there is no comprehensive workload model for grids available.

This paper aims to provide a starting point for grid performance evaluation from a practical point of view: a selection of requirements, objectives, and guidelines (including both well-known metrics from parallel workload modeling and newer, more grid-specific measurement gauges) is suggested to give an overview of what could be considered within a Grid performance evaluation system, and steps towards a common framework for adoption in real-world environments for the purpose of verification, analysis and benchmarking are shown. Our main contribution is thus twofold: (1) our approach is the first to deal programmatically with different critical grid modeling issues like co-allocation, job flexibility, data management, and failures; and (2) we gauge our approach as a standardization effort, by providing the necessary theoretical framework, and an early toolset to work with it.

The remainder of the paper is organized as follows. Section 2 presents three different evaluation scenarios. Section 3 analyzes a set of typical performance objectives which are commonly used in grids. Sections 4 and 5 focus on the features and requirements for modeling workloads for grids. While the modeling aspects in Section 4 contain strong links to existing work from the High-Performance Computing (HPC) community, Section 5 discusses in detail a selection of six grid-specific aspects: computation management, data management, locality/origin management, failure modeling, and economic modeling. Section 6 describes the GRENCH-MARK system, its current status, and the foreseen extensions towards the additional requirements presented in this paper. The discussion in Sections 4 and 5 acts as a guideline for added functionality to the GRENCHMARK framework. We conclude with a brief summary and a preview of our future research in this area, in Section 7.

2   System Scenarios

The common definition and proposed visions for grids go in the direction of a large-scale heterogenous computing platform with varying resource availability. This inherently dynamic and distributed nature is the root of the specific problem of evaluating grids: the sheer size and the dynamic behavior of grids renders difficult the evaluation of their performance. In this context, two questions need to be answered: 1. What is the actual scenario for which performance evaluation is done? and 2. What kind of performance objectives are sought after?

Clearly, a single evaluation system will not be able to fulfill all needs. For example, performance evaluation in simulated systems can be done by restricting the environmental description to a few[1] parameters (the number of clusters and of machines, the machine's speed distribution etc.) and allows the analysis of long-term usage as well as non-typical configurations. Simulated systems are, however, restricted to whatever the simulation designer has considered, and their results should not be seen as actual performance values, but more as indicators towards them. In contrast, the use of an actual grid system allows the derivation of current system data on the performance, stability, and usability of a real installation. Still, long-term assessments are inherently difficult, due to the non-exclusive access to the system itself or its configuration. Moreover, the evaluation produces results that are difficult to reproduce, even in the same scenario. To avoid the disadvantages of the previous two scenarios, emulated systems come into place: here, a high-accuracy simulation is done, and performance evaluation is occurs just like in a real environment. This, of course, requires the representation of the simulated infrastructure to match as closely as possible the

---

[1] Of course, the description of the simulation environment can also influence evaluation, but this discussion is out of the scope of this work.

technical description of the system to be emulated, which leads to a trade-off between the achieveable precision and the evaluation speed. Furthermore, the emulated environment needs to run itself on top of a large-scale distributed system. While the theoretically reachable precision of the evaluation results is very high, it is extremely difficult to prove the correctness of the emulation due to the combinatorial explosion of parameter values that can be varied.

We assume that all three approaches, simulation, emulation, and real system testing, are of significance in their domain. Thus, a performance evaluation system should ideally (a) support all of them and (b) allow a comparison of results on a technical level.

Nevertheless, the applied workload and job models, as well as the underlying grid model, are crucial for the evaluation. It is clear that, in a scenario in which a scheduling and management strategy for grids is quantitatively analyzed, the applied workload and the examined grid configuration are highly dependent. If for instance the requested load extends the system's saturation level, more and more jobs will be queued over time: the wait time for users will increase over time to an unrealistic level, which destabilises many performance objectives and, in the end, makes the results from such evaluations mostly useless. As a counter example, if the requested load is significantly lower than the saturation level, the scheduling problem degenerates to trivial job dispatching. Due to the strong dependence between a grid configuration and the applied workload, evaluation is very complex, as it is not possible to re-use the same workload for grid configurations which deviate largely in performance. One solution to the problem can be the dynamic adaption of workload generation based on the grid performance. However, such an approach has high impact on the performance objectives that can be assessed. We will investigate this problem in more detail in Sections 4 and 5.

3   Performance Metrics

The evaluation of the Grid performance highly depends on the given scenario (see Section 2), and the provider and user objectives. However, some typical standard evaluation metrics exist that can be applied in most cases. In this section we shortly present many of these metrics, and propose a selection of metrics for general purpose use.

Although we base the evaluation of grid systems on the seminal work in the context of parallel production environments by Feitelson et al. [25,24], our notation is in some cases modified according to the standards defined for operational research scheduling by Graham et al. [28]. For an overview of this notation we refer to [43]. Rooting our work in these approaches enables us to build on established results, and to have a good base of comparison with previous performance evaluations.

Within the Grid we assume m machines[2] and a job system τ. Within the system, each job $j \in \tau$ can further be divided into tasks $k \in j$. The number of

---

[2] Note that this term is used loosely and may specify any type of resource.

jobs in the system is $|\tau|$; the number of tasks for job j is $|j|$. Sometimes, such tasks are modeled as individual jobs that are connected by precedence constraints; especially then, the tasks of a job j are not executed in parallel.

Each job j and all its corresponding tasks $k \in j$ are released at time r_j. Grids typically work in an online scenario, that is, r_j is not known in advance for most jobs and tasks. As they arrive, jobs are scheduled to run, that is, a suitable set of resources is allocated for the future job run. For rescheduling capabilities, we define the *final schedule* for a period of time T as the schedule of all jobs arriving during time 0 and time T in which no job can be further rescheduled.

3.1   Time-, Resource- and System-Related Metrics

Within the final schedule S, the task $k \in j$ is completed at time $C_k(S)$. Hence, job j leaves the system at time $C_j(S) = \max_{k \in j} C_k(S)$. The processing time of task $k \in j$ is p_k. Hence, the processing time p_j of job j can be calculated by $C_j(S) - \min_{k \in j}(C_k(S) - p_k)$. Besides the maximum lateness $L_{max} = \max_{j \in \tau}(C_j(S) - d_j)$, which may be used as an analysis criterion (and needs to be minimised for grid systems), the number of tardy jobs $\text{TJ} = \sum_{j \in \tau \wedge C_j > d_j} 1$ also is of interest, as it provides information about the number of user requests that could not be fulfilled.

The resource consumption RC_k of a task is defined by the product of the corresponding processing time and the used machines ($\text{RC}_k = p_k \cdot m_k$). Consequently, we can define the resource consumption of a job by $\text{RC}_j = \sum_{k \in j} \text{RC}_k$ and of a whole schedule by $\text{RC}(S) = \sum_{j \in \tau} \text{RC}_j$. Using this total resource consumption we can also define the utilization U of the available machines, see Equation 1. The resource provider usually[3] selects as objective the maximization of the system utilization.

$$U = \frac{RC(S)}{m \cdot (\max_{j \in \tau} C_j(S) - \min_{j \in \tau}(C_j(S) - p_j))} \tag{1}$$

With task execution failures being common in grids (see Section 5.6), jobs may fail during execution, and be run several times before they successfully complete. We therefore define the true resource consumption $\text{RC}_{\{k,j\}}^{true}$ and the true utilization U^{true} as corollaries respectively, so that also the failed job's consumption of resources is measured. The sum of the resource consumption of such faulty jobs is defined as the waste metric $\text{WASTE} = U^{true} - U$, which gives a hint on the dynamic reaction to failures of the grid system and is to be minimized by the resource owner.

---

[3] In some cases (when certain users or user groups are willing to pay for the utilisation of a machine or have an affiliation to a certain organisation, etc.), the utilization might be of less importance.

As grid systems are belonging to several stakeholders, measuring the fairness of use is becoming an interesting point. A possible, but rather simple metric for measuring resource use fairness is the average wait time deviation [46], as defined in Equation 2; here, the objective is to minimize the $AWDT$ for each grid stakeholder.

$$AWTD = \frac{1}{|\tau|} \sqrt{\sum_{j \in \tau}(WT_j)^2 - (\sum_{j \in \tau} \frac{WT_j}{|\tau|})^2} \tag{2}$$

3.2   Workload Completion and Failure Metrics

In nowadays grids, the ability to complete the execution of a given workload can be even more important than the speedup obtained through this execution[4]. Grids require the redefinition of the *application failure* notion: a grid application which was not able to finish successfully within its budget generates an application failure event upon the first detection of its inability to complete successfully. For example, an application fails if its requested computation resources cannot be found, because of having a deadline assigned, but exceeding it, or because of running out of credits (even during execution). Using this notion, *fault tolerance* becomes postponing the application failure as much as possible, while there are realistic chances of finishing the application, possibly to the point where the application finishes successfully. In this section we describe metrics pertaining to workload completion and failures.

We propose as a metric the workload completion (WC), computed as given by Equation 3. This helps to identify the limitations of the grid system, and its maximization should be used as a major objective both by the user and by the resource owners. However, the workload completion has limitations from the resource owners' point of view, as jobs with a smaller number of tasks have a higher influence on this value. As complementary metrics, we propose the task completion (TC), given by Equation 4, and the enabled task completion (ETC), given by Equation 5. Note that in the latter the enabled tasks are those tasks which can be run, after their previous tasks dependencies have been completed. The resource owners' objective is to maximize the enabled task completion. If the TC and the ETC metrics differ greatly, special care must be taken by the resource owners to fulfill critical tasks (tasks which are present in the dependency lists of many other tasks), for example by automatically launching redundant runs of these tasks.

$$WC = \frac{\sum\limits_{j \in \tau \wedge j \ completed} 1}{|\tau|} \tag{3}$$

---

[4] Note that the jobs executed in grids may be much more complex than the jobs executed in traditional parallel environments, e.g., workflows vs. batches of jobs.

$$TC = \frac{\sum\limits_{j \in \tau \wedge k \in j \wedge k \ completed} 1}{\sum\limits_{j \in \tau} |j|} \quad (4)$$

$$ETC = \frac{\sum\limits_{j \in \tau \wedge k \in j \wedge k \ completed} 1}{\sum\limits_{j \in \tau \wedge k \in j \wedge k \ enabled} 1} \quad (5)$$

We further propose as a metric the system failure factor (SFF), as the ratio between the number of failures observed for all the tasks that were started and the number of tasks that were started. Note that SFF is equal to $1 - ETC$ for a system with no retry capabilities, but may vary greatly otherwise. The SFF metric may be an effective performance evaluator for the ability of the grid system to detect and correct failures in the system, e.g., if a resource becomes unavailable, repeatedly sending jobs to it for execution would increase the number of observed failures, and prove a lack of dynamic response to partial system failures. The objective of the resource owner is minimize the value of the SFF metric. Note that it is possible to have a high value for the waste metric and a small value for the system failure factor at the same time, for instance when a few tasks fail, but their failure occurs or is observed after the tasks have been running for an extensive period of time. Besides this system-oriented metric, the *expected task failure*, that is, the probability that a task will fail upon being run, may be used to evaluate the performance of grids where the availability of resources is very dynamic [37].

3.3   Metrics Selection

Given the number of proposed metrics, the selection of an appropriate subset is still an open question. Recent works by Feitelson et al. show that *all* quantitative metrics should be reported and considered for a representative systems evaluation [22,23]. Therefore, a scheduling performance evaluation could be done after considering the detailed resource consumption report, and the following aforementioned metrics: the system utilization **U**, the workload completion percentage **WC**, the enabled task completion **ETC**, the wasted resources **WASTE**, the system failure factor **SFF**, and the average wait time deviation **AWTD**. Besides that, we also consider the response time **AWRT**, the wait time **AWWT**, the slowdown **AWSD**, (all average), all used in their weighted versions, by which all jobs with the same resource demand have the same influence on the schedule quality. Without the weighting mechanism, a job using few machines would have the same impact on these metrics as a job that uses many machines, see Schwiegelshohn et al. [45]. To prevent this effect, bounds can be imposed for these metrics, e.g., bounded slowdown [25]. Specific time-based summaries of the consumption report and the nine metrics are sometimes needed, e.g., for normal, peak, and clear months, or for week days and week-end. Different providers will then be able to weight those metrics according to their system use scenario.

In some cases, metrics need also be computed per user or per user group, in addition to metrics for the full system. This may be needed, for example, for grids where the machine providers have different commercial relationships to different grid participants, and therefore specific objectives for different users or user groups [3]. An early example is the fair-share utilization concept used in the Maui scheduler [33], where separate policies are defined for different users and groups.

4 General Aspects for Workload Modeling

Most research on workload modeling for single HPC parallel computers focus on the characterization of the overall features of workloads. Since the evaluation of scheduling strategies for parallel computers focus on the optimization of a global performance metric, like to minimize the *overall* response time, or the makespan or to increase machine utilization, a general descriptive model is often sufficient for workload modeling [39,11]. Here, a collection of probabilistic distributions are sometimes suitable for various workload attributes (e.g. runtime, parallelism, I/O, memory). By sampling from the corresponding distributions, a synthetic workload is generated. The construction of such a workload model is done by fitting the global workload attributes to mathematical distributions.

In a grid environment the scheduling objectives depend more on the individual choice of the users. Here, some users may prefer the minimization of cost, while others accept a longer waiting time in favor of a better quality of service, e.g. more or faster processor nodes available. Therefore, a different knowledge of the workload characteristics is needed for a realistic evaluation of grid systems. Unfortunately, there is currently no actual grid workload trace publicly available, such that only assumptions can be made about the actual use of grids. For the time being, it can however be assumed that the current user communities from HPC sites are at the forefront of using grids. Thus, we argue that modeling techniques that have been employed for HPC traces can be (at least partly) applied also in the case of grids, and that existing workload traces taken from parallel computers at HPC sites may be useful as a first start for modeling grid workloads. Within the context of this assumption, the 17 HPC traces from the Parallel Workloads Archive[5] provide valuable modeling data. In this section we present the general aspects of HPC workload modeling.

4.1 User Group Model

While it is clear that the individual users' characteristics need to be emphasized in grid environments, the main challenge in the construction of a group and/or user model is to find a trade-off between two extremes: the summarization in a general probability model for all job submissions on the one hand, and unique models which are created for each user based on information about her past actions on the other. We further address the dimensions of the required modeling effort.

---

[5] Available at `http://www.cs.huji.ac.il/labs/parallel/workload/`.

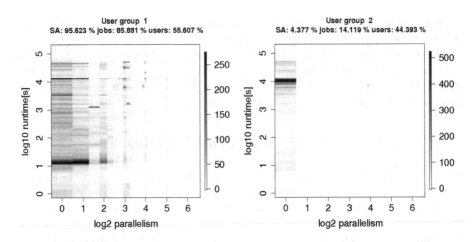

Fig. 1. Dominant set of groups of size 2 for the KTH workload

We call a set of users or a set of groups dominant if it covers the majority of jobs and is responsible for the majority of consumed resources (from hereon, *squashed area*, or *SA*). When the size of the dominant set of groups or users is reduced, e.g., less than 10, the detailed modeling approach may be used. In [38], the top-5 groups and the top-10 users form dominant sets, respectively, and unique models for each group and user are created. However, this approach does not scale for larger communities, e.g., using hundreds of distributions for different users. In this case, the approach suffers from two significant problems. First, there is usually not enough information available for all users, as some only have a few job submissions. Second, the overall number of parameters will be quite large so that the interpretability and scalability of the model is lost. As a consequence, a trade-off on the level of user groups is anticipated. That is, users are clustered into groups with similar but distinct submission features. This user group model allows to address the user submission behaviors while maintaining simplicity and manageability.

In [48] such a user group model has been proposed which clusters users into groups according to their job submissions in real workload traces. The analysis showed that for the examined workload, there exists a dominant set of groups of size 4. If the clustering would be even more pronounced, a dominant set of size 2 can be found, with the first group covering more than 95% of the squashed area (see Fig. 1).

In the presented research work, the analysis and modeling was restricted to the job parameters *run time* and *number of requested processors* which were sufficient for single parallel computer scheduling. However, modeling on the level of these groups provides the possibility to assign additional workload features, e.g. necessary for grids, to these groups. Some examples of such additionally required features are discussed in Section 5.

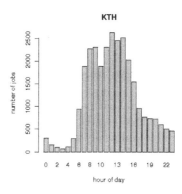

Fig. 2. Job arrivals during the daily cycle

4.2   Submission Patterns

The users of grids have their own habits to request resources and to submit jobs, which is referred to as *patterns*. Here, we take the daily cycle as an example. The daily cycle could refer to the habit of submitting more jobs during day time than night, and to the considerably distinct submission distributions during the day and the night. Fig. 2 shows the daily arriving patterns of jobs, for the KTH workload. There is an obvious daily cycle: most jobs arrive during the day and only a few of them at night. Obviously, these patterns might blur in grid environments because of users living in different timezones [17]; however, they are still important to the local sites (and the local schedulers).

Similar patterns can be found through the week, e.g., users tend to submit more jobs during the week-days than during the week-end, or year, e.g., an outstanding increase in the number of job submissions may be observed during several months of the year [38], or during short periods [9].

These effects can be described by classical statistical methods. For example, Downey [13] modeled the daily cycle using combined Poisson distributions; Calzarossa [7] found that an eight-degree polynomial function is a suitable representation of all the analyzed arrival processes. However, this does not necessarily hold because of dependencies within the workload (see [19,18]), e.g. sequential dependencies.

Therefore, temporal modeling is an important aspect. For example, one of these temporal effects is *repeated submission* [19], namely, users do not submit one job once but several similar jobs in a short time frame. Even if the successively appearing jobs are disregarded, temporal relations can still be found, as shown in [18]. It can be seen that the successors of jobs with a large parallelism value also tend to require more nodes.

Such temporal characteristics are useful for the many grid scheduling scenarios, including resource reservation and load balancing. The application of various techniques, e.g., stationary and non-stationary analysis as well as stochastic processes, provides a good representation of the temporal relations in users' submissions. In [47], correlated Markov chains are used to model the temporal characteristics of job sequences. The idea to correlate the Markov chains is that since the job parameters are correlated, the transformations of their corresponding Markov chains are related as well. In [41], a model based on Markov chains is used for the number of jobs consecutively submitted by a user during a single submitting session.

Besides that, analysis has shown that users also tend to adapt to the performance of the available system. That is, users may change their job submissions according to the available online information, e.g. system states and quality of services as shown in [20,21]. Therefore, it is reasonable to model the users' submissions with the considerations of such feedback behaviors. Thus, the workload generation should be coupled to the system with a feedback loop.

In many cases, the explicit feedback tags are missing; therefore it is not feasible to determine whether feedback factors do affect job delivery. For example, if a user seldom delivers jobs at noon, it might result from a regular lunch at this time, or has a real feedback implication: the user finds many waiting jobs at noon and then stops his or her submissions.

However, it is possible to elicit whether feedback factors affect a job's profile (like parallelism and runtime), since the job profiles can be compared along different situations of influential factors. To this end, the correlations between the feedback factors and the job attributes should be analyzed.

5   Grid-Specific Workload Modeling

In this section we present the grid-specific workload modeling requirements. Due to the lack of publicly available traces[6] of real grids operation, we restrict our presentation to the main characteristics that could become subject of near-future modeling.

5.1   Types of Applications

Grid jobs may have a complex structure which may be handled only with advanced support from the submission middleware. From this point of view, we consider two types of applications that can run in grids, and may be included in generated grid workloads: i. *unitary applications*, which include sequential or parallel (e.g. MPI) applications and at most require taking the job programming model into account (launching additional naming or registry services, for example) and ii. *composite applications*, which include bags, chains or DAGs of tasks and additionally require special attention by the grid scheduler regarding inter-dependencies, advanced reservation and extended fault tolerance.

---

[6] There is, of course, one public trace of a HPC site participating in the EGEE/LCG production grid; however, due to the fact that only the batch system log is available, but no information whatsoever on the grid infrastructure layer, this workload degenerates to a standard HPC site trace.

Note, in the remainder of this section we use the term application at some points. By this we understand a certain user problem that has to be calculated. In this sense, application and job are the same.

5.2 Computation Management

Another grid-specific problem is the *processor co-allocation*, that is, the simultaneous allocation of processors located at different grid sites to single applications which consist of multiple components. Co-allocation models need to describe the application components and the possible resource co-allocation policies. To model the application components, we need to define the number of components (NoC) and the component size (CS), and furthermore must allow multiple configurations, such that sets of (Noc, CS) tuples or even ranges can be then specified. In practice, the typical configurations for processor co-allocations are selected such that they fill completely clusters of resources, to keep the inter-cluster communication low [5]; load-balancing across the number of sites can also be used for jobs requiring large numbers of resources [4]. Obviously, there are three possible resource co-allocation policies: 1. *fixed*, where each job has predefined resource preferences; 2. *non-fixed*, where jobs have no resource preferences at all and 3. *semi-fixed*, where only some job components require certain resources, whilst others can be dispatched at the scheduler's discretion. Experience with co-allocation in a real environment is described in [42,31]. However, no statistical data regarding the use of co-allocation by real communities of users is publicly available.

In addition, *job flexibility*, that is, the (in)ability of a job to run on a changing number of resources, raises many more problems in grids than in traditional parallel environments. Flexibility models need to describe the flexibility type and (possibly) the number and dynamics of computing resources that may be allocated to a job. There are four possible flexibility types: rigid, moldable, evolving, and malleable [25]. To model the application flexibility, at least one job shape (cf. [12], a tuple comprising the minimum and maximum number of computing resources, the configuration constraints, e.g., n^2 processors, and the resource addition / subtraction constraints) must be defined per job. Statistical data for moldable jobs for a real supercomputing community is given by Cirne and Berman [12]; experiments with moldable applications in a real environment have been presented by Berman et al. [2].

Finally, one has to consider that, in production grid environments, there often exists a certain *background load*: many processing resources are shared with the grid by a local community, and may have local jobs running outside the grid resource management. Also, it is expected that usage of resources must differ greatly depending on the *project stage* of a certain user community which generates the usage. Considering a long-term project, there might be a startup and a transition phase, in which infrastructure and application test are produced, an execution phase, which contains the main body of work for the project, and an ending phase, in which jobs with characteristics and submission patterns totally different from the previous stages might appear. From such a projects' point of view, the modeler needs to be able to characterize each individual stage.

5.3 Data Management

We now discuss the modeling requirements of data management. Grid jobs need input data for processing, and generate output data to make the computed results persistent. The data needs to be present before[7] the job can start, and the stored results must be fetched after the job has finished, or streamed as they are produced. Hence, the modeler needs to specify at least the identifiers of the input and of the output files. For composite applications (see Section 5.1), it is also necessary to specify data dependencies between the jobs, that is, which of a job's output files represent another's input, and which input files are shared by several jobs.

Similarly to specifying an estimated computation time or size for their applications, it would be desirable that users specify an estimation of the needed input and output space within the job description. Also similarly to the estimated/actual runtime discrepancies, the information specified by the user may not be reliable and available, e.g., the user provides imprecise estimations or the job determines result data sets during runtime. We argue that such information can be added easily, as many applications have well-studied I/O requirements, both when running individually, or when running in batches [49].

For many applications, data is obtained from remote large-scale storage devices, usually with very different access times than the locally available data. Additionally, unexpected difficulties can occur regarding the access time for files which appear to be locally available, i.e., files might seem to be accessible on a local filesystem but essentially have been moved to tertiary storage. This is especially the case for HSM[8] systems, where the restoration of files can take a long time. In this case, a model should provide detailed information about the source and destination storage, for the input and output files, respectively.

Sometimes, the same file is replicated on several storage sites in the grid. Modeling this aspect can be reduced to specifying lists of input and/or output files locations for each unique file identifier. Note that the information in the list may need to be combined with information on the data storage device.

5.4 Network Management

When introducing data management into workload models for grids, it is obvious that also networks between sites have to be considered. The available bandwidth for transfers of input or output data is limited and thus has an impact on the data transfer time. This can influence the decision which site is used for a certain computation and whether data has to be replicated to this site in order

---

[7] There also exist I/O models that introduce remote data access with read-ahead and/or caching mechanisms, but these are out of the scope of this work.

[8] Hierarchical Storage Management.

to run the job. There are also other application scenarios in which network management is a critical feature, like the management of bandwidth in Service Level Agreements between remote resource allocations, e.g. for parallel computation, large-scale visualization, or consistent data streaming from experimental devices [26]. Therefore, the end-to-end bandwidth between different nodes in the grid must be described and managed.

Ideally, the total bandwidth of every end-to-end connection would be known and dedicated reservations could be enforced. However, this is often not supported: in IP networks, end-to-end connections are virtual (since the packet route can change) with a maximum weakest-link-in-chain bandwidth. Hence, in many realistic scenarios often no precise information about the service quality between two ends is available. However, there are means which can ameliorate this situation. For example, the NWS system [52] measures and records the available bandwidth between two nodes periodically. This data is then used to predict the expected average bandwidth in the future based on historic patterns. In cases where reservation of bandwidth is not feasible, there are still possibilities to shape network traffic. However, abiding agreements on an certain QoS level cannot be settled normally. Regarding network latency, which is important for applications requiring large numbers of small network packets (e.g. streaming), the situation is akin.

Besides that, there is always a certain amount of background (not grid workload-related, that is) traffic on a network, which lowers both bandwidth and latency. However, due to the lack of reservation capabilities, the impact of background traffic is not predictable at all. Even when predictions expect high network availability and the known future utilization is low, a single data-intensive file transfer can suddenly produce a high, previously unexpected network load.

On the whole, realistic network depiction in workload models is difficult and will have to be subject to further research; first steps into the direction of grid-specific data staging and network modeling have been taken in the SDSC HPSS work [44] and Tan et. al [50]. However, it would be useful that a grid performance evaluation system provides support for network resources and consequently for network related workload requirements in order to have a testing platform for future models. Such an extension would include the addition of network information and requirements to jobs as well as evaluated grid configurations on which the workload is executed.

5.5   Locality/Origin Management

Another requirement for some evaluation scenarios in grids is the realistic modeling of the origin of job submissions. While some may argue that grid workload is created decentralized and on a global scale, many usage scenarios still need information about the locality of job creation. A typical example of such a scenario is the collaboration between HPC centers which want to share their workload to improve quality of service to their local user community. While the sites may agree on sharing the workload, it is quite common that certain policies or rules exist for this sharing (balancing between local and "foreign" users, for instance).

Other examples can be conceived, in which the submitting user plays a role, as he may belong to a certain virtual organization and may have subsequently special privileges on certain grid resources [33]. Support for these scenarios can be helpful for P2P grids, where resource access is mostly user-centric and not dependent on a particular site policy.

5.6 Failure Modeling

Due to the natural heterogeneity of grids and their sheer size, failures appear much more often than in traditional parallel and distributed environments, occur at infrastructure, middleware, application, and user levels, and may be transient or permanent. Furthermore, different fault tolerance mechanisms can be selected by the user, for each job or workflow in the workload. Hence, the modeler must use a dynamic grid model, combined with a realistic failure model. Then, she must take into account the fault tolerance mechanisms, i.e., the failure response mechanism selected by the user or employed automatically by the system. Furthermore, experiments such as comparing two middleware solutions may require deterministic failure behavior.

Failures in the grid infrastructure may be caused by resource failures (e.g. node crashes), or by other resource outages (e.g. maintenance). To model resource failures, the traditional availability metric, *mean-time to failure* [34], the length of failure (*failover duration*), and the percentage affected from the resource, must be specified for each resource. To model other resource outages, the following parameters must be specified: outage period, announced and real outage duration, percentage affected from the resource affected, and (optional) the details of the failures, e.g., which resources or resource parts did fail [8].

Failures in the grid middleware may have various causes. One source of errors is the scalability of the middleware; another is due to the middleware configuration: according to the survey in Medeiros et al. [40], 76% of the observed defects are due to configuration problems. For modeling purposes, starting points could be static mechanisms like mean-time to failure, and the length of the failures, again.

Regarding *failures in grid applications*, it has been observed by Kondo et al. [37] that jobs submitted during the weekend are much more error-prone. Therefore, an application failure model should contain a *fault inter-arrival time* distribution.

User-generated failures can be modeled similarly to the distribution of the jobs' inter-arrival time. Faults due to user-specified job runtimes have been a topic of interest in parallel workload modeling, other issues like missing or expired credentials and disk quota overrun [10,14,31], invalid job specifications [36] or user-initiated cancellations [11] are other sources of user-generated failures.

To respond to the numerous sources of failure, various *fault tolerance schemes* may be applied in grid, and possibly need to be modeled (see for example [29]); the technique type then needs to be specified for each job or workflow in the workload, coupled with the specific technique parameters.

5.7 Economic Models

There is a lot of discussion on the connotation of access to grid resources not being free of charge [35,15,6]. Especially the support for commercial business models will include support for economic methods in grids. Therefore, it is clear that the allocation of jobs to resources may incur cost in certain grid scenarios. Adopting cost has many implications to the allocation of jobs to grid resources: providers will require the implementation of pricing policies for the access to resources. To the same extend, users will need support for managing budgets for job executions and preference constraints on how jobs should be executed (e.g., price vs. performance). First economic models have been published by Ernemann et al. [15] and Buyya et al. [6].

While it is not the task of an evaluation system to tackle the technical implications of economic models, like whether cost occurs in virtual credits or actual money, it can be conceived that there are requirements to model budget information for either jobs, users or virtual organizations. This is even necessary if grids are modeled in which users or groups have a certain quota on resources; a precondition to optionally support budget constraints in the evaluation system.

Another step could be the support for different optimization goals that are economy-related. For instance, users may prefer a cheaper (in terms of cost) execution of a job in contrast to an early execution. This, however, requires the extension of the performance metrics to include cost-related parameters, in a possibly parametric fashion. For example, in Ernemann et al. [15], grid users provide parametric utility functions, and the systems performs automated request-offer matching.

6 GRENCHMARK: A Framework for Grid Performance Evaluation

GRENCHMARK is a framework for synthetic grid workload generation, execution, and analysis of execution results. It is *extensible*, in that it allows new types of grid applications to be included in the workload generation without a change in the design, *parameterizable*, as it permits the user to parameterize the workloads generation and submission, and *flexible*, as it can be used for analyzing, testing, and comparing common grid settings. GRENCHMARK is currently developed at TU Delft[9].

6.1 Current Features

In our previous work we have shown how GRENCHMARK can be used to generate and submit workloads comprising unitary and composite applications, to replay-scale-mix traces from the Parallel Workloads Archive, and in general to analyze,

---

[9] A reference implementation is available from
http://grenchmark.st.ewi.tudelft.nl/

test, and compare common grid settings [32,31]. Therefore, we only point out prominent features, and invite the reader to consult our work.

GRENCHMARK offers support for the following workload modeling aspects. First, it supports unitary and composite applications as well as single-site and co-allocated jobs. Second, it allows the user to define the job submission pattern based on well-known statistical distributions. Third, it allows the workload designer to combine several workloads into a single one (mixing). This allows for instance the definition of separate user groups (see Section 4.1), further combined into a single grid workload. Furthermore, it supports the generation, storage, modification, replay and analysis of workloads based on user-defined parameters.

6.2   Extension Points

GRENCHMARK has been designed with an incremental approach in mind, and facilitates future extensions at many levels.

Based on the dynamics of the grid workload generation process, we identify two types of grid workload generation: statically-generated workloads, and dynamically-generated workloads. *Statically-generated workloads* do not change at execution time with modifications in the execution environment. Currently, GRENCHMARK incorporates rather simple models (statistical distributions for submission patterns, for example, without correlations to other parameters or feedback functionality). However, due to the extensibility, more complex notions such as temporal models and parameters correlation (see Section 4.2), data and network management (see Sections 5.3 and 5.4), or locality/origin management (see Section 5.5) can be easily adapted. To introduce support for *dynamically-generated workloads* into GRENCHMARK, the framework design needs to be extended with the ability to react to system changes for both workload generation and submission. Since the reference implementation already uses feedback for the submission process (for composite job submission and reacting to execution errors [31]), the implementation of such functionality seems feasible and, as such, we plan to address this issue in future work.

From the perspective of operating in a dynamic system, GRENCHMARK can already respond to the situation when the background load can be extracted from existing traces and, as such, is known, and offers adequate modeling capabilities. For handling the background load as a separate workload, an extension is still required. For a variable background load in a real environment (the most difficult case), the desired load could, for example, be controlled by coupling GRENCHMARK to existing monitoring services. Then, dummy jobs can be launched to ensure a fixed level of background load during all experiments, as in Mohamed and Epema [42]. However, the modeling itself remains an open issue.

Another important extension issue is the use of GRENCHMARK in different system scenarios (cf. to Section 2). We have already used GRENCHMARK in real environments. For simulated environments, the reference implementation needs to be extended to event-based simulation, which is work in progress.

Summarizing, GRENCHMARK provides a framework for Grid performance evaluation which already contains basic modeling techniques, but needs to incorporate more sophisticated modeling capabilities in order to generate and analyse Grid workloads.

7 Conclusion

In this work we have presented an integrated approach for generic grid performance evaluation. For this purpose, we have first presented several grid performance objectives, and made a selection for the general case. We have then combined traditional and grid-specific workload modeling aspects, and synthesized the requirements for realistic grid workload modeling. Finally, we have presented an existing framework for workload generation and analysis and pointed out extension points on both modeling and infrastructure issues.

In order to validate our work with experimental results, we are currently working on extensions to the GRENCHMARK framework to accommodate the changes detailed in Section 6.2 with the goal to have a powerful, yet extensible framework for workload modeling and analysis. We hope that this work will become the basis for a common performance evaluation framework for grid environments.

Acknowledgements

This research work is carried out under the FP6 Network of Excellence Core-GRID funded by the European Commission (Contract IST-2002- 004265). Part of this work was also carried out in the context of the Virtual Laboratory for e-Science project (www.vl-e.nl), which is supported by a BSIK grant from the Dutch Ministry of Education, Culture and Science (OC&W), and which is part of the ICT innovation program of the Dutch Ministry of Economic Affairs (EZ).

References

1. The Parallel Workloads Archive Team . The parallel workloads archive logs, June 2006. [Online]. Available: http://www.cs.huji.ac.il/labs/parallel/workload/logs.html.
2. Francine Berman, Richard Wolski, Henri Casanova, Walfredo Cirne, Holly Dail, Marcio Faerman, Silvia M. Figueira, Jim Hayes, Graziano Obertelli, Jennifer M. Schopf, Gary Shao, Shava Smallen, Neil T. Spring, Alan Su, and Dmitrii Zagorodnov. Adaptive computing on the grid using apples. *IEEE Trans. Parallel Distrib. Syst.*, 14(4):369–382, 2003.
3. N. Beume, M. Emmerich, C. Ernemann, L. Schï£jnemann, and U. Schwiegelshohn. Scheduling Algorithm Development based on Complex Owner Defined Objectives. Technical Report CI-190/05, University of Dortmund, January 2005.
4. Anca I. D. Bucur and Dick H. J. Epema. The performance of processor co-allocation in multicluster systems. In *Proc. of the 3rd IEEE Int'l. Symp. on Cluster Computing and the Grid (CCGrid)*, pages 302–309, 2003.

5. Anca I. D. Bucur and Dick H. J. Epema. Trace-based simulations of processor co-allocation policies in multiclusters. In *Proc. of the 12th Intl. Symposium on High-Performance Distributed Computing (HPDC)*, pages 70–79, 2003.

6. R. Buyya, D. Abramson, and S. Venugopal. The grid economy. In *Special Issue of the Proceedings of the IEEE on Grid Computing*. IEEE Press, 2005. (To appear).

7. Maria Calzarossa and Giuseppe Serazzi. A characterization of the variation in time of workload arrival patterns. *IEEE Trans. Comput.*, C-34(2):156–162, Feb 1985.

8. Steve J. Chapin, Walfredo Cirne, Dror G. Feitelson, James Patton Jones, Scott T. Leutenegger, Uwe Schwiegelshohn, Warren Smith, and David Talby. Benchmarks and standards for the evaluation of parallel job schedulers. In Dror G. Feitelson and Larry Rudolph, editors, *Proc. of the 5th Int'l. Workshop on Job Scheduling Strategies for Parallel Processing (JSSPP)*, volume 1659 of *Lecture Notes in Computer Science*, pages 67–90. Springer, 1999.

9. Brent N. Chun, Philip Buonadonna, Alvin AuYoung, Chaki Ng, David C. Parkes, Jeffrey Shneidman, Alex C. Snoeren, and Amin Vahdat. Mirage: A microeconomic resource allocation system for sensornet testbeds. In *Proc. of 2nd IEEE Workshop on Embedded Networked Sensors (EmNetsII)*, 2005.

10. Greg Chun, Holly Dail, Henri Casanova, and Allan Snavely. Benchmark probes for grid assessment. In *Proc. of the 18th International Parallel and Distributed Processing Symposium (IPDPS)*, 2004.

11. Walfredo Cirne and Francine Berman. A Comprehensive Model of the Supercomputer Workload. In *4th Workshop on Workload Characterization*, December 2001.

12. Walfredo Cirne and Francine Berman. A model for moldable supercomputer jobs. In *Proc. of the 15th International Parallel and Distributed Processing Symposium (IPDPS)*, pages 59–79, 2001.

13. Allen B. Downey. A parallel workload model and its implications for processor allocation. *Cluster Computing*, 1(1):133–145, 1998.

14. Catalin Dumitrescu, Ioan Raicu, and Ian T. Foster. Experiences in running workloads over grid3. In Hai Zhuge and Geoffrey Fox, editors, *Grid and Cooperative Computing (GCC)*, volume 3795 of *Lecture Notes in Computer Science*, pages 274–286. Springer, 2005.

15. C. Ernemann and R. Yahyapour. *Grid Resource Management - State of the Art and Future Trends*, chapter Applying Economic Scheduling Methods to Grid Environments, pages 491–506. Kluwer Academic Publishers, 2003.

16. Carsten Ernemann, Volker Hamscher, Uwe Schwiegelshohn, Ramin Yahyapour, and Achim Streit. On advantages of grid computing for parallel job scheduling. In *Proc. of the 2nd IEEE Int'l. Symp. on Cluster Computing and the Grid (CCGrid)*, pages 39–49, 2002.

17. Carsten Ernemann, Volker Hamscher, and Ramin Yahyapour. Benefits of global grid computing for job scheduling. In *Proceedings of the 5th IEEE/ACM International Workshop on Grid Computing*, Pittsburgh, November 2004. IEEE Computer Society.

18. Carsten Ernemann, Baiyi Song, and Ramin Yahyapour. Scaling of Workload Traces. In Dror G. Feitelson, Larry Rudolph, and Uwe Schwiegelshohn, editors, *Job Scheduling Strategies for Parallel Processing*, volume 2862 of *Lecture Notes in Computer Science*, pages 166–183. Springer, October 2003.

19. Dror G. Feitelson. Packing Schemes for Gang Scheduling. In Dror G. Feitelson and Larry Rudolph, editors, *Job Scheduling Strategies for Parallel Processing*, volume 1162 of *Lecture Notes in Computer Science*, pages 89–110. Springer, 1996.

20. Dror G. Feitelson. The forgotten factor: facts on performance evaluation and its dependence on workloads. In B. Monien and R. Feldmann, editors, *Euro-Par 2002 Parallel Processing*, volume 2400, pages 49–60. Springer, 2002. Lecture Notes in Computer Science.

21. Dror G. Feitelson. Workload Modeling for Performance Evaluation. In Mariacarla Calzarossa and Sara Tucci, editors, *Performance Evaluation of Complex Systems: Techniques and Tools*, volume 2459 of *Lecture Notes in Computer Science*, pages 114–141. Springer, 2002.

22. Dror G. Feitelson. Metric and workload effects on computer systems evaluation. *IEEE Computer*, 36(9):18–25, 2003.

23. Dror G. Feitelson. Experimental analysis of the root causes of performance evaluation results: a backfilling case study. *IEEE Transactions on Parallel and Distributed Systems*, 16(2):175–182, Feb 2005.

24. Dror G. Feitelson and Larry Rudolph. Metrics and benchmarking for parallel job scheduling. In Dror G. Feitelson and Larry Rudolph, editors, *Proc. of the 4th Int'l. Workshop on Job Scheduling Strategies for Parallel Processing (JSSPP)*, volume 1459 of *Lecture Notes in Computer Science*, pages 1–24. Springer, 1998.

25. Dror G. Feitelson, Larry Rudolph, Uwe Schwiegelshohn, Kenneth C. Sevcik, and Parkson Wong. Theory and Practice in Parallel Job Scheduling. In Dror G. Feitelson and Larry Rudolph, editors, *Proc. of the 3rd Int'l. Workshop on Job Scheduling Strategies for Parallel Processing (JSSPP)*, volume 1291 of *Lecture Notes in Computer Science*, pages 1–34, Geneva, April 1997. Springer-Verlag.

26. Ian Foster, Markus Fidler, Alain Roy, Volker Sander, and Linda Winkler. End-to-end quality of service for high-end applications. *Computer Communications*, 27(14):1375–1388, September 2004.

27. Michael A. Frumkin and Rob F. Van der Wijngaart. Nas grid benchmarks: A tool for grid space exploration. In *Proc. of the 10th Intl. Symposium on High-Performance Distributed Computing (HPDC)*, pages 315–326, 2001.

28. R. L. Graham, E. L. Lawler, J. K. Lenstra, and A. H. G. Rinnooy Kan. Optimization and approximation in deterministic sequencing and scheduling: A survey. *Annals of Discrete Mathematics*, 15:287–326, 1979.

29. Soonwook Hwang and Carl Kesselman. Gridworkflow: A flexible failure handling framework for the grid. In *Proc. of the 12th Intl. Symposium on High-Performance Distributed Computing (HPDC)*, pages 126–137, 2003.

30. Alexandru Iosup, Catalin Dumitrescu, D.H.J. Epema, Hui Li, and Lex Wolters. How are real grids used? the analysis of four grid traces and its implications. In *The 7th IEEE/ACM International Conference on Grid Computing (Grid)*, Barcelona, ES, Sep 28-29 2006. (accepted).

31. Alexandru Iosup and D.H.J. Epema. GrenchMark: A framework for analyzing, testing, and comparing grids. In *Proc. of the 6th IEEE/ACM Int'l. Symp. on Cluster Computing and the GRID (CCGrid)*, May 2006. (accepted).

32. Alexandru Iosup, Jason Maassen, Rob V. van Nieuwpoort, and Dick H.J. Epema. Synthetic grid workloads with Ibis, KOALA, and GrenchMark. In *Proceedigs of the CoreGRID Integrated Research in Grid Computing, Pisa, Italy, November 2005*. LNCS, 2006.

33. David Jackson, Quinn Snell, and Mark Clement. Core algorithms of the Maui scheduler. In Dror G. Feitelson and Larry Rudolph, editors, *Proc. of the 7th Int'l. Workshop on Job Scheduling Strategies for Parallel Processing (JSSPP)*, volume 2221 of *Lecture Notes in Computer Science*, pages 87–102. Springer, 2001.

34. R. Jain. *The Art of Computer Systems Performance Analysis: Techniques for Experimental Design, Measurement, Simulation, and Modeling,*. Wiley-Interscience, New York, NY, USA, May 1991. Winner of "1991 Best Advanced How-To Book, Systems" award from the Computer Press Association.
35. Chris Kenyon and Giorgos Cheliotis. Architecture requirements for commercializing grid resources. In *Proc. of the 11th Intl. Symposium on High-Performance Distributed Computing (HPDC)*, pages 215–224, 2002.
36. George Kola, Tevfik Kosar, and Miron Livny. Phoenix: Making data-intensive grid applications fault-tolerant. In Rajkumar Buyya, editor, *GRID*, pages 251–258. IEEE Computer Society, 2004.
37. Derrick Kondo, Michela Taufer, Charles L. Brooks III, Henri Casanova, and Andrew A. Chien. Characterizing and evaluating desktop grids: An empirical study. In *Proc. of the 18th International Parallel and Distributed Processing Symposium (IPDPS)*, 2004.
38. Hui Li, David Groep, and Lex Wolters. Workload characteristics of a multi-cluster supercomputer. In Dror G. Feitelson, Larry Rudolph, and Uwe Schwiegelshohn, editors, *Job Scheduling Strategies for Parallel Processing (JSSPP'04)*, pages 176–194. Springer-Verlag, June 2004.
39. Uri Lublin and Dror G. Feitelson. The workload on parallel supercomputers: Modeling the characteristics of rigid jobs. *Journal of Parallel and Distributed Computing*, 63(20):1105–1122, 2003.
40. Raissa Medeiros, Walfredo Cirne, Francisco Vilar Brasileiro, and Jacques Philippe Sauvé. Faults in grids: Why are they so bad and what can be done about it?. In Heinz Stockinger, editor, *GRID*, pages 18–24. IEEE Computer Society, 2003.
41. Emmanuel Medernach. Workload analysis of a cluster in a grid environment. In Dror G. Feitelson, Eitan Frachtenberg, Larry Rudolph, and Uwe Schwiegelshohn, editors, *Proc. of the 11th Int'l. Workshop on Job Scheduling Strategies for Parallel Processing (JSSPP)*, volume 3834 of *Lecture Notes in Computer Science*, pages 36–61. Springer, 2005.
42. H.H. Mohamed and D.H.J. Epema. Experiences with the koala co-allocating scheduler in multiclusters. In *Proc. of the 5th IEEE/ACM Int'l Symp. on Cluster Computing and the GRID (CCGrid)*, May 2005.
43. M. Pinedo. *Scheduling: Theory, Algorithms, and Systems*. Prentice-Hall, 2nd edition, 2002.
44. Wayne Schroeder, Richard Marciano, Joseph Lopez, and Michael K. Gleicher. Analysis of HPSS Performance Based on Per-file Transfer Logs. In *Proc. of the 16th IEEE Mass Storage Systems Symposium*, pages 103–115, San Diego, March 1999. IEEE Computer Society.
45. U. Schwiegelshohn and R. Yahyapour. Fairness in parallel job scheduling. *Journal of Scheduling*, 3(5):297–320, 2000.
46. Hongzhang Shan, Leonid Oliker, and Rupak Biswas. Job superscheduler architecture and performance in computational grid environments. In *SC*, pages 44–54. ACM, 2003.
47. Baiyi Song, Carsten Ernemann, and Ramin Yahyapour. Parallel Computer Workload Modeling with Markov Chains. In Dror G. Feitelson, Larry Rudolph, and Uwe Schwiegelshohn, editors, *Proc. of the 10th Job Scheduling Strategies for Parallel Processing (JSSPP)*, volume 3277 of *Lecture Notes in Computer Science*, pages 47–62. Springer, October 2004.
48. Baiyi Song, Carsten Ernemann, and Ramin Yahyapour. User Group-based Workload Analysis and Modeling. In *Proc. of the 5th Int'l. Symp. on Cluster Computing and the Grid (CCGrid)*. IEEE Computer Society, 2005.

49. Douglas Thain, John Bent, Andrea C. Arpaci-Dusseau, Remzi H. Arpaci-Dusseau, and Miron Livny. Pipeline and batch sharing in grid workloads. In *Proc. of the 12th Intl. Symposium on High-Performance Distributed Computing (HPDC)*, pages 152–161, 2003.
50. Mitchell D. Theys, Howard Jay Siegel, Noah B. Beck, Min Ta, and Michael Jurczyk. A Mathematical Model, Heuristic and Simulation Study for a Basic Data Staging Problem in a Heterogenous Networking Environment. In *Proc. of the 7th Heterogeneous Computing Workshop*, pages 115–122, Orlando, March 1998. IEEE Computer Society.
51. G. Tsouloupas and M. D. Dikaiakos. GridBench: A workbench for grid benchmarking. In P. M. A. Sloot, A. G. Hoekstra, T. Priol, A. Reinefeld, and M. Bubak, editors, *Proc. of the European Grid Conference (EGC)*, volume 3470 of *Lecture Notes in Computer Science*, pages 211–225. Springer, 2005.
52. Rich Wolski, Neil Spring, and Jim Hayes. The network weather service: A distributed resource performance forecasting service for metacomputing. *Journal of Future Generation Computing Systems*, 15(5-6):757–768, October 1999.

A   Grid vs. Parallel Production Environments

In this section we make a brief comparison of offered computational power for the parallel production environments with traces in the Parallel Workloads Archive, and Grid systems for which we have analyzed partial traces in our previous work [30].

Table 1. Grid vs. Parallel Production Environments: processing time consumed by users, and highest number of jobs running in the system during a day. The "Type" column shows the environment type: PProd for parallel production, or Grid.

Environment	Type	Data Source	CPUYears/Year	Jobs Spike
NASA iPSC	PProd	[1]	92.03	876
LANL CM5	PProd	[1]	808.40	5358
SDSC Par95	PProd	[1]	292.06	3407
SDSC Par96	PProd	[1]	208.96	826
CTC SP2	PProd	[1]	294.98	1648
LLNL T3D	PProd	[1]	202.95	445
KTH SP2	PProd	[1]	71.68	302
SDSC SP2	PProd	[1]	109.15	2181
LANL O2K	PProd	[1]	1,212.33	2458
OSC Cluster	PProd	[1]	93.53	2554
SDSC BLUE	PProd	[1]	876.77	1310
LCG 1 Cluster	Grid	[30]	750.50	22550
DAS-2	Grid	[30]	30.34	19550
Grid3 1 VO	Grid	[30]	360.75	15853
TeraGrid	Grid	[30]	n/a	7561

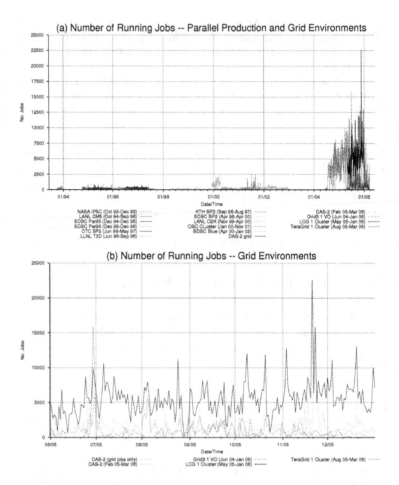

Fig. 3. Running jobs during daily intervals for grid and parallel environments: (a) comparative display over all data for grid and parallel environments; (b) comparative display for data between June 2005 and January 2006, for grid environments only.

Table 1 depicts the processing time consumed by users (averaged and expressed in CPUYears/Year), and the highest number of jobs running in each environment during a day; Figure 3 shows the number of running jobs in all the environments from Table 1 as a function of time.

The users of current grid systems *have already consumed* more than 750+ CPUYears/year in a cluster (the RAL cluster in CERN's LCG), and 350+ CPUYears/year in combined use by one VO (ATLAS VO in Grid3). Spikes in number of jobs running in a system can be around or over 20000/cluster (DAS-2 and LCG RAL cluster, respectively). The number of jobs completed per day in current grid systems is on average over 4000 jobs/day in LCG's RAL cluster, and 500 to 1000 for Grid3 and DAS2, rates sustained for periods spanning more than one year [30]. By comparison, large parallel production environments offer 50 to 1300 CPUYears/year, have on average less than 500 completed jobs/day, and spikes below 5500 jobs (results hold for each individual parallel production environment trace from the Parallel Workloads Environments; note that LPC EGEE and DAS FSx are not parallel production environments, but clusters in grid environments).

Author Index

Lecture Notes in Computer Science

For information about Vols. 1–4294

please contact your bookseller or Springer

Vol. 4345: N. Maglaveras, I. Chouvarda, V. Koutkias, R. Brause (Eds.), Biological and Medical Data Analysis. XIII, 496 pages. 2006. (Sublibrary LNBI).

Vol. 4344: V. Gruhn, F. Oquendo (Eds.), Software Architecture. X, 245 pages. 2006.

Vol. 4342: H. de Swart, E. Orłowska, G. Schmidt, M. Roubens (Eds.), Theory and Applications of Relational Structures as Knowledge Instruments II. X, 373 pages. 2006. (Sublibrary LNAI).

Vol. 4341: P.Q. Nguyen (Ed.), Progress in Cryptology - VIETCRYPT 2006. XI, 385 pages. 2006.

Vol. 4340: R. Prodan, T. Fahringer, Grid Computing. XXIII, 317 pages. 2007.

Vol. 4339: E. Ayguadé, G. Baumgartner, J. Ramanujam, P. Sadayappan (Eds.), Languages and Compilers for Parallel Computing. XI, 476 pages. 2006.

Vol. 4338: P. Kalra, S. Peleg (Eds.), Computer Vision, Graphics and Image Processing. XV, 965 pages. 2006.

Vol. 4337: S. Arun-Kumar, N. Garg (Eds.), FSTTCS 2006: Foundations of Software Technology and Theoretical Computer Science. XIII, 430 pages. 2006.

Vol. 4335: S.A. Brueckner, S. Hassas, M. Jelasity, D. Yamins (Eds.), Engineering Self-Organising Systems. XII, 212 pages. 2007. (Sublibrary LNAI).

Vol. 4334: B. Beckert, R. Hähnle, P.H. Schmitt (Eds.), Verification of Object-Oriented Software. XXIX, 658 pages. 2007. (Sublibrary LNAI).

Vol. 4333: U. Reimer, D. Karagiannis (Eds.), Practical Aspects of Knowledge Management. XII, 338 pages. 2006. (Sublibrary LNAI).

Vol. 4332: A. Bagchi, V. Atluri (Eds.), Information Systems Security. XV, 382 pages. 2006.

Vol. 4331: G. Min, B. Di Martino, L.T. Yang, M. Guo, G. Ruenger (Eds.), Frontiers of High Performance Computing and Networking – ISPA 2006 Workshops. XXXVII, 1141 pages. 2006.

Vol. 4330: M. Guo, L.T. Yang, B. Di Martino, H.P. Zima, J. Dongarra, F. Tang (Eds.), Parallel and Distributed Processing and Applications. XVIII, 953 pages. 2006.

Vol. 4329: R. Barua, T. Lange (Eds.), Progress in Cryptology - INDOCRYPT 2006. X, 454 pages. 2006.

Vol. 4328: D. Penkler, M. Reitenspiess, F. Tam (Eds.), Service Availability. X, 289 pages. 2006.

Vol. 4327: M. Baldoni, U. Endriss (Eds.), Declarative Agent Languages and Technologies IV. VIII, 257 pages. 2006. (Sublibrary LNAI).

Vol. 4326: S. Göbel, R. Malkewitz, I. Iurgel (Eds.), Technologies for Interactive Digital Storytelling and Entertainment. X, 384 pages. 2006.

Vol. 4325: J. Cao, I. Stojmenovic, X. Jia, S.K. Das (Eds.), Mobile Ad-hoc and Sensor Networks. XIX, 887 pages. 2006.

Vol. 4323: G. Doherty, A. Blandford (Eds.), Interactive Systems. XI, 269 pages. 2007.

Vol. 4320: R. Gotzhein, R. Reed (Eds.), System Analysis and Modeling: Language Profiles. X, 229 pages. 2006.

Vol. 4319: L.-W. Chang, W.-N. Lie (Eds.), Advances in Image and Video Technology. XXVI, 1347 pages. 2006.

Vol. 4318: H. Lipmaa, M. Yung, D. Lin (Eds.), Information Security and Cryptology. XI, 305 pages. 2006.

Vol. 4317: S.K. Madria, K.T. Claypool, R. Kannan, P. Uppuluri, M.M. Gore (Eds.), Distributed Computing and Internet Technology. XIX, 466 pages. 2006.

Vol. 4316: M.M. Dalkilic, S. Kim, J. Yang (Eds.), Data Mining and Bioinformatics. VIII, 197 pages. 2006. (Sublibrary LNBI).

Vol. 4314: C. Freksa, M. Kohlhase, K. Schill (Eds.), KI 2006: Advances in Artificial Intelligence. XII, 458 pages. 2007. (Sublibrary LNAI).

Vol. 4313: T. Margaria, B. Steffen (Eds.), Leveraging Applications of Formal Methods. IX, 197 pages. 2006.

Vol. 4312: S. Sugimoto, J. Hunter, A. Rauber, A. Morishima (Eds.), Digital Libraries: Achievements, Challenges and Opportunities. XVIII, 571 pages. 2006.

Vol. 4311: K. Cho, P. Jacquet (Eds.), Technologies for Advanced Heterogeneous Networks II. XI, 253 pages. 2006.

Vol. 4309: P. Inverardi, M. Jazayeri (Eds.), Software Engineering Education in the Modern Age. VIII, 207 pages. 2006.

Vol. 4308: S. Chaudhuri, S.R. Das, H.S. Paul, S. Tirthapura (Eds.), Distributed Computing and Networking. XIX, 608 pages. 2006.

Vol. 4307: P. Ning, S. Qing, N. Li (Eds.), Information and Communications Security. XIV, 558 pages. 2006.

Vol. 4306: Y. Avrithis, Y. Kompatsiaris, S. Staab, N.E. O'Connor (Eds.), Semantic Multimedia. XII, 241 pages. 2006.

Vol. 4305: A.A. Shvartsman (Ed.), Principles of Distributed Systems. XIII, 441 pages. 2006.

Vol. 4304: A. Sattar, B.-H. Kang (Eds.), AI 2006: Advances in Artificial Intelligence. XXVII, 1303 pages. 2006. (Sublibrary LNAI).

Vol. 4303: A. Hoffmann, B.-H. Kang, D. Richards, S. Tsumoto (Eds.), Advances in Knowledge Acquisition and Management. XI, 259 pages. 2006. (Sublibrary LNAI).

Vol. 4302: J. Domingo-Ferrer, L. Franconi (Eds.), Privacy in Statistical Databases. XI, 383 pages. 2006.

Vol. 4301: D. Pointcheval, Y. Mu, K. Chen (Eds.), Cryptology and Network Security. XIII, 381 pages. 2006.

Vol. 4300: Y.Q. Shi (Ed.), Transactions on Data Hiding and Multimedia Security I. IX, 139 pages. 2006.

Vol. 4299: S. Renals, S. Bengio, J.G. Fiscus (Eds.), Machine Learning for Multimodal Interaction. XII, 470 pages. 2006.

Vol. 4297: Y. Robert, M. Parashar, R. Badrinath, V.K. Prasanna (Eds.), High Performance Computing - HiPC 2006. XXIV, 642 pages. 2006.

Vol. 4296: M.S. Rhee, B. Lee (Eds.), Information Security and Cryptology – ICISC 2006. XIII, 358 pages. 2006.

Vol. 4295: J.D. Carswell, T. Tezuka (Eds.), Web and Wireless Geographical Information Systems. XI, 269 pages. 2006.